The Palaeolithic Age

CROOM HELM STUDIES IN ARCHAEOLOGY

General Editor: Leslie Alcock, University of Glasgow

SURVEYING FOR ARCHAEOLOGISTS AND OTHER FIELDWORKERS
A.H.A. Hogg

CELTIC CRAFTSMANSHIP IN BRONZE
H.E. Kilbride-Jones

EARLY MAN IN BRITAIN AND IRELAND
Alex Morrison

The Palaeolithic Age

John Wymer

CROOM HELM
London & Sydney

© 1982 J.J. Wymer
Croom Helm Ltd, Provident House, Burrell Row,
Beckenham, Kent BR3 1AT
Croom Helm Australia Pty Ltd, First Floor,
139 King Street, Sydney, NSW 2001, Australia
Reprinted 1984
First paperback edition 1984

British Library Cataloguing in Publication Data

Wymer, J.J.
    The palaeolithic age.
    1. Stone age
    I. Title
    930.1'2   GN768

ISBN 0-7099-2710-X

20 04003 595

Printed and bound in Great Britain by
Biddles Ltd, Guildford and King's Lynn

Contents

Contents

Figures

Figures

Tables

Preface

'. . . since nobody knows what he can do until he tries, the only clue to what man can do is what man has done. The value of history, then, is that it teaches us what man has done and thus what man is.' – R.G. Collingwood

It is unlikely that Palaeolithic man ever concerned himself with anything of the past beyond his own experience. The same is true of societies in much of historical time. The present tendency to look back rather than forward is unquestionably a phenomenon of modern, complex societies, and is a study in itself. This book can make no attempt to justify or explain this phenomenon, other than to observe that there has always been a pattern of change, but only in the past few centuries has the speed of that change exceeded the comprehension of individual generations. All of us now die in a world far different to that into which we are born. It is little wonder that we should ponder on how it all started, and this means retracing the history of Man to the time when it becomes difficult to be sure whether we are really dealing with our own species. This spans the Palaeolithic or Old Stone Age, covering the first two million years of Man's existence, ending when hunting societies gave way to farming and ultimate urbanisation.

There is little to show for most of this enormous period of time: only those artifacts made of imperishable materials, or the bones of butchered animals and, very rarely, the bones of the men themselves. Several good summaries of the Palaeolithic age have been published but, generally, details can only be found in the proceedings of various learned journals. This book has been written in the hope that it might help bridge this gap. It is, inevitably, an archaeological study, and thus concerned with things and places. I have tried to express this evidence in terms of human physical and cultural evolution, and to balance it geographically. Some of this is very subjective, but I believe the general theme will stand. Behind the descriptions, classifications and tables is a continuity that will hopefully be recognised, a continuity of human development seen on a global scale, not by particular peoples or nations but as a species, sometimes successful, sometimes less so, sometimes more so.

Alternatively, I hope the book may prove of use to those who wish to pursue the subject further and more profoundly. Thus I have included references at both general and specialised levels. The bibliography is by no means exhaustive and, in some cases, preference has been given to non-original sources on the grounds of availability. Sometimes there is no source other than obscure publications, but everything cited is available, even if only in University or society libraries. In this respect, like many other archaeologists, I am indebted to Mr John Hopkins, librarian at the Society of Antiquaries, who has cheerfully guided me over the years to the correct shelves, often when the required book is under my nose. I owe acknowledgement to many colleagues whose writings and discussions have so influenced my viewpoints, although they may not agree with them, especially Dr K.P. Oakley, Dr D.A. Roe, Dr P. Mellars, Professor R. Singer, Professor K.M. Clayton, Dr G.S. Boulton and Dr E.R. Shephard-Thorn. Dr M.D. Leakey has kindly allowed me to reproduce some of her drawings of Olduvai artifacts and I am grateful to the people or institutions who have permitted the reproduction of the photographic plates. My wife, Mollie, patiently typed, re-typed and re-typed the manuscript. Mrs A.M. Wilkinson compiled the index.

Chapter 1

Time, Change and Method

The Palaeolithic age spans the time between the appearance of the first humans and the final retreat of glacial ice in the northern hemisphere about 8500 BC. This is a period of some two million years. The recent end is tidily defined by geological stratigraphy and absolute radiocarbon years, but the distant end is obscured by our not being too sure how we can define the first humans, or really knowing how far back in time they may be found. The biggest difficulty is knowing how far to go back or, turning our thoughts upside down, where do we start? When do the non-human hominoids become our respectable ancestors? Some definition is required as to what constitutes a Human Being. It is easy to define the differences between ourselves and our nearest relatives, the existing apes (by physical anatomy, language, etc.), but how can this be done when there is nothing in the fossil record for comparison but a few broken bones of human aspect, especially when it is realised that some of the bones of existing apes are very similar? Dr K.P. Oakley has modified Benjamin Franklin's original definition of Man as 'a tool-making animal' to a 'tool-making primate' with the cautious qualification that the tools must be made to a 'set and regular pattern'. Even this needs further qualification, as it has been shown that chimpanzees will make tools of sorts. However, chimpanzees do not make stone tools to a 'set and regular pattern' and it seems reasonable to use this as a criterion. The problem thus becomes: what are the oldest tools? This cannot be answered without a consideration of the problem of time.

Readers who are not familiar with prehistory may be bewildered by the concept of time in units of thousands and millions of years. It is difficult to conceive such a vast span in which the building of the pyramids of Egypt becomes a recent event. It is perhaps less difficult when calendar years are involved, even if they are given to the nearest 500 or 1,000 years. There is some consolation and reality in knowing that the ice of the Last Glaciation finally melted in Britain by about 8500 BC but dates such as 46,000 years ± 1,500 or 1.75 million years may make little real impression. However, the order in which events occur is more important than calendar years when considering remote time. It is critical to know whether one event is older or more recent than another. This is termed relative dating. Some framework of known happenings is required, within a scale of the likely order of time, even if it is measured in units of tens or hundreds of thousands of years. There is obviously no point in quibbling whether a tool was made 46,681 or 46,682 years ago and as one goes further back the importance of precise dates becomes proportionately less.

The starting-point for any framework is the geological time scale, so some geological matters need to be considered first. The geological periods which concern human evolution are, in ascending order of time:

Pleistocene	0-2 million years ago
Pliocene	2-7 million years ago
Miocene	7-26 million years ago
Oligocene	26-38 million years ago

The Pleistocene belongs to the Quaternary period, as does the Holocene, which is merely the relatively brief time between the last retreat of glaciers in the northern hemisphere until the present day. Some geologists reject the Holocene and regard the present as part of the Pleistocene, thus making the terms Pleistocene and Quaternary synonymous. Although strictly an epoch, the Pleistocene is usually more loosely referred to as a period (see Table 1.1). The Pliocene, Miocene and Oligocene belong to the Late Tertiary. The latter will concern us very little, except that here will be found the beginnings of the evolutionary changes among the higher primates leading to *Homo*. It is the Pleistocene period which contains the Palaeolithic period. To give some order of time in years, the present assessment for the Pliocene-Pleistocene boundary, based on palaeontological change and radiometric dating, is about two million years. This is just a date of convenience, for there is obviously no fixed line between one geological period and another. The Pleistocene may be defined as the period with true horses and elephants, but such creatures did not appear overnight. Nor did Man, although the first clear indications of his presence appear around the end of the Pliocene and beginning of the Pleistocene, which we will refer to as the Plio-Pleistocene. Evolution is a lengthy business and the pace will vary from area to area, so boundaries based on the appearance or disappearance of particular species are very imprecise. This is of no consequence in the older geological epochs, when a few million years one way or the other really make no difference, but in terms of geologically recent events it is very unsatisfactory. Thus, a stratigraphical boundary has been agreed upon as an arbitrary division between the Pliocene and the Pleistocene, namely the oldest marine deposits that have been recognised in the Mediterranean, referred to as the Calabrian Stage. Anything older than the Calabrian is Pliocene, anything younger is Pleistocene. It is a technical point, but essential if muddles are to be avoided.

Knowledge of Pleistocene events is not yet complete enough to permit a succession of named stages or other divisions which can be applied on a world basis, although we shall see that the evidence from deep-sea cores and radio-active dating methods promises this may be so in the future. The glacial chronology of the Alps has been used in the past, and unsuccessful attempts made to identify and correlate wet (pluvial) periods in Africa with it. It seems best to abandon this approach and, in the meantime, use stages which can be identified in any one geographical region on the basis of stratigraphy and fluctuations in temperature. This can be done with some confidence in a particular region, but correlating events in one region with those in another is difficult. Table 1.1 illustrates the principle of world, regional or local sequences.

As an example of local terminology, the names given to the subdivisions or stages of the Pleistocene in Britain are shown in Table 1.2. The type localities are the places where there is sufficient stratigraphical evidence to demonstrate where the deposits representing a particular stage occur in the sequence. They may overlie or be covered by deposits of another stage identified elsewhere.

Nowhere in Britain is there one site where all the stages can be found in a neat, unbroken column so, although the order is correct, there may be gaps. Also shown on the table is the prevailing climate of each stage.

Table 1.1: Geological Terminology

World				Regional	Local
Era	Period	Epoch	Stage		
		Holocene		Alpine	Britain
Caenozoic	Quaternary	Pleistocene	Late, Middle and Early	Würm, Riss, Mindel, Gunz	Flandrian, Devensian, Ipswichian, etc.
	Tertiary	Pliocene			

Table 1.2: Stages of the British Quaternary Period

Stage of Pleistocene	Name and type locality		Climate
Late	Flandrian	(begins at 8500 BC)	Warm
	Devensian	Four Ashes, Staffs	Cold
	Ipswichian	Bobbitshole, Ipswich, Suffolk	Warm
	Wolstonian	Wolston, Warwicks	Cold
Middle	Hoxnian	Hoxne, Suffolk	Warm
	Anglian	Corton, Suffolk	Cold
	Cromerian	West Runton, Norfolk	Warm
Early	Beestonian	Beeston, Norfolk	Cold
	Pastonian	Paston, Norfolk	Warm
	Baventian	Easton Bavents, Suffolk	Cold
	Antian	Ludham, Norfolk	Warm
	Thurnian	Ludham, Norfolk	Cold
	Ludhamian	Ludham, Norfolk	Warm
	Waltonian	Walton-on-the-Naze, Essex	Cold

Sources: Mitchell, Penny, Shotton and West, 1973; and Sparks and West, 1972.

Many of the Palaeolithic sites that are to be described can be fitted into a local or regional geological sequence. Sometimes, sediments associated with the sites can be dated by one or more of a number of techniques. Before these methods are surveyed it is necessary to consider some of the complications involved in the subject of dating. A distinction has already been made between dates in calendar years (absolute or chronometric dates) and dates based on the order of events, i.e. whether one thing is younger or older than another (relative dates). The respective merits of these two ways of assessing time need to be examined. Absolute dates are obviously the best dates because, if they are reliable, then comparison may be made of the dated sites or objects anywhere in the world. Instantly it can be seen whether one is earlier, more recent or contemporary with another. However, in practice, their reliability may be suspect. Either the dating method may be in doubt or the validity of the sample being dated is questionable. For example, a radiocarbon date on wood from an archaeological site may give an erroneous date for the site itself, for the wood may have come from a tree already many hundreds of years older than the date of the occupation of the site. Similarly, radiocarbon-dated shells in a river deposit may have been derived from earlier deposits; thus the date applies to the shells and not the deposit where they were found. There is also the problem of contamination of samples submitted for radiocarbon dating; modern rootlets may produce a boost of radioactive carbon and thus make the date too recent. Careful, laboratory pre-treatment of samples can usually eliminate these possible sources of error, but similar contamination by lime-rich water may create greater difficulties and subsequent errors. Conversely, contamination by dead carbon such as coal could give a much older date than the correct one.

All so-called absolute dates produced by a variety of ingenious measurements, usually of some radioactive substance, are really dates expressed in terms of probabilities. Radiocarbon dates, for instance, are always quoted with a plus or minus figure of years. This does not mean that the date must lie within the range of this number of years each side of the actual date, but that there is a degree of probability in the order of two to one that the real date does lie within it. This is one 'standard deviation', so, as an example, if a radiocarbon date of 5000 years ± 200 years is quoted, then there is a 2:1 chance that the date lies between 4800 and 5200 years. However, if two standard deviations are taken, so that the range is between 4600 and 5400 years, then the probability is correspondingly increased to 19:1. Such methods of dating are described briefly below, but these aspects of absolute dating are mentioned so that the value of relative dating can be compared.

Relative dating is merely a statement of the relationship in time of one thing to another, not in terms of calendar years but in the sense of earlier or later than. Its great advantage is that in certain circumstances it is unequivocal. The laws of stratification still constitute the most powerful dating instrument although their application may be limited to regions, areas or just individual sites. Stratification is, of course, a geological concept: literally, the relationship of successive strata, i.e. different layers of geological deposits. It is obvious that, if a fine, silty sediment is found on top of a coarse river gravel, the former must be more recent than the latter, whatever time may have elapsed between the deposition of them. It may be possible to find rare instances of glacial ice thrusting an early deposit bodily over a later one, or overthrust faulting in certain parts of the world subject to major earthquakes doing the same thing, but this is unlikely to happen without the deposits in question being distorted or rearranged in some manner that is easily recognised. More important, to the archaeologist, is the interpretation of archaeological material found within stratified sediments. The simple law of stratigraphical succession will always apply, but it also has to be remembered that these laws apply to the deposit and not to any objects found within it. Thus, if the litter from one phase of human occupation is buried beneath an accumulation of sediment such as lake mud, river silt or volcanic ash, it will be earlier than the time when that deposit formed. If conditions should then allow any phase of human occupation on top of that deposit, then we have the happy situation of being able to place two phases of human occupation in relative order. In practice it is rarely so simple. These matters are vital for any study of the Palaeolithic period for such is the long period of time involved that the archaeological record is inextricably mixed with the geological one. Later prehistory, from the Neolithic period, is much less concerned with geological matters, for the landscape in most parts of the world has had little time to change since then. Certainly it has changed very little in comparison to the Pleistocene period, especially in the northern hemisphere where glaciations have drastically altered whole aspects of the topography. This is the main difference between Palaeolithic sites and those of later periods. It will be seen that, with rare exceptions, it is only in the latter part of the Pleistocene that we have archaeological sites where human activities have been a major factor in the accumulation of deposits, such as the occupational litter that builds up under rock shelters. With such sites, normal archaeological techniques of excavation and interpretation can be used, but for the most part the human history of the Palaeolithic period has to be unravelled from the effects of geological change. This is not necessarily a disadvantage, for the deposits concerned may be the only hope of reconstructing the contemporary environment, and a means of putting archaeological sites or objects into a relative sense of order. It is the latter aspect that requires a little elaboration, for a misunderstanding of the evidence will make, and in some instances has made, a mockery of all subsequent interpretations.

The simple case cited above of two human phases of occupation, neatly separated by an intervening sediment, and thus relatively dated, depends entirely upon a careful judgement of the archaeological material itself. It must first be demonstrated that the evidence of human occupation or activity is *in situ*, in other words is in the place where it happened. If the evidence consists of a few stone tools and broken bones, can it be certain that they are lying where they were dropped by the people responsible? If so, then they may be said to be in a *primary context* and all is well; but the sediment concerned may be a river gravel, and the stone tools and the broken bones may have been derived from an earlier surface or deposit, in the same way as all the other stones and sand which constitute the gravel. Then they are in a *secondary context* and, reflecting on the laws of stratification, it can be said that they could be earlier than the time when the gravel accumulated. They could be contemporary, but they cannot be younger. At least there is a minimum date, in relative terms.

Is it possible to assess whether archaeological material within sedimentary deposits is in a primary or secondary context? In most cases this should be possible, by a consideration of the nature of the material and the deposit itself. There are no rigid rules and certainly a subjective element is introduced, for the archaeologist must take each case on its own merits. Some examples will help to make this clear. Fragile material, such as delicate bones or the razor-sharp edges of freshly struck stones, cannot be moved without some destruction, so if it is in a completely unchanged condition it is likely to be in primary context. Material in deep-water accumulations must have been derived from elsewhere unless dropped in. Where similar impossible conditions for human habitation are implied by the type of deposit, any archaeological objects are almost certainly derived. Habitation on the surface of glaciers is unthinkable, so nothing in boulder clay could be in a primary context. Nor could anything in the torrent gravels formed by violent flooding, or in raised beaches formed by wave action. It is easier to make a list of situations in which archaeological material is found in a derived state than otherwise, for the very nature of geological change is not conducive to preservation of material in primary contexts. Fortunately there are exceptions, such as the example first mentioned of fine river silt. Such gentle sedimentation can bury a surface with only the slightest disturbance of anything lying on it, or none at all. Lake muds are ideal in this respect, and many of the most important Palaeolithic sites owe their existence to the rise of the water table around a lake. Volcanic ash is particularly useful for sealing sites, as in the famous Olduvai Gorge. Blown sand can sometimes be a little too drastic and lead to drifting rather than interment, but the fine wind-blown soil of the periglacial regions, loess, has preserved magnificent sites in western Europe. Sometimes it may be possible to demonstrate, by careful recording or excavation, that the distribution of material in a restricted area forms a pattern that could only be the result of human activity, and could not possibly be formed by the random scattering of natural agencies. It is then obviously in a primary context. So would be any pits, features or structures in the archaeological sense if they existed. Unfortunately these are almost non-existent until the last 50,000 years or so of the Palaeolithic period.

Relative dating by geological stratification may be extended from one site or region to another when particular deposits have a wide range and can be identified with confidence. The glacial till or boulder clay of East Anglia is mainly assigned to one geological stage, so it is possible to refer to deposits as distant from each other as Essex and Norfolk as being younger or older than this stage, depending on whether they overlie or underlie the till. 'Marker horizons' may be identified, such as a particularly distinctive volcanic tuff around Lake Turkana referred to as the KBS Tuff. Sea levels and river terraces have been similarly used as a means of correlation over wide areas, but this is a divergence from the laws of stratification and is correspondingly suspect. The identification of ancient sea levels and river terraces usually depends on two factors: altitude and topography. These are the sphere of geomorphology, the study of the shape of the land, and quite distinct from stratigraphy, although the latter may often come to its rescue.

River terraces are the remnants of former river courses or, more exactly, their flood plains. They have been left high and dry as the river has deepened its valley, especially in response to the low sea levels which prevailed during various stages of the Pleistocene. In general, it may be assumed that the higher a terrace is above its present flood plain, the older it is, but this is not always so: sometimes sediments may accumulate in a river valley to such an extent that former, higher terraces are covered by them. This may be caused by floods transporting great quantities of rock waste downstream until the water no longer has the power to move it and it accumulates on the flood plain. Such aggradations may result from the tumultuous conditions caused by melting ice or snow in glacial or periglacial episodes. Conversely, during interglacial periods, a rise in sea level could make a river very sluggish in its lower reaches and cause it to deposit the fine material held in suspension. Such aggradations may be followed by the lowering of the river once again, with the result that there are sediments left on a high terrace younger than those buried beneath them. These older deposits may be re-exposed by the later recutting. By the time that erosion has reduced these ancient flood plains to small, isolated remnants, it may be impossible to unravel the complexity. This is particularly unfortunate as so much of the evidence for the Palaeolithic period is found in river terrace deposits. There is also the complication of different modes of deposition and erosion, dependent on the distance of the river from the sea. It is easy to see how tidal range must affect terrace formation in the lower reaches of a river and, correspondingly, how erosion is likely to predominate over deposition in the upper reaches.

The relative ages of former sea levels are normally assessed on the altitude of the remains of their ancient beaches or rock cut platforms. They may make impressive features and are particularly well developed in the Mediterranean, where a flight of them may be recognised at intervals of about 30 m or less down from the highest at 200 m above the present sea. Traces of ancient sea levels are to be found around all the continents of the world and, on the principle that water must find its own level and making due allowance for tidal discrepancies and crustal disturbances, there might here be a geological method of correlating these features on a world scale. However, only if there is corroborating evidence from the deposits which are often associated with these old sea levels is there much likelihood of ever achieving this. The complications are even greater than with river terraces. Sea levels have changed throughout the world in response to glacial and interglacial periods. During the former, an enormous quantity of the water of the oceans is locked up as ice. The normal cycle of evaporation and precipitation, followed by run-off from the land and so back to the sea, is interrupted by the greater amount of snow which does not melt but builds up glaciers and ice sheets. As more and more of the sea water fails to return to the sea, so the level drops. Conversely, as the climate ameliorates into an interglacial, the ice gradually melts and the sea rises correspondingly. Some interesting calculations have been made as to what would happen if all the ice now at the north and south poles were to melt and flow back into the sea. It is calculated that the sea level would rise about 60 m, which would mean that Londoners who wanted to keep their feet dry would be restricted to parts of Hampstead and Blackheath. World geography would be altered out of all recognition, but it seems unlikely that anything will happen on this scale, for, if the present is considered as mid-interglacial, little more ice will melt before it begins to accumulate again. There is certainly plenty of evidence to show that the sea level has fallen at times to perhaps 100 m below its present level, so world maps during glacial periods would look considerably different from present ones.

There are two other factors to consider. Firstly, the sea has oscillated up and down in response to the ice ages many times, so it will have traversed the same ground on different occasions, and features at any one level are not all necessarily the same age. Secondly, contrary to common experience, the solid ground beneath our feet is anything but solid and is likely to rise and fall in response to pressures and tensions in the geological structure, of local, regional or even continental magnitude. Earthquakes and tremors are the violent expressions of these tensions, but gradual, imperceptible movements may also be operating. Moreover, the land mass is also sensitive to weight upon it, and the weight of ice sheets during glacial phases has temporarily depressed the land beneath or around it. There has then been corresponding uplift of the land as the ice has melted. Scandinavia may be rising about 15 cm a century at the present time. Uplift and depression of the land mass is referred to as isostasy; rise and fall of the ocean as eustasy. The interplay of one with the other makes the interpretation of former sea levels very difficult, except in the Later Pleistocene since there has been less time available for one event to obliterate another.

There is one other curiosity concerning former sea levels. It has been mentioned that if all the present ice in the world melted the sea would rise by about 60 m, yet there are traces of Pleistocene sea levels throughout the world considerably above this height. It is difficult to believe that there has been a general, uniform rise in continental land masses. Various theories have been suggested to account for these traces: the seas may be drying up or, much more credible, the world is expanding and the same amount of water cannot reach so far. This does not have much bearing on relative dating in the Pleistocene, other than to emphasise that, in spite of some of the objections mentioned, there is still a general rule that high sea levels and high terraces are more ancient than low ones.

Radiocarbon dating is one of the most useful techniques available to prehistorians, but its drawback for Palaeolithic studies is that it cannot with any reliability be applied to anything beyond the Upper Palaeolithic period. This is because the amount of measurable radiocarbon in a sample over about 30,000 years is so very small. Dates earlier than about 30,000 years obtained by this method are suspect; in fact some would attach little faith to those beyond 20,000 years. This may be a little over-cautious but, until there are other methods to use as cross-checks, it is safer to be sceptical. The bland acceptance of radiocarbon dates by some archaeologists is the despair of the physicists who produce them. As will be seen in a later chapter, radiocarbon dating is so important for assessing the chronology of Upper Palaeolithic sites that a brief account of the method is warranted. The principle is straightforward but its practical application is complicated, with numerous sources of error not always taken into account. It is based on the existence of two different isotopes of the element carbon: carbon 14 and carbon 12. Carbon 12 (^{12}C) is stable, whereas carbon 14 (^{14}C) is radioactive and therefore unstable. The proportion of one isotope to the other in the carbon of the atmosphere, in the form of the gas carbon dioxide, remains fairly steady for as fast as the unstable ^{14}C decays it is replaced by the effect of cosmic rays converting atmospheric nitrogen into further ^{14}C. The proportion concerned is a minute one, for there is only about one atom of the radioactive carbon 14 to a million million atoms of ordinary carbon. However, as carbon is contained in the structure of all living things, so they all contain the same proportion of ^{14}C to ^{12}C. This even applies to marine life, as carbon dioxide is dissolved in the ocean. The dating method is based on the fact that, once a living organism dies, it no longer absorbs carbon dioxide, the unstable ^{14}C decays and is not replaced, so the proportion of ^{14}C to ^{12}C changes,- with the former becoming less and less as time elapses. It has been calculated that in 5,730 ± 30 years there will only be one half remaining of the number of ^{14}C atoms originally present. This is termed the half-life. Hence, if the amount of ^{14}C in a sample is measured, it is possible to calculate its age or, to be more precise, the period of time that has elapsed since the sample of living matter died. Wood charcoal is an ideal substance for sampling, but bone, antler and shell can all be submitted to the physicist for dating by this method.

However, as has been stated, if the sample to be dated has a real age of more than about 30,000 years, the amount of radioactive carbon present will be so small that the measurement of it is a problem. Because of this, most dates of more than 30,000 years are generally expressed as 'greater than'. By about 50,000 years, the amount of radiocarbon left is infinitesimal, which is why the technique cannot be used for the long time span of most of the Palaeolithic period.

Apart from possible contamination of a sample by such things as groundwater containing 'dead' carbon (i.e. non-radioactive carbon), there is the problem of radiocarbon dates versus 'real' dates (i.e. calendar years). It can be demonstrated that they do not equate exactly and the further back in time, the greater is the difference between them. The method depends on the assumption that the level of radioactive carbon in the atmosphere has always been the same and now it would seem that this may not be true. It is certainly much higher at present than it has ever been because of the effect of man-made nuclear explosions since 1945. Cross-checking of radiocarbon and real dates on samples of wood of bristlecone pine trees in America, back to about 6000 BC, has shown that the radiocarbon dates tend to be younger than they should be. In order to avoid confusion a convention has now been adopted to use small letters for radiocarbon years (bc) and capital letters for calendar years (BC), or bp (radiocarbon years before the present) as opposed to BP. The present is conventionally regarded as 1950 AD. BC is used here for broad dating estimates, but radiocarbon dates are all bc as no suitable calibration scale is yet available for dates beyond the bristlecone pine scale. As mentioned, it is essential to regard radiocarbon dates as probabilities and not statements. For this reason, it is much more sensible to express radiocarbon dates on charts by bars to indicate a range in time, taken to one, two or more standard deviations. Such a latitude is usually of little consequence for dates in the Upper Palaeolithic, so the dating method is particularly useful for this branch of archaeology.

There are several other radioactive methods of dating, all based on various isotopes which decay at known rates. Some of them have such long half-lives that dates can only be assessed to the nearest million years or so, which may be very useful for geologists, but not for archaeologists. The most useful one for Palaeolithic archaeology is the potassium/argon method of dating, based on the decay of the isotope potassium 40 (^{40}K) to the gas argon (^{40}Ar). Dates can be assessed for a range covering the whole Pleistocene, up to about 100,000 years ago. However, in samples as 'recent' as the last few hundred thousand years there has been so little radioactive change that some scientists would contend that it is impossible to measure with sufficient accuracy. There is a considerable difference of opinion among scientists engaged in research on K/Ar dating and some of the results are conflicting, but it remains the most valuable technique so far devised for dating the critical period of the Early Pleistocene when Man first appeared. Potassium 40 is present in volcanic rocks, which has made the technique particularly applicable to numerous sites in East Africa, where sites along the Rift Valley have been covered by the ashes and lavas of volcanic eruptions.

The drawback of potassium/argon dating for Palaeolithic archaeology, apart from doubts concerning the method itself, is that it is dependent on the existence of volcanic rocks, whereas most Palaeolithic sites are not associated with volcanic activity. At present, there is a great absence of absolute dates for the whole middle of the Pleistocene period. There is potassium/argon at one end and radiocarbon at the other, but nothing in between. However, there are some other radioactive dating methods that may eventually prove reliable and success-fully fill this gap. Uranium series dating offers the best chance. This is based on the gradual decay of uranium to lead. It is a complex process, for about a dozen isotopes are formed in a series of successive stages. Uranium 238 and uranium 235 remain longest in the succession and the varying proportion of one to the other allows time to be calculated. Other isotopes in the series (thorium 230 and protactinium 231) have also been used successfully, particularly for fossil corals, but so far they have proved unsuccessful with shell. The method has been applied to bones from Clacton and Swanscombe and given dates of 245,000 and greater than 272,000 years respectively, which seem to be in the right order of time.

Another method of dating which promises to be useful and fill the difficult gap in the middle is that of amino-acid dating of bone or shell, dependent on the variation in the ratio of certain amino-acids contained in bones with time. Unfortunately this process is influenced by both temperature and chemical conditions and, as these will vary from site to site, the method has obvious limitations.

Fission-track dating is a technique resulting from the discovery that certain minerals and natural glasses (obsidian) which contain uranium bear distinctive marks caused by the decay of radioactive particles. These marks, or damage tracks as they are termed, may be between 5 and 20 microns long and can actually be observed under a microscope. A micron is one millionth of a metre, or one thousandth of a millimetre. The number of tracks increases with age. However, it is not a sensitive method of dating and has so far had little applica-tion to Palaeolithic archaeology.

Burnt clay and stone have the property of trapping 'energy' produced by minute quantities of radioactive impurities within them, which are released if they should be reheated, emitting light. It is thus called thermoluminescent dating. The amount of 'energy' trapped increases in time and can be measured by heating. This dating method can be usefully applied to hearths and burnt flints and, although little applied yet to Palaeolithic material, promises to be very useful.

The chemical analysis of bone can be of value for assessing the relative ages of bones at a particular site, especially where there may be doubt as to whether a specimen came from a particular level or is intrusive. A bone rarely survives in the soil for any period without undergoing considerable chemical change; some elements decrease or disappear, others increase through absorption from the soil. Thus the fluorine and uranium content of bones will tend to increase in time, while the nitrogen content decreases. The rate of such change is almost entirely dependent on the nature of the soil in which a bone may be buried, so the method is only applicable to bones found in the same deposit. It can also give a general guide to the antiquity of a particular bone that may have no known context, as was done with such impressive results on the Piltdown skull and jawbone.

The ideal time scale for the Pleistocene demands some continuous process which can be measured in terms of calendar years and be related to geological events such as glaciations. Such a process does exist for there is one situation where sediments have gradually accumulated throughout the entire Pleistocene period, and where present conditions may be regarded as indicative of the past. This is on the floor of the deep oceans. Fine material eroded from the continental land masses eventually finds its way, suspended in ocean currents, to the deeper parts and gradually settles on the bottom. The rate of accumulation will vary according to a number of factors such as the geography of the ocean floor and the depth of water. Moreover, other complications have to be considered such as the movement of sediment along the ocean bottom by turbidity currents and the constant reworking of the upper few centimetres by animals. Rates are generally from about one to several centimetres per thousand years, and the disturbance of sediments can be recognised and compensated for accordingly. It may be thought that even if it is possible to calculate how many metres of sediment formed in so many years, this could have only academic interest and be unrelated to geological or human events on the distant continents. However, ingenious analyses of the sediments have created the most valuable framework yet devised for understanding the scale and variety of events during the Pleistocene. It is the interplay and cross-checking of one method or approach against another within the same sediment that makes this possible. The first task is, of course, to obtain a long sample of the sediment, and this is done by extracting a core from the bottom of the sea with a piston corer which takes out cylindrical sections 5 cm in diameter.

About 40 per cent of the ocean floor is covered with *Globigerina*-ooze, consisting of clay and calcium carbonate. The latter is derived mainly from the shells of microscopic Foraminifera. As might be expected, there is also an element of debris from other marine life, including fish teeth, radiolaria and diatoms. The terrestrial component may include volcanic ash. Some material may be the result of chemical precipitation within the ocean, and even traces of meteorites from outer space may be included. Greater amounts of coarser sediment correspond to periods of low sea level during glacial periods, when so much of the water of the oceans was locked up as ice. This meant greater erosion around the edges of the continents and thus a thicker accumulation. Radioactive methods of dating have been applied to the deep-sea cores (radiocarbon and protactinium/thorium methods) and have produced absolute dates for the last 150,000 years. Beyond then, it is reasonable to extrapolate but, as will be seen, palaeomagnetism can be used as a check.

The major importance of deep-sea cores is that it is possible to calculate the surface temperature of the ocean at the time a particular level of ooze was deposited. This is done by identifying the species of Foraminifera, some of which only live in water of a certain range of temperature, and, with greater sensitivity, by oxygen isotope analysis. This involves a measurement of the ratio of the two stable isotopes of oxygen, O^{18} and O^{16}, found in the calcium carbonate of the Foraminifera shells. This ratio will vary according to the temperature of the water at the time the shell was formed and is connected with the storage of sea water within continental ice sheets during glaciations. It has thus been possible to build up a time scale of temperature variations of the surface water of the ocean during the whole of the Pleistocene period. Peaks of low and high temperatures must coincide with climatic oscillations as preserved in the geological evidence for glacial and interglacial episodes. Figure 1 shows the temperature variations for the last two million years as recorded in a deep-sea core taken in the western equatorial Pacific. It will be seen that these variations are more marked from about 800,000 years ago to the present day and this may well reflect the major glaciations of the northern hemisphere. However, as yet it is not possible to relate with confidence any of these temperature variations to terrestrial events, but there are some strong implications. It is generally agreed that Isotope Stage 5 represented the Last Interglacial period and, as described on page 109, the Mindel or Anglian Glaciation was probably Stage 12. It is to be hoped that definite correlations will soon be made between some of the events recorded in the deep-sea time scale and terrestrial deposits for, once the two can be linked, many of the chronological problems of the Pleistocene will have been answered.

Also on the deep-sea time scale is the palaeomagnetic record, showing the major epochs when polarity was either normal or reversed (i.e. the magnetic pole was at the south instead of the north as at present), together with some brief 'events' when the polarity was opposite to that prevailing during the epoch. It is not known why the earth's magnetic field should behave in this manner; we are all familiar with the minor variations of magnetic north from true north, as shown on Ordnance Survey maps, but the compass merely varies by a few degrees. It has been shown from a study of the sediments at the bottom of Lake Windermere that since the end of the Last Glaciation, about 8300 BC, there has been a magnetic oscillation of about 20° from the mean at a frequency of about 2,700 years.

This information has been achieved because some sediments contain ionised particles, which lie in accordance with the earth's magnetic field at the time of their deposition. Thus, unless the orientation of the rock itself has moved, this direction may be measured. Lake sediments and volcanic ash are especially helpful. It is surprising to discover that within the last two million years there has been a particularly long period or epoch, known as the Matuyama, when polarity was reversed, that is the south pole was the magnetic one. This is obviously a world-wide phenomenon and it has a useful application for Pleistocene dating. It is particularly fortunate that volcanic rocks are often the most suitable for measuring palaeomagnetism, for the same rocks are generally suitable for radioactive dating by the potassium/argon method. These dates can then be applied to the appropriate place within the palaeomagnetic sequence recorded in the deep-sea cores, where absolute dating is not possible. Thus the critical swing from reversed to normal polarity at the beginning of the current Brunhes epoch is dated to 730,000 years. This date can be marked on to the deep-sea cores, and can thus corroborate the dates arrived at independently by extrapolation. It also means that long sequences of reversed polarity must be older than 730,000 years.

Mention has already been made of climatic changes. There have also been drastic geographical changes during the immense period of time in which Man evolved. The Miocene witnessed great movements of the earth's crust which crumpled and buckled the ancient sedimentary rocks on a global scale, forming the Himalayas and the Alps. The repercussions of these forces folded much of the strata of southern Britain, pushing up the chalk to form the now familiar North and South Downs. The geography of the continents and oceans was considerably different from that of today and it was not until the Later Pliocene

Figure 1: Framework and Basis for Time Scale for the Pleistocene Period
The temperature curve records the oscillations of climate for about the last two million
years, as shown by oxygen isotope analysis of deep-sea sediments. The adjacent vertical bars
indicate the major cooler (even numbers) and warmer (odd numbers) stages, which are
thought to be linked with the various glacial and interglacial periods of the northern hemisphere. The rate of deposition of sediment for the last 30,000-40,000 years is known, for it
can be measured by radiocarbon dating, and it is in the order of 1.7 cm per 1,000 years. To
obtain a time scale for the Pleistocene period it is reasonable to extrapolate this figure.
Actual calculations are complicated by such factors as changes in sediment particle size,
gaps in sedimentation and movements of the ocean floor. The curve below is based on core
V28-239, taken in the western Pacific ocean and is thought to represent about 2.1 million
years of accumulation (Shackleton and Opdyke, 1976). A cross-check with certain terrestrial deposits is possible by a combination of palaeomagnetic measurements and potassium/
argon dating.

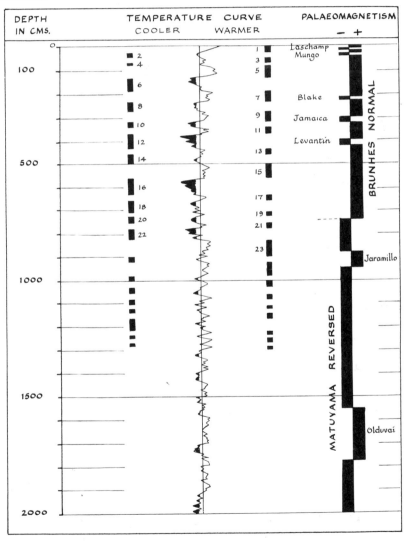

period that the land and sea masses of the world began to take on their present shape. Also in the Miocene there is evidence that there were marked changes in world climate: subtropical conditions gave way to temperate and, especially in Africa, forests were reduced in size and gave way to dry, grassy plains. Animals had to adapt to such changes or perish, and it is possible that this was one of the major factors which led to the eventual evolution of Man.

Oscillations of climate, shown so clearly by the palaeotemperature curve on the time scale (Figure 1), resulted in alternating periods of extreme cold and temperate conditions in the northern hemisphere, for most of the Pleistocene. During the cold periods the polar ice cap spread southwards, rendering much of Europe and Asia uninhabitable. Between these glacial periods were interglacials. This perpetually changing environment had a profound effect on human distribution and activity, although it is unlikely that any of the changes were sudden enough to have been apparent, even from one generation to the next.

Interglacials have been described as periods in which the climate becomes sufficiently warm for a long enough period to allow the development of a mixed oak forest, such as in Britain today. It may become warmer, but if it only ameliorates sufficiently to allow a vegetational climax of conifer forest before reverting to Arctic conditions, it is referred to as an interstadial period. Past vegetational successions are determined by analysis of pollen contained in sediments which formed during the various interglacial phases. An ideal situation is a deposit which slowly formed on the bed of a glacial lake and continued to do so during the whole of the subsequent interglacial period, so that there is a complete pollen record through the whole glacial-interglacial cycle. The fossil pollen grains are extracted from their mineral matrix and by taking samples at intervals throughout the vertical sequence of the sediment it is possible to reconstruct the vegetational changes that occurred. Every pollen grain, examined microscopically, has a distinctive form which allows its parent plant to be identified. Pollen from every species of plant that was growing in the vicinity may be present. In practice, it is generally only the tree pollen grains which are carefully identified and counted, for the character of the nearby contemporary woodland is the best indicator of the climate at the time. The proportion of tree pollen to non-tree pollen is also usually calculated for this gives valuable information on the open or closed aspect of the landscape. Such a site, where the whole of an interglacial is represented by a pollen profile, is Marks Tey, Essex (Figure 2).

The sequence of different types of woodland shows clearly in the diagram, with birch and pine dominating the cold periods at the beginning and end of the interglacial, and mixed oak forest in the middle. Apart from climate, there are other factors which govern the growth of woodland, such as the condition of the soil and the amount of light available for plants beneath an ever-increasing tree cover. There is an interaction between the plants, the light, the temperature and the soil, so that the latter develops from raw mineral, devoid of humus, to a basic or neutral one. This soil is subject to leaching processes and gradually, towards the end of an interglacial, becomes acidic and true podsols may occur. Local conditions such as altitude and the nature of the underlying rock obviously have an effect, but the general succession is the same. Thus, any interglacial may be divided into zones. The accepted scheme is as follows:

Figure 2: Interglacials — Pollen Diagram from Marks Tey, Essex

The glaciation of the northern hemisphere has been interrupted many times by recession of the ice sheets and a reversion to milder climate in formerly glaciated areas. The pollen diagram (after Turner, 1970) is from Marks Tey, Essex, and shows the vegetational changes throughout an entire interglacial. This has been determined by studying the fossil pollen contained in lake sediments which gradually accumulated from the time when the ice retreated and later returned. Laminations in the sediment correspond to yearly discharges and suggest a duration of about 15,000-20,000 years for the whole interglacial. When Palaeolithic sites can be fitted into such a framework, much environmental and chronological information is obtained.

Note the deforestation period at the end of sub-zone 11c, indicated by a decline in the pollen of hazel, yew and oak, and a corresponding rise in grasses. The same is to be seen in the pollen diagram for Hoxne in the neighbouring county of Suffolk (see page 127).

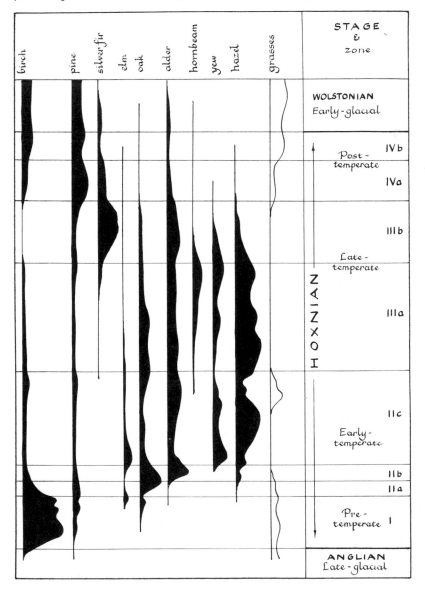

Zone I   Pre-temperate zone: birch and pine woodland gradually replaces the harsh, open landscape of a late glacial period. Light-demanding herbs and shrubs also thrive.

Zone II Early-temperate zone: this is the period of the development of mixed oak forest, producing a shaded, closed landscape. The soil becomes slightly acid.

Zone III Late-temperate zone: temperate trees such as silver fir and hornbeam are established in this zone, and there is a general decline of the mixed oak forest, mainly due to the increasing acidity of the soil.

Zone IV Post-temperate zone: there is a return to birch and pine woodland as the temperature declines and the leaching of the soil reaches a maximum. Temperate forest trees become virtually extinct and podsols give rise to damp, open heaths.

Letters are sometimes added to these zone numbers in order to distinguish sub-zones, which may be the result of local factors or just the length of a particular zone. The value of the environmental information available from such pollen studies is inestimable for interpreting Palaeolithic sites, apart from any chronological information they may impart. They constitute an ever-increasing aspect of importance to Palaeolithic archaeologists, particularly in the northern hemisphere. Pollen has also been used to demonstrate changes of climate in Africa during the Pleistocene, from dry to wet rather than cold to warm. It is not understood why the Pleistocene period is one of alternating glacial and interglacial cycles, for there is nothing in the geological record to show that such conditions prevailed in the preceding Tertiary period. However, it can be demonstrated that the rotation and orbit of the earth are subject to regular oscillations and movements. Astronomers have observed these movements since the eighteenth century and various theories have since been put forward to explain the glaciations of the northern hemisphere as a result of them. Certainly, changes in the angle of inclination of the earth's axis to the sun must affect the amount of annual radiation received at particular latitudes, and it would be difficult to refute that there is some connection here between these global movements and oscillations of climate. If so, it suggests that some astronomical event at the end of the Pliocene epoch could have been responsible. The major advocates of the astronomical theories of glaciation were Croll and Ball in the nineteenth century and Milankovitch in the twentieth. The late Professor Zeuner based his chronology of the Pleistocene on the elaborate calculations of the latter. The dated record of climatic changes which is now building up through the study of deep-sea cores offers a valuable check against the predictions of the astronomical theory of Milankovitch. They do not agree in detail, but it can hardly be a coincidence that both indicate a more or less continuous cycle from cold peak through a warm interval to another cold peak about every 40,000 years. The estimate for the duration of the interglacial represented by the laminated clays of Marks Tey, Essex, is in the order of 20,000 years. The framework of a Pleistocene time scale does seem to be emerging.

There are other ingenious theories connected with glaciations, some of which should not be taken seriously. One that does need to be considered is that of Antarctic ice surges. It can be argued that some late interglacial deposits appear to have been formed rapidly and represent a high sea level. The explanation offered is that vast portions of the Antarctic ice sheet, on a continental scale, have broken away from the land and fallen into the ocean, with the result that the world sea level has risen rapidly, almost overnight, by several metres. It is further suggested that this phenomenon is the inevitable result of a build-up of the ice sheet in Antarctica during an interglacial period, and that the effect of the great mass of ice in the ocean is to cool the waters and bring about a glacial phase; thus the whole process begins again. Advocates of this theory point in particular to the several sites of the Last Interglacial in England where, in the latter part of the sequence, large numbers of mammalian bones occur – animals, it could be argued, which drowned in the catastrophic rise in sea level which affected the lower reaches of rivers. It is a sobering thought that, if an expanse of the Antarctic ice sheet did slide into the sea on this scale tomorrow, London would be inundated. However, there is certainly no proof that this has ever happened and it must remain a theory. There is a Noah-like flavour and an element of unfashionable 'catastrophism' to this theory that do not appeal to most geologists, but it should not be ignored.

Geological processes may give some idea of time; sea cliff erosion is particularly obvious and, where the rocks are soft, the recession of a coastline may be measured at so many feet a year. Thus estimates can be made as to where the coastline was so many years beforehand. Mud may accumulate in a river delta at so much thickness a year; therefore a particular depth of sediment may be translated into terms of years. Deltaic sediments were used to obtain the first estimates for the time when Alpine glaciers retreated, and it was a general comprehension of the whole geological process of build-up and denudation that prompted John Frere at the end of the eighteenth century to make his famous remarks about the flint tools from Hoxne being of 'a very remote period indeed; even beyond that of the present world'. The obvious disadvantage of any assessments of age based on sedimentation or erosion rates is that they can only have any validity if past rates were the same as present ones. There is no way of assessing this. Earth movements, changes in sea level, changes in climate and numerous unknown factors are likely to have caused major and minor differences so, beyond indicating a general order of time, this method of dating is very limited. However, some sediments may be deposited in regular cycles for hundreds of even thousands of years in a manner which does allow their rate of accumulation to be calculated. The laminated clays (varves) which are found in lakes that formed in front of slowly retreating glaciers are the best examples of sediments of this type, for alternations of coarse and fine material are the result of annual, seasonal discharges. The resulting laminations may be counted and taken to correspond with the number of calendar years involved. In this way, absolute dates have been estimated for the retreat of Scandinavian glaciers because, in theory, it is possible to work back from varves which are forming at the present day to those which formed as the climate ameliorated. In practice there are several difficulties, the main one being that there is no unbroken sequence in one place, so it is necessary to correlate sequences of varves in one place with those in another and thus carry the succession forwards or backwards. This is not unwarranted, for seasons vary and the varves vary accordingly in thickness; one set may therefore be compared to another and keyed in with confidence. In the same way, seasonal variation in geographical regions will affect the annular growth of trees and produce distinctive patterns of tree rings. This is the principle of dendrochronology, for it allows the rings in one tree to be correlated with another, provided that at one time they were growing contemporaneously. Living trees may give a time scale going back several centuries. Their earliest ring pattern may be keyed in with older trees preserved in peats or other favourable circumstances. The great redwood and pine trees of North America have enabled a dendrochronological time scale to be constructed back to over 5,000 years before the present. There seems little chance of finding sufficient fossil wood ever to carry back this reliable dating method to the Palaeolithic period, but it is indirectly important as it has been used to check the validity of radiocarbon dates which do extend back to the Upper Palaeolithic period at least. It has been found that the radiocarbon dates for the oldest tree rings are about a thousand years too young.

Varves cannot give an absolute time scale beyond the final phases of the Last Glaciation in the northern hemisphere, but laminated clays produced by similar seasonal events are known from lakes which gradually silted up in interglacial periods, such as the example at Marks Tey in England mentioned above.

The vastness of geological time is difficult to comprehend, rather like astronomical distance. In human terms, a million years is a staggering duration, yet the Palaeolithic goes back two million years or more, and the evidence for our relatively close primate ancestors, several more millions. In this time the world has undergone many changes: continents have altered their shape, mountain ranges have formed, rivers and seas have been endlessly wearing away the rocks and transporting them from one place to another. Changes in the climate have occurred on a global scale, transforming arid zones to wet ones, or vice versa, or causing ice sheets and glaciers to render great tracts of the earth uninhabitable to all living forms. Animals, particularly mammals, have evolved or become extinct, and our own species is no exception; in fact it is the outstanding example of the appearance on the earth of a new type of animal, so different from anything else that many would reject the association. The archaeology of the Palaeolithic period covers this almost unbelievable rise of Man from his humble ape-like origin virtually to the beginnings of agriculture.

Palaeolithic archaeologists, collaborating with their colleagues in related fields such as geology, palaeobotany, palaeontology and an ever-increasing number of other natural and physical sciences, can, within very restricted limits, reconstruct past human events. A framework has to be made which includes time, environment and achievement, yet, for much of the Palaeolithic period, human activity and development have to be assessed from chipped stones, broken bones and very little else. It may seem unreasonable to use the term 'culture' for the mode of life and apparent traditions of a group of people represented in such a manner, but it is unavoidable if any attempt is made to humanise the evidence. Interpretations must vary, especially as more and frequently conflicting evidence appears. Provided interpretations are not presented as facts, there seems no harm in this. Some would claim that it is possible to extract far more information of an objective nature from statistical analyses of the material, even to the extent of formulating laws which govern human cultural evolution. Cynics may be excused for doubting this on the grounds that it seems impossible to discover laws governing present populations, let alone past ones, but it would be unwise to ignore such possibilities. Until such can be demonstrated, a subjective 'historical' approach must suffice, and that is what is attempted in this brief outline of the Palaeolithic period.

Culture is used here in the broad sense of Childe: 'Culture must correspond to a social group which sanctifies the distinctive conventions and carries the social tradition.'[1] The 'distinctive conventions' of most of the Palaeolithic period are nothing else but traditional methods of stone working. From these alone have to be assessed the degree of achievement of the society concerned. There seems little objection to comparing the primitive stone tools of the earliest hominids with the elaborate equipment of Upper Palaeolithic societies and concluding that the latter represents a much higher level of achievement. It is less easy when considering the varied industries of the long period in between.

Industry is the archaeological term for a particular method and tradition of stone working that may be recognised in numbers of assemblages, not necessarily contemporary. They presumably reflect the material requirements of a society, and it is further assumed that societies with the same industry are likely to be at the same level of economy and organisation. This may not be so but, with minor exceptions, there are stronger arguments for this assumption than against it. Opponents of such an assumption claim that many industries merely reflect a brief period of activity and that, depending on the type of activity, so the industry will differ. The imitative and conventional behaviour of man is at variance with this: habits are ingrained and most of us react against things which disturb those habits. It seems unlikely that early man was much different, and the astonishing standardisation of certain stone industries over long periods of the Pleistocene adequately confirms this. In simple, hunting economies, there would be little variation in the major activities on which life depended. It is not surprising that many Palaeolithic industries are found at butchering sites or, more accurately, are found in association with numerous bones of large mammals which are presumably the remains of their butchering. Some of these sites abound with stone tools called hand-axes, others with more roughly made chopper-cores. There is no reason to think that the animals could not have been butchered by either set of equipment. Unless there was some other activity which has left no trace it seems reasonable to conclude that the differences in the industries result from social tradition. These are the assumptions made for the purpose of setting out the evidence in this book.

There are many stone industries recognised throughout the world, and a corresponding number of names; a name is generally derived from the place where the industry was first recognised. However, they can all be placed in one of four major different traditions of stone working, called industrial complexes. Three are easy to define:

1. chopper-core industries without hand-axes;
2. hand-axe industries;
3. leptolithic industries (see p. 177).

The fourth is best described as an industrial complex, transitional in technology between the first two and the third. Few would refute the validity of this classification. It is the general conclusion from over a century of archaeological investigation. These industrial complexes will be explained and defined in subsequent chapters, but it is their significance which needs a little consideration first, especially if it is accepted that they may represent cultural stages in the evolution of human society. If this is correct, we might expect to find them occurring in a neat lineal succession. If it is wrong, they should not occur in temporal order but often be contemporary with each other. Both cases are true, or partly so. The problem is identical to the problem we shall encounter in the next chapter, namely that of putting the early hominids into a time scale. The fact that at least three different types of hominids were all living at about the same time in Africa at the beginning of the Pleistocene does not refute any argument that they could represent three stages of human evolution. In the same way, the occurrence of hand-axe industries and chopper-core industries at the same time in the Middle Pleistocene does not invalidate the argument that hand-axes are a technological advance on chopper-cores. There are distinct parallels between human physical and cultural evolution which certainly reinforce the idea that culture is part of our hominid evolutionary process. As will be seen in subsequent chapters, the elaborate and refined equipment of the leptolithic or blade and burin industries of the Late Pleistocene stands in marked contrast to the crude stone bashing of the earliest hominids. There is undoubtedly a cultural gulf between them greater than that between the communities represented by leptolithic industries and ourselves and it seems reasonable to apply the terms 'savagery' and 'barbarism' to their economies respectively. 'Savagery' is not meant in the popular sense of primitive and cruel, but in the sense of an economy dependent on catching or gathering food that is naturally available, in the same way as other animals, so that a balance is achieved between the different species. 'Barbarism' implies food production. Normally, it would only be considered that Neolithic societies had reached such a stage. Childe would have assigned the whole of the Palaeolithic and Mesolithic to savagery.[2] Here it will be suggested that the term 'barbarism' should also be applied to the Upper Palaeolithic societies for, although there was no question of arable farming or domestication of animals in the sense we are familiar with, hunting and food-gathering methods attained such a pitch of efficiency that the distinction between catching and slaughtering, or gathering and reaping, is too slight to separate them. It is more a matter of Upper Palaeolithic barbarism and Neolithic barbarism.

It will be seen in the succeeding chapters that, although there is no clear unilinear succession of stone industries throughout the world, there are obvious technological developments that proceed from one tool type to another. At least it can be stated that:

1. the first industries were the chopper-core industries;
2. there were no hand-axes at the beginning, and none at the end of the Pleistocene;
3. industries transitional between leptolithic industries and earlier ones do not occur until late in the Middle Pleistocene;
4. there were no leptolithic industries until the Late Pleistocene.

Thus it is reasonable to interpret the four industrial complexes as successive stages in a series of progressive refinement and elaboration of material equipment, which is reflecting cultural advancement in a social and economic sense. If this is so, and the order is accepted of

1. chopper-core industries
2. hand-axe industries
3. transitional industries
4. leptolithic industries

then any industry that occurs after the appearance of the succeeding group may be regarded as a survival.

Industries are frequently divided into sub-stages, where typology and stratigraphy can demonstrate a successive evolution. Sub-stages are rarely applicable in anything but a limited region. Table 1.3 shows how these various terms are related to each other.

Table 1.3: Palaeolithic Terminology

Period	Culture	Economy	Industry	Stage or facies
	Mesolithic		Leptolithic industries (Maglemosian, etc.)	
		Barbarism		
	Upper Palaeolithic		(Aurignacian, Solutrian, etc.)	Aurignacian I, etc.
	Middle Palaeolithic	Transitional	Transitional industries (Mousterian, etc.)	Mousterian (La Quina)
		Savagery		
	Lower Palaeolithic		Chopper-core and hand-axe industries (Acheulian, Oldowan, etc.)	Early Acheulian, Middle Acheulian, etc.

(Period column, rotated: Palaeolithic)

If cultural advancement in the Pleistocene is identified by series of stone industries then, as stated, it is clear that it has not advanced everywhere at the same speed. Also, it would seem that there have been centres of advancement. Everything, at present, points to Africa, especially the eastern side of the continent, being the centre at the very beginning of hominid experimentation. The first stone tools of the chopper-core industries are found there, and so are the first hand-axes. Thereafter there seems a great human dispersal over much of what is termed the Old World. The Middle Pleistocene probably saw the most stable and uniform culture the world has ever known, and stone industries in Africa, India and Europe have astounding similarities with each other.

Chopper-core industries survived in much of the world, but only in South East Asia to the exclusion of hand-axes. Uniformity may almost have been reached, but there appears to have been a burst of change and adaptation in the Middle Pleistocene, coinciding with evidence for severe glaciation of much of the northern hemisphere. Centres of advancement would appear, at this stage, to have been in Europe, Africa and the near east. Leptolithic industries seem earliest in Africa but their later development occurs mainly in the Near East and Europe.

The term 'Palaeolithic' has been in archaeological use for over a century. Sometimes it is used in a cultural sense, sometimes in a chronological one. The two are virtually synonymous so confusion is not likely to arise, but when subdivisions of the Palaeolithic are made it is a different matter. If the term 'Upper Palaeolithic' is used, what is meant may not be what is understood. There should, of course, be a noun to follow the term, for it is adjectival, but common usage allows *the* Upper Palaeolithic. If we refer to the Upper Palaeolithic in an archaeological or cultural sense, i.e. leptolithic industries based on blade production, with gravers, end scrapers, points and other tools made from them, then this is very different from the chronological sense of an Upper Palaeolithic period. The latter only has real meaning in a restricted geographical area, where the archaeological evidence is sufficient to indicate that only Upper Palaeolithic industries existed during the time implied. Elsewhere in the world, contemporary industries may be of Middle or Lower Palaeolithic type. This was certainly so in parts of South East Asia, where chopper-core industries were contemporary with the Upper Palaeolithic industries of Europe and elsewhere. If such simple, unevolved industries are termed Upper Palaeolithic just because they belong to the Late Pleistocene, all manner of confusion will arise between culture and chronology. In this account of human history from the end of the Pliocene epoch to the beginning of the Flandrian Stage of the Pleistocene (see Table 1.2) any subdivision of the Palaeolithic has a cultural implication irrespective of time. Thus, it is not contradictory to write that Lower Palaeolithic industries continued in parts of south east Asia into the Late Pleistocene, and it is hoped that the meaning will be clear.

That culture and time are not synonymous is obvious from the varied cultures that have coexisted in the world in historical time and, to a lesser and lesser extent, still do. The archaeological evidence for the Palaeolithic indicates it may have always been so from the very beginning. The only hope of assessing the developments and trends in this complex cultural process lies in placing the evidence into a chronological framework. The evidence must consist not just of pure archaeology (i.e. deductions made from artifacts and their direct associations), but of everything found with them that can help reconstruct the environment as near to its totality as possible.

Notes

1. Childe, 1942, p. 18.
2. Childe, 1944, p. 8.

References

There are several excellent and readily available books on the application of scientific methods to the many aspects of archaeology, especially D. Brothwell and E. Higgs (eds),

Science in Archaeology (1969). K.P. Oakley, *Frameworks for Dating Fossil Man* (1964) and F.E. Zeuner, *Dating the Past* (1958) are standard works. More general works such as M.J. Aitken, *Physics and Archaeology* (1974), E. Pyddoke (ed.), *The Scientist and Archaeology* (1963) and S. Fleming, *Dating in Archaeology* (1976) have relevant chapters. Geological aspects are covered by R.G. West, *Pleistocene Geology and Biology* (1968), K.W. Butzer, *Environment and Archaeology* (1968) and D.Q. Bowen, *Quaternary Geology* (1978). Specifically for the British Isles are W. Sparks and R.G. West, *The Ice Age in Britain* (1972) and J.G. Evans, *The Environment of Early Man in the British Isles* (1975). The classic work of F.E. Zeuner, *The Pleistocene Period* (1959), although now much outdated by further discoveries and techniques, remains an essential source book for many things mentioned in this chapter.

The following references provide details and sources of particular subjects:

Astronomical theories:	Zeuner, 1958, 1959.
Antarctic ice surges:	Hollin, 1969.
Potassium/argon dating:	Evernden and Curtis, 1965; Emiliani, 1968; Miller in Bishop and Miller (eds), 1972.
Radiocarbon dating:	Aitken, 1974; Fleming, 1976.
Pollen analysis:	West, 1968.
Deep-sea cores:	Emiliani, 1967; Shackleton and Opdyke, 1976.
Palaeomagnetism:	P. Evans, 1971; Mackereth, 1971.
Stages of British Quaternary:	Mitchell *et al.*, 1973.
Typology:	Bordes, 1950, 1961.
Metrical analysis:	Roe, 1968b.

Chapter 2

The First Humans

Fossil bones of higher primates (that is the order to which the Anthropoidea belong, which includes monkeys, apes and humans, to use the conventional classification system) are rare in comparison to the fossil bones of most other mammals. One reason for this could be their relatively greater intelligence, which might prevent them doing the kind of thing that would ensure their death and ultimate fossilisation, such as sinking into liquid mud. Otherwise, the Anthropoidea are subject to the same factors which affect all other living creatures as regards fossilisation.

The Hominoidea, that is the apes and humans which constitute that super-family, are classified into three families:

1. Pongidae – the living apes;
2. Oreopithecidae – apes represented by fossil bones, some of which are related to the living apes and others which became extinct;
3. Hominidae – ourselves (*Homo sapiens sapiens*) and a few extinct forms, some of which may not be related to us.

It is convenient to refer to the first two families as hominoids, and the latter, including ourselves, as hominids.

Several types of fossil apes have been found in Oligocene sediments and classified into various genera (*Dryopithecus, Oreopithecus, Propliopithecus, Limnopithecus*). Others come from Miocene sediments (*Ramapithecus*). A particularly important group of Lower Miocene age are referred to as *Proconsul*. The greatest number of fossil apes have been discovered in Africa, but they have also been found in India and Europe and it should not necessarily be assumed that Africa was the most important centre. It is fair to state, though, that on the evidence available, this would seem to be the case.

These fossil apes, frequently represented by little more than a few teeth, parts of mandibles or skull fragments, have to be assessed by the combinations of physical characteristics; some have teeth patterns, for instance, more like the living apes, others more like our own. In fact, *Ramapithecus* is regarded by some as a true hominid. Limb bones are particularly informative and one generalisation which is permissible is that the long forearms of the living apes, useful for their swinging or brachiating habits among the trees, are a specialisation: their ancestors had arms much more like ours in size and proportion to their bodies. In this respect it is the living apes which are specialised, not ourselves. True upright walking on two legs (bipedalism) is certainly a hominid characteristic and several of the fossil apes have limb bones which suggest they were not far from walking erect. From this pithecine mixture, although the details are hazy, were derived the living apes and ourselves. Several genera of apes which are now extinct were also derived from it. Likewise, it is apparent that there were derived some other hominids which became extinct.

Classification and nomenclature provide a perpetual subject for debate. Some anthropologists (the 'splitters') prefer to give a new generic name for almost every fossil they find, others (the 'lumpers') prefer to accept great variety within one genus and only give specific recognition with reluctance. The latter will be followed here, even if there is a danger of oversimplification.

A wealth of information for the period from the Late Pliocene to the middle part of the Pleistocene, say up to a million years ago, is now available from East Africa. Within the last 20 years, the discoveries at Olduvai Gorge by the Leakeys and the international expeditions in northern Kenya and Ethiopia have produced large numbers of fossil hominids, often associated with stone tools, within sediments with the optimum conditions for obtaining environmental information and dating.

The nomenclature for fossil hominids is a subject on which there is much disagreement and confusion. The author has neither the qualifications nor the temerity to put forward anything which goes beyond an assessment of the evidence and a favoured interpretation of it. In the period under consideration there would appear to be five fairly distinct types of hominids, two of the genus *Australopithecus* and three of *Homo*. Most anthropologists accept the distinction between the two genera, and to a somewhat lesser extent the specific differences. These hominids can be referred to as:

Australopithecus africanus
Australopithecus robustus
Homo habilis
Homo erectus
Homo sp. indet. (species indeterminate)

Table 2.1 helps to clarify some of the old and current terminology.

One, at least, of these hominids made stone tools and primitive structures from small boulders. One, at least, is presumably the ancestor of *Homo sapiens*, who does not appear until the latter part of the Middle Pleistocene. Their qualifications for these distinctions will be considered in turn.

Australopithecus africanus

There has been much argument among human palaeontologists as to whether the Australopithecines should be grouped together as one species or subdivided into two or more species. Certainly, there are two particularly distinct forms, one being a light, slender hominid (the 'gracile' form), and the other a heavier-faced stocky hominid (the 'robust' form). *Africanus* is the gracile form, represented by the discoveries at Taung, Botswana and in the Makapan and Sterkfontein caves, South Africa. At the latter site, a fine specimen of a skull, generally regarded as a female because of the association of a female pelvis, is referred to familiarly as 'Mrs Ples', as this genus was originally known as *Plesianthropus* (Plate I). Several individuals of *africanus* are represented in this rich cave by more than a hundred

Table 2.1: Some Published Synonyms of Fossil Hominids in Africa

As given here:	*Australopithecus africanus*	*Australopithecus robustus*	*Homo habilis*	*Homo erectus*	*Homo sp. indet.*
As published by: Dart, date as shown	*Australopithecus africanus* (Taung) (1925) *Australopithecus prometheus* (Makapansgat) (1948)				
Broom, date as shown	*Australopithecus transvaalensis* (Sterkfontein) (1936) *Plesianthropus transvaalensis* (Sterkfontein) (1937)	*Paranthropus robustus* (Kromdraai) (1938) *Paranthropus crassidens* (Swartkrans) (1949)			*Telanthropus capensis* (Swartkrans) (Broom and Robinson, 1949)
Robinson, date as shown	*Australopithecus transvaalensis* (Sterkfontein) (1954) *Homo africanus* (Sterkfontein) (1972)	*Paranthropus robustus* (Kromdraai) (1954) *Paranthropus boisei* (Olduvai) (1960)	*Homo africanus* (Olduvai) (1972)		*Homo erectus* (Swartkrans) (1961)
Arambourg, 1954				*Atlanthropus mauritanicus* (Ternifine)	
L.S.B. Leakey, 1959		*Zinjanthropus boisei* (Olduvai)			

Table 2.1: contd

L.S.B. Leakey, Tobias and Napier, 1964			*Homo habilis* (Olduvai)		
Oakley, 1964	*Australopithecus africanus* (Sterkfontein, Makapansgat)	*Paranthropus robustus* (Swartkrans, Kromdraai) *Paranthropus boisei* (Olduvai)	*Australopithecus capensis?* (Olduvai)		*Australopithecus capensis* (Swartkrans)
Campbell, 1964		*A. robustus* (Kromdraai) *A. r. crassidens* (Swartkrans)			
Tobias, 1967		*Australopithecus boisei* (Olduvai)			
Howell, 1969	*Australopithecus cf. africanus* (Omo)	*Australopithecus cf. boisei* (Omo)			
R.E.F. Leakey, 1970		*Australopithecus cf. boisei* (Koobi Fora)			*Homo sp.* (Koobi Fora)
M.D. Leakey, 1972				*Homo erectus* (Olduvai)	
Clarke, Howell and Brain, 1970					*Homo sp. indet.* (Swartkrans)

Table 2.1: contd

Wolpoff and Lovejoy, 1975	*Australopithecus africanus* (Sterkfontein, Swartkrans, Kromdraai, etc.)	*Australopithecus africanus* (Sterkfontein, Swartkrans, Kromdraai, etc.)	
M.D. Leakey, Hay, Curtis, Drake, Jackes and White, 1976			*Homo sp.* (Laetolil)
Johanson and Taieb, 1976	aff. *Australopithecus africanus* (Hadar)	aff. *Australopithecus robustus* (Hadar)	*Homo sp.* (Hadar)

For a review of the problems of nomenclature see B.G. Campbell, 1965.
For details of discoveries see Oakley and Campbell, 1967, and Day, 1977.

teeth and fragments of skulls, jawbones and limb bones. At present the site is difficult to date with any more precision than Early Pleistocene, on the basis of associated animal bones. Stone tools have been found at Sterkfontein but it has now been demonstrated that they come from a level above the breccia containing the Australopithecine remains and this could represent a gap of about a million years between them.

A spectacular discovery at Hadar, in the central Afar region of Ethiopia, is the partial skeleton of an individual within sediments radioactively dated to about three million years. Also a female, she is known affectionately as 'Lucy', and is regarded as a rather less advanced type of *africanus* than is represented at Sterkfontein. This is by far the most complete example of this type of hominid ever found, consisting of skull fragments, the mandible, most of both arm bones, some vertebrae, ribs, half the pelvis and some of the leg bones. She is thought to have been about 40 years old when she died, and little more than a metre high. The forearms are longish but there can be little doubt that she walked erect. No tools have been reported from the Hadar sediments, but, even if they had, 'Lucy' might not have made them for she is not the only hominid represented there. Contrary to Sterkfontein, where there were no other associated hominids, there are two upper jawbones from Hadar of *Homo* with nearly complete dentition. These jawbones appear to have some affinities with *Homo erectus*. There is also part of a skull that is probably the other robust form of Australopithecine.

West of Lake Turkana (formerly Lake Rudolf) in northern Kenya, *africanus* has been recorded from Kanapoi in sediments dated to greater than 1.8 million years by the potassium/argon radioactive dating method,[1] and in the same area within sediments ranging well back into the Pliocene, and possibly 4 million years old.[2] At Kanapoi there were no stone tools directly associated, but those found on the surface nearby were probably contemporary. Other gracile Australopithecines have come from the Lower Omo Basin in Ethiopia.

The other well-known site for remains of this hominid is Makapansgat in the northern Transvaal, South Africa.[3] Palaeomagnetism suggests a date of greater than 3.06 million years. Professor Dart has claimed that many of the animal bones found with the twelve individuals represented by the remains were purposely selected and utilised. In the absence of any other hominid it would seem likely that this Australopithecine had been responsible, but most archaeologists are not convinced that the bones in question were either purposefully selected or used.

The famous site at Olduvai in Tanzania, thought to date back to about 1.75 million years, has not yielded remains of *africanus*, but there is a suspicion that some of the *Homo habilis* remains may really belong more with this group than with *Homo*. Such are the difficulties of attempting to reconstruct evolutionary history from sparse fragments, and this particular problem is mentioned again below in the brief survey of *habilis* himself. What does seem fairly clear is that the gracile Australopithecines flourished in the Late Pliocene but did not extend very far into the Pleistocene. Nor, on present evidence, do they appear to have spread out of South and East Africa (Figure 3). They are certainly contemporary with the production of stone tools, but whether they made any of them or not is unproven.

Figure 3: Map of Hominid Sites of the Pliocene and Early Pleistocene Periods
With only one possible exception in China, they are confined to Africa and one site in the Near East.

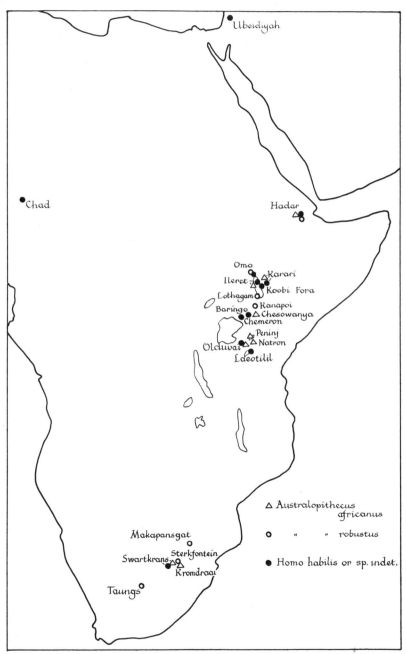

Australopithecus robustus

It seems a remarkable coincidence that this hominid is best represented in old cave deposits at Swartkrans, less than a mile away from the Sterkfontein cave. Large numbers of Australopithecine bones have been laboriously extracted from their limestone matrix, including near-complete skulls and several mandibles (Plate II). Generally, *robustus* is, as the name suggests, an individual with a strong heavy face. In many cases there is a ridge of bone (sagittal crest) along the top of the skull, as in a modern gorilla, to accommodate the large muscles which had to be attached to it. The jaw is usually massive. The main arm bone (humerus) is very similar to modern man and there is no doubt that *robustus* walked upright.

Dating at Swartkrans is difficult and, as at the other South African Australopithecine sites, is dependent on the associated fauna. This correlates best with that from the Shungara formation in East Africa, dated by palaeo-magnetism to 1.8-1.4 million years. The conclusion is that Swartkrans is not as old as Sterkfontein. The same may be said for another nearby cave, Kromdraai, which has also yielded remains of *robustus*. There is no definite association of stone tools at Swartkrans or Kromdraai, although some have been found there. At Swartkrans there is also another hominid present, once known as *Telanthropus*, which will be discussed below.

Robustus, himself, has had a plethora of generic names put upon him and, of course, these retain some validity if the grouping or 'lumping' of these various discoveries is discounted. At Sterkfontein he was *Paranthropus crassidens*, *Paranthropus robustus crassidens* or even elevated to *Homo transvaalensis*. There is now *Australopithecus boisei* for the Olduvai specimens. Whether all the differences seen in the various discoveries may really be regarded as a range of variation within a species is a palaeontological problem not yet resolved. This applies also to the previous Australopithecine considered above and, to a lesser extent, to all the hominids under discussion. More relevant to this broad survey is the notion that both *robustus* and *africanus* are really one species, and their separation is unwarranted, even at the level used here. At one time it was thought that the robust Australopithecines were the males, and the gracile ones the females, of just one species. This is not such a far-fetched suggestion as it may seem for, to take a modern parallel, the skeleton of a tall Masai warrior would look very odd against the skeleton of a female West African pygmy. This would be an extreme variation within the present species, but the sexual dimorphism in any modern population is considerable. However, the explanation of the differences between *robustus* and *africanus* as being due to sexual dimorphism or an extreme range of variation within one species[4] is a difficult one to accept and is not generally supported.[5] Several facts argue against it, particularly the absence of gracile forms at Swartkrans and the absence of robust forms at Sterkfontein. There would also appear to be a time difference in the range of these species: only *robustus* continues well into the Pleistocene. Also, most convincing of all, in the sites around Lake Turkana the numbers of *robustus* specimens now found produce a range of variation that would be consistent with the differences that might be expected between males and females.

Perhaps the most famous and important robust Australopithecine found is the one from the lower part of Bed 1 at Olduvai Gorge, Tanzania. He was named Zinjanthropus or 'nutcracker man' on account of his enormous molar teeth. This was the first one to be found in a datable context, and radioactive methods would put the date at about 1.6 million years. Stone tools were found with him, so, for a few months, he topped the list of possible suspects for the role of tool maker. As will be seen below, he was rapidly ousted from this distinction by the discovery of another hominid at Olduvai at a near-contemporary level.

Robustus has an ancestry, like *africanus*, well back in the Pliocene, as has been proved by the discoveries around Lake Turkana in northern Kenya (Figure 4). He continues well above the KBS Tuff (a rock formed of fragments thrown out by a volcanic eruption and later consolidated) which is a marker horizon in that area originally dated to 2.61 ± 2.6 million years,[6] although some new measurements suggest that a date of 1.80 ± .01 million years is more accept-able.[7] He is certainly contemporary with stone industries at Karari and Ileret, to name just two of these sites.

As with *africanus*, there are no known examples of this hominid outside South and East Africa, with the exception of one claim from China. A few other claims or suggested affinities with *Australopithecus* from sites outside Africa, such as Ubeidiyeh in Israel, would now be regarded as coming more within the sphere of *Homo habilis* or *Homo sp. indet.*

Homo habilis

This hominid (Plate III) was first discovered at Olduvai Gorge, at a level just below that of *Zinjanthropus*, and there can be little difference of time between them. Other discoveries at Olduvai and around Lake Turkana have shown conclusively that *habilis* belongs to the same Plio-Pleistocene time span as *robustus*. Skulls, teeth and limb bones indicate a gracile hominid. Foot bones for one individual suggest a height of about 1.40 m. There are clear similarities with *africanus* and many anthropologists would see no generic difference. However, the brain size is larger, being about 650 cc; *africanus* had a cranial capacity of rarely more than about 500 cc.

Some of the hominid material found around Lake Turkana and the Omo Valley has been classified as *habilis*. In the latter area it appears in a dry period with zebra and antelopes, indicating open, grassy plains. There is also an associated stone industry of small flakes.

There seem valid reasons for regarding the type specimens from Olduvai as something distinct and worthy of a new name, but it becomes very difficult with some of the other material. It is not just that the affinities of some of the characteristics are more or less with the gracile Australopithecine, *africanus*, but that they are frequently more or less with the next hominid to be con-sidered, *Homo erectus*. Little more can be said about *habilis* until *erectus*, himself, has been considered.

Figure 4: Stratigraphy and Chronology of Sites East of Lake Turkana, Kenya

On this simplified chart are shown some of the numerous hominid discoveries that have been found at various localities east of Lake Turkana. The numbers are those given by the Kenya National Museum to individual discoveries. Open circles have been used on the chart to indicate *Australopithecus robustus*, closed ones *Homo sp. indet.* It can be seen that the two species are contemporary but *Homo* was presumably responsible for the KBS industry (Industry 1), in and just below the KBS Tuff, and also the later Karari industry (Industry 2) (see Figure 7) (based on Brock and Isaac, 1976; R.E.F. Leakey, 1976 a and b; Wood, 1976; and others).

The chronometric dates are based on K/Ar dating. These were originally calculated to give much older dates (Fitch and Miller, 1976), with the KBS Tuff at 2.6 million years. Further works (Curtis *et al.*, 1978; Drake *et al.*, 1980) strongly support a more recent date of about 1.8 million years for the KBS Tuff. The fauna and palaeomagnetism support the younger date, but fission-track dating (see page 22) gives a date of 2.4 million years. Such are the present complexities and difficulties of dating the Pliocene-Pleistocene boundary.

For the geology of these critical sites see Behrensmeyer, 1970; Bowen and Vondra, 1973; and Bishop (ed.), 1978.

KNM-3733 has been compared to *Homo erectus* and is the most advanced hominid known at this early date. It is illustrated on Plates IV and V. KNM-1470 is illustrated on Plates VI and VII.

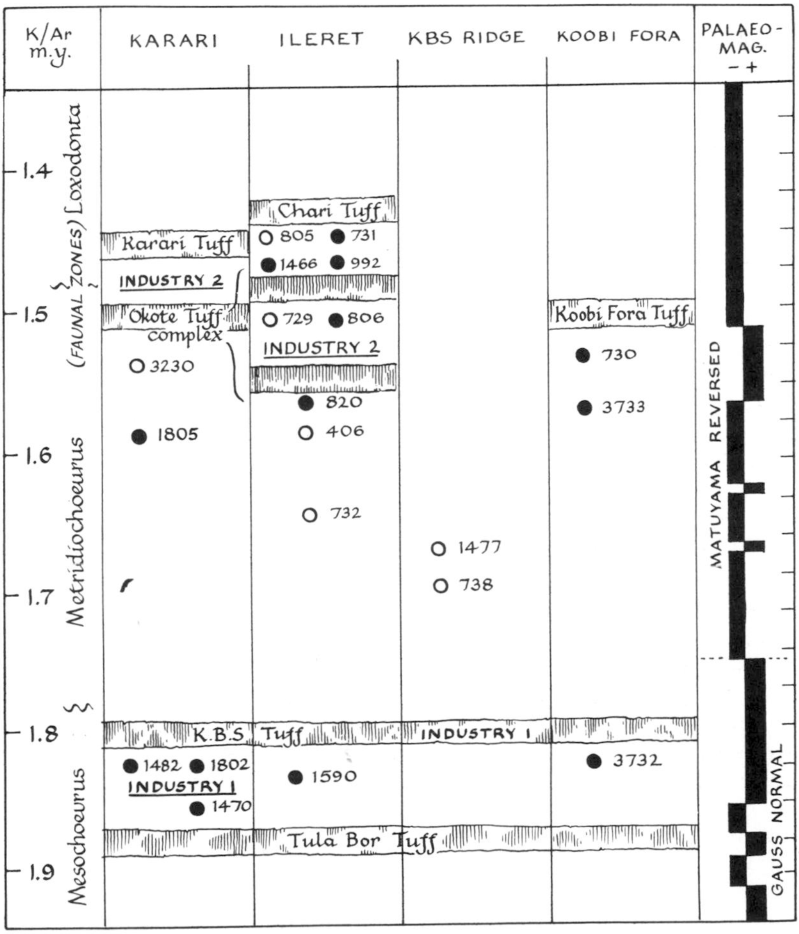

Homo erectus

It is always more sensible and scientifically acceptable to work from the known to the unknown so, rather than become confused by the evidence concerning this species in the Plio-Pleistocene, and its affinities with its contemporary hominids in East Africa, it seems best to jump to the earlier Middle Pleistocene period and work backwards. Significantly, this takes us out of Africa for a while. Peking Man has been well known for over forty years, under the name of *Sinanthropus pekinensis*. It is now mainly agreed that he can be lumped together with several other discoveries, including Java Man, as *Homo erectus*. The Peking finds were made in a disused limestone quarry at Choukoutien, near Peking (see Figure 15), in deposits infilling an ancient cave system. A population of over forty individuals, men, women and children, is represented from this one site. Peking Man was a heavy-faced, large-jawed person with very thick brow ridges; a muscular, stocky individual about 1.6 m tall. His brain size varied from about 900 to 1,225 cc (modern man is about 1,450 cc) (Plate XI). He used fire, made stone tools and successfully hunted large game. Dating cannot be precise as it depends on the animals associated with him, but it is an assemblage belonging to the Middle Pleistocene and unlikely to be any earlier. Less than half a million years is a sensible guess, although one attempt to get an absolute date by amino-acid racemisation process gave a date of 300,000 years. Other finds of *Homo erectus* in Middle Pleistocene contexts come from Hungary, East and West Germany, France, Spain, North and East Africa (see Figure 19). In most cases there is an accompanying stone industry.

There can be no doubt about the *Homo* status of *erectus*, even if we would rather give him a separate specific name. The time gap between *erectus* in South East Asia and the earlier hominids found in South and East Africa is large; it may span over a million years, and this seems ample time to have allowed *erectus* to evolve either from them or from something similar elsewhere. *Erectus* fossils that are earlier than Peking Man fit well into such a scheme. The most famous group is that from Java, found at a number of localities and not all of the same age. The earlier Trinil and Sangiran skulls probably date to about 700,000 years (Plate X). Estimations of the cranial capacities of these three skulls vary from 750 to 940 cc. This is considerably smaller than their Peking counterparts and approaching *habilis* and some of the other Plio-Pleistocene hominids from East Africa. Surprisingly, no stone tools have been found associated with the Java skulls, although a simple stone industry is known from the country and might well be expected to have been associated with them. There is another find of *Homo erectus* in China: a skull cap and mandible from Lantian, in the province of Shensi. This is probably earlier than the Choukoutien fossils. The brain size is 778 cc and it was associated with at least one stone hand-axe, a type of tool not known from Choukoutien.

Erectus is well represented in the upper part of the Olduvai sequence by so-called 'Chellean Man' (Plate IX). The discovery consists of a near-complete skull but devoid of the face and the mandible. This was found in Bed II at Olduvai, but above a hiatus in the sedimentation, which could mean a gap of about half a million years between this skull and the *habilis* and *robustus* remains beneath. Radioactive dating by the potassium/argon method has given a date of about 500,000 years, but there must be doubt about the validity of this date, and an earlier one seems more likely. Chellean Man had a brain size of about 1,000 cc and is associated with a hand-axe industry. A broken cranium of *erectus* and leg and pelvic bones also come from Bed IV at Olduvai, thought to date to about 300,000 years. There is also most of an ulna bone thought to belong to this hominid, from Bed II.

Finds of *erectus* in the later Middle Pleistocene, or of human fossils of that time with *erectus* traits, will be discussed in later chapters, where appropriate, but it is important at this point to see how or when he originated, especially in relation to the other types of hominids that were certainly living in East and South Africa in the Plio-Pleistocene, as listed above. Mention has been made of hominids with *erectus*-like traits from the sites around Lake Turkana. There is a finely preserved skull from Koobi Fora (referred to as KNM 3733), found in the Upper Member of the sediments there (Figure 4), dated to about 1.3 to 1.6 million years (Plates IV-V). It has a brain capacity of between 800 and 900 cc, and such are its similarities with some of the Chinese discoveries that its finder is prepared to regard it as *erectus*. There are also two skulls from levels below the marker KBS Tuff in the same region, from Karari and Ileret, much earlier than the Koobi Fora specimen: older than 1.8 million years. These are numbered KNM-ER 1470 (Plates VI-VII) and KNM 1590 respectively. The brain size of the skull from Koobi Fora is about 800 cc, far in excess of all the other hominids known to be contemporary with it. Anthropologists are hesitant to name these fossils. As Richard Leakey, the discoverer of KNM 1470 puts it, 'the maxilla and facial region are unlike any known hominid. Only the flat fronted, wide palate is suggestive of *Australopithecus*.' There are differences from *erectus*, as described from the classic sites in China and Java. There are even points of resemblance with *Homo sapiens*, especially among some associated limb bones. Another site, 30 miles south of the famous Olduvai Gorge, has now produced remains of 13 hominids from deposits known as the Laetolil Beds, and extended the problem well back into the Pliocene. This site has also revealed a spectacular line of human footprints, but not a single stone tool. The Laetolil Beds have been dated by potassium/argon to 3.59-3.77 million years, yet some of the affinities of these fossils are thought to be with *Homo*. Comparison has been made with the upper and lower jaw fragments found with 'Lucy' at Hadar, mentioned above. There is clearly a taxonomic dilemma and the evidence is demanding a new approach to the problem. It may be focusing our attention on to reality and revealing something of the actual mechanics of evolution among these early hominids. So, rather than invent a multitude of new specific names, it seems wise to place these and several other hominid fossils into a broad, non-committal category: *Homo sp. indet.*, i.e. an indeterminate species of *Homo*. Under this heading it is convenient to examine the likely manner in which *Homo erectus* appears to emerge in the earlier part of the Pleistocene, when the other hominids fade away.

Homo sp. indet.

It has already been stated that hominid traits can be detected in some of the Miocene and Pliocene hominoids, even if these traits are mainly assessed on such small items as the cusp patterns of teeth. By the end of the Pliocene these traits are shared by a variety of hominids which, in turn, are exhibiting their own specific traits. When these are distinctive enough it has been found convenient to give their owners a name. There are many ways of looking at the problem, but there is a general acceptance that *robustus, africanus, habilis* and *erectus* do warrant some title in order to separate them. Is it, however, really justifiable to do this, and what does such separation imply? If they are given separate generic status this should imply, to a biologist, that there can be no interbreeding, yet some of the hominid remains appear to have affinities with more than one species. Somewhere along the line there must have been an interbreeding population, part of which developed certain characteristics that eventually distinguished it from the remainder. Is there any reason to think that the Plio-Pleistocene hominids had developed beyond such a stage when one species, as identified by us, was incapable of producing fertile offspring with another? The similarities between *africanus* and *habilis* do not support such a notion. However, the differences between *robustus* and *habilis* are greater and perhaps it is likely that this hominid had diverged from a common ancestry a long way back in the Pliocene and remained apart from his relations for so long that, even if interbreeding was still possible, differences in physique and mode of life made it abhorrent or otherwise undesirable. There seems nothing to suggest that *robustus* had anything to do with the appearance of *Homo*, but had adapted himself to a particular ecological niche with which he coped quite successfully until the earlier part of the Pleistocene, when it would seem he died out. It is probably no coincidence that his demise takes place as *erectus* emerges.

The idea of several hominids living in one area at the same time has never appealed to ecologists. If we relegate *robustus* to one niche, we are still left with three others. Their specific status may be questioned, but not their characteristics or traits. Before any assessment can be made as to which of these hominids made stone tools and can really be regarded as 'human', or even if they all made stone tools, it is necessary to consider in a little more detail the mechanics of evolution in what is, in biological terms, a very closely related group. There are no clear answers, only speculative ideas or models which can be tested against the evidence as it appears. Many models can be devised, and have been, but most anthropologists would now see them as reduced to two. The first is one which sees slow changes within a population through time, so that there might be marked differences from one end of the scale to the other, but a distinct similarity throughout the whole population at any one time. This is called 'phyletic gradualism'. It would mean that the hominids which have been classified as *habilis* and *erectus*, because they are virtually contemporary, must represent two different populations which may have diverged from a common stock, but at a considerable time beforehand.

The other model is 'allopatric speciation', which sees new species evolving rapidly by the splitting of the population of one lineage. This might be induced by selective breeding within a combination of factors such as advantageous traits and geographical isolation. This could mean the development of a new 'species' in such a short time that it would contrast with the remaining population from which it had sprung. Thus *habilis* and *erectus* could well be contemporary and, in a sense, facies of one population. There could then be hybridisation of these groups, which might eliminate certain characteristics that had developed, increase or modify them in some other way and perhaps give rise to yet other distinct groups. This model, otherwise called the spectrum hypothesis, implies a very wide range of existing or possible variation within one species. It allows endless permutations, and the control can only be the possibilities of variation dependent on the common gene pool and their effect on chances for survival. It does demand the isolation of elements within a population for periods long enough to allow characteristic features to appear. Conversely, if the population is constantly intermixed and no one group ever becomes isolated it cannot happen, and the model of 'phyletic gradualism' would be more applicable.

The 'allopatric speciation' model does seem to fit the evidence for the Plio-Pleistocene period in East and South Africa. It is expressed diagrammatically by Figure 5. It may explain the coexistence of different hominids, but it does little to help us elucidate the circumstances which led to the advantage that one group may have had over another. Here, again, we can only speculate. It is also reasonable to assume that what did happen in Africa might also have happened elsewhere in the world where hominids were present, such as parts of Asia and southern Europe.

Brain size has been mentioned and, as might be expected, there is a fairly general increase in brain size from the Plio-Pleistocene hominids to the present day. Brain size and humanity are connected. It would be more accurate to say brain size and shape, and much depends on the number of cells that exist for potential use. Suggestions have been made that there may be a threshold of about 900 cc, over which, connected with physical changes of the jaw structure, tongue and larynx, language is possible. A modern *sapiens* baby, for instance, is said not to be able to speak until its brain has grown to about this 900 cc capacity. It is possible that a similar threshold could exist below which conscious organisation among a number of hominids was impossible; but beyond which conceptual thought and tool making for visualised eventualities could be possible. Apart from the rare hominid fragments, there is no way in which such matters can be assessed, but Palaeolithic archaeology can to some extent reconstruct human situations. It cannot do so without artifacts — that is, anything made or used by a human being — and then only if these are related to every available scrap of associated evidence. There are sites in East Africa, particularly around Lake Turkana and in the Olduvai Gorge, where it would be reasonable to consider that traces remain of the first human adaptation to the complex world. If not the very first sites, they are probably at the first level of the human activity which was to make the species dominant. If, as probably happened, this activity occurred elsewhere in the world, it is likely to have been along similar lines. East Africa can safely be regarded as a model for this initial stage of human progress.

Subsequent chapters will be more concerned with the archaeological aspect of human groups throughout the Pleistocene, and the manner in which they appear to have developed, but it is first worth considering what circumstances induced certain hominids, at about the end of the Pliocene period, to adopt a way of life that was to prove so successful. Necessity for survival must be the only answer. World changes in climate, even slight ones, can greatly affect some animals and make little difference to others. Some change that was radical to hominids is implied about this time. There is some evidence from faunal assemblages and lake levels that there were dry periods. This would mean greater dependence on the fewer water sources and a shorter supply of vegetable food.

Figure 5: Diagram of Possible Model of Human Evolution
This is based on traits transmitted genetically by an interbreeding population, with relatively marked and rapid changes taking place as a result of the isolation of certain groups by such reasons as geographical barriers, selective breeding or cultural divisions. This model is known as 'allopatric speciation' or the 'spectrum hypothesis'.

The time span represented by the diagram is Late Pliocene to Early Pleistocene, with *habilis* occurring at about the boundary between them. *Robustus* is assumed to have split from the *Ramapithecus/Australopithecus* lineage further back in the Pliocene, but his traits may still have influenced the emerging *Homo* species; hence skull KNM-ER 1805 from Karari, East of Lake Turkana (see Figure 4), which, in spite of *Homo*-like features, possessed bony crests on the skull like *robustus*.

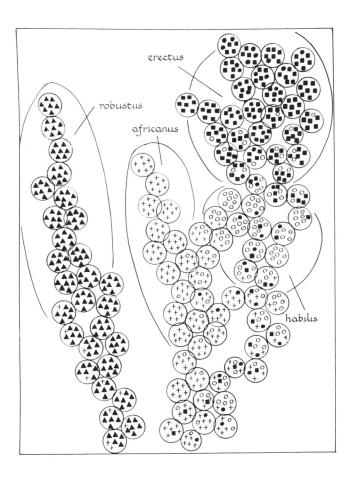

●	traits of *Homo sapiens*
■	traits of *Homo erectus*
○	traits of *Homo habilis*
▲	traits of *Australopithecus robustus*
+	traits of *Australopithecus africanus*

Hominids had the evolutionary advantage of having teeth and digestive systems which could tackle both meat and vegetables. The hunting of animals, or at least the scavenging of meat from carnivore kills or other deaths, may thus have become more important. However, the quantity of meat to be found was probably quite small and individual or small groups of hominids may have found this type of existence hazardous to the point of starvation for, while they were searching for dead animals, they could not be gathering fruits and vegetables. The danger of exposing themselves in open areas would have been a serious factor, and this is just where carnivore kills might be found. It would be suicidal to grub around for roots and seeds on the open savannah, even if they could be found. The hominids would need to have all their faculties concentrated on keeping alive. Strength, fleetness and cunning were clearly advantageous. Child-bearing females, or children, could not have survived with the meat scavengers, but they could concentrate their activities on the vegetable foods to be found in the safer areas of water courses or other places where trees or rocks gave some shelter. A divergence of activity may have been unavoidable. However, male and female individuals or, more likely, small groups would obviously meet. The foraging success of one may have been greater than the other and food may have been voluntarily exchanged. This idea is favoured by some of the anthropologists who have worked on these early sites, and has been put forward as the trigger for developments which become almost inevitable. Food sharing is suggested as the method by which some hominids adapted to the reduction of the food supply in their changed ancestral environment.

The concept of daily food sharing in such a manner, as a means of existence, may only have been possible with hominids possessing a large enough brain to comprehend and act upon it. The formation of a 'home base' becomes automatic, for there must be some agreed place at which to meet and share the food. It also implies some concept of time and the formation of routine. If a 'home base' was found to be favourable it may have been used consistently for long periods. The known East African sites of this period are mainly on the sides of the lower reaches of small streams, or around the edges of the lakes into which streams debouched. Trees could be expected to exist where there was adequate water, especially along the stream beds. Trees supplied protection from the sun and some security from predators, and there can be little doubt that for some millions of years most hominoids and hominids had adapted themselves to a wooded landscape. Ingrained within the first humans may have been an almost instinctive compulsion to seek such shelter.

Food-sharing activities of this nature demand some form of communication; signs, gestures and grunts would hardly have sufficed even at this primitive level of human existence. Attempts to teach chimpanzees to speak have had no success, although chimpanzees reared in human society can learn to identify objects with gesticulated signs. Abstract ideas cannot be conveyed and this may well be connected with their failure to comprehend language which, as has been stated above, could be connected with the size and shape of their brains. There may also be physiological reasons preventing chimpanzees from forming articulate sounds, although they make a variety of calls. If these deductions are correct, it follows that a larger brain will allow both the possibility of conceptual thought, without which food sharing of the type envisaged was probably impossible, and adequate means of communication. The latter was probably restricted to sounds for concrete needs and a few abstract ideas. Language and speech are terms which imply sophisticated forms of tonal communication far beyond anything possible at this stage of humanity, but it would be safe to think that the basis was being laid. Most significantly, there is the strong implication that a larger brain would have been an advantage for survival. Those hominids with *erectus* traits had the largest brains, and it is they who survived into the Middle Pleistocene, so they are best regarded as forerunners of ourselves; other hominids, such as *habilis*, were either absorbed by them or, if genetically isolated, failed to develop the traits required for survival. Their weak position may even have made them prey for their near-relations. The disappearance of *habilis* from the fossil record in the early part of the Pleistocene does not seem surprising when viewed in this way.

There is one further aspect of this early human activity that the evidence allows us to consider: tool making. More correctly, it should perhaps be seen that the crude stone tools which are found at this period indicate a requirement for equipment. Some of the stone artifacts were tools in their own right, but others (or the same ones used for other purposes) were the means by which other materials could be worked into useful objects. Unfortunately, apart from a few dubious used bones, none of the other materials has survived. Wood, bark, vegetable fibres, skin and sinew are the obvious raw materials available but, if any of these materials were used, they have perished without trace. We can only guess at the requirements of these first human groups and, as before, reckon that the familiar maxim of necessity being the mother of invention must have applied. Food sharing means food distribution and there are obvious drawbacks to passing a joint of meat around for everyone to have a bite at; the distribution of similar-sized pieces would seem essential if the food-sharing principle was to work at all, and this demands the use of some form of knife. Any convenient sharp-edged stone would serve as a crude cutting instrument and it would soon be apparent that a freshly broken stone was much more efficient than one blunted by natural weathering. The next step almost suggests itself: one stone was bashed against another and the resulting splinters examined for those which were of convenient size and sharpness to hold between the fingers and use as a knife. The advantages of being able to make a tool as opposed to searching for a natural one are self-evident. It was also a happy coincidence that the stream beds and lakeside favoured as home bases were the very places where natural erosion and water movement caused pebbles and boulders to accumulate. It soon became apparent which types of rock split easiest and gave the best cutting edges. Quartzites, lavas and silcretes splintered well, sandstones and tuffs were often too soft, basalts and other igneous rocks were frequently too hard.

Apart from cutting up the food supply, we can guess at other requirements: some form of container for collecting nuts, seeds and small fruits; storage containers for water; wind-breaks or roofs where the natural shelter at a home base was insufficient; digging sticks for buried edible roots; means of reaching inaccessible fruits.

The bashing of one stone upon another to produce useful splinters is such a crude business that the term 'industry', as used by archaeologists for the resulting products, seems far too elaborate. However, astonishing as it may be, it is clear that by the beginning of the Pleistocene the haphazard smashing of one stone upon another had already been supplanted by a certain amount of technique to which the terms 'method' and 'skill' are not inappropriate.[8] It is obvious that skilful, controlled knapping of a stone could produce far more useful pieces of sharp stone than haphazard bashing which would tend to produce a large number of very small splinters of no use. Knapping is the term used to describe the purposeful hitting of one stone with a hammer, usually another stone, in order to detach flakes. It involves the selection of suitable surfaces in relation to the angles of nearby edges. The rudiments of flint knapping are described in many books and, although there was no flint in East Africa, the same principles apply to the rocks used. These rudiments had been acquired and Figure 7 shows a few typical tools from the KBS site east of Lake Turkana, below a marker tuff dated to 1.8 million years. Whatever the exact age, it is certainly at the lowest technological level of human stone industrial activity. There are three main elements to the industry: the cores from which flakes have been struck, the flakes themselves, and other flakes which have been further trimmed in order to modify their shape or edge qualities. Some of the cores may have been used as choppers, while some may have been made purposely as choppers. The edge chipping or secondary working of flakes implies the need for some specialised tool. This is the level from which developed the various stone industries of the Pleistocene, which will be described in subsequent chapters.

It will be seen that by the latter half of the Pleistocene there are industries which contain highly specialised forms of stone implements. The tool kit of the Upper Palaeolithic period is particularly rich and fits well with our interpretation of the people of that period as being a highly advanced hunting society. However, there are other industries at various periods in the Pleistocene which show very little technical advance over those figured from Lake Turkana at the beginning of it all. Some caution is required in assessing the achievements of past populations merely by their stonework, for many factors may be involved. Elaborate equipment might be produced from the crudest flakes. Bamboo can make good knives. Human groups might exist without having to resort to stone tools in any form and, if everything else perished, there would be no trace of their existence. There is also the danger that, because we feel an affinity for the hominid who could flake a stone with some control and method, we might credit him with too much humanity, and see him more like ourselves than is justified. Conversely, we might discredit some of our ancestors by attributing to them a savagery and inhumanity that would be equally out of proportion. Until the last 50,000 years at least, there is virtually nothing but stone tools to guide us, yet what they reflect is consistent with the complexity of events that led from these early hominid beginnings to modern society.

Notes

1. Patterson, Behrensmeyer and Sill, 1970.
2. Bishop and Chapman, 1970.
3. Brain, 1958; Mason, 1962.
4. Wolpoff and Lovejoy, 1975.
5. R.E.F. Leakey and Walker, 1976.
6. Fitch and Miller, 1970, 1976; Fitch, Hooker and Miller, 1976.
7. Drake, Curtis, T.E. Cerling, B.W. Cerling and Hampel, 1980.
8. Isaac, 1978.

References

Most of the detailed descriptions of the discovery or interpretation of the remains of Plio-
Pleistocene fossil man are contained in the journals, memoirs and proceedings of learned
societies, especially the *Journal of the Royal Anthropological Institute*, the *American
Journal of Physical Anthropology*, *Memoirs of the Transvaal Museum*, *Proceedings of the
Pan African Congresses* and the *South African Journal of Science*. New discoveries are
generally reported in *Nature*, published weekly and usually available in public reference
libraries.

The following standard works or more general publications are listed below as a guide to
further reading; most of them contain bibliographies with full references to the original
sources.

Evolution

History of the Primates by W. le Gros Clark and *Evolution* (Anon.) are two inexpensive
handbooks published by the British Museum (Natural History) which make admirable
introductions to the subject. Le Gros Clark's *The Fossil Evidence for Human Evolution*
(1964) and *The Antecedents of Man* (1959) are more detailed. Unfortunately, they predate
the wealth of material since discovered in East Africa, the impact of which is only beginning
to have its effect on earlier evaluations. Similarly, F. Clark Howell and François Bourlière
(eds), *African Ecology and Human Evolution* (1963) lacks this material but is a large volume
of authoritative papers on this aspect of human evolution. There are many excellent papers
in A.L. Kroeber (ed.), *Anthropology Today* (1953).

Also highly recommended as general works on human evolution are B.G. Campbell's
Human Evolution (1974), and J. Pfeiffer's *The Emergence of Man* (1970). L.S.B. Leakey's
Adam's Ancestors (1953) is outdated but still makes useful reading; it has good photographs
of several fossil hominids and chapters on stone working and African sites.

A popular and readable account of human evolution is William Howells's *Mankind in the
Making* (1964). Although Robert Ardrey's *African Genesis* (1961) could not be recommended as a source of information, nor many of the conclusions taken uncritically, it is an
immensely stimulating book, and the enthusiasm and searching mind of the author could
well inspire the reader to probe deeper.

Discoveries of Fossil Man

The most useful book is Michael Day's *Guide to Fossil Man*, the third, expanded edition of
which, published in 1977, includes a wealth of information and critical assessment on the
more recent numerous discoveries in Africa. There are brief descriptions, usually illustrated,
of each find with information neatly tabulated under the headings of synonyms, site, found
by, geology, associated finds, dating, morphology, dimensions, affinities, originals, casts and
references. It is not, of course, restricted to Early Pleistocene hominids, but the sections on
the Australopithecines are particularly useful. There are also three comprehensive *Catalogues
of Fossil Hominids* published by the British Museum (Natural History) under the editorship
of Drs Oakley, Campbell and Molleson (1967, 1971, 1975), and C. Jolly's *Early Hominids
of Africa* (1978). An excellent recent survey is by Pilbeam (1975). References to specific
early hominids are given at the end of Chapter 3.

Definition of Man:	Oakley, 1957, 1962.
Ape behaviour:	Washburn, 1962; Devore and Washburn, 1963; Schaller and Emlen, 1963; Goodall, 1971.
Australopithecus 'Lucy':	Johanson and Taieb, 1976.
Laeotilil hominids and footprints:	M.D. Leakey, Hay, Curtis, Drake, Jackes and White, 1976; M.D. Leakey and Hay, 1979.
Stone-working technology:	Introductory: Oakley, 1949; Watston, 1950; Timms, 1974. Specialised: Bordes, 1950; Swanson, 1975.

Chapter 3

Unspecialised Hunter-Gatherers: Chopper-core Industries

Some speculation has already been made in Chapter 1 as to the circumstances which produced the first human groups in the Plio-Pleistocene period. The earliest known sites with stone tools are in East Africa. Not surprisingly, the stone-working technique is simple and the range of tool types small. There are numerous irregular flakes and also various heavier tools made from the cores from which the flakes were struck. It will be seen that such a simple stone-working technique, with few or no tools that follow a standard pattern, was used for an enormous span of time. The Oldowan industry is separated from the Clactonian of Europe by at least a million years, yet the basic technique is little changed.

Archaeologists may define distinctions between these simple industries which are quite valid, but on the basis of the stone tools alone it would be difficult to recognise much change in the behaviour of their makers. This refers, of course, only to the simple industries described below, not to the industries containing elegant, standardised tools such as hand-axes, many of which are contemporary with the latter half of the period concerned. Unquestionably, over much of the Old World in the Early and Middle Pleistocene are found stone industries that comprise little else than pebbles or chunks of rock, flaked from one or more sides (unifacial or bifacial) to produce heavy hand tools, many of which could certainly be used as choppers, and flakes that are sometimes modified in a non-standardised way by secondary working. Such industries have prompted the concept of 'pebble-tool cultures', but it was Professor Hallam Movius who defined them as chopper/chopping tool industries, in contrast to industries containing hand-axes. A chopper was unifacially flaked, a chopping tool bifacially. Other archaeologists have begged the question of their use by referring to both types as chopper-cores — thus chopper-core industries. This term is reasonably descriptive and non-committal so it is used here. The matter is complicated because some chopper-core industries contain a few hand-axes, as in the developed Oldowan of Olduvai Gorge. The intriguing question of just what this double industrial theme means is considered later. In the meantime, for the purpose of this account, emphasis is placed on the unspecialised nature of the tools: there is an almost total absence of the standardised tool forms which constitute such a remarkable feature of most later industries. By a process perhaps not legitimate, but because it is the hunters themselves who are our ultimate concern, the epithet has been transferred to them from the tools. Hence the title of the chapter: unspecialised hunter-gatherers — a description already applied by the distinguished African archaeologist, Professor J. Desmond Clark.

Sites have to be considered from four main aspects: distribution, time,

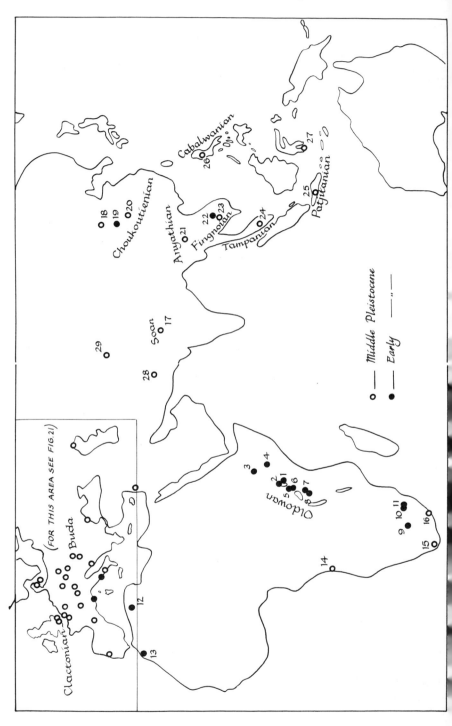

context and behaviour. Each aspect can be subdivided, and all are intercon-
nected. Some sites may only allow one aspect to be considered; for instance, a
surface find of an industry with chopper-cores and flakes will give information
only on distribution. One in a stratified context, but in derived condition, will
give information on distribution and, to a limited degree, time. A stratified site
in a primary context will give information on distribution, time, context and
possibly behaviour. Distribution is generally a simple matter, although derived
stone tools may have travelled some distance from their place of manufacture or
use. Time is either relative or chronometric. Context consists of the associated
faunal and floral remains which may be present and allow reconstruction of the
former environment, or geological aspects which may indicate the choice of site:
river or lakeside, cave or rock shelter, high or low ground, open or closed landscape. Behaviour may be implied by the context, or by purely archaeological
interpretations of the material, for instance by proportions of different tool
classes: choppers and flakes + a butchered animal skeleton = a kill or butchering
site; high numbers of scrapers and flakes with secondary working = domestic
sites. There are all manner of permutations and qualifications and the best
approach method is to take sites individually. It would be ideal if the more
important sites could be taken in order of time, irrespective of their distribution
throughout the world. Unfortunately, few sites are dated chronometrically and
it is generally impossible to correlate accurately well-stratified, and hence
relatively dated, sites in one part of the world with another. Thus it seems more
sensible in our present state of knowledge to list the sites by geographical
distribution. The subdivisions used are: Africa, India and Pakistan, China, the
Far East, central and western Asia and Europe. There is nothing to indicate
that there was any human occupation of Australia and the New World during
the whole of this immense period of time.

Associated with some of these sites, directly or indirectly, are the rare skeletal
remains of the hunters themselves. These will be described briefly and, at the
end of the chapter, some assessment will be attempted as to what is implied in
terms of human physical and cultural evolution.

Figure 6: Map of Chopper-core Industries, Early and Middle Pleistocene

1. East of Lake Turkana (formerly Rudolf) including Karari and KBS Ridge	15. Paarl
	16. East London
2. Omo Basin	17. Potwar region
3. Melka-Kontouré	18. Choukoutien
4. Plain of Gadeb	19. Lantian
5. Kanapoi	20. Ke-He
6. Lake Baringo	21. Upper Irrawaddy
7. Olduvai	22. Mae Tha
8. Lake Ndutu	23. Fing Valley
9. Vaal River	24. Kota Tampan
10.-11. Swartkrans and Sterkfontein	25. Java
12. Ain Hanech	26. Philippines
13. Morocco	27. Celebes
14. Luanda — Baia Farta	(remainder as on Figure 21)

None is known in Australia or anywhere in the New World.

Africa

East of Lake Turkana

A remarkable series of sites has been discovered in the region immediately east of Lake Turkana in Kenya, within part of the great Rift Valley of Africa. Sediments, mainly lacustrine, rest on lava, part of which has been uplifted so the sediments are frequently tilted and faulted. During the Late Pliocene and Early Pleistocene periods there were outbursts of volcanic activity; at various intervals eruptions caused rock fragments and ash to exude from local volcanoes, which consolidated to form a rock referred to by geologists as tuff. Sometimes the ash became mixed with the silt forming in rivers and lakes. This was happening at a time when hominids were living on the low land near the edge of the lake, often in the dry channels of seasonally active rivers. At times of volcanic eruptions they would have retreated to a safer place, as present-day people still do in the Rift Valley. Their inconvenience is our benefit, for the combination of the geology and the volcanics has created optimum conditions for investigating their living sites. Their stone tools, butchered animal bones and even some of their own bones have been found securely stratified within the sediments at different levels.

There are four major sites: Karari, Ileret, Koobi Fora and the so-called KBS Ridge. All are within about 30 km of each other, between the present waters of Lake Turkana (formerly Lake Rudolf) and the higher ground of the Surgei Cuesta. Later earth movements and erosion do not allow a continuous horizontal sequence of sediments to be traced between these sites, but one can be correlated with another by the identification of the various tuffs. Furthermore, the tuffs are ideal rocks for dating by the potassium/argon (K/Ar) method. One tuff in particular, the KBS Tuff, acts as a firm marker at all the sites. It has been dated to about 1.8 million years, although other geophysicists have calculated the age as 2.6 million years (see Figure 4). Evidence at the moment is more in favour of the younger date.

Many of the sediments are also very suitable for measuring the former magnetic polarity. Measurements of the KBS Tuff have indicated normal polarity,[1] i.e. the magnetic pole was still near the earth's northern polar axis as it is today. This was originally identified with the Gauss normal epoch (see Figure 1) but later work[2] has shown that this result is unreliable. Correlation with the Olduvai event is possible. What does seem certain is that the reversed polarity above the KBS Tuff is that of the Matuyama epoch which continued until about 730,000 years ago.

Yet another cross-check for relative dating and correlations is provided by the fauna.[3] Four zones have been recognised, three of which relate to the Plio-Pleistocene periods represented by the sediments. Below the KBS Tuff is the *Mesochoerus limnetes* zone, and above the KBS Tuff is the *Metridiochoerus andrewsi* zone (both archaic pigs). Above the latter is the *Loxodonta africana* zone (African elephant).

The stratigraphy of these four sites is presented diagramatically in Figure 4, combined with the K/Ar dates and palaeomagnetic determinations. Into this impressive framework can be fitted the archaeology and the associated hominid remains.

The earliest industry is either in or just below the KBS Tuff and is referred to as the KBS industry as it is well represented at at least three separate sites along the KBS Ridge.[4] It also occurs at Karari. Both are in the *Mesochoerus limnetes* zone. Excavation of one of the sites (designated FxJjl)[5] yielded 139 stone artifacts at one level associated with a scatter of broken animal bones. They lay on the sand of a dry river bed and the excavators thought the site may have been chosen because of the trees and bushes that were likely to have been growing along the old water course. Animals represented include porcupine, pig, gazelle, waterbuck and hippo and it seems reasonable to conclude that these are the remains of portions of carcasses brought back to the 'home base'. Whether they were scavenged or hunted can only be guessed. At one of the other sites (designated HAS), about a kilometre away, were a similar number of artifacts associated with the bones of a single hippo, so this may have been a kill site.

The KBS industry[6] comprises cores, flakes and flake fragments (Figure 7). The cores have been classified as choppers, polyhedrons, discoids, scrapers, proto-bifaces and sundry. It is interesting that at the possible 'kill site' there was a smaller percentage (2 per cent instead of 5 per cent) of core tools, suggesting perhaps less varied activities.

A younger industry is associated with the *Loxodonta africana* zone in the Upper Member of the Koobi Fora Formation and, as can be seen from Figure 4, K/Ar dates are about 1.4 million years. This younger industry is well represented at Karari and is thus known as the Karari industry. In spite of the apparent long time interval there are no very striking differences in the stone industry. However, many of the tools are made with greater precision, and scrapers made on cores or flakes are very characteristic, some having denticulate edges. Choppers, proto-bifaces, discoids and polyhedrons occur as with the earlier KBS industry, and there are various worked flakes of unspecialised forms (Figure 7). The Karari industry is also found at Ileret, between the Lower and Middle Tuffs, in the same *Loxodonta africana* zone. A few hand-axes and cleavers may be a component of the industry but have not been found in definite association. There are numerous other surface occurrences of this industry in the area. They indicate that the hominids were active along the lake margin, in stream channels and on the alluvial plains between the high ground to the west and the lake, and also on alluvial fans at the foot of the high ground. In almost every case, the sites were never further than a few hundred metres from a water course. Apart from the need for water and the protection and shelter of trees and bushes, stream courses would be an available source of raw material for their stone tools. Basalt was especially favoured for its flaking qualities, but the hominids had learned to select numerous other suitable rocks: lavas, chert and chalcedony.

Well over a hundred specimens of hominid have come from this area east of Lake Turkana, varying from single teeth to near-complete skulls.[7] The stratigraphical position of some significant ones is shown in Figure 4. Three different types of hominid are present: *Homo sp. indet.*, *Homo erectus* and *Australopithecus robustus*. Two *Homo sp. indet.* specimens come from below the KBS Tuff, one at Karari and one at Ileret (KNM 1470 (Plates VI-VII) and 1590), the latter associated with the KBS industry. Another near-complete cranium comes from the Upper Member at Koobi Fora (KNM 3733) (Plates IV-V). KNM 806 is associated with the Karari industry at Ileret and is also considered as *Homo sp. indet.* There are at least three other specimens of the same hominid from between the Middle and Chari Tuff at Ileret.

Figure 7: The KBS and Karari Industries

The KBS Industry (Industry 1 as in Figure 4)

1. and 4. Chopper-cores (1. polyhedron; 4. discoid). 2. Flake with secondary working. 3. Flake of fortuitous blade-like shape. All from the KBS Tuff. This is the earliest evidence in the world for the systematic making of stone tools. This industry is represented at three separate sites at least along the KBS Ridge and also occurs at Karari. Excavation of one site (FxJjl) yielded 139 artifacts *in situ* at one level with a scatter of broken animal bones. They lay on the sand of a dry river bed. It is interpreted as a 'home base site', whereas another site 1 km distant had a similar number of artifacts around the bones of a single hippo, and hence is regarded as a 'kill site'. The proportion of core tools was less (2 per cent instead of 5 per cent) at the latter.

The Karari Industry (Industry 2 as in Figure 4)

5. Unifacial chopper; 6. Well-struck flake. This younger industry is in the Upper Member of the Koobi Fora Formation. In spite of the long gap between this and the KBS industry there are no striking differences although many of the tools are made with greater precision. Scrapers, made on cores or flakes, are very characteristic, some having denticulate edges.

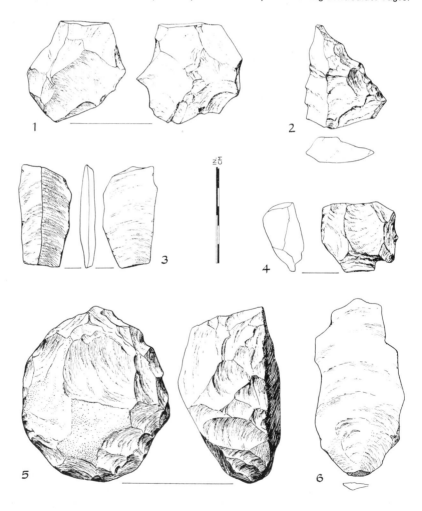

The Lower Omo Basin, Ethiopia

The River Omo flows into the northern end of Lake Turkana through a complex series of tilted and faulted Pliocene and Pleistocene rocks. A great series of lacustrine, fluviatile and deltaic sediments, known as the Shungura Formation, records the response of the ancestral Omo to the many movements within the Rift Valley. The formation is at least 700 m thick and is interleaved with numerous tuffs caused by frequent volcanic eruptions in the area.[8] The tuffs are good material for K/Ar radioactive dating methods and measurements indicate a date of 3.75 million years for the base of the formation, and about 1.4 million years for the top. This conveniently covers the critical period which is the concern of this chapter and, as the formation outcrops for about 200 square kilometres, there have been good opportunities for surface exploration, with follow-up excavation at selected sites.

The tuffs in the Shungura Formation have been designated A to J, in chronological sequence from the bottom. The earliest archaeological material is in F, K/Ar dated to 2.04 million years, in flood-plain sediments 35 m thick. A K/Ar date for the overlying Tuff G gave a slightly younger date of 1.93 million years, but this only emphasises the fact that these calculated dates are not really dates in the sense of precise calendar years, but statements of probability. The standard deviations, here in about the order of 0.10 million years, have been omitted.

Two archaeological localities in these sediments have been excavated,[9] one yielding 95 artifacts and no bone, the other 130 artifacts associated with bones of elephant, hippo and bovids. The excavators concluded that the material was not in a primary context but had been washed into the sediment, so the association of the artifacts and bones might be fortuitous. If not, it is a further instance of these very early hunters exploiting large animals. The stone industry was mainly small pieces of shattered milky white vein quartz. The small size and crudity of the industry probably only reflects the raw material which was available; vein quartz is very intractable but, when broken, does produce fragments with useful, razor-sharp edges. There was no intensive secondary working on any of the pieces, but there were some traces of edge damage. There were also a few lava and chert artifacts. At least one bifacially worked chopper has come from the sediments of Bed E. It is made of quartz and the edges are damaged, as though by heavy use.

Hominid remains have been found throughout the Shungura Formation, and also in the overlying Kibbish Formation which is Late Middle Pleistocene.[10] At least four types of hominids are represented: both robust and gracile Australopithecines (our *A. robustus* and *africanus*), *Homo habilis* and *Homo sapiens* or *erectus*. The latter is best represented by an almost complete skull and mandible. There is a well-developed chin eminence on the mandible, much more akin to *sapiens* than *erectus*, but the skull itself is more comparable to those from Solo in Java, which are *erectus*! However, this specimen (Omo II) comes from the Upper Kibbish Formation and is probably too recent to be connected with our unspecialised hunters.

A rare discovery was a complete hominid forearm bone in Member E of the Shungura Formation, immediately underlying the sediments containing the industry described above. It resembles a modern human forearm bone but with some significant differences in its length, curvature and cross-section, so it is considered to be Australopithecine.

The robust Australopithecine has been found throughout the Shungura Formation and is convincing evidence for the continuation of this type of hominid until well into the Pleistocene period.

Melka-Kontouré, Ethiopia

Melka-Kontouré is 50 km south of Addis Ababa in the valley of the River Awash. As elsewhere in this region, phases of uplifting and volcanic activity have had drastic effects upon the drainage. The River Awash has alternately eroded or filled its valley in response to the many changes, and the complexity of the resulting sediments that remain can be seen in the diagrammatic section, Figure 8. The presence of stone artifacts within the various deposits is also indicated on the diagram and the principle of stratification allows them to be put into relative order.[11] Those in the lowermost sediments are obviously the earliest, and very rich collections have been made in these of simple stone industries without hand-axes. They have been typologically compared with the classic sequence within Beds I and II at Olduvai Gorge (see below), where two industries precede the Acheulian industries there: Oldowan and a later Developed Oldowan. As can be seen from the diagram, the Developed Oldowan is, as at Olduvai, stratified above the Oldowan.

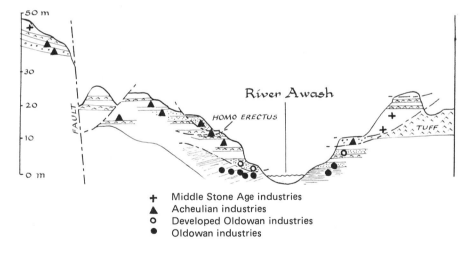

+ Middle Stone Age industries
▲ Acheulian industries
○ Developed Oldowan industries
● Oldowan industries

Figure 8: Section across the River Awash at Melka-Kontouré, Ethiopia
This shows the stratigraphical succession of stone industries (after Chavaillon, 1971).
    As can be seen from the diagram, the Developed Oldowan is, as at Olduvai, stratified above the Oldowan.

The most important localities for these Oldowan sites are Gomboré 1 (five levels of Oldowan), Kella (two levels of Developed Oldowan), Garba IV (five levels of Oldowan and Developed Oldowan) and Karre (five levels of Oldowan).

The Plain of Gadeb, Ethiopia

This area is dissected by the headwaters of the River Webi Shebele. Formerly, in Late Tertiary times, volcanic activity had blocked the drainage and caused a large lake to form, about 150 km long. The main river and its tributaries now cut through and expose some of the lacustrine and fluviatile sediments of Plio-Pleistocene age, and at three localities, Gadeb 2, 2B and 2C, stone artifacts have been found in alluvium.[12] These have been compared to the Developed Oldowan industry, although a few Acheulian cleavers are included. Some of the workmanship is surprisingly refined. The great interest of these sites is that they are out of the Rift Valley, on a high plateau between 2,300 and 2,500 m, with nearby mountains rising to 4,000 m. This is the highest elevation at which a stone industry of this age and type has been found, and shows that these early hominids were capable of adapting to a very different environment from the hot and arid low-lying floor of the Rift Valley, where most of their remains have been found.

Kanapoi, Kenya

At the southern end of Lake Turkana, on its western side, are Pleistocene sediments with a K/Ar date of about 2.5 million years and reversed palaeomagnetic polarity. Oldowan-type artifacts are found on their surface and it seems almost certain that they are eroding out from the sediments and are thus of that age.

Further west at Lothagam there is a remarkable sequence of deposits extending back through the Pliocene and into the Miocene. In Member 1, K/Ar dated to between 5 and 6 million years, was found a jawbone of a gracile Australopithecine (*?A. africanus*)[13] which has the distinction of being the oldest fossil hominid, (unless *Ramapithecus* is also regarded as a hominid) apart from the Fort Ternan, Kenya, jawbone,[14] reckoned to be 14 million years old, and a tooth from the Ngorora Formation in the northern Kenya Rift Valley, dated 0-12 million years.[15] No stone artifacts are known from the Lothagam site, although claims have been made that some broken bones and battered lava pebbles at Fort Ternan were the work of that hominid.[16]

Around Lake Baringo, Kenya

On the eastern side of this lake, at Chesowanja, a series of lake sediments and tuffs known as the Chemoigut Formation is exposed on the surface due to the erosion of a local anticline,[17] as shown in the diagram in Figure 9. It can be seen that this formation is overlain by the Chesowanja Formation. This contains an Acheulian industry, but the earlier one has only yielded artifacts comparable to the Oldowan/Developed Oldowan complex (Figure 10).[18] These have been found at five separate levels within the sequence, which is 25-30 m thick. Numerous faunal remains show that the environment had been one of bush-grassland, with giraffe, elephant, rhino, antelope, horses and pigs. There were also hippos, crocodiles and turtles, so this richly vegetated landscape must have been close to the lake.

The only hominid remains are the fragment of a skull and some teeth of *Australopithecus robustus*.[19] The industry comprises choppers of various forms, polyhedrons, discoids and proto-bifaces. Light-duty scrapers are made on flakes.

The industry is made from a variety of stones including trachytes, phonolites, welded tuffs and basalts (Figure 10).

Dating is based on palaeomagnetic measurements and the presence of an early form of elephant, *Deinotherium bosazi*, which is not found above Tuff J in the Shungura Formation at Omo (see above), dated at 1.34 million years. The polarity is reversed so the deposits must lie somewhere within the Matuyama reversed epoch, i.e. between 0.7 and 2.4 million years.

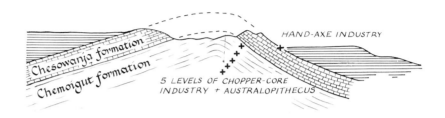

Figure 9: Diagrammatic Section across the Anticline East of Lake Baringo, Kenya
The Chemoigut Formation is 25-30 m thick and, as shown in the diagram, has yielded artifacts comparable to the Oldowan/Developed Oldowan industries at five separate levels, with a rich fauna indicating bush-grassland.

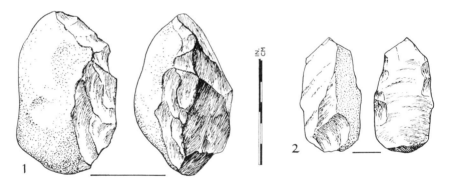

Figure 10: Stone Industry from the Chemoigut Formation
1. Chopper. 2. Flake with secondary working.

This industry has affinities with the Developed Oldowan and includes choppers, polyhedrons, discoids and proto-bifaces. Light-duty scrapers are made on flakes (e.g. no. 2). The rocks used include trachytes, phonolites, welded tuffs and basalts. K/Ar dating suggests a date between 1.9 and 1.3 million years. (After Gowlett in Harris and Bishop, 1976; see also Bishop *et al.*, 1978, and Isaac, 1978).

On the other, western, side of Lake Baringo are the Chemeron Beds, which are of Plio-Pleistocene age. A hominid temporal bone has come from the surface of these beds and, although excavation could not confirm it, had presumably eroded out of them.[20] It is considered to be Australopithecine, but with *habilis* and *erectus* traits, so is best placed in our *Homo sp. indet.* category. Unfortunately, no stone tools are recorded.

There is an important Acheulian site in the Kapthurin Beds, which overlie these Chemeron Beds.[21]

Olduvai Gorge, Tanzania

The famous Olduvai Gorge is a steep-sided gash about 100 m deep through the Serengeti Plain, revealing a complicated sequence of ancient lake beds, tuffs and other sediments. It has yielded many hominid bones, the finest sequence of stone industries of Lower Palaeolithic age in Africa, a wealth of associated faunal remains, and suitable sediments for K/Ar dating and palaeomagnetic measurements. It is also the most intensively excavated site of its type in the world, and three large, magnificently produced volumes have already appeared on the findings.[22] There is also a fine, detailed survey of the geology, with reconstructions of the landscape and environment for each phase as represented by the sediments.[23] Figure 11 is based on this wealth of information.

The geological sequence at Olduvai is divided into four Beds, numbered I-IV, from bottom to top. Bed I is composed mainly of lake and river sediments overlying a basalt that has been K/Ar dated to 1.89 million years. The whole of Bed I is thought to have formed in the relatively short (geologically speaking) time of 150,000 years. During this time a perennial lake existed in this part of the Serengeti Plain, about 22 km across. Lower Palaeolithic unspecialised hunters occupied the flat land around the south east margin of the lake, where freshwater streams drained into it. The lake itself, like many of the present lakes in the Rift Valley, was saline. The various tuffs make convenient markers for identifying deposits in different parts of the gorge, and the one at the top of Bed I, Tuff IF, defines the junction between Beds I and II. Ignimbrite is a special type of volcanic rock and it makes a valuable marker in the lower part of Bed I.

Similar conditions appear to have prevailed during the early part of Bed II, but the stability of the region was then upset by a number of earth movements and, shortly after the deposition of the Lemuta Member, a wind-borne tuff, these movements caused radical changes in the drainage system, with the result that the lake was partially drained. Lacustrine and fluvial tuffs still formed but a considerable time interval may have existed between the lower and upper parts of Bed II. The middle of Bed II is K/Ar dated to about 1.3 million years.

Beds III and IV continue the sequence upwards, with further fluvial and lacustrine silts, aeolian sediments and tuffs. Bed III is reddened and can easily be recognised. The uppermost Masek Beds are estimated to be about 400,000 years old.

Vast numbers of animals must have dwelt in this area of the Serengeti throughout the Lower and Middle Pleistocene. The fauna of Bed I contains many extinct forms, including an early elephant (*Deinotherium bosazi*), archaic pigs, a large horned giraffe (*Libytherium*) and various bovids. This faunal assemblage is thought to be earlier than the fauna found at Omo, which equates better with that from the lower part of Bed II at Olduvai. The upper part of Bed II above the Lemuta Member contains a very different fauna with both 'archaic' and later elements. Some of the forms were very spectacular, including a giant sheep-like creature, *Pelorovis oldowayensis*, with a span of some three metres across its horns. There are few faunal remains preserved in Bed III. Bed IV is rich and contains several modern species (gazelles, antelopes, horse and rhino),

Unspecialised Hunter-Gatherers

Figure 11: Diagram of the Sequence at Olduvai Gorge, Tanzania
The Pleistocene sediments exposed in the Olduvai Gorge of the Serengeti Plain are over 100 m thick. They have formed in response to alternating fluviatile or lacustrine environments. Human activity was much in evidence where freshwater streams entered lakes which, at times, were saline. Volcanic activity and earth movements (faulting) occurred at intervals both during and since the formation of the various geological beds. The region, like most of the Gregory Rift Valley, is still unstable today.

The positions of some of the more important, numerous hominid remains are shown by their site catalogue numbers: H5 is the skull of *Zinjanthropus* (Nutcracker Man) found in 1959, H9 is *Homo erectus* (Chellean Man) found in 1960, and H7 the type specimen of *Homo habilis* also found in 1960. Some excavation sites, identified by code letters, are shown in another column. (After M.D. Leakey, 1971; M.G. and R.E.F. Leakey, 1978; Hay, 1976; and Day, 1977)

Details of selected hominid discoveries at Olduvai:

Cat. no.	Locality	Bed	Skeletal parts discovered	Described as
OLD H2	MNK II	IV	Few fragments of cranial vault	*Homo erectus?*
OLD H4	MK I	I	Mandible fragment and two molars	*Homo habilis*
OLD H5	FLK I	I	Nr. complete cranium plus dentition	*Zinjanthropus boisei*
OLD H6		I	Two molars and part of cranial vault	*Homo habilis*
OLD H7	FLKNN I	I	Parietals, part of occipital, mandible, upper molar and hand of juvenile (Pl. III)	*Homo habilis*
OLD H8	FLKNN I	I	Clavicle, hand fragments and near complete foot	*Homo habilis*
OLD H9	LLK	II	Cranium (Pl. IX)	*Homo erectus* 'Chellean Man'
OLD H12	VEK	IV	Skull fragments, maxilla and teeth	*Homo erectus?*
OLD H13	MNK II	II	Part of vault of small cranium and mandible	*Homo habilis?*
OLD H14	MNK	II	Skull fragments of juvenile	*Homo habilis?*
OLD H15	MNK	II	Three teeth	*Homo erectus?*
OLD H22	VEK/MNK	surface III or IV	Mandible fragment	*Homo erectus?*
OLD H20	HWK	surface I or II	Femur fragment	*Australopithecus boisei*
OLD H24	DK East	I	Cranium and some teeth	*Homo habilis*

NB: OLD H1 is the complete skeleton of *Homo sapiens* found on an early expedition in 1913, now regarded as an intrusive burial in Bed IV.

Figure 11

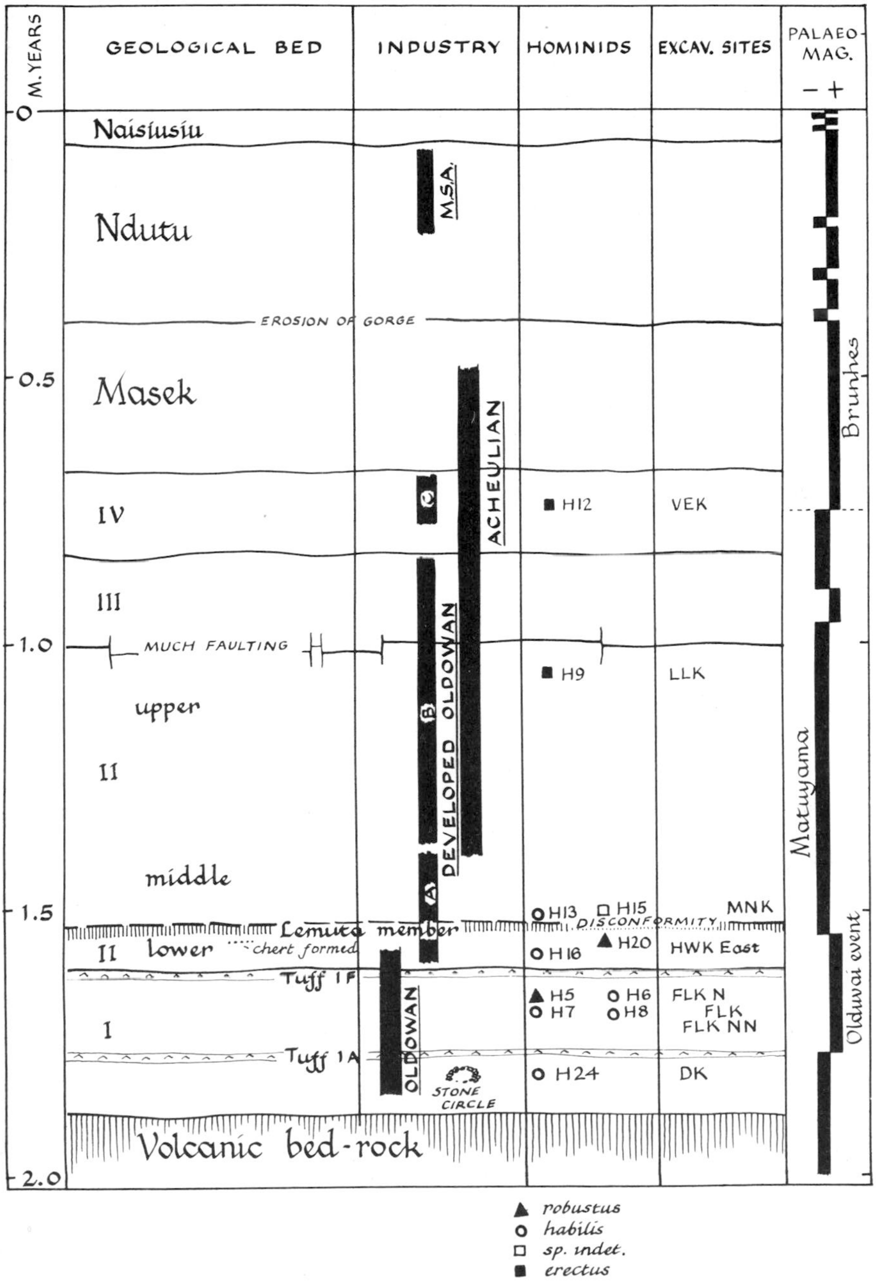

M. YEARS	GEOLOGICAL BED	INDUSTRY	HOMINIDS	EXCAV. SITES	PALAEO-MAG. − +
0	Naisiusiu				
	Ndutu	M.S.A.			Brunhes
	— EROSION OF GORGE —				
0.5	Masek	ACHEULIAN			
	IV		■ H12	VEK	
	III				
1.0	MUCH FAULTING	DEVELOPED OLDOWAN	■ H9	LLK	Matuyama
	upper II				
	middle		○ H13 □ H15	MNK	
1.5	II lower ⁝⁝chert formed Lemuta member		○ H16 ▲ H20	HWK East	Olduvai event
	Tuff IF	OLDOWAN	▲ H5 ○ H6 ○ H7 ○ H8	FLK N FLK FLK NN	
	1 Tuff IA	STONE CIRCLE	○ H24	DK	
2.0	Volcanic bed-rock				

DISCONFORMITY

▲ robustus
○ habilis
□ sp. indet.
■ erectus

but it still has several species now extinct.

Dating at Olduvai is supplied by K/Ar measurements and palaeomagnetism. Below the top of Bed III, polarity is reversed, except for two relatively brief events, the Jaramillo and Olduvai events. The upper part of Bed IV and the Masek Beds have normal polarity. The K/Ar date for the cranium of 'Chellean Man' (=*Homo erectus*, H9 on Figure 11) in the upper part of Bed II given as 490,000 years appears anomalous.

The figure marks the stratigraphical positions of the more important hominid discoveries. *Homo habilis*[24] (Plate III) and *Australopithecus boisei* (H5 on Figure 11, classified here as *A. robustus*) coexisted during the time of Bed I. *Homo erectus* (Plate IX) appears in Bed II and is also found in Bed IV.[25] Who made the stone tools remains a question unsolved. Certainly, *Homo erectus* can be credited with those from the upper part of Bed II onwards, but were those in Bed I made by *habilis*, or by some ancestor of *erectus* not yet found, perhaps the *Homo sp. indet. cf. erectus* of other sites in East Africa who appears to be contemporary or even earlier? *Robustus* is dismissed as a tool maker, although this could be doing him an injustice.

Three stone industries are marked on the table: Oldowan, Developed Oldowan and Acheulian.[26] Only the first two concern this chapter, although the last two were partly contemporary. As they are better represented at Olduvai than anywhere else, they will be described in some detail. It seems reasonable to use these assemblages for comparison against other similar assemblages found in East Africa, as has already been done at a few of the sites listed above. It might be dangerous to apply these comparisons geographically too far afield.

The difference between the Oldowan and the Developed Oldowan is not just the introduction of new tool types in the later industry, but a change in the proportions of certain tool classes (Figure 12). Some of the later artifacts are better made, indicating that their makers had achieved a mastery over the material that was mainly lacking in the Oldowan. Examples of the various tool classes are shown in Figure 13.

Some of the Developed Oldowan tools, especially the light-duty scrapers, are so neat and cleanly made that it is difficult to reconcile them with the lowly human state of their makers. This was partly caused by the availability of some fine-quality chert in the upper part of Bed II, a rock which flakes easily and cleanly. Otherwise, lava, basalt and quartzites had to be used and, considering their relative intractability, it is remarkable that the average tools were made as well as they were. This chert actually formed within the lacustrine silt of Lower Bed II and was later exposed when the earth movements already mentioned caused changes in the drainage and some streams eroded deeper channels.

A few hand-axes occur in the Developed Oldowan B and C industries, as though the idea had been 'borrowed' from the contemporary Acheulian industry but never 'caught on'! (Figure 14). However, the coexistence of two separate, contemporary industrial traditions is an astonishing fact.

Figure 12: The Oldowan Industry — Histograms of Tool Forms
Tool forms as classified by Mary Leakey in Oldowan assemblages at Olduvai Gorge in Beds I-IV, and the varying proportions of different types throughout the sequence. See also Figures 11 and 13. (After M.D. Leakey, 1971 and 1975)

Figure 12

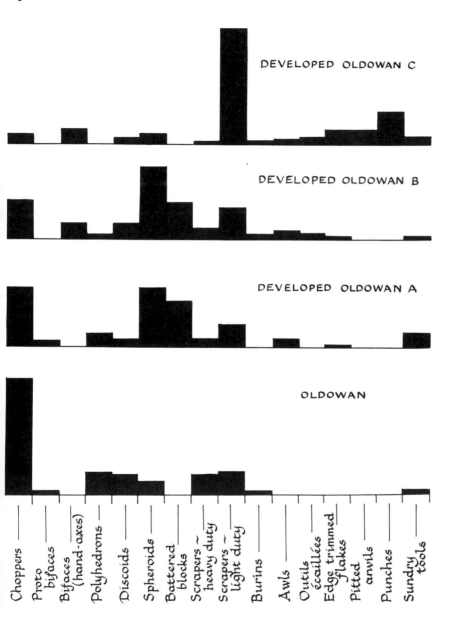

Figure 13: Oldowan Industry — Artifacts from Bed I
From the *'Zinjanthropus'* level (H5) at Site FLK, Bed I, Olduvai Gorge.
1. Side chopper of lava. 2.-3. End choppers of lava. 4.-10. Light-duty quartzite scrapers.
(From M.D. Leakey, 1971)

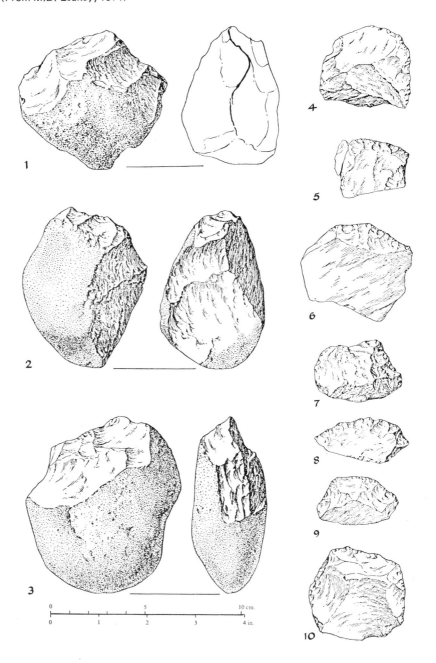

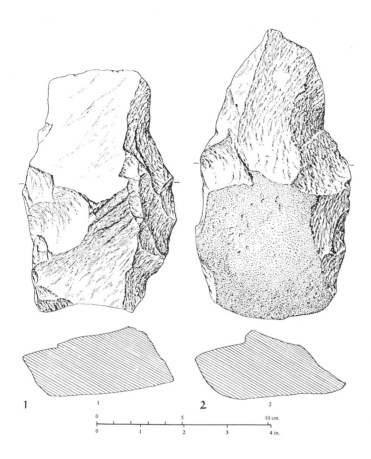

Figure 14: Developed Oldowan Industry
From the upper part of Middle Bed II, Olduvai Gorge.
1. Cleaver. 2. Hand-axe. Both made on flakes of lava. (From M.D. Leakey, 1971)

Another unusual discovery at Olduvai, which is at variance with preconceptions we may have of the lowly cultural state of these unspecialised hunters, is an actual structure, constructed of stones that must have been carried several kilometres. At DK, the archaeological reference letters for this particular site near the base of Bed I, stones had been loosely piled to form a circle about 4 m in diameter. Most of the stones were lumps of basalt about 10-15 cm across, although some were as large as about 24 cm. There were also six separate piles, and it is impossible to dismiss this whole assembly as anything else but human handiwork. It is beneath the ignimbrite of Bed I, close to the basalt K/Ar dated as 1.89 million years, and within the Olduvai event of normal polarity. On present evidence it must be about 1.7 million years old. What was the purpose of this structure? Some form of shelter is a sensible guess: stones placed around the rim of a circle of branches perhaps, with supporting poles steadied by the separate piles. Or is it possible that they had already learnt how to utilise skins, and the circle of stones remains from the weights on the edge of a circular, tepee-like structure? This sounds far-fetched, but some shelter would have been almost essential from the blazing sun in a treeless area, and the stone tools we describe as scrapers may really have been used for scraping skins.

Another suggestion for some form of structure comes from site FLK, where *Zinjanthropus* was discovered. One occupational level was meticulously excavated and recorded, and the resulting distribution of artifacts showed a gap of about 1.5 m between the main concentration and concentric strips of more artifacts.[27] A semi-circular wind-break of woven branches may have stood on one side of this gap, thus preventing the spread of material being thrown down or kicked about.

The actual number of stone tools in the Developed Oldowan is prodigious. At HWK East, eroding out of a sandy conglomerate beneath the aeolian tuff of the Lemuta Member, stone artifacts cover the present surface of the gorge in their thousands. They are always present in similar numbers wherever else in the gorge the same bed is exposed and, if the same concentration is present everywhere, it is estimated that some 2,000,000 artifacts remain for the archaeologist to study!

Lake Ndutu, Tanzania

Sediments in this area have been correlated with the Masek beds of Olduvai Gorge and would thus be of Middle Pleistocene age, c. 500,000 years.[28] An amino-acid date has been calculated which is 500,000-600,000 years[29] but, as has already been stated, dates obtained by this method cannot yet be accepted with confidence. A skull of *Homo erectus* has been found,[30] associated with animal bones and a stone industry. Two hundred and seventy artifacts were found, including 20 indeterminate cores or polyhedrons, but no hand-axes or cleavers.

Terraces of the Vaal River, South Africa

The valley of the Vaal is wide and gently sloping. Gravels on the slopes each side of the river are remnants of former, higher courses and, in the Windsorton area of the Cape, these terrace gravels have been studied in considerable detail.[31]

As with any river system of great age, the terrace sequence is complex. Past observations and interpretations tend to contradict each other, and attempts to fit the terraces into a framework of pluvials and interpluvials (wet and dry periods) are now discounted. The most recent work suggests that there are only three main terraces, at 66, 33 and 23 m (200, 100 and 70 ft) above the present level of the river, and that the 'younger gravels' below 23 m belong to one long stage culminating in the present flood plain. It is the younger gravels which contain Acheulian and more recent industries,[32] but chopper-cores, proto-bifaces and crude hand-axes have been found in the higher, older gravels. It is not easy to be confident that these early-looking stone artifacts really do come from the undisturbed body of these ancient Vaal gravels, for later erosion and hillwash may have disturbed them. Thus it is satisfactory to have evidence from a controlled excavation at Suurkree, near Barkly West, that stone artifacts do really exist in the primary, alluvial gravel of the 66 m terrace.[33] Finds were limited to a proto-biface and two flakes, but they seem incontrovertible. There were also chopper-cores and flakes in a different level that had probably been derived from the same primary gravel.

The dating of the 33 m terrace is Middle Pleistocene on the basis of the fauna contained within it, so the higher terraces must be considerably older. A date of 4.8 million years has been suggested for the 66 m terrace on the calculation of the time taken for the river to erode its valley since then; but, if the dates for similar material in East Africa are relevant, this date seems far too old, and it must be suspect until more reliable methods of dating can be applied.

There are other sites along the Vaal River with chopper-cores and crude hand-axes which seem to come from similar very early contexts, especially at Klipplaatdrif.[34]

Sterkfontein and Swartkrans, Transvaal, South Africa

These two caves are famous, respectively, for the rich discoveries of *Australopithecus africanus* (Plate I) in one, and *A. robustus* (Plate II) in the other.[35] Stone tools have been reported from both sites, and their relationship with the Australopithecine remains is critical. At Sterkfontein the relationship seems clear: all the Australopithecines come from a breccia without stone tools, in association with a fauna that, in East Africa, would be dated to between 2.5 and 3 million years.[36] The stone tools belong to an overlying breccia, and a gap of about a million years could exist between them. They comprise choppers, cores, polyhedrons, discoids and flakes with or without secondary working.[37] There are also a few hand-axes and proto-bifaces and the industry can be classified as similar to the Developed Oldowan or Early Acheulian. Of great significance is the discovery of most of the skull and some of the mandible and teeth of an individual comparable to *Homo habilis* in this tool-bearing breccia.[38] There seems a strong possibility that he made the tools.

The associations between the numerous stone tools found at Swartkrans and the hominid discoveries is less clear, but the industry is similar, with a few hand-axes and at least one well-made cleaver.[39] It now seems likely that these are to be linked with the hominid referred to as *Telanthropus*, and a near-complete skull and face with resemblances to *Homo erectus*. They are both best put into the *Homo sp. indet.* category, as perhaps should be the *habilis*-like individual from Sterkfontein.

Makapansgat, Transvaal, South Africa

Claims have been made that many of the bones found with *Australopithecus africanus* within the same cave filling had been purposely selected and used; also that stalactites had been used as tools and that dolomite pebbles had been split and flaked.[40] Furthermore, baboon skulls showed depressed fractures considered to have been the result of being struck by the distal end of antelope humeri. This was all thought to be the work of *Australopithecus*. Most, or all, of this evidence has been disputed.[41] The supposed stone artifacts can certainly be dismissed as naturally broken stones, and there may be other reasons than Australopithecine scavenging for the demonstrably selected nature of the bones, such as the disproportionate number of antelope skulls, mandibles, humeri and shoulder blades, and hyaena jawbones. Some archaeologists still accept a few of these bones as having been purposefully selected and utilised and, as no other hominid is known from the site, *Australopithecus* could have been responsible.

Ain Hanech, Algeria

At the opposite end of Africa to the sites above is the important site of Ain Hanech, one of many between the Atlas Mountains and the Mediterranean coast. High-level fluviatile and marine deposits result from relative changes in the level of land and sea. They frequently contain rich assemblages of fossil bones and, at Ain Hanech, there is a typical Villafranchian (the name of a stage in the Mediterranean succession = Early Pleistocene) fauna, within sandy clay overlying gravel. It was during the course of collecting this fossil fauna that some crude artifacts were found, made on limestone pebbles.[42] They comprise polyhedrons and flakes and constitute evidence for the presence of unspecialised hunters in this part of Africa, almost within sight of Europe.

Morocco

The succession of raised beaches in Morocco has enabled a detailed local succession to be established, with its own terminology of stages. The Moulouyen, Messoudian, Saletien and Maarifien stages cover the Early Pleistocene, and simple industries of chopper-cores and flakes have been found in all of these stages.[43] Those in the earlier two stages are considered to be less evolved than those in the later. The similarity of this sequence to that in East Africa is apparent, and the estimated dates for these stages are about the same. If movements of population are envisaged, it would seem that the Sudan and Sahara Deserts did not then present the formidable barrier that they do today.

Other sites in Africa

The sites listed above have been selected mainly because there is some information on their likely date and associations. However, there are numerous places where simple tools of Oldowan type have been discovered but it would be dangerous to conclude that, because of their typology, they must relate to the earlier part of the Pleistocene. It can be demonstrated that such tools (choppers, chopper-cores, discoids, large and small flakes, etc.) are often found as a component of more evolved Acheulian hand-axe industries, so when they are found on the surface or in a derived state within gravels it may be impossible to know what they really represent. Sometimes the evidence is more definite as, for instance, the chopper-cores and flakes that are found in the 80-100 m raised beach in North East Angola, from Luanda to Baia Farta,[44] or in raised beaches at several sites in South Africa, such as East London, Keurbooms River and Paarl, or along the Natal coast.[45] Oldowan-like industries have been reported from Namaqualand, in Katanga, in Rhodesia, Malawi, Uganda and elsewhere.[46] Those from Uganda, at Kafu, were some of the first to be 'recognised' but it is now certain that some, if not all, of this 'industry' is the result of natural fracturing of stones.[47] This is a further problem with such simple industries, as many of the products may be difficult to distinguish from natural breakages, and so consequently many reports have to be treated with suspicion. The sites that have been selected are beyond such criticism.

India and Pakistan

Potwar Region, Northern Punjab

This region, between the Salt Range and the Indus Valley, is drained by the River Soan, which has given its name to a series of simple stone industries, reminiscent of the Oldowan of Africa. Subdivisions have been made of Pre-Soan, Early Soan and Late Soan, based on the discovery of artifacts within gravels on the higher terraces of the Soan and Indus Rivers.[48] The geology is complex for not only has the region been affected by the advance and recession of Himalayan ice sheets, but there was a major uplifting of the land in the Middle Pleistocene, which raised the great Himalayan Mountains to their present height and position.

Five terraces have been identified in the Soan-Indus Valley, with fluvial gravels resting in most cases on what have been described as boulder conglomerates.[49] The Pre-Soan industry comes from the highest of these conglomerates, near Rawalpindi, and could be regarded as evidence for hunters being active in the region in the early part of the Middle Pleistocene. However, several archaeologists doubt that the 'flakes' which constitute this Pre-Soan industry are of human manufacture, but believe they are the result of turbulent conditions during the deposition of the sediment. Also, unless these alleged artifacts are thought to predate the formation of this conglomerate, they would suggest that hunters were occupying the valley at a time of intensive flooding coupled with a barren, cold landscape, which seems very unlikely. The coarse gravels which later became consolidated to form this Upper Boulder Conglomerate are clearly the discharge from receding glaciers. This appears to have been during the time of the maximum glaciation of the Himalayas, and, for this reason, is correlated with the Mindel Glaciation of Europe (see time chart, Figure 25). It was also at this time that the final uplifting of the mountains took place.

The first indisputable evidence for human occupation in India is the Early Soan industry in the fluvial gravels of the highest terrace, Terrace I, which succeeds the Upper Boulder Conglomerate. It consists of unifacial and bifacial choppers, discoids and flakes, usually without any secondary working. Such tools have been found in large numbers and this is not surprising as the early hunting groups in this area had access to unlimited material in the form of waterworn pebbles. Fine-grained quartzites and lavas flaked cleanly. Unfortunately, in spite of this wealth of stone material, none of it can be regarded as being in a primary context. The most important information to be gained is that the Soan industry appears to continue with very little change well into the Late Pleistocene period. It is still to be found in Terrace 2, at a lower level in the valley, probably of Last Interglacial age. The same crude choppers and flakes are to be found, but there are also smaller, neater forms, flake tools and the use of a prepared core or Levalloisian technique (see pp. 115-17).

Sites of the Soan industry are also known about 560 km south east of Rawalpindi, still in the southern foothills of the Himalayas and Siwalik Hills. A few hand-axes have come from the Soan Valley and, conversely, a few Soan-like choppers are found with the Acheulian hand-axe industries of central and southern India.

China

Choukoutien, near Peking

This is the most famous and important Lower Palaeolithic site in the Far East. Numerous remains of *Homo erectus*, otherwise known as *Pithecanthropus pekinensis, Sinanthropus pekinensis,* or popularly called Peking Man, have come from deposits associated with stone tools and faunal remains (Plate XI). The stone tools are of a chopper-core industry and it can be said that Peking Man lived in caves, used fire and was a successful hunter with a preference for deer meat.

Choukoutien is a large hill of Ordovician limestone, extensively quarried commercially. Most of the archaeological material has come from the fillings of fissures in the limestone. *Homo erectus* is best represented at Locality I.

Figure 15 shows the general stratigraphy at Choukoutien and it can be seen that Locality I is a vast cavity in the limestone filled with a succession of sands, clays, breccias, travertines and rock fall. It is 50 m deep and the changes have been so extensive that it is difficult to reconstruct the original shape and form of the cave. The cave mouth has disappeared and most of the roof collapsed, but when it was first used by these early hunter/food gatherers the cave must have had cathedral-like proportions. Assuming that the mouth was similarly large, light would have penetrated far back into the cave. However, it is unlikely to have been a very cheerful place, for the entrance is thought to have faced north-east and the sun could not ever have shone into the interior. This entrance area has all been eroded or quarried away and what remains is part of the interior, showing numerous occupational layers separated by deposits which formed in periods when sand and clay were washed into the cave, or when the roof partly collapsed, or when dripping, lime-rich water produced layers of stalagmite.

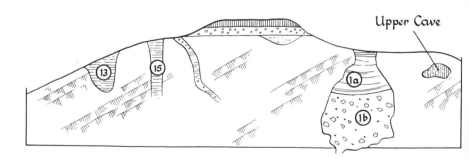

Figure 15: Section through Choukoutien Hill, near Peking, China
The hill is composed of tilted Ordovician limestone and is 60 m high. Fissures and caves have developed in the limestone and subsequently filled with sediments. Numbers in circles indicate archaeological localities.
  1. *Sinanthropus* (= Peking Man = *Homo erectus*) deposits a) upper zone of ashes and clay, b) lower zone of sands and breccias. Middle Pleistocene.
 13. Red clays. Early Middle Pleistocene.
 15. Loams. Early Late Pleistocene. Upper Cave. Late Pleistocene. (After Movius, 1949)

The cave filling of Locality 1 is divided into an upper and lower zone, separated by a layer of stalagmite. It is unlikely that there is a long time interval between these two zones, but the total accumulation of about 50 m of deposit could represent a very long span of time. There is no way of assessing this and the only dating evidence available is that given by the fauna. This does not significantly vary from one zone to the other so the whole deposit can be regarded as one phase somewhere within the Middle Pleistocene. A date of about the time of the Mindel Glaciation is the usual estimate.

As with any cave site, it is impossible to know whether the animals represented by the discovered bones died in the cave, were dragged in by carnivores or scavengers, or were brought in as carcasses by the hunters themselves. The latter seems a probable explanation for most of the bones at Choukoutien, because 70 per cent of the faunal remains are deer bones, and human selection seems the only way to account for this. Other animals include leopard, cave bear, sabre-toothed tiger (*Machairodus inexpectatus*), a giant hyaena, elephant, rhinoceros, camel, bison, water buffalo, wild boar, roebuck, antelope, big-horned sheep and musk ox. Presumably, the hunters cooked their meat as there is abundant evidence of the use of fire: hearths, ashes, charcoal.

Homo erectus is represented by an impressive amount of excavated material, tragically lost during the Second World War. There were 14 skulls, 11 mandibles, 147 teeth, 7 femora shafts, 2 humeri fragments, a tibia fragment and a broken clavicle. The teeth indicate that about 32 individuals have been found, divided into 20 adolescents or adults, and 12 children. There is a marked variation in the size of the teeth and this is thought to be the result of sexual differentiation. The limb bones are similar to those of modern man.

The stone industry has been called 'Choukoutien'. It is not plentiful and is mainly made from quartz and greenstone. A local stream bed appears to have supplied the hunters with pebbles of sandstone and quartz, but vein quartz, rock crystal and chert had to be brought in from elsewhere. These rather intractable rocks were flaked into choppers and chopping tools and the resulting flakes utilised as they were or further flaked into non-standardised tools (Figure 16).

Stone tools occur throughout the massive accumulation of cave filling at Locality 1. As stated, a long period of time must be represented by this filling, yet the stone industry at the bottom differs little from that at the top. There are more flakes with secondary working in the upper part, but this may only be reflecting the greater use of some good-quality chert.

Other important localities at Choukoutien where stone tools have been found are Locality 13 and Locality 15. The former is a fissure deposit with numerous animal bones, some of them burnt. The fauna is considered to predate that from Locality 1 and, on these rather tenuous grounds, a chopping tool of cleaver-like form that was found here is considered to be the earliest evidence for man at the site. The industry from Locality 15 is considerably more specialised and the fauna is suggestive of a Late Pleistocene date.

North China

Stone industries have been reported from Pleistocene contexts at several hundred sites in North China, particularly in the provinces of Shansi, Shensi and Honan. The most important are Lantian, Ke-He and Ting-ts'un where stone tools have been found in and on gravels capped by red clays and sands. Dating is mainly

Figure 16: Stone Industry from Choukoutien, China
1. Cleaver-like tool of chert from Locality 13, associated with some burnt bones and a fauna of an earlier type than that found at the other localities at this site. 2.-4. Flakes with some secondary working or marks of use, made of sandstone or quartz, neither of which is a very suitable flaking material. 5. Large chopper made from a sandstone pebble. 2-5 are from Locality 1 in association with *Homo erectus* (= *Sinanthropus* = Peking Man). (After Movius, 1949)

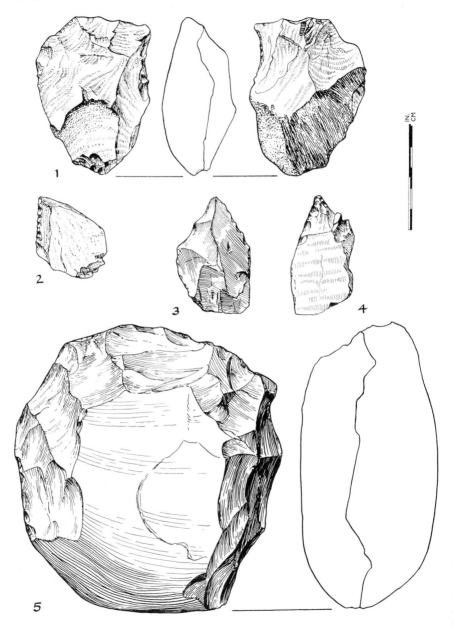

dependent on associated faunal remains. The earliest is Lantian, which is considered to predate all the discoveries at Choukoutien. Here a jawbone and skull cap of *Homo erectus* have been found, associated with a stone industry of large flakes and core tools.[50] One of the latter, made of quartzite, is a large (17.5 cm) pointed, bifacially worked implement that can be described as a hand-axe. These discoveries were made at the base of an enormous thickness (c. 80 m) of loess. Several of the animals represented are known from Choukoutien, Localities 1 and 13, but three species are characteristic of the Lower Pleistocene of China and are unknown at Choukoutien. This is the evidence for the early date. The fauna also suggests a considerably warmer climate than that of Choukoutien.

At Ke-He (or K'oho) stone tools have come from a consolidated pebble bed beneath 4 m of sands and 20 m of red, loessic loam. The inclusion of such animals as *Stegedon zdanskyi*, an archaic form of elephant, renders it unlikely that the site is more recent than the beginning of the middle of the Pleistocene. These industries have been referred to as part of the Fenho complex and comprise the ubiquitous flakes, choppers and chopping tools, but also some crude pointed pick-like forms and at least one quartzite hand-axe. Similar forms of tools, hand-axes and cleavers, have come from a much more recent, probably Late Pleistocene, site at Ting-ts'un.[51] Chinese archaeologists are reluctant to call these tools hand-axes as this implies association with Acheulian industries of Africa and Europe.

South East Asia

Burma

Five river terraces have been recognised in the Upper Irrawaddy, and stone tools have been found in the top four of them. The oldest is thought to date to about the time of the Mindel Glaciation of Europe, like the upper terrace of the River Soan in northern India. The industry has been named Anyathian (which merely means: Upper Burma) and, apart from increasing our knowledge of the distribution of chopper-core industries, it is significant for two reasons: it emphasises the great duration of time over which such industries appear to have existed in Asia without developing, and it is a perfect example of the effect of a particular raw material on the typology of the artifacts.

The stone tools in the higher terraces (T.1 and T.2) are classified as Early Anyathian, and those in the lower (T.3 and T.4) as Late Anyathian. This must represent a time range of Middle and well into Late Pleistocene, yet the basic technology persisted with little or no change. The usual components are to be found: flakes, choppers, chopping tools, proto-bifaces and scrapers. Most of the tools were made on fossil wood which occurs in great quantity all along the valley. It is a useful, siliceous material which will produce a good, sharp edge but, unlike most other rocks used for knapping, it has a longitudinal grain and therefore only flakes easily in one direction. This property has determined the shape of many of the tools, and a so-called hand-adze is common (Figure 17). Silicified tuff was also used, and this flakes well in all directions. This was used to make choppers, chopping tools and other forms similar to those found in any simple industry of this type.

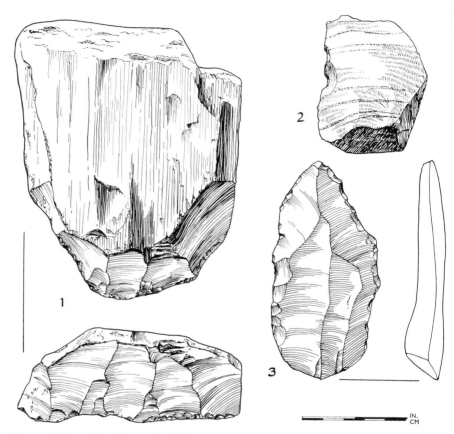

Figure 17: Stone Tools from South East Asia
1. Anyathian chopper-core made from fossil wood. Upper Burma. 2. Tampanian flake of quartzite. Kota Tampan, Perak, Malaya. 3. Patjitanian flake with secondary working of silicified limestone. South-Central Java.
(1 and 3 after Movius, 1949; 2 after Walker and Sieveking, 1962)

Thailand

A simple pebble tool industry has been recognised in Thailand and called the Fingnoian, as it occurs in gravels of a 20 m terrace of the Fingnoi Valley at Bhan-Kao. It is also found in the Kwae Noi Valley near the Burmese border. The only clue to its date is the height of the terrace above the river and a terrace at this height could be of Late Pleistocene age.

Much more convincing evidence for Palaeolithic sites in Thailand comes from a series of sites in the north, in the basins of the Lampang and Phrae Rivers.[52] A rich chopper-core industry has come from a pebble conglomerate at Mae Tha, on the highest terrace of the river. The pebble conglomerate is considered to be a cemented fluviatile deposit, part of the same sedimentary cycle as the underlying river sand. The industry is confined to the top of the conglomerate, which has undergone an intense laterisation, a soil process of tropical climates generally producing hardpans. This laterite is covered by a superficial layer of sand that is not laterised. However, this evidence alone would not be sufficient to warrant the acceptance of an early date for the industry, for there are many unknown factors in the formation of a laterite soil. More significant is that this conglomerate can be traced laterally in the region and, at a point only 2.5 km distant, it is covered by volcanic basalt. This basalt has been measured for palaeomagnetism and it is of reversed polarity. Even closer to Mae Tha is another site with a series of basalt flows over the same conglomerate, and the lower one is also of reversed polarity while the upper ones are normal. Any doubts on the position of the actual industry in relation to the basalt would appear to be dispelled by a site 12 km away at Ban Don Mun where pebble tools have been claimed from a gravel beneath basalt with a reversed polarity. This palaeomagnetism indicates an age that is unlikely to be younger than the Matuyama reversed epoch/Brunhes normal epoch boundary, i.e. about 730,000 years ago on present reckoning.

Malaya

Another rich pebble tool industry was found at Kota Tampan in northern Malaya, and thus called the Tampanian. It is found in a river gravel about 80 m OD which is thought to be the same age as the higher terraces of the Irrawaddy and Soan-Indus systems. There is no fauna in the gravel at this site to support such a correlation, but the tooth of an archaic elephant, *Elephas nomadicus*, comes from similar gravels further south. The industry is one of choppers, chopping tools, proto-bifaces, cores and flake implements. Some of the rolled tools of quartz and quartzite are, from the published photographs, difficult to distinguish from naturally broken pebbles.

Java (Indonesia)

The well-known discoveries of Java Man (*Homo erectus*, otherwise known as *Pithecanthropus erectus* (Plate X)) have come from three sites along the Solo River: Sangiran, Trinil and Modjokerto. This is a volcanic area and there has been considerable uplift and movement since the formation of the deposits in which the human remains were found. These tilted 'Solo Beds' are divided into three stratigraphical units: the Djetis, Trinil and Ngandong strata. They are ancient fluviatile sediments, mainly consolidated into conglomerates, containing volcanic material. On the basis of the contained fauna, a Lower Pleistocene date has been claimed for the oldest unit, the Djetis Beds, but it is now thought that both the Djetis and Trinil Beds are Middle Pleistocene. A K/Ar date of 550,000 years has been obtained for the Trinil Beds from basalt, although formerly a date of 1.9 million years had been obtained from pumice a few metres below the site of the Modjokerto skull.[53] Another conflicting date comes from the Trinil Beds at Sangiran, mentioned below.

It is surprising that, in spite of the long years of methodical investigation, not a single stone tool has been found with these famous human fossils, yet there is known in Java a chopper-core industry of a type that would be expected to be associated with them. Termed the Patjitanian, it is a bold industry of large flakes, chopper-cores, proto-hand-axes and apparent hand-axes. The raw material used was mainly a silicified tuff, but silicified limestone and fossil wood was also employed. Some of the initial flakes are over 30 cm long, and there are numerous, neat, small scrapers of various forms. The 'hand-axes' are distinctive in being made by longitudinal flaking from the pointed end.

The dating of this industry is difficult. At the type site, Patjitan, the industry is found in a gravel of relatively recent age, only 9 m above the present river. The artifacts are mainly in a rolled condition, so it is thought that they have been derived from an older deposit, yet they have not been found in the higher 18 m terrace. An argument against their antiquity is that the rocks used for their manufacture were not exposed until the Middle Pleistocene. A late Middle to Upper Pleistocene date is inferred, but this seems too late for the industry to be associated with the human remains. Some archaeologists regard the industry as Late Pleistocene or even more recent. Although no tools have been found with the *erectus* remains, they have now been found at Sangiran in the Trinil Beds and can be regarded as contemporary.[54] So far, only small flakes of a siliceous rock are known, but it does confirm that *Homo erectus* in Java was, like his rather more recent counterpart in China, using stone tools. There is another K/Ar date for the Trinil Beds in this area of 830,000 years.

The Philippines and Celebes

Chopper-core industries are known from both of these East Indian islands and, although the dating is not secure, they are probably Middle Pleistocene. In the Philippines, a quartzite industry called the Cabalwanian is found in beds containing the extinct form of elephant, *Stegadon*, so, provided the industry is really contemporary with the fauna, an early date is proven. Similarly, in the Celebes, near Tjabenge, there is an industry made on chalcedony and jasper which comes from a terrace deposit 40 m above the Walanae River, and this same deposit contains an extinct pygmy elephant, *Archidiskodon*, and giant tortoise. This industry from the Celebes contains short, thick flakes, some of which are worked into points.

The great interest of the discoveries in these places is the problems they raise concerning the distribution of human populations during the Middle or latter part of the Pleistocene.

The present geography of South East Asia would be radically altered if the sea level were to drop by about 100 m, for the present major islands of Borneo, Java and Sumatra are only the higher parts of the shallow Sunda Shelf which stretches to the mainland of Malaya, Thailand and Indochina. Such a fall in sea level would extend the land mass of the Asian continent almost to Australia. There have certainly been world-wide low sea levels during periods of the Pleistocene and there can be little doubt that it was then that the early Lower Palaeolithic hunters spread to Java. The Celebes, however, are separated from the Sunda Shelf by the 1,800 metre-deep Macassar Strait and, even with a low sea level, it is estimated that there would always have been a sea barrier 40 km wide between those islands and Java. It seems inconceivable that such a sea voyage could be achieved by hunters at this lowly cultural level, so the only possible migration route would have been through the Philippines along the narrow shelf which, at times of low sea level, would have emerged to form a land bridge running sinuously from the Celebes to Formosa.

Western and Central Asia

Ladiz River, Northern Baluchistan, Iran

Lower Palaeolithic sites are very rare in Iran, and Ladiz River is the only known site of a chopper-core industry. Two localities (LT2 and LT8) are known on a high terrace of the River Ladiz and they have produced choppers, cores, flakes, flake tools but no hand-axes. Unfortunately they are surface sites, but their Palaeolithic date is supported by the discovery of some flakes within coarse gravels at another locality (LT9) in the same area.

Kara Tou Mountains, Southern Tadjikistan, USSR

A chopper-core industry has been excavated at a site 50 km south east of Dushanbe, above the River Vaksh at a height of 1,125 m. This area is in the foothills of the great mountain ranges which divide the USSR from China, Afghanistan and India. Immense thicknesses of loess have accumulated on the sides of the Kara Tou Mountain Ridge, up to 100 m thick, and the industry comes from within such loess at a depth of 64 m from the surface, associated with one of several buried soils. Some of the tools are made of flint, the remainder in metamorphosed rocks.

Faunal remains from other sites with which this loess has been equated suggest a Middle to Late Pleistocene date. There is a thermoluminescence date of 200,000 years, which would fit this interpretation, but this method of dating cannot yet be regarded as reliable for such early periods.

Ubeidiya, Israel

This important site lies on what may have been a corridor between Africa and Asia. Earth movements have severely disrupted the earlier Pleistocene deposits of the Near East and at Ubeidiya ancient lake beds have been so distorted that they are now nearly vertical, posing a strange problem for the archaeological investigators. Stone tools have come from four different levels: the lower three have yielded a chopper-core industry which has been compared to the Oldowan, whereas the upper one has produced an industry with crude hand-axes. It is from this latter level that part of a human skull and some teeth were found, probably of *erectus*.

Of the chopping tools, 70-80 per cent are made of flint, whereas spheroids are made of limestone and the later hand-axes of basalt, which seems to suggest that the different classes of tool were used for different purposes for which particular rocks were more suitable.

Palaeomagnetic measurements show that the human occupation occurs between levels of reversed and normal polarity and this is probably the Matuyama/Brunhes boundary of about 730,000 years. K/Ar dates of 640,000 and 680,000 years seem to confirm this.

Europe

Greece

A few flakes and chopping tools have been reported from the island of Kephallenia.[55] They are surface finds and therefore their date is suspect, but they seem to be confined to the 75-85 m ancient shorelines of that island and, if they really do relate to it, they can be regarded as early Middle Pleistocene, or even earlier.

Yugoslavia

Some support for the antiquity of the previous findings comes from a cave at Sandalja, near Pula. A bone breccia within the cave has been excavated. There is a rich fauna of horses, rhinoceros, pigs, deer and bovids of species that are generally found in Middle and Upper Villafranchian deposits, so an early Middle Pleistocene date is fairly secure. The archaeological importance of the site is that it has also produced a human tooth and one chopper, i.e. a unifacially flaked pebble of quartzite. The tooth has been justifiably claimed as evidence for the oldest man in Europe. Similarly, this may be the first evidence for a chopper-core industry in Europe.

Ukraine and Roumania

There are several records of cores, chopping tools and flakes being found over a wide area from the east coast of the Black Sea, particularly around Majkop, on the 50 m terrace of the Dniester, through Moldavia to the Caucasus. They are mainly isolated surface finds, and there are a few hand-axes in the same area. It is impossible to know at present whether these tools really represent the movement of hunters in the region during the Middle Pleistocene but, in view of the material from stratified sites in parts of eastern and central Europe, it seems likely that it does. A chopper-core industry has been reported from Gherasimovka near Taganrok, on the shores of the Sea of Azov. It is thought to be of Middle Pleistocene date.

The same applies to the choppers and chopping tools found in the Valley of the Olt. A site at Burgiulesti has yielded a Villafranchian fauna and it has been claimed that many of the bones have been broken by human agency, but this is such a difficult thing to prove that it is not very convincing.

Vértesszöllös, Hungary

This is the most important Lower Palaeolithic site in central Europe, discovered by commercial quarrying of travertine about 50 km west of Budapest. It lies on a high terrace of a small tributary of the Danube and the human occupation probably relates to a time when the river was flowing near this level, for travertine, a form of tufa resulting from lime-rich water and aquatic plants, had already formed prior to the first occupation. Hunters settled on its dry surface, but it does not seem to have been long before wet conditions prevailed again and more travertine was formed, neatly sealing the litter left behind. The site was reoccupied during a further dry period before loess accumulated and then further travertine.

The stone industry, at both levels, is thus in primary context, and the calcareous nature of the deposits has preserved, in superb condition, faunal and floral remains. There are casts of leaves and, in one place, the actual footprint of one of the hunters, where he trod in the plastic, calcareous mud before it solidified. More important is the discovery of an occipital bone of *Homo erectus*. Dating is fairly secure, on the basis of mammalian remains, including a rich micro-fauna. Larger animals are horse, deer, *Bos* and wolf; beavers, including the extinct giant beaver, *Trogontherium*, suggest a wooded landscape with wide sheets of shallow water, around which the hunters camped. There is no charcoal, but many of the bones are burnt. This fauna is thought to belong to an interstadial period within the Mindel Glaciation, called the Biharian.

The industry is an unusual one and is best described as a microlithic chopper-core industry. The largest chopping tools of quartzite are about 8 cm wide, but those less than 5 cm are much more numerous (Figure 18). The flakes are correspondingly minute, generally less than 3 cm, yet some of them show secondary working of considerable refinement. Various types of rocks were used: quartz, quartzite, flint, chert and limestone. A statistical analysis of 500 artifacts showed a mean length of 2.40 cm, ranging from 1.1 to 6.2 cm. The reason for the diminutive size is almost certainly the lack of anything larger in the immediate area to use. It is called the Buda industry on account of the earlier site noted below.

Buda-Várhegy, Budapest, Hungary

Travertine is also present on Terrace 4 of the Danube at Budapest itself, and the cellars of houses on Castle Hill are cut into it. A few chopping tools and flakes are recorded from this travertine, together with a Biharian fauna, both of which correspond to those at Vértesszöllös.

Stranská Skála, Czechoslovakia

This site is a low hill of Jurassic limestone 5 km north east of Brno. The remnants of Pleistocene cave fillings have been exposed by commercial quarrying and large collections of faunal remains have been made. On the slopes of the hill successive layers of talus overlie loess and river deposits.

The fauna from all these levels is considered to be Biharian, probably equivalent to an interstadial stage of the Mindel Glaciation. About two dozen artifacts of hornstone have been found. Hornstone is a siliceous rock that differs from flint or chert in being laminated, so it splits very easily along one plane. The natural pressures caused by soil movements will tend to split this rock and, not surprisingly, many such natural fractures are in the scree slopes that have been excavated. This makes the identification of artificial pieces difficult, but numerous archaeologists are quite satisfied that at least two dozen are the work of man.

Přezletice, Czechoslovakia

This is another well-excavated and documented site, 20 km north of Prague. Four archaeological horizons have been found within a series of lacustrine marls and sands. Fossil pollen, mammals, fish, molluscs and ostracods all indicate that this lake was silting up in the first half of an interglacial period, and that this was almost certainly earlier than the Elster Glaciation and therefore, in western European terms, Cromerian.

A typical chopper-core industry comes from all of the four levels, although none of them is thought to be in a primary context. Some of the bones found are also considered to be tools. One molar tooth is all that remains of the hunters themselves.

Figure 18: European Chopper-cores
1.-3. Vértesszöllös, Hungary. 4. Vallonet, France. 5. Wimereux, France. 6. Swanscombe (Lower Loam), England. 7. Clacton-on-Sea, England.
(1-3 after Kretzoi and Vertes, 1965; 4 after de Lumley, 1976a; 5 after Tuffreau, 1971; 6 from Waechter and Conway, 1969)

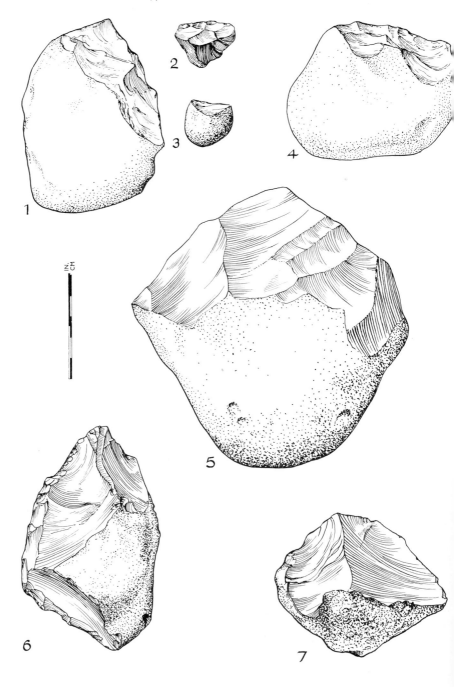

Bečov, Czechoslovakia

Two sites are known here: Bečov I, thought to be pre-Elster Glaciation and probably about the same age as Přezletice, and Bečov II, thought to be of Elster age, so possibly contemporary with Vértesszöllös in Hungary. Both have yielded a chopper-core industry although the later one is considered to be more evolved. This may only be due to the industry from Bečov I being made of quartzite, and that from Bečov II being made of lydite, a rock with far better flaking qualities.

Other sites in Czechoslovakia

Further evidence for the activity of unspecialised hunter/food gatherers in this part of central Europe during the early Middle Pleistocene comes from Praha-Suchdol, where lake marls containing a chopper-core industry have been dated on the basis of contained molluscs and soil formations. Later occupation is demonstrated from another site near Prague, Sedlec, where a chopper-core industry has been found on the surface of a terrace that dates to the Mindel Glaciation. It may belong to the Holstein Interglacial and, as will be seen below, there are several sites of chopper-core industries of this time in Germany and further west.

Another rich chopper-core industry has been found on the surface at Mlazice, near Mělník, and has been compared to that of Sedlec.

Bilzingsleben, East Germany

Many of the sites in Germany where isolated examples or industries of chopper-cores have been found have either no secure associations for their dating or are unsatisfactory in some other way. It is consoling to have this rich and important site in the mountains of northern Germany, 35 km north of Erfurt. The material is in a primary context within consolidated lake-shore sediments and is dated by fauna and pollen to the Holstein Interglacial period, almost certainly the equivalent of the Hoxnian of Britain. Furthermore, two conjoining fragments of a human occipital bone have been found, and also part of a frontal. This hunter was clearly *Homo erectus*.

The stone industry is not a normal chopper-core industry. Some of the larger worked flakes are of pointed cordate shape and resemble hand-axes, and there are also some small, bifacially worked flakes. Unlike the earlier, simple chopper-core industries, there is a large proportion of flakes with secondary working, including scrapers, borers and denticulates, the edges of which are retouched with bold, steep flaking. There is also a very high proportion of diminutive pieces, reminiscent of the Hungarian Buda industry; only 2 per cent of the flakes are greater than 3 cm, and 66 per cent of the flakes with secondary working are between 1 and 3 cm long.

Claims for the early working of bone have frequently been made and, in most or all of the cases, it is very difficult to substantiate that they really are artifacts. Many are obviously the result of natural breakages, chemical dissolution or gnawing carnivores; others remain as puzzling possibilities. Yet it would have been strange if human ingenuity had not found any use for the numerous bones that must have littered the camp sites. Here, at Bilzingsleben, is definite proof that it did so. Bone tools had been made from broken splinters of bone, flaked or cut into shape, mainly to produce stubby points. Some of these points are polished as if by use. By themselves they would not be very convincing, but there is a remarkable series of 40-50 deer antlers, all with the brow tine shortened and the beam severed below the trez tine, and this could not have happened fortuitously. There is a great resemblance to the flint miners' picks of the Neolithic, and it seems likely that these worked antlers were intended as digging tools. Even more remarkable is a collection of six long, pointed objects made of elephant ivory. They look like the smooth pointed ends of tusks and are of the same proportions. One at least is 60 cm long. Yet it is claimed that these have been actually carved out of solid ivory. It is difficult to know what purpose they could have served, and the amount of labour employed on their manufacture seems at variance with the casual aspect of the stone industry or any other activity we know of these people.

This site is still being excavated and promises to give a wealth of information on the activities of these Middle Pleistocene hunters.

Other sites in Germany

There are numerous sites in Germany where artifacts have been found which, typologically, could belong to chopper-core industries, particularly at Leipzig, Hundisburgh, Wangen and Wallendorf. They have come from gravels which probably date to the Saale Glaciation. There is a rich surface collection from Oberhessen and a site in Schleswig-Holstein with at least eight flakes in a deep, 23 m, interglacial section, but the pollen diagram does not seem to equate with either the Cromerian, Holstein or Domnitz stages. Artifacts have been claimed from the famous bone-bearing deposit of the former course of the River Neckar at Mauer, which has produced a mandible of *Homo erectus*, and is considered to be of Mindel Interstadial date. The supposed artifacts from Mauer are made of a rough quartzitic sandstone and most archaeologists are hesitant to accept them as anything but natural. Similarly, the so-called 'Altona Culture' from near Hamburg[56] cannot be considered a human stone industry, although it is possible that some of the pieces are genuine artifacts.

Denmark and the Low Countries

Crude chopper-cores, proto-bifaces, cores and flakes are found on the shores of Isefjord in Zealand. Excavation has proved an interglacial beach deposit between two moraines, and the lower one is probably that of the Riss Glaciation. The industry appears to be eroding out of this moraine. Similar finds are known from Asnaes, the island of Samso and Hokkelbjerg in South Jutland. These sites may be the most northern extent of chopper-core industries.

A rich site that has been known since the beginning of the century is the gravel pit known as the Carrière Hélin, near Spiennes, Belgium. The gravels are probably of Riss age and the industry is of the good-quality flint which abounds in the area and was later mined by Neolithic people. It includes chopper-cores and flakes with elaborate secondary working, but hand-axes are also said to have been found.

Italy

It is possible that at certain times during the earlier part of the Pleistocene a land bridge may have existed between North Africa and Sicily, so the discovery of a few chopper-cores in the territory of Agrigento on that island may be significant.

They have been found on the high 200 m Calabrian marine terrace but whether they are contemporary with it is unproven. Unfortunately, several of the find spots in Italy of chopper-cores are surface ones, but some have come from gravels at Arce and Pozzo Camillo which are thought to date from the end of the Mindel or the beginning of the Riss Glaciation. More conclusive of human activity in Italy during the early Middle Pleistocene is the presence of a couple of flakes in sand and gravel at Valchetta Cartoni in Rome. This deposit is regarded as older than a lava-flow at Acqua Acetosa from the Sabatino volcano, and palaeomagnetism indicates a date of more than 750,000 years for this lava.

Spain and Portugal

There are several mainly surface discoveries of chopper-cores in Spain and Portugal but little more can be said of them, although those from high-level raised beaches (at 100 and 60 m) in Estramadura, Portugal, are probably Middle Pleistocene. There is a claim that some have come from a deposit of Villafranchian age at the base of the Montserrat Mountains in Catalonia, and a mandible of *Homo erectus* has been found in cave sediments at Atapuerca, 40 km east of Burgos. There were no artifacts with this important find and dating is, on the basis of associated fauna, also just broadly Middle Pleistocene.

Vallonet, France

On the hills above Roquebrune-Cap-Martin, near Menton, is the opening to the small cave of Le Vallonet, overlooking the Mediterranean 108 m below. This site confirms the presence of hunters with a chopper-core industry in southern France in the earlier part of the Middle Pleistocene. It also shows that caves were being utilised for shelter at this time, for the archaeological material is in a primary context, within sandy clays that gradually accumulated in a period which, to judge from the fauna, was cooler than the present.

The industry is made from local quartzite and limestone (Figure 18), and dating is based on the fauna, which includes beasts such as the extinct southern elephant, *Elephas meridionalis*, and is thus equated with the Villafranchian. The presence of the extinct pine vole, *Pitymys arvaloides*, is also consistent with this, and a date equivalent to the Cromerian of North West Europe seems likely, but a much earlier date is claimed on the basis of the positive polarity of the palaeomagnetism. This is connected with the Jaramillo event estimated at 900,000 years.

The hunters presumably sought shelter in the cave from the cold climate, yet no trace of fire was found.

Other sites in Southern France

There are several places where chopper-cores have been found, particularly in the Rhone Valley, Provence, Languedoc, Haute Garonne and Auvergne. Many are surface finds but there are several from high-level gravels and, although this may not give their exact age, it certainly shows they are Middle Pleistocene or earlier. Mondavezan in Haute-Garonne is one of the most important in this respect, for chopper-cores occur on the surface of a terrace 110 m above the river, and in a rolled condition within the 60 m terrace below, where they are mixed with hand-axes in a fresher condition. At Soleilhac in Auvergne they are well stratified in a gravel which, from its contained fauna, is considered to be immediately post-Villafranchian. Here, there are chopper-cores of basalt, flint and quartz.

Northern France

No chopper-core industries are known from the classic deposits of the Somme Valley, although some flakes associated with an extinct form of horse, *Equus stenonsis*, in the highest terrace, and another at Boismont further down the valley, would appear to predate any Acheulian industry in the area.[57] A chopper-core found at Senart, 20 km south of Paris, comes from solifluction gravel (i.e. gravel that has sludged down a slope in a semi-frozen state) 50 m above the River Seine, but its date must be suspect. More convincing are the sites at Achenheim and nearby Hangenbieten,[58] both close to Strasbourg. Twenty metres of clays and sands overlie gravels and in the former is a rich fauna that is comparable to the famous site of Mauer (see above). On these grounds the deposits are of Mindel or pre-Mindel age, and at least two chopper-cores have been found in this context.

On the coast of the Channel, near Boulogne, at Wimereux, flint chopper-cores and flakes have been found on the beach. It seems that they are eroding from a thin deposit of gravel exposed in the low cliff, only 2-3 m above the beach, but this has not been proved. In spite of its low altitude, this gravel could be Middle Pleistocene or earlier, for only 12 km further along the coast at Wissant is a gravel at a similar height which contains remains of *Elephas meridionalis*. A similar flint industry has also been reported from Montfarville in Normandy, also at sea level.

Clacton-on-Sea and Swanscombe, England

From Clacton pier to Jaywick Sands, gravels, marls and clays fill or spread over what appear to be a series of ancient channels of a former river, at about present sea level. A rich chopper-core industry, referred to as the Clactonian (Figures 18, 19), is found in these sediments, either in the underlying gravel, or *on* it in a primary context, covered by marl also containing the same industry. Numerous bones of straight-tusked elephant, *Bos*, fallow deer, red deer, horse and rhinoceros testify to the success of the hunters, and a rare wooden spear (Plate XII) gives an insight into their hunting methods.

Bore-hole investigation and archaeological excavation have given much information on this site. Pollen indicates that the upper part of the sequence, at least, is of Hoxnian Interglacial age. However, geological considerations suggest that the earliest part of the sequence may have been in a milder period at the end of the Anglian stage.

An identical flint industry to that found at Clacton-on-Sea comes from the lower part of the complex sequence at Swanscombe in Kent (Figure 20). At this site it is stratified below and thus earlier than an Acheulian hand-axe industry.

The Cultural Level and Distribution of Unspecialised Hunter-Gatherers

The archaeological evidence for chopper-core industries throughout the world has been summarised, but what does it mean in terms of human physical and cultural evolution? Confining the problem to the Early and Middle Pleistocene,

Figure 19: Flake Tools from Clacton-on-Sea, Essex
A series of flakes with secondary working, typical of the Clactonian industry.

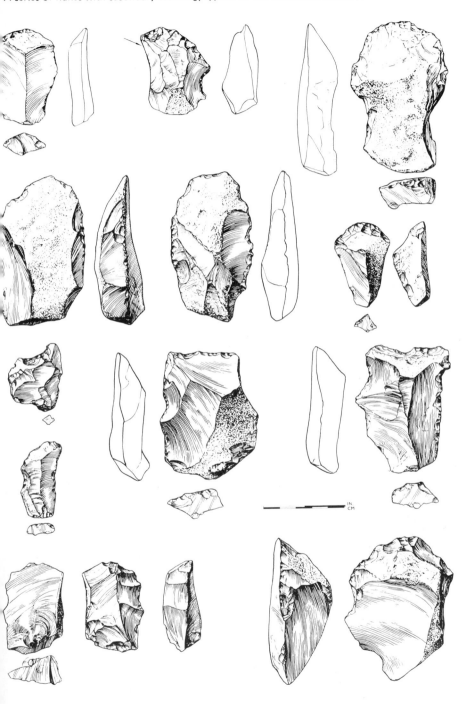

Figure 20: Acheulian Industry from Swanscombe, Kent

The industry in the middle gravels at Swanscombe is dominated by pointed hand-axes, often of very fine workmanship (e.g. 1 and 4). Equally common are numbers of small, crude, stone-struck hand-axes (e.g. 3). Some of the vast numbers of primary or finishing flakes, struck in the manufacture of hand-axes, were fashioned by secondary working into flake tools, such as the end scraper (5). The small hand-axe (2) was found close to and in the same stratum as one of the human skull fragments. Associated animal remains include giant ox, horse, red deer, giant deer, fallow deer, straight-tusked elephant, rhinoceros, wolf, lion, hare and birds.

The middle gravels at Swanscombe are about 30 m above the present level of the River Thames, and are subdivided into lower and upper units. The two parietal bones and occipital of the 'Swanscombe Skull' all came from within the upper middle gravel, but it is unlikely that there is much of a time interval between the lower and upper middle gravels. The middle gravels rest on the lower loam, which contains a Clactonian industry in primary context. This, in turn, rests on the lower gravel which contains a Clactonian industry in derived context. No hand-axes are known from the lower loam or lower gravel, and it is possible that there was a long time interval between the lower loam and the middle gravels. (1, 3 and 5, lower middle gravel; 2 and 4, upper middle gravel)

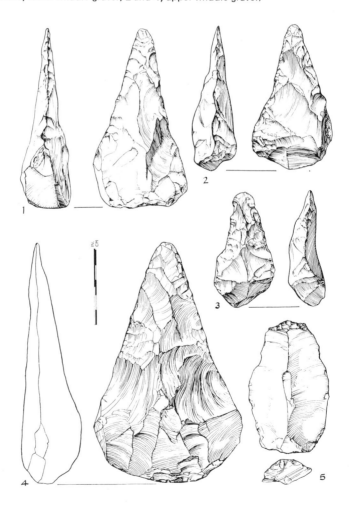

what can be concluded?

Archaeology can demonstrate that chopper-core industries appear in Africa at the time of the Plio-Pleistocene boundary, and constitute the only kits of stone tools until about 1.4 million years ago. This is the first stage to consider. Then hand-axes appear in the tool kits of some human groups, but not in others. Geographical distribution appears to be an important factor. A third stage is marked by the appearance in the Middle Pleistocene of chopper-core industries in much of the old world prior, it would seem, to the appearance of most hand-axe industries in the same places. Hand-axes form an artifact category that has not yet been described and which constitutes a major element of the next chapter. It is the premise of this account that they *do* represent a different type of human cultural group from that symbolised by the non-hand-axe chopper-core industries. For this reason it is the latter groups that are the concern of this chapter.

In the previous chapter it was pointed out that Miocene and Pliocene hominoids have been found in India and Europe, as well as in Africa. Such are the anatomical similarities that the evolutionary distance between such hominoids as *Dryopithecus* and *Ramapithecus* and the hominids, *Australopithecus* and *Homo*, is a small one, yet these hominids are found at the end of the Pliocene only in Africa. Conditions must have been particularly conducive to their evolution there and not so elsewhere. Furthermore, it is not the whole of the African continent that was the arena for this remarkable evolutionary acceleration, but apparently a narrow strip defined by the great Rift Valley. *Australopithecus* appears a little further south in the Transvaal, but it is the area from Tanzania to Ethiopia that can be fairly regarded as the birthplace of Man. There, as has been seen, at the beginning of the Pleistocene, was a hot, dry landscape, looking much as it does today. Seasonal streams discharged into perennial lakes, most of which were saline. Game of every sort abounded and smoke hung over the tops of a few volcanoes. Occasionally, the earth would shudder from some subterranean movement. In this habitat walked two species of *Australopithecus*. There was, in addition, *Homo habilis* and a form of *Homo erectus* and, as well, someone sharing the traits of the latter two. These *Homos* can be regarded either as different non-interbreeding species, or as just one species with a wide range of variation. The latter seems far more probable, and it may be that the one we like to call *erectus* merely possessed more of the traits which were successful in the evolutionary sense. By the normal processes of selective breeding, temporary geographical isolation and ability to survive, these traits gradually dominated. We can only speculate upon what situation produced such a variation in the hominid lineage in the latter part of the Pliocene. There is evidence that the climate became drier, which would have had a marked effect upon the vegetation and hence upon the food supply, but similar environmental circumstances must have occurred previously during the long history of the higher primates.

There are many theories, but our concern is with assessing the level of humanity in the first groups of these hominids that made tools. It is reasonable to talk of groups because all our closest relatives live in groups: chimps, gorillas, orang-outangs and gibbons. So do our distant relatives, the monkeys. This is a cultural trait that must have been inherited. Hominids are certainly gregarious in this sense, but what size of group would have been likely for the earliest human hunters in the Rift Valley of Africa, two million or more years ago? Archaeology can supply no definite answers, but there is nothing to indicate that they were large groups. Possibly they were very small with perhaps a dozen or so individuals mainly of common descent, although the concept of family as a social grouping was presumably lacking. The size of groups among the living apes varies greatly. Observations on some gorillas in central Africa showed that numbers varied from five to 27 gorillas in ten groups. Chimpanzees, our closest living relatives, form into larger groups of up to a hundred or more individuals, as do baboons. If food sharing really was one of the major factors in the organisation of the earliest human groups, then this would have had a powerful effect on the size of groups: above a certain number the problem of dividing foodstuffs into equal parts would have been so fraught with difficulties that inevitable squabbling would have negated the beneficial effects of the system. Unless some idea of numeration existed, sharing would have been impossible, and group feeding would have degenerated to the 'grab what you can' and 'strongest takes most' behaviour of non-food-sharing primate groups. Division into fair, if not equal, shares seems essential, and already this is implying concepts of notation and morality, which we would regard as human attributes and which are noticeably lacking in the living apes. On these grounds alone it is reasonable to estimate groups in the order of 10-20 individuals. The boulder circle in Bed I at Olduvai was probably the remains of some form of shelter, and of a size to accommodate such a number, although there are too many unknown factors to use this as evidence to support these suggestions.

Most ape groups have leaders, generally dominant males, so it seems likely that some form of leadership existed in these earliest human groups. It is impossible to go much further in basing speculation on the behaviour of groups of our nearest living relatives, let alone the behaviour of other classes or orders of animals. Territorial instincts have been emphasised by some as the motivating cause of much human behaviour,[59] mainly because it can be demonstrated that it is a powerful instinct in many animals. It seems better to regard territorialism as just one factor, together with aggression and many other attributes common to humans and other animals. It is better still to concentrate on the tangible remains of these groups — the stone tools — for they alone give us an insight into the activities of their makers.

The different categories of stone tools found in this first human industrial stage, to use archaeological parlance, have been described above (see especially Figures 7, 10, 12-14, 16-18). As with many archaeological typologies, the differences may be more evident to the archaeologist than to the people who made and used the actual tools. The original functions of choppers, chopping tools, cores, hand-axes and proto-hand-axes may have been all the same, with perhaps minor modifications in the shape for immediate purposes or dictated by the raw material. Chopping bones and digging must have been common activities, and crude tools of this nature could have assisted in both. Flakes must have been used for their cutting properties, and cutting meat is an obvious purpose for them. Small flakes with rounded, blunted edges, generally termed 'scrapers', are of less obvious purpose. If they were used for scraping skins, what were the skins required for? Clothing is possible, but unlikely to have been necessary. Skins, however, can be used to make useful containers for food gathering or water carrying. This raises another aspect of stone tools: some were only intended for the working of other materials into useful objects. The equipment of *Homo erectus* in the earliest part of the Pleistocene may have been far more varied and impressive than the crude stone tools indicate. It would be strange if the human ingenuity employed in skilfully splitting somewhat intractable rock into useful tools was not employed in a hundred other ways that have left no archaeological trace.

Some tool categories are more likely to have had specific functions; discoids may have been missiles, polyhedrons and spheroids used for grinding vegetable food, 'outils écaillés' for wedges to split bone or wood, and awls for boring holes in skins prior to tying pieces together.

These earliest industries in East Africa have been described above as the Oldowan, Developed Oldowan, KBS and Karari industries. Later, over much of the Old World, it is seen that crude stone industries without hand-axes are referred to by archaeologists by a multitude of different names. This is essential for several reasons, but the similarities are sufficient to warrant the use of one term to describe them all. The term chopper-core industries is used here. Up to the time of the middle part of Bed II at Olduvai it seems in order to equate a chopper-core industry with a level of human attainment or culture but, at this time, estimated at about 1.4 million years, there is a change; an industry appears with well-made, symmetrical bifacial tools of pointed or oval shape, called hand-axes. Also, a few hand-axes appear in the Oldowan industry, now somewhat evolved and referred to as Developed Oldowan (Figure 14). This Oldowan chopper-core industry occurs, as has been seen, at various levels throughout Bed I and the lower part of Bed II. Mention was made of the prodigious quantities of stone artifacts at the level of HWK East in Bed I at Olduvai. It is possible that 2,000,000 artifacts of the Developed Oldowan industry occur at this level and this, at first sight, suggests a population explosion, but it could merely mean a more intensive use of the gorge because of especially favourable conditions. The figure is less impressive if it is considered that the production of one chopper would produce at least ten flakes, so if ten individuals attend one kill only once a week this would mean ten choppers and a hundred flakes. Thus, in one year there would be 520 choppers and 5,200 flakes = 5,720 artifacts. 2,000,000 ÷ 5,720 = 349 years, a negligible period considering the total time involved!

The relationship between the Developed Oldowan and the Acheulian industry with hand-axes is puzzling. The latter presents such a contrast to the former that the excavator of Olduvai thinks that the hand-axe industry was intrusive into the area, and that the people responsible for the Developed Oldowan copied the idea and made an occasional hand-axe. This begs the question of where the hand-axe people came from and why the tool was such a dominant feature of one industry and not in the other. There is also the alternative explanation that there was really only one industry and that the hand-axe had been developed for a particular purpose, so its absence or presence merely indicates some different activity. A more objective approach has been to define the Acheulian industries by the proportions of hand-axes contained in them, i.e. more than 40 per cent of all the bifacially worked pieces are hand-axes = Acheulian, less than 40 per cent = Developed Oldowan. Unambiguous as this may be, it is not satisfactory as it does not take into account all the other features of the industries. The preferred interpretation is that there are two different industrial traditions. The whole question of hand-axes is the subject of the next chapter, but at this point it is necessary to emphasise that industries with large numbers of hand-axes are contemporary with chopper-core industries throughout the whole of the Olduvai sequence up to the top of Bed IV.

Elsewhere in Africa, in the Vaal Valley to the south and Morocco to the north, chopper-core industries appear a little later, in the Upper Villafranchian, or later part of the Early Pleistocene. The site of Vallonet, in southern France, shows that the Mediterranean had been crossed. Chopper-core industries also appear in Greece, Yugoslavia and possibly Italy and Spain at this time. This could well represent a spread of these unspecialised hunting groups from East Africa, but can the same be said for the near-contemporary material in China and Java? Lantian Man is associated with a chopper-core industry and at least one hand-axe. Java Man probably had a similar tool kit. More important is the presence of *Homo erectus* in the Far East during the latter part of the Early Pleistocene, probably contemporary with Upper Bed II at Olduvai. Lantian may be a little more recent, at the beginning of the Middle Pleistocene. Even if these dates are imprecise, neither Java nor Lantian Man can be as old as the earliest discoveries of hominids and stone tools in Tanzania, Kenya and Ethiopia. So does this time gap represent the time required for *Homo erectus* to wander across the southern part of Iran, through India into South East Asia and China? If so, there are vast areas in between with no evidence to confirm it, although Ubeidiya in Israel may belong to this stage. Perhaps some of the undated chopper-cores in Baluchistan, India, Burma and elsewhere were left en route, but where they can be dated they seem to be considerably more recent. Some Chinese and Indian anthropologists prefer the notion of the separate evolution of *Homo erectus* in the Far East and point to the presence of *Ramapithecus* in the Pliocene of the Siwalik Hills. This would mean a degree of parallel evolution difficult to accept, apart from the independent invention of tool making. Migration offers the easiest explanation.

The third stage, well into the middle of the Pleistocene, has been interpreted by several archaeologists in very distinct terms of population movements,[60] and it seems to be connected with the major glaciation of the northern hemisphere. This is the period that culminated in Europe with the Mindel Glaciation (Figure 21). Ice sheets and glaciers, on several occasions, spread southwards over most of Europe and Asia. Beyond the ice sheets, glaciers formed on the higher mountain ranges such as the Alps, the Elburz and the Himalayas, fanning out to meet the main mass. Human occupation of these regions during glacial maxima was obviously impossible, but there were alternating periods of warmer interstadials, or even full interglacials. These may have lasted ten or twenty thousand years or more and given adequate time for much of the ice to melt and the land to be occupied. Prior to these drastic effects on the landscape, as has been mentioned, unspecialised hunters with chopper-core industries had penetrated into southern Europe and South East Asia and China. Similar hunting groups continued to occupy much of Africa, from the Cape to the Mediterranean. A few sites show that China and at least parts of Europe were inhabited in the warmer phases.

The Peking Man site of Choukoutien belongs to this time, as does Vértesszöllös in Hungary, Stranská Skála and Přezletice in Czechoslovakia. The Mauer jaw of *Homo erectus* proves his presence in Germany. Numerous, insecurely dated finds of chopper-cores from Germany to the Ukraine may be contemporary, but more likely they belong to the period after the retreat of the

Figure 21: Map of the Maximum Extent of Glaciation in Europe

The greatest spread of the glaciers and ice sheets in the northern hemisphere occurred some time in the Middle Pleistocene, during part of the Mindel Glaciation of the Alpine sequence (= Anglian of the British stages). This was probably a long, complex glacial stage with numerous periods of retreat and advance of the ice, in response to oscillations of climate, with corresponding intervals of warmer interstadials or even interglacials. The temperature curve from the deep-sea cores (Figure 25) suggests dates of between 460,000 and 400,000 for these events.

Sites of chopper-core industries are indicated, although in some instances the 'industry' comprises little more than a few flakes (e.g. Sandalja, Valchetta Cartoni). Contemporary hand-axe sites are omitted. The broad separation of the chopper-core sites into those prior to or after the maximum extent of this glaciation is difficult to justify at some of the sites (see text).

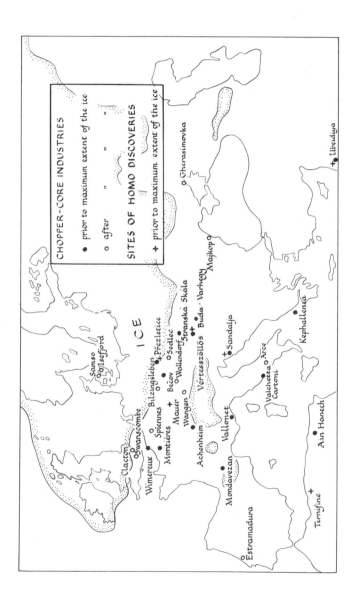

Mindel ice sheets. As the climate ameliorated so these hunters appear to have followed the vast herds of deer, *Bos*, horse, elephant and rhino across the central European plains. Sites in East Germany and England are firmly dated to the interglacial which followed the ice retreat, and there is tentative evidence that several others in West Germany, Denmark and Belgium are of the same period. These European sites are of particular interest because they seem to predate the main arrival of hand-axe industries in the same areas, after the Mindel ice retreat. This is a convincing argument for seeing these unspecialised hunters as quite separate and distinct from the other hunting groups using hand-axes. Meanwhile, chopper-core industries continued to flourish in China, India and South East Asia. As far as can be seen, they had virtually disappeared in Africa.

The span of time between the first chopper-core industries in East Africa and those of Middle Pleistocene date discussed above may be in the order of about one and a half million years. It is difficult to comprehend such slow development. Man had certainly evolved physically: he was now bigger both in stature and in brain capacity. The adaptations in group organisation, which were probably imperative for survival at the beginning of the Pleistocene in East Africa, had been successful. Division of activities, initially between hunting and food gathering, may have expanded and, as hunting prowess increased, allowed the formation of larger groups. Communication would have been essential, and some form of language must have developed. The invention of the spear, the use of shaped missiles and the ability to work in unison would have made *Homo erectus* a lethal hunter. From an insignificant, scavenging primate, unnoticed or ignored by the large mammals, by the Middle Pleistocene his appearance would probably strike as much fear into a herd as a pack of wolves. He could make and control fire, as defence or to enable him to live in cold and damp places. Digging sticks and stone pounders and choppers would have allowed the collection and use of a wide variety of vegetable foods, and the expanding brain permitted the accumulation of store-houses of information. Trial and experience could be retained and, with the beginnings of language, passed on from generation to generation. The dextrous use of simple stone tools would have produced many items of equipment made of materials that have entirely disappeared from the archaeological record. Contrary to the popular notion of a semi-starving, savage, wailing beast, by the Middle Pleistocene at least these first human hunting groups had sufficient security and comfort to survive in a highly successful manner. Once this existence had been established there was little or no reason to change it. Probably the major difficulty in maintaining the success of such a hunting group was in its numbers. Apart from the obvious drawbacks of having to share food among larger numbers of people, when the group organisation could only produce so much food within a given area, there were probably social reasons that made any group above a certain size incapable of working and living together. *Homo erectus* may already have discovered that his worst enemy was *Homo erectus*! This problem possibly had something to do with the other groups of hunters who are the subject of the next chapter.

Notes

1. Isaac and Brock, 1974; Brock and Isaac, 1976.
2. Brock, 1978.
3. Maglio, 1972.
4. M.D. Leakey, 1970b; Isaac, R.E.F. Leakey and Behrensmeyer, 1971; Harris and Isaac, 1976; Isaac, 1976; Merrick and Merrick, 1976.
5. Isaac, Harris and Crader, 1976.
6. Harris and Herbich, 1978.
7. R.E.F. Leakey, 1970, 1971, 1972, 1973a, 1973b, 1974, 1976a, 1976b; Walker, 1976; M.G. Leakey and R.E.F. Leakey, 1978; Day, R.E.F. Leakey, Walker and Wood, 1975.
8. Butzer, 1969, 1970, 1971; W.W. Bishop, 1978.
9. Merrick, Heinzelin, Haesaerts and Howell, 1973; Merrick and Merrick, 1976.
10. Howell, 1969; Day, 1969; R.E.F. Leakey, Butzer and Day, 1969; Chavaillon, 1970; Howell and Wood, 1974; Howell and Coppens, 1976.
11. Chavaillon, 1971.
12. Clark and Kurashina, 1979a.
13. Patterson, Behrensmeyer and Sill, 1970.
14. L.S.B. Leakey, 1969.
15. Bishop and Pickford, 1975.
16. L.S.B. Leakey, 1968.
17. Bishop, Pickford and Hill, 1975; Bishop, Hill and Pickford, 1978.
18. Harris and Bishop, 1976.
19. Carney, Hill, Miller and Walker, 1971.
20. Martyn and Tobias, 1967.
21. M.G. Leakey, Tobias, Martyn and R.E.F. Leakey, 1969.
22. L.S.B. Leakey, 1965; Tobias, 1967; M.D. Leakey, 1972.
23. Hay, 1976.
24. M.D. Leakey, Clarke and L.S.B. Leakey, 1971.
25. M.D. Leakey, 1971.
26. M.D. Leakey, 1975.
27. M.D. Leakey, 1972.
28. M.D. Leakey, Hay, Thurber, Protsch and Berger, 1972.
29. Mturi, 1976.
30. Clarke, 1976.
31. Lowe, Söhnge and Visser, 1937; Lowe, 1952; Partridge and Brink, 1967.
32. Goodwin, 1928.
33. Mason, 1967.
34. Mason, 1962.
35. Brain, 1958.
36. Partridge, 1978.
37. Robinson and Mason, 1962.
38. Hughes and Tobias, 1977.
39. Brain, 1970; Clarke, Howell and Brain, 1970; M.D. Leakey, 1970a.
40. Dart, 1959.
41. Mason, 1965; Wolberg, 1970.
42. McBurney, 1960; Coles and Higgs, 1969, p. 181.
43. Biberson, 1961; Coles and Higgs, 1969, pp. 170-3.
44. Clark, 1963, 1966a.
45. Clark, 1959, p. 117.
46. Clark, 1959, pp. 116-17.
47. Clark, 1958.
48. Movius, 1949; Drummond and Paterson, 1962; Mohapatra, 1966.
49. Terra and Paterson, 1939.
50. Woo, 1966.
51. Movius, 1956.
52. Sorensen, Shouls and Laming, in press.
53. Bartstra, 1978; Jacob, 1972.
54. Koenigswald and Ghosh, 1973.

55. Cubuk, 1976.
56. Rust, 1962.
57. Bourdier, 1969.
58. Thévenin, 1976.
59. Ardrey, 1961.
60. Collins, 1969.

References

Africa

Michael Day's *Guide to Fossil Man* (1977) gives excellent accounts of most of the major sites, including those in East Africa found since 1967, together with references to the original published sources. Most textbooks predate these later spectacular discoveries, but are still essential for obtaining the history and background to African Lower Palaeolithic archaeology. Penguin Books have published J. Desmond Clark's *The Prehistory of Southern Africa* (1959), Sonia Cole's *The Prehistory of East Africa* (1954) and C.B.M. McBurney's *The Stone Age of Northern Africa* (1960). L.S.B. Leakey, *Adam's Ancestors* (1953) is a good introduction to the subject of African early hominoids. Volumes I and II of *Olduvai Gorge* by L.S.B. Leakey (1965) and M.D. Leakey (1972) give detailed, authoritative accounts of this major African site, the geology of which is also in R.L. Hay's *Geology of the Olduvai Gorge* (1976). There are several relevant chapters in W.W. Bishop and J.D. Clark (eds), *The Background to Evolution in Africa* (1967) and F.C. Howell and F. Bourlière (eds), *African Ecology and Human Evolution* (1963), and the Lake Turkana region is well documented in Y. Coppens, F.C. Howell, G. Ll. Isaac and R.E.F. Leakey (eds), *Earliest Man and Environments in the Lake Rudolf Basin* (1976) and in C. Jolly (ed.), *Early Hominids of Africa* (1978). There is much relevant material in W.W. Bishop (ed.), *Geological Background to Fossil Man* (1978). South Africa is documented by chapters in R.J. Mason, *The Prehistory of the Transvaal* (1962) and North Africa in P.J. Biberson, *Le Paléolithique Inférieur du Maroc Atlantique* (1961) and H. Alimen, *The Prehistory of Africa* (1957). Good summaries of most of the sites are in J.M. Coles and E.S. Higgs, *The Archaeology of Early Man* (1969), F. Bordes, *The Old Stone Age* (1968) and D.K. Bhattacharya, *Palaeolithic Europe* (1977). Publication of much of the more recent works is scattered throughout the pages of *Nature* or in the proceedings of various learned societies and institutions. Some of the more relevant ones are indicated in the text by numbers, the full reference to which can be found in the bibliography at the end of this volume. A general survey of chopper/chopping tool cultures, by Hallam Movius Jr, is in the *Transactions of the American Philosophical Society* (1949).

India and Pakistan

The Punjab area was first investigated for its archaeology, and related to the climatic and geological events of North West India, by T.T. Paterson and H. de Terra, described by them in a publication by the Carnegie Institute in Washington (Terra and Paterson, 1939), but see also Movius (1949), Drummond and Paterson (1962) and Mohapatra (1966). More accessible summaries of the Soan industry in its geological context can be found in F.E. Zeuner, *Dating the Past* (1958), K.P. Oakley, *Frameworks for Dating Fossil Man* (1964) and J.M. Coles and E.S. Higgs, *The Archaeology of Early Man* (1969).

China

Choukoutien and Peking Man. There is no monograph on the archaeology of Choukoutien but numerous preliminary reports and papers, particularly Black, de Chardin, Young and Pei (1933) and Pei (1934). Summaries, with relevant references are in Movius (1949), Oakley (1964) and Coles and Higgs (1969). Details of the human skeletal material are in Day (1977), with appropriate references to the monographs by Black and Weidenreich. Discoveries in North China are summarised in Oakley (1964) and Coles and Higgs (1969). An absorbing account of the loss of the Choukoutien human fossil collection is in H.L. Shapiro, *Peking Man* (1976).

Lantian Man: Aigner and Laughlin, 1973; Day, 1977.

South East Asia

A recent survey is in F. Ikawa-Smith, *Early Palaeolithic in South and East Asia* (1978). Apart from the more general works already cited (especially Movius, 1949; Coles and Higgs, 1969; Oakley, 1964) in which adequate references to detailed papers will be found, the following are particularly relevant or additional:

Anyathian industry:	Terra and Movius, 1943.
Fingnoian industry:	Sorensen, 1962.
Tampanian industry:	Walker and Sieveking, 1962.
Homo erectus in Java:	Day, 1977; Jacob, 1967.
Contemporary stone industry of Java Man:	Koenigswald and Ghosh, 1973.
Cabalwanian industry:	Fox and Peralta, 1972.

Eastern and Central Asia

Most of the literature is in Russian but the following are more accessible:

Ladiz River:	Hume, 1967, 1976.
Kara Tau:	Ranov, 1974.
Ubeidiya:	Stekelis, 1966; Stekelis, Bar-Yosef and Schick, 1969; Bar-Yosef and Tchernov, 1972; Bar-Yosef, 1975.
K/Ar dating:	Horowitz, Siedner and Bar-Yosef, 1973.
Barda Balka, Iraq:	Wright and Howe, 1951.

Europe

A very useful summary of the European evidence is contained in the papers in *Current Anthropology* on Vértesszöllös by Kretzoi and Vértes (1965), and on central and eastern Europe by Valoch (1968). Germany is summarised by Schwabedissen (1973), and France in H. de Lumley (ed.), *La Préhistoire Française*, vol. 1 (1976). Britain is surveyed in D.A. Roe, *The Lower and Middle Palaeolithic Periods in Britain* (in press). Otherwise, the general works already quoted should be consulted, as should the following papers on specific sites or subjects:

Sandalja cave:		Malez, 1974.
Gherasimovka:		Boriskovsky, 1958.
Vértesszöllös:		Kretzoi and Vértes, 1965; Vértes, 1975.
	Homo erectus:	Vértes, 1965b.
	Industry:	Vértes, 1965a.
Stranská Skála:		Musil and Valoch, 1968.
Přezletice:		Fejfar, 1969.
Bečov:		Fridrich, 1976.
Bilzingsleben:		Mania, 1974.
Leipzig:		Grahmann, 1955.
Denmark:		Madsen, 1963, 1968; Baudet and Jepsen, 1968.
Sicily:		Bianchini, 1969.
Valchetta Cartoni:		Blanc, 1936.
Spain:	*Homo erectus:*	Aguirre, Basabe and Torres, 1976.
Wimereux:		Tuffreau, 1971.
Vallonet:		Lumley, 1976a.
Clacton-on-Sea:		Warren, 1951; Singer, Wymer, Gladfelter and Wolff, 1973; Wymer, 1974.
Swanscombe:		Swanscombe Committee, 1938; Waechter, Newcomer and Conway, 1970, 1971.

Chapter 4

Specialised Hunter-Gatherers

Hand-axe Industries

The greatest enigma of Lower Palaeolithic archaeology is the hand-axe. It is a tool which, in its various forms, was in use for about a million years, yet it defies any simple explanation. All theories of the purpose of hand-axes are fraught with contradictions. They may be pointed, heart-shaped, oval, discoidal, or transitional between these shapes. They may be crudely chipped by the use of stone hammers, or finished by refined techniques into symmetrical objects of elegance and beauty. They are usually described as 'all-purpose tools' but it is clear that certain forms would be particularly suitable for certain tasks. They are bifacially flaked, although often made on flakes with minimal working on one side. The more technical aspects and typologies are considered below, but the one thing that all hand-axes have in common is that they do conform to types; there is a degree of standardisation that is lacking in the chopper-core industries.

There is a simple evolutionary sequence from chopper-core to pointed chopper-core, proto-biface and hand-axe and the line between the last two can be regarded as a threshold, beyond which tool making became something more than the production of functional working edges. Specialisation is apparent and, as with the previously described unspecialised hunting groups, the epithet is transferred to the hunters themselves. It is difficult to believe that the life of these people was not considerably different from that of the unspecialised hunter/food gatherers, but the archaeological evidence needs to be summarised before such speculation can be amplified.

The problem would be easy to understand if it could be demonstrated that the advent of hand-axes coincided with greater hunting success; that these efficient tools allowed the biggest animals such as elephant, rhinoceros and hippopotamus to be butchered, whereas the clumsy chopper-cores could not cope with such massive beasts. This is assuming that some of the hand-axes were actually used for butchering and, as at least two hand-axes from Hoxne bear traces of microwear consistent with the cutting of meat, this seems likely. Certainly, some of the thin, pointed hand-axes look admirably suited for making the initial incisions through tough hides. However, there are two serious objections to the suggestion that this use of a hand-axe would have made any difference to the efficiency of butchering activities: firstly, the remains of the same large beasts are found with chopper-core industries and, secondly, the evolved hunting communities of the Upper Palaeolithic had no use for hand-axes. They may have been used for butchering, but this is not a complete explanation.

Another possibility is that some of them were weapons. The very first hand-axe ever discovered, near Kings Cross Station in London, was likened 'unto the head of a lance', and they were often referred to by gravel diggers as 'fighting stones'. The traditional 'comic cuts' figure of a cave man with a pointed stone stuck on the end of a spear may not be too fanciful. This could account for the disappearance of the hand-axe, for it cannot be entirely coincidental that its demise occurs at the same time as recognisable stone spearheads and other projectile points appear in the Late Pleistocene. On the other hand, there is nothing to indicate that they ever were hafted, either as heavy spearheads or clubheads, and many of the acutely pointed hand-axes have irregular, untrimmed butts that would make hafting difficult, if not impossible. They would have been useless as hand weapons, unless hunters were fighting each other, which may have occasionally happened.

Some of the large, pointed forms of hand-axes could have been used for digging, but experiments show that they are not much use in this respect, and far less efficient than a suitably shaped stick, if it is long enough to allow the principle of the lever to facilitate the work. Also, constant use in soil would impart distinctive marks of wear on the implement, and these have not been detected.

A further unexplained fact about hand-axes is that at a few carefully exca- vated sites they have been found on their edges, as though they had been pressed into soft ground to form a kind of edged anvil. This has been noticed in Africa at Isimila, Elandsfontein and Doornlaagte. Another puzzle is that the commonest form of hand-axe in many Acheulian industries is a very small (less than 10 cm long) poorly made tool that does not look useful for anything. At the other end of the scale are large, magnificently made hand-axes which seem too good (Plates XIII-XIV) or too heavy (Figure 22) to use. It is also hard to reconcile the large numbers of hand-axes found at some sites, such as Olorgesailie in Kenya, with small populations. Hundreds, sometimes thousands, of hand-axes at one site give an impression of large bands of hunters but, although the average size of hunter-gatherer groups was probably considerably greater than that of the unspecialised groups, it is most unlikely that numbers ever ran into hundreds. It is more likely a matter of artifacts accumulating over the years at a particularly favoured spot.

Hand-axe industries are referred to as Acheulian industries after a prolific site at St Acheul near Amiens in northern France, where many discoveries were made in the nineteenth century. It was at first thought that there was a gradual, technological improvement in their manufacture through time, with crude hand-axes at the beginning and elegant, refined types at the end. This seemed to correspond with the methods of manufacture: crude stone-struck hand-axes preceding those finished by neat, shallow flaking produced by using a bar-hammer of wood, bone or antler (Figure 23). It is now evident that there is no such tidy, logical progression. Once again, the key site is that of Olduvai Gorge in Tanzania. Not only is this one of the earliest sites where hand-axes have been found, dated to about 1.3 million years, but the long vertical succession through Beds II to IV show conclusively that there is no evolutionary 'improvement' in them from the bottom to the top. There are considerable variations, but the industry in the middle of Bed II is best matched by another in Bed IV, and the most elegant specimens come from an intermediate layer. It would seem that once the idea of a hand-axe had been realised, the degree of craftsmanship employed on its manufacture was dependent on matters other than a slow gaining of skill. Once the necessity to produce a hand-axe of a particular form was there, new techniques were probably mastered rapidly and passed from generation to generation. For the most part, evolutionary 'improvement' was the learning process of individuals and not scores of generations. However, such is the skill required to flake flint or other stone, and make hand-axes of exceptional regularity and symmetry, that some form of apprenticeship may have been practised. Constant working of stone over a few years would have been required to acquire the degree of skill shown in such superb examples as the giant hand-axe from Furze Platt (Plate XIII). There is an argument here for the specialist knapper. This could have had significant social implications.

Figure 22: Acheulian Industries in Britain
Giant hand-axe found in gravel at Shrub Hill, Feltwell, Norfolk. The gravel forms a low 'island' only about a metre above the surrounding fenland and is unrelated to any present-day drainage pattern.

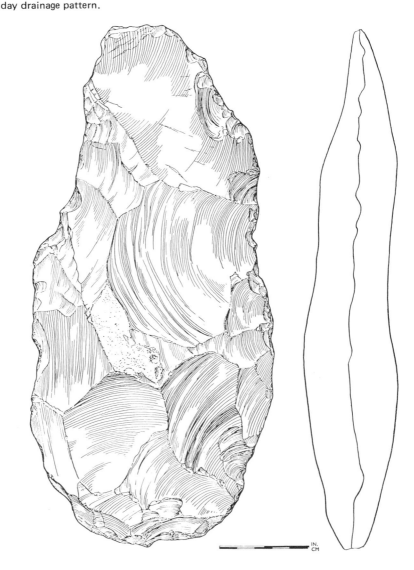

Figure 23: Acheulian Industries in Britain and France
1. Elegant cordate hand-axe with cutting edge at tip formed by a tranchet blow. Hoxne, Suffolk: Lower industry. 2. Side scraper. Hoxne: Upper industry. 3. Hand-axe finishing flake struck with a bar-hammer of wood, bone or antler. Hoxne: Lower industry. 4. Scraper made on cortical primary flake. Hoxne: Lower industry. 5. Ovate hand-axe. Found in dune sand at Vron, north of Abbeville, Somme, France. 6. Cleaver made on large primary flake. Note the pronounced cone of percussion at the bottom caused by the use of a hammer-stone. Gravels of the River Yare at Whitlingham, Kirby Bedon, near Norwich, Norfolk. 7. Proximal end of flint blade. Hoxne: Lower industry. Although the platform appears to have been carefully dressed before the flake was struck, this blade is probably a fortuitously shaped hand-axe finishing flake, as no prismatic blade cores are known in this industry. (5 from Baudet, 1959)

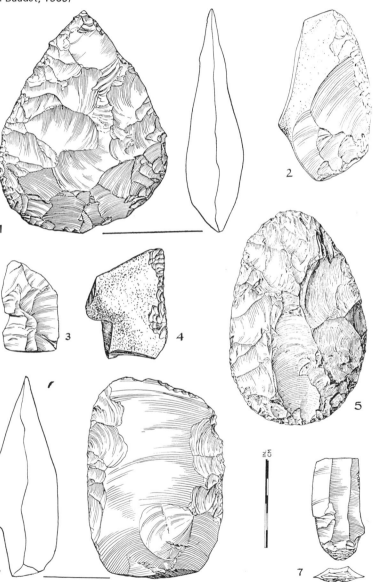

Another astonishing aspect of the Acheulian stone worker's craft was his ability to produce superb results from very intractable rocks. Highly siliceous rocks such as flint and silcrete flake easily and predictably, but quartzites, lavas and fine-grained igneous rocks are very difficult. In spite of this, most of the quartzite hand-axes of Africa equally match in refinement their European counterparts in flint.

Acheulian industries often include another distinctive tool termed a cleaver, made bifacially or on a large flake. There can be little doubt how this tool was used; the cutting edge is wide and straight, at right angles to the major axis, and the heavy butt affords a good grip (e.g. Figure 24, no. 2). A cleaver is a well-designed efficient tool and could have been used for butchering, chopping trees, working wood, smashing bones or cutting up vegetables. The surprising thing is that it is very common in Africa and becomes increasingly less so in Europe, being virtually absent at rich sites like Swanscombe.

Hand-axes can be classified into many different types, although one type will tend to grade into another, which is the problem of most archaeological typology. Pointed and cordate or ovate forms dominate and might be expected to have served different functions. Even this seems unlikely, for some Acheulian industries consist predominantly of pointed forms, while others consist almost entirely of cordate or ovate hand-axes. Metrical analyses of hand-axes from different sites demonstrate the reality of this phenomenon. If a tradition of shape preference is the reason, it suggests that both forms were being used for the same purpose. Sometimes both forms *are* present in one industry, and just how much tradition or immediate need dictated the shape of hand-axes is impossible to say. For many everyday purposes it is difficult not to believe that a good, well-struck flake of reasonable size with razor-sharp edges would have been more useful than a hand-axe. There is a suspicion that tradition may have outweighed rational behaviour.

One or two features of hand-axes may have temporal significance, even if present knowledge is not sufficient to demonstrate it conclusively. Cordate and ovate hand-axes that have been skilfully sharpened by the removal of tranchet flakes, in the manner of some cleavers (see Figure 23, no. 1), do not seem to occur before the latter part of the Middle Pleistocene, after the time of maximum glaciation. Nor do those hand-axes with a peculiar reversed S twisted section. Elegant hand-axes with plano-convex sections are probably confined to the Late Pleistocene, as are those of flat-butted sub-triangular form (see Figure 36, no. 9). Long, acutely pointed 'ficron' hand-axes also seem to occur mainly in late contexts. Hand-axe typology is an involved subject and some archaeologists are of the opinion that, treated objectively, it can increase our knowledge of the relationship of one industry with another. This is possible, but it is unlikely that such methods will ever penetrate the circumstances which determined the differences between one industry and another, or why hand-axes were made at all. There are so many puzzling factors about hand-axes that the answers may well be outside a straightforward, rational explanation and lie in the realms of human behaviour rather than function.

The industry from the middle gravels at Swanscombe is a good example of an Acheulian industry (see Figure 20). Hand-axes are the predominant tool form almost to the total exclusion of anything else except a few flake tools. The number of cores and choppers made unifacially or bifacially is negligible. Flake

Figure 24: Acheulian Industries in Africa
1. Elegant cordate hand-axe made of silcrete. Elandsfontein, Hopefield, Cape Province, South Africa. This is of the same age as the fauna which is thought to be associated with the 'Saldanha Skull' (so-called because Elandsfontein is not far from Saldanha Bay). Dating remains imprecise, at broadly Middle Pleistocene.
2. Cleaver of quartzite. Geelhoutboom, Eastern Cape Province, South Africa. This tool is made on a large flake. Such cleavers are commonly found in the Acheulian industries of Africa but are much rarer in Europe and elsewhere.

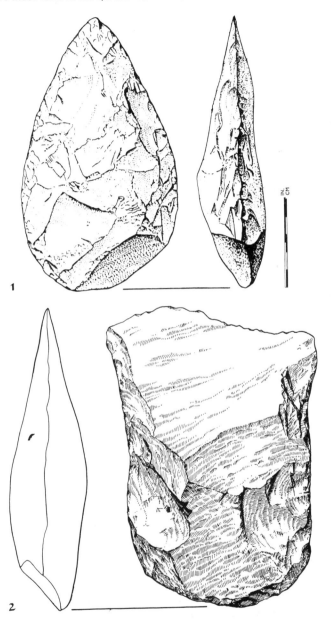

tools of a specialised nature are rare, but are particularly distinctive as their dorsal surfaces bear the characteristic scalar pattern produced by soft-hammer flaking found on the finished hand-axes.

The quantity of flakes produced in the manufacture of a hand-axe is considerable, as experiments by archaeologists can demonstrate. One very carefully controlled experiment[1] produced a hand-axe weighing 230 g by removing 51 flakes and 4,618 minute chips which would not pass through a 1 mm sieve. The original piece of flint weighed 2,948 g. In practice, about 50-60 recognisable flakes would be an average number produced in the making of one hand-axe. The excavation of the Lower industry at Hoxne in mainly a primary context produced seven hand-axes and 557 flakes, including spalls less than 2.5 cm long. This gives an average of 80 flakes per hand-axe, but there were also eleven cores. There are too many unknown factors in such calculations to allow any very useful conclusions, but they do give the approximate order of numbers of flakes. Similar totals were obtained from the unselective collection of artifacts in the middle gravels at Swanscombe. It would thus seem that any Acheulian occupation or activity area would abound with the waste flakes from hand-axe manufacture. These were doubtless utilised as knives, scrapers or other tools either with or without any further secondary working.

If such an industry is taken as a yardstick, the differences between other types of Acheulian industries become more apparent. Many of the differences are a matter of proportions of tool classes, e.g. many more cores, a greater number of specialised flake tools, no evidence of bar-hammer technique, or the addition of flakes struck from specially prepared cores.

Acheulian industries abound throughout Africa, the Near East, India and western Europe (Figures 22, 23, 24). In these regions they are far more common than the chopper-core industries which are contemporary with some of them. It would be impossible in this account to enumerate all the localities where Acheulian industries have been found, nor is it necessary; a few, selected sites reveal the general pattern. These sites are mainly ones where a combination of favourable circumstances, chance preservation and archaeological excavation or investigation give positive information on chronology, the contemporary environment or the mode of life of the hunters.

Acheulian Sites Prior to the Major Glaciation of the Northern Hemisphere

It has already been mentioned that the earliest hand-axe industries known in the world are in the middle of Bed II at Olduvai Gorge, Tanzania,[2] thought to be about 1.3 million years (Figure 11), and at Gadeb,[3] about 1.4 million years, so Africa can be accepted as the source of this second cultural advance of our ancestors. Apart from Olduvai and Gadeb there are, however, few sites in East and southern Africa where Acheulian industries can be positively dated to such an early phase. An Acheulian industry west of Lake Baringo[4] is associated with a mandible probably of *Homo erectus*. Hand-axes and cleavers occur frequently in high-level gravels of the Vaal and other rivers, but the dating of these gravels is very insecure,[5] and Middle Pleistocene seems more likely than Early. The levels at Sterkfontein and Swartkrans, South Africa, with stone tools and *Homo ?habilis* (see p. 73) is certainly earlier than Middle Pleistocene on the basis of fauna and palaeomagnetism but, on the small assemblage, it is difficult to assess whether it is a Developed Oldowan type of industry or Acheulian. The stone artifacts from the pink breccia of Swartkrans[6] include chopper-cores of quartz and quartzite, discoids, spheroids and other typical components of a chopper-core industry, but also three hand-axes and a well-made flake cleaver. This industry is probably contemporary with the one from Sterkfontein[7] and, particularly on the basis of the cleaver, can be regarded as Acheulian. These South African sites provide a fascinating repetition of the situation in Bed II at Olduvai, with the suggestion of a hand-axe element in an Early Pleistocene chopper-core industry, both coupled with remains of *Homo habilis* or *erectus*.

At the other, northern end of Africa, and just into Asia, there is a little evidence to show that hunters with hand-axes had reached the shores of the Mediterranean prior to or about the time of the great glaciations of the northern hemisphere. The important site of Ternifine in Algeria,[8] 22 km east of Mascara, is one of many Palaeolithic sites along this coastline, where sands, gravels and consolidated dunes remain from the periods when the Mediterranean was at various higher levels than its present one. Mention has already been made in the previous chapter of the chopper-core industries at Ain Hanech and elsewhere. The Ternifine hand-axe site is in a gravel pit at Palikao in Oran Province, and dating is based on the associated animal remains. These are mainly species which are typical of the Middle Pleistocene, but the presence of a giant warthog (*Phacochoeroides sp.*), a giant extinct form of ape (*Cynocephalus*) and sabre-toothed tiger (*Machairodus*) which are all typical of the end of the Early Pleistocene, point to an early date for this site. The industry comprises mainly pointed hand-axes and cleavers made on massive flakes. Most significant is the discovery with the artifacts and faunal remains of three human mandibles and a parietal bone, proving the presence of *Homo erectus*, otherwise known here as *Atlanthropus mauritanicus*. It is possible that the hand-axe industry from the basal layer of a complex series of deposits at Sidi Abderrahman,[9] near Casablanca, is of the same age.

A site at the eastern end of the Mediterranean, which would seem to belong to this early pre-major-glaciation period, is one that has already been mentioned in connection with a chopper-core industry, namely Ubeidiya in Israel.[10] The fauna, as with Ternifine, suggests a late Early to early Middle Pleistocene. There is a hand-axe industry stratified above three levels of a chopper-core industry. As seen, it is associated with some fragmentary human remains, probably of *erectus*. Some fragmentary remains of *Homo erectus* have also come from Hazorea in Israel,[11] but they were ploughed accidentally out of context and it is impossible to relate them to any particular stone industry.

There is nothing in India or the rest of Asia to show that hand-axe industries were present there before the great glaciation, although the artifacts from Lantian in China[12] and a few other sites seem to point to a hand-axe element.

Examination of the temperature chart (Figure 1) does show two major occasions in the Middle Pleistocene when different cycles of coldness tended to merge with each other and produce extended periods of immense duration with mainly very low temperatures. There is one between 630,000 and 570,000 years (Stage 16 on Figure 25) and another between 400,000 and 460,000 years (Stage 12 on Figure 25). If the deep-sea temperature curve really does reflect actual events (and it is difficult to believe that it does not), one of these long periods is most likely to represent the time of the maximum growth of ice sheets and glaciers. To use the British sequence, the interglacial period before the Anglian Glacial Stage is known as the Cromerian (see Table 1.2). The fauna of this stage still contains some Villafranchian elements, but there is now a mammoth-like elephant and several other features to indicate that it is Middle Pleistocene. It is stratified beneath Anglian glacial till, so an early Middle Pleistocene date seems certain, and it seems reasonable to suggest that the Cromerian fits broadly into the space between the two long cold periods. A date prior to this is very unlikely because, apart from anything else, the palaeo-magnetism of Cromerian deposits shows normal polarity. It is the second of these periods, the Anglian, which appears to have seen the maximum extension of the ice sheets, equating with the Elster and Mindel Glaciations of continental Europe. This is also thought to be the time of the maximum extension of the ice in the Himalayas, but there are many uncertainties.

This interpretation may help explain the distribution of hunters throughout the Old World in the late Early to early Middle Pleistocene. Prior to the cold period commencing about 630,000 years ago, activity had seemingly been confined mainly to South and East Africa and the Far East, although it was spreading into North Africa and the Middle East. The early hand-axe sites of Ternifine and Ubeidiya probably date to this time, as would the Vallonet cave with its remains of unspecialised hunting groups. After this time the climate may have discouraged any migration northwards further than North Africa, or east-wards past the barrier of the Himalayas. The amelioration of the climate at the beginning of the Cromerian seems to have encouraged the northward march of hunters into southern Europe: hunters mainly with hand-axes. Their known sites are few: Torralba and Ambrona in Spain,[13] Abbeville in northern France[14] and possibly Kent's Cavern, near Torquay, England.[15] The earliest securely dated artifacts in Britain are from Westbury-sub-Mendip,[16] but it is not certain whether they belong to a chopper-core or Acheulian industry. Other claims for 'Early Acheulian' in Britain[17] are difficult to substantiate. This meagre total is sup-ported by a few more sites possibly of the same age, but more uncertain. Only Abbeville seems fairly securely dated on the grounds of associated fauna, includ-ing the sabre-toothed tiger, *Machairodus latidens*, which became extinct after the Cromerian. This is the main reason for accepting the Kent's Cavern site as Cromerian, for sabre-toothed tiger was found there with a few crude, stone-struck hand-axes. Unfortunately, the association of the two is unproven. At Abbeville the industry is also one of crude hand-axes and, apparently, cores and flakes more consistent with a chopper-core industry. It is odd that both these sites have an industry of crude hand-axes, which is in harmony with the nineteenth-century preconceptions of slow technical development in contra-diction to the evidence of Olduvai Gorge, where refined hand-axes are found in Early Pleistocene contexts. The Spanish sites are dated by the excavators as inter-Mindel, i.e. an interstadial period of the glaciation following the Cromerian.

The Himalayas may have remained a physical barrier to migration throughout the whole of the Cromerian, and unspecialised hunting groups resident in the sunnier climes further east had no contact with the west. Africa remained little changed and hunting groups, mainly specialised types with hand-axes, existed successfully wherever the environment was favourable. However, in the latter part of the Mindel or Anglian stages in Europe, a warm spell, the so-called

Figure 25: Time Scale for Part of the Early and Middle Pleistocene
The temperature curve is based on isotopic analysis of deep-sea cores (see Figure 1), adapted to a time scale by a calculation of the rates of sedimentation. Alternate vertical bars on the chart are assumed to correspond with glacial periods (even numbers) and interglacial periods (odd numbers). There is not yet any certain way of relating the terrestrial geological record of glacials and interglacials with this marine record, but Stage 11 is probably equivalent to the Hoxnian Stage of the British sequence. Other tentative correlations are made.

The major palaeomagnetic reversal at the Brunhes-Matuyama boundary seems reliably dated by the potassium/argon method at about 730,000 years. The Cromerian deposits of Britain have normal polarity, so they cannot be older than this.

The chronometric dates and correlations with geological stages are based on the interpretations of Kukla (1977). Other workers prefer a 'shorter chronology' and would equate Stage 6 with the Wolstonian, 7 with the Hoxnian, 8 with the Anglian and 9 with the Cromerian.

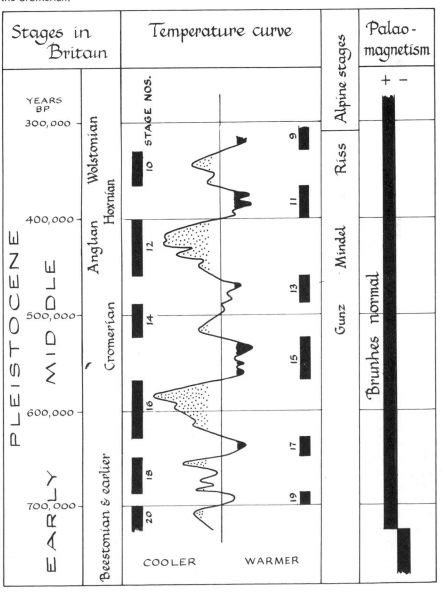

Biharian (around 450,000 years perhaps), there may have been a movement of people from the east into Europe, people belonging to unspecialised hunting groups. At the same time, specialised hunting groups were in southern Europe. As the ice eventually retreated so there appears to have been a rapid expansion of human activity into North West Europe. This seems to coincide broadly with a great development of specialised hunting groups in Africa, the Near East and India. A turning-point in human history had been reached, to judge by the wealth of archaeological material that now appears. The succeeding warm period, Hoxnian in the British terminology, Mindel-Riss in the continental, and also the following cold period, the Wolstonian or Riss, saw the climax of these early hunting groups, as savagery accelerated along the path to barbarism. It must have been a complex period of invention and innovation: small-scale by modern standards, but profound when seen against the background of the previous one and a half million years. Some of this change is reflected in the variety of stone-working techniques and different industries that existed.

Specialised Hunting Groups with Hand-axes after the Mindel-Anglian Glaciation

This period coincides with the end of the Middle Pleistocene and the beginning of the Late (see Table 1.2). Most of the hand-axe sites in Africa, North West Europe, the Near East and India date to this time, where they can be dated at all. Particularly important in Europe are the numerous discoveries of hand-axes in gravels of the Rivers Thames and Somme, for it can be demonstrated that these gravels are mainly more recent than the maximum southward extension of the ice sheets, but older than the Last Interglacial. Unfortunately, discoveries of stone industries in river gravels have limited value, for they are in a derived state, and so little can be learnt of the mode of life of the hunters responsible for them. However, their great numbers in these river valleys and many others do emphasise the preference for settlement on the banks of major rivers. Settlement is not really the correct term, because it implies some permanence of occupation in one place or region. It could be argued that the hunting groups moved constantly from one type of habitat to another, and that the presence of large quantities of visible flint on the edge of a river bed merely prompted them to concentrate their industrial activity there. Such an interpretation suggests that necessary tools were made beside the river and then taken away for use elsewhere. The numbers of finely made, unbroken hand-axes found at such sites as Swanscombe and many hundreds of other sites in England alone do not support this, although it is almost certain to be partly true. There are several sensible and obvious reasons why these hunting groups chose to have their base camps beside a river or a lake: drinking water, available flint or other suitable stone for tools, abundant game and ease of movement in a predominantly wooded landscape.

The map, Figure 26, shows the distribution of hand-axe industries in North West Europe during this critical post-major-glaciation period. Sites with associated hominid remains have been distinguished. Neither these, nor others in the world, can be summarised in detail here, but some interpretation of the evidence is offered in terms of the organisation of their society at the end of this chapter, under the following headings: habitat, food supply, domestic activities,

Figure 26: Distribution of Hand-axe Industries
The dotted areas indicate the general spread and density of Acheulian hand-axe industries. The numbered, closed circles are sites of human skeletal remains associated with hand-axes (see table on pp. 135-8) or thought to be of similar age, i.e. mainly prior to the Last Interglacial, c. 130,000 years ago. The majority are considerably older.

1. Swanscombe.	7. Arago.	13. Ferme Bouassa.
2. Biache-St Vaast.	8. Lazaret.	14. Mt Carmel.
3. Steinheim.	9. Grimaldi.	15. Kanjera.
4. La Chaise.	10. Rabat.	16. Makapansgat.
5. Orgnac.	11. Temara.	17. Elandsfontein.
6. Montmaurin.	12. Sidi Abderrahman.	18. Ternifine (Palikao).

Major Regions or Investigated Sites of Acheulian Industries

Southern Africa
Cape Province and Transvaal: Clark, 1967a, *Atlas of African Prehistory*: with detailed distribution maps for the whole of Africa at various stages of the Palaeolithic.
Stellenbosch, Cape: Seddon, 1966, 1967.

Figure 26: contd

Montagu Cave, Cape:	Keller, 1973.
Elandsfontein, Hopefield, Cape:	Singer and Wymer, 1968.
Vaal River Terraces, Transvaal:	Mason, 1967.
Doornlaagte, Transvaal:	Butzer, 1974.
Wonderboom, Transvaal:	Mason, 1962.
Cave of Hearths, Makapan, Transvaal:	Mason, 1962.
Kalambo Falls, Zambia:	Clark (ed.), 1969b.

East Africa

Isimilia, Tanzania:	Howell, Cole and Kleindienst, 1962.
Olduvai, Tanzania:	M.D. Leakey, 1972.
Olorgesailie, Kenya:	L.S.B. Leakey, 1952; Isaac, 1977.
Kariandusi, Kenya:	S. Cole, 1954, pp. 144-6.
Nsongezi, Uganda:	G.H. Cole, 1967.
Somaliland:	Clark, 1954.
Sudan:	Arkell, 1949.
Hadar, Ethiopia:	Corvinus, 1975, 1976.

North Africa

Sidi Abderrahman, Morocco:	McBurney, 1960, pp. 114-17; Freeman, 1975.
Ternifine:	McBurney, 1960, pp. 99-102; Freeman, 1975.
Sidi Zin, Tunisia:	McBurney, 1960, pp. 103-9; Freeman, 1975.
Valley of the Nile, Egypt:	Sandford and Arkell, 1929-39.

Near and Middle East

Latamne, Syria:	Clark, 1967b, 1969a.
Jisr Banat Yaqub:	Stekelis, 1960.
Barda Balka, Iraq:	Wright and Howe, 1951.

India

Madras area and Punjab:	Allchin and Allchin, 1968.
Narmada River, Deccan:	Wainwright, 1964.
Chirki-on-Pravara:	Corvinus, 1970.

Eastern Europe

Santani Dar, Armenia:	Kernd'l, 1963; Klein, 1966.
Ukraine:	Klein, 1966.

Western Europe

Torre in Pietra, Italy:	Blanc, 1958.
Torralba and Ambrona, Spain:	Freeman and Butzer, 1966; Freeman, 1975.
Lazaret, Provence, France:	Lumley, 1976b.
Terra Amata, Provence, France:	Lumley, 1976b.
Orgnac, Ardèche, France:	Combier, 1967.
Somme Valley Terraces, France:	Bourdier, 1969.
L'atelier Commont, St Acheul, Somme, France:	Bordes and Fitte, 1953.
Cagny-la-Garenne, Somme, France:	Tuffreau, 1978.
Markleeberg, Germany:	Grahmann, 1955.
South East England and Thames Valley Terraces:	Roe, 1968a; Wymer, 1968.
Swanscombe, Kent, England:	Ovey (ed.), 1964.
Hoxne, Suffolk, England:	Wymer, 1974.

equipment and structures and the physical type of the hunters themselves. These aspects cannot be considered until something has been said of the stone industries without hand-axes that flourished in the latter part of this period, up to the beginning of the Last Glaciation.

Industries with few or no Hand-axes prior to the Last Interglacial

From the time of the recession of the glaciers and ice sheets of the major Mindel Glaciation (the Anglian Stage of Britain, the Elster of Germany) until the beginning of the Last Glaciation, about 80,000 years ago, North West Europe and the Near East appear to have been the main centres of advancement in the world. One reason for this may have been the conditions created by the glacial stage in the middle of this period: the Riss or Saale of the continental schemes, the Wolstonian of Britain. The French recognise three very cold phases in the Riss, separated by two interstadials, on the basis of loess deposits and buried soils. In Britain the evidence is less clear. During the later part of the Wolstonian, ice may have partly blocked what is now the English Channel, and this could explain some of the significant differences between the Palaeolithic sequence in France and Britain.

What does seem certain is that ice did *not* cover South East England or France for most of the time. There may have been periods when the expansion of the Alpine and northern British ice sheets made living conditions so intolerable, even in the summer months, that hunting groups retreated to more favourable localities. The important point is that they do not appear to have abandoned the region as a whole, but they used their ingenuity to adapt. To some extent this may have been forced upon them by such things as geographical barriers, dependence on particular herds of game, or even population pressures. Adaptation meant greater use of fire for heating, wearing clothes, utilising natural shelters or constructing artificial ones. The archaeological evidence for this is meagre, but some caves were occupied, floors of rocks and pebbles were laid on soft, damp ground, larger stones were sometimes placed as though to delimit a living space, a central hearth is associated with a few such areas, and flimsy shelters are suggested by apparent post holes at least at one site. These items are described in more detail below. A considerable change in social organisation is suggested, and old patterns of behaviour had to give way gradually to new. This would eventually lead to the near-revolutionary formation of what we shall later refer to as advanced hunting communities.

Broadly, it can be said that this long period of human history witnessed the apex of hand-axe industries and their slow decline. Large flakes and flake-blades take their place; scrapers and a variety of small flake tools become more numerous. However, as always in times of change, development does not proceed at the same pace everywhere, with the result that at any one time many stages will be coexistent. The stone industries provide no exception.

It has already been suggested that the ultra-standardisation of hand-axes may have reached a point where it exceeded their effectiveness. A poorly made hand-axe is not so efficient a skinning and butchering tool as a large, well-struck flake, and a well-made hand-axe is no better. An ingenious technique for producing large flakes of suitable shapes was devised, termed the Levallois

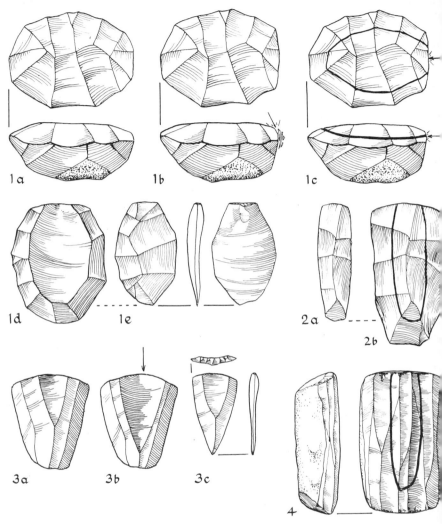

Figure 27: Diagrams to Illustrate Levallois Technique

This was an ingenious method of producing good, serviceable flakes of predetermined shape, devoid of cortex and with clean, straight cutting edges.

1a.-1e. Stages in the production of a Levallois flake.

1a. An oval flake is required so a core is dressed by simple, hammerstone, alternate flaking to an oval shape in plan.

1b. A striking platform is prepared at one end of the core.

1c. A well-directed blow with a hammerstone detaches the required flake.

1d. The struck core which, from its resemblance in side view to the carapace of a tortoise, is known as a 'tortoise' core.

1e. The Levallois flake as struck from the core. Its distinctive features are the flattish, radial flaking on its dorsal face, and the faceting of the striking platform. Bulbs of percussion are generally prominent.

The grace of this method is that all the unsightly concavities produced by the initial blocking out are left on the discarded core. The disadvantage of this method is that only one flake technique after the type site near Paris. To some extent it was an adaptation of the skilful methods used by the craftsmen who made the finest hand-axes. It was based on the production of the exact angle between the striking platform and the direction required for detachment of a flake. In the final flaking of elegant hand-axes, in order to achieve symmetry, the knapper had to apply very careful control, so that the flakes he struck came off the tool exactly where he wanted them to. The edge of the near-complete hand-axe was the striking platform so, if it were a little irregular or at too shallow an angle, it was first trimmed by some gentle secondary work. The resulting flake bears the mark of such trimming on its striking platform, and is referred to as a faceted striking platform or butt. On a hand-axe finishing flake this will, of course, still be very small. Several of the finishing flakes from the sites of Swanscombe, Kent, and Cagny-la-Garenne, Somme, show this feature. Given such control over the direction in which a flake could be detached, the advance was now to apply this technique to a core. A nodule of good-quality flint was selected and flaked by the use of a heavy stone hammer until, in plan view, it bore the general shape of the flake required by the knapper, usually oval. One end of the core was then carefully trimmed to make a striking platform at the correct angle and the final stage was the detachment of one large flake of predetermined shape from the core. It is easier to comprehend this Levallois technique visually, as shown in Figure 27.

The grace of this technique is that all the deep, unsightly concavities, caused by the use of a stone hammer to block out the core, are left on the core itself, and the reverse side of the final flake has a clean face devoid of them. The struck core, because of its plano-convex section when viewed from the side, resembles the shell of a tortoise, and is thus called a 'tortoise core'. The disadvantage of this method of producing useful flakes is that it is extremely wasteful. Sometimes a further attempt to remove a second flake behind the first was made, usually unsuccessfully in that the edge of the second flake transgressed the edge of the core and was, as a result, irregular. Not surprisingly, industries with great numbers of tortoise cores from which large flakes have been struck are generally found where there is a rich source of flint available, such as at Northfleet, Kent,[18] and Onival, on the coast of Normandy.[19] At Northfleet, where a site known as Baker's Hole has produced tens of thousands of Levallois flakes and cores, there is an outcrop of upper chalk containing much good flint. Knappers

s obtained from a large nodule of stone. It is thus very wasteful of raw material and, not surprisingly, the richest Levallois sites are those where good-quality stone such as flint outcrops naturally in quantity (e.g. Northfleet in Kent; Onival, Somme, France).

2a.-b. Blade-like flake produced from an elongated core. The flaking of the core is still radial and the resulting flake does not fulfil the description of a true blade, which has longitudinal, near-parallel facets on its dorsal face.

3a.-c. Stages in the production of a Levallois point.

3a. Prepared core of conical shape with dressed striking platform.

3b. Struck core.

3c. Required point with distinctive facets on its dorsal face and faceted striking platform. This is a very common type in African Middle Stone Age industries. With or without a little additional secondary working, they were used as projectile points.

4. Elongated core with platforms prepared at both ends. This is the true prismatic blade core and it has the great advantage of producing numerous blades from one core. It only occurs in late industries and is the forerunner of the two-platform prismatic blade core which dominated the leptolithic industries of the Upper Palaeolithic.

of a hunting group, at some time near the end of the Wolstonian Stage, must have discovered this flint and grubbed it out of the hillside. It seems unlikely that they mined the flint, but this will never be known, because near-glacial conditions, probably not long afterwards, caused the whole of the chalk slope to sludge down the small tributary valley of the Thames. If the flint was grubbed out, this suggests a very thin vegetation cover so that it was visible. The latter would also indicate a cold climate.

Levallois flakes could be used just as freshly struck, but they were sometimes modified by high-quality bar-hammer secondary working (Figure 28). A few hand-axes are sometimes found with Levallois material so it would seem that this was a special technique adopted by hunters with a hand-axe tradition. In this case it is really an Acheulian industry with Levallois technique. However, at some sites there are no hand-axes, and there is every gradation in between, from industries with many hand-axes and a few Levallois flakes to the opposite, often referred to as Acheulo-Levalloisian or Levalloiso-Acheulian industries. These were particularly well developed in the Near East at the time of the Last Interglacial.

At a perhaps slightly earlier time in the Wolstonian Stage in Britain there was another industry which can only be described as Proto-Levalloisian. It is well represented at Purfleet, Essex,[20] where, as at Baker's Hole, a wealth of flint was available in the upper chalk. The industry has none of the skill and elegance displayed in true Levallois industries, but gives the impression of the technique being applied by people who had only an elementary knowledge of flint knapping. Much of the work is simple, alternate flaking and the resulting cores and flakes are indistinguishable from their Clactonian counterparts. Several, however, have one end prepared and quite large, albeit irregularly-shaped, flakes have been struck from them. The flakes, with their wide, faceted striking platforms, are distinctive, and there is nothing of this nature in the Clactonian industry. No hand-axes were found at Purfleet that can definitely be associated with these crude Levallois flakes, although the gravel containing this industry overlies a chalk surface on which a few elegant cordate and ovate hand-axes were found. None of the cores are methodical enough to be classified as tortoise cores. It is as though the technique of preparing a striking platform in order to produce a large flake had been discovered, but not the idea of predetermining the shape of the flake by careful preparation of the core. This Proto-Levalloisian industry is found at a few other sites in the Thames Valley and in East Anglia, but in association with other types of artifacts in a derived condition, so there must be some doubt as to whether it really is a separate industry or part of another. The latter seems more likely (Figure 29).

True Levallois technique is not confined to producing large flakes of predetermined shape from tortoise cores, but includes the production of flake-blades and pointed flake-blades from other types of methodical cores. The production of flake-blades is particularly important, as it formed the basis of the later blade technique which dominated the Upper Palaeolithic industries. The evolution from tortoise core to blade core is a neat, logical one, as shown in Figure 27.

Levallois flake-blades tend to be thick, especially at their bulbar end, and rarely have both edges and all reverse facets exactly parallel with each other. A typical site in the Thames Valley of such an industry is Crayford, Kent, probably of early Last Interglacial date. Where known, this type of industry is always

Figure 28: Levalloisian Industry from Brundon, Sudbury, Suffolk
Found in alluvium of the River Stour probably dating to the Ipswichian or Wolstonian Stage. Associated animal remains include wolf, cave bear, lion, horse, rhinoceros, red deer, giant deer, giant ox, bison, straight-tusked elephant and mammoth.
1. Large flake struck from 'tortoise' core, trimmed all round by bar-hammer flaking. 2. Struck 'tortoise' core. 3. Long, blade-like Levallois flake.

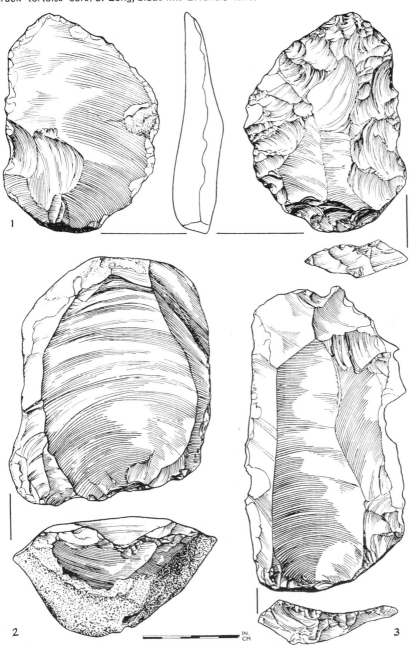

Figure 29: Levalloisian Industry
1. Levallois flake rejoined to its parent 'tortoise' core. Montieres, Somme, France (after Breuil and Koslowski, 1932).
2. 'Tortoise' core from which one blade-like flake has been struck. Barnham, Suffolk. The top view shows the well-prepared striking platform, but the core lacks the refinement or skill generally found in Levalloisian industries. When found in numbers, together with much cruder examples and alternately flaked chopper-cores, as at Purfleet in the Lower Thames Valley, the term 'Proto-Levallois' is justified.

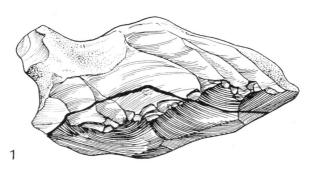

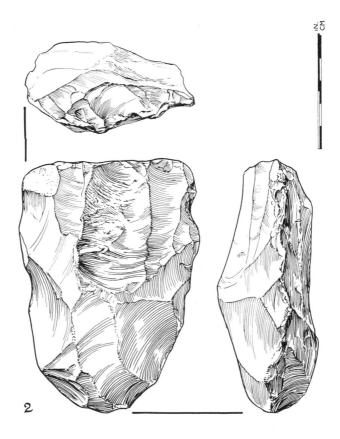

post-Riss in continental terms. The Crayford site was in primary context, and Levallois flakes lay in numbers around the bones of butchered rhinos and other animals. Knapping had been done on the spot, for the excavator was able to rejoin a mass of flakes and reconstruct the original flint nodule. This nodule had been dressed into a core, which had been taken away to another part of the site for the removal of flake-blades from it, so there was a cavity in the centre of the rejoined flakes. Plaster of Paris poured into this cavity reproduced a cast of this missing core! A few hand-axes were among the equipment of this specialised hunting group at Crayford,[21] so it could be referred to as a Levalloiso-Acheulian industry.

In France, during the Riss Glacial period, there was an industry called Tayacian. This comprised many different tool types and large numbers of usually small, often very crudely struck flakes. There could be chopper-cores, scrapers of various forms, denticulate tools and points. Levallois technique was sometimes used and hand-axes occur occasionally. Even leaf-shaped bifacial points make their rare appearance. The industry is named after a site at La Micoque, near Tayac, in the Dordogne,[22] although it seems there to be part of an Acheulian industry. At La Caune de l'Arago, Tautavel, in the eastern Pyrenees,[23] in cave deposits of Riss date, and associated with human mandibles and a nearly complete skull, is an industry of this type. Quartz was the main raw material and this must have affected the typology as it is much less tractable than flint. It is a non-Levallois Tayacian industry with many choppers and chopping tools, polyhedrals and some rare hand-axes. There are also points and micro-choppers reminiscent of a much earlier chopper-core industry at Vértesszöllös in Hungary (see p. 84). At La Baume Bonne in Provence[24] there is a little Levallois technique, some rare blades, many convex and transverse scrapers, points, notched scrapers, a few chopping tools and many choppers. Hand-axes are included in the later levels, as are some leaf points. This site is also dated to the time of the Riss. A similar industry to that from Tautavel is at La Grotte d'Aldène in Hérault,[25] and it may be a little earlier than Riss. Similar industries of about the same Riss date have been reported from Taubach in Germany.[26] There is an unusual industry from Remenham in the Thames Valley, near Henley,[27] which may belong to this complex.

It is difficult to assess the origins of the Tayacian; it may have developed from local Acheulian traditions, as the presence of hand-axes and occasional Levallois technique suggests, or have its roots in the industries of unspecialised hunting groups, with their emphasis on chopper-cores and flakes. However, although its origins are obscure, it would certainly seem to contain the elements from which later Mousterian industries developed. The latter industries belong mainly to the period of the Last Glaciation and are thus described in the next chapter, but some Tayacian-like industries during the Riss appear to have such resemblances to later Mousterian industries that they have been described as Pre- or Proto-Mousterian. The industry at La Grotte de Rigabe in Provence[28] is so described. It contains Levallois flakes, a few made into tools, and many convergent scrapers (Figure 30). Another early or Pre-Mousterian site is at Ehringsdorf, Germany,[29] but is of Last Interglacial age.

A somewhat similar industry to the Tayacian has been found in the lowest levels of the cave at Et Tabun, Mount Carmel,[30] referred to as the Tabunian. This was followed by a hand-axe industry. Hand-axes remain an important element in

Figure 30: Tayacian or Proto-Mousterian and Allied Industries

1.-7. Tayacian. La Caune de l'Arago (after de Lumley, 1976a). 1. Chopper-core. 2. Double convex/concave scraper. 3. Scraper. 4.-6. Points. 7. Bifacial scraper.

8.-11. Tayacian. La Baume Bonne (after de Lumley, 1976b). 8. Double-convex side scraper. 9. Point. 10. Denticulate. 11. Unifacial leaf point.

12.-14. Remenham, Berkshire (after Wymer, 1968). 12. Unifacial point. 13.-14. End scrapers.

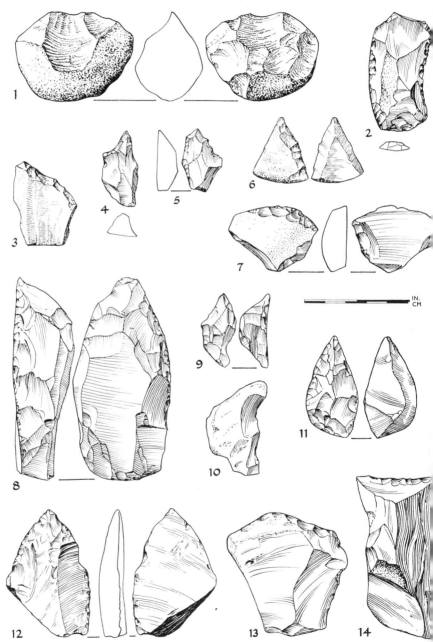

ther flint industries in the Near East of Last Interglacial age, but are superseded by the Jabrudian,[31] an industry of flakes and scrapers reminiscent of the Mousterian of Europe (Figure 40), with an occasional hand-axe. There is also a blade industry, known as the Amudian[32] (Figure 59), which has been found in contexts both earlier and later than the Jabrudian.

There was thus, in Europe and the Near East, during the later part of the Riss and continuing into the Last Interglacial, a bewildering mixture of stone-working traditions, with several new techniques and tool types. Whether this implies a mixing of actual hunting groups and the exchange of ideas cannot be proved but, in a rising population in various parts of Europe, geographical and other restrictions may have caused this. By the later part of the Last Interglacial, Mousterian-type industries were becoming prevalent in much of southern, western and central Europe, North Africa and the Near East.

The succession in southern and eastern Africa does not seem quite the same. There are a few sites where an industry of flakes and unspecialised flake tools occur, contemporary with Acheulian industries. Such a flake industry, known as the Hope Fountain, occurs on two of the numerous, stratified land surfaces at Olorgesailie, Kenya,[33] and it could well be the result of some particular activity by people who normally made and used hand-axes. It is also found in Bed III at Olduvai Gorge.[34] Otherwise, in all but South Africa, Acheulian industries appear to flourish up to a time equivalent to the Last Glaciation in the northern hemisphere (Figure 24). Levallois technique of a kind was practised in southern Africa, where it is called Victoria West technique, after a site in Cape Province.[35] It was part of an Acheulian tradition, for the flakes struck from side-struck prepared cores were frequently used as blanks for the making of hand-axes. Levallois technique also appears in China[36] and India[37] in the Late Pleistocene but, in the absence of securely dated sites, it is impossible to know how it fits in with the European sequence, whether it evolved independently or was the result of migrating hunters spreading the idea. Siberia, Australia and the whole of the American continent were still unpopulated.

The mode of life of these specialised hunting groups can now be considered.

Habitat

Mention has already been made of the preference for living sites beside fresh water. This is true throughout the whole of the world inhabited by these specialised hunting groups. It is the reason why so many of their tools are found within the sands and gravels of ancient river systems, washed into them from the original living sites beside the water. Lakes, seasonal or permanent, have always attracted hunters. There are many more Palaeolithic lakeside sites known in Africa than in Europe, mainly because of the much larger number of lakes that have always existed along the great Rift Valley. At Olorgesailie and Kariandusi in Kenya, particularly at the former, hand-axes occur in large numbers, to be measured in hundreds or thousands. Lakes are also a feature of a landscape recently emerged from ice sheets, as can be seen by a glance at a modern map of Scandinavia. Hoxne, Suffolk, is a good example of a site of this nature, where the initial occupation around the edge of the lake was in the Early-temperate zone of the interglacial.

Spring sites, such as Sidi Zin in northern Tunisia,[38] are uncommon, but many such sites in the northern hemisphere may have been destroyed by later erosion during glacial episodes.

The evidence for the choice of coastal sites is sufficient to show that some sea beaches attracted occupation. The most impressive discovery is that of Terra Amata, near Nice in southern France, where an actual dwelling was constructed on the beach. Hand-axes in marine deposits, such as raised beaches, presumably indicate coastal activity. The southern coast of the Mediterranean, especially in Morocco and Algeria, seems to have been well favoured to judge by the numerous sites, including Sidi Abderrahman which has yielded contemporary remains of the hunters themselves. Baia Farta in South West Angola is one of the few on the west side of Africa, but coastal sites are common along the southern coast of the Cape.[39] Most of the latter sites are surface discoveries, but the tough Palaeozoic rocks of this area can have eroded little since the Middle Pleistocene, and the ancient coastline must virtually coincide with the present one. Similarly, coastal sites in Somaliland[40] exist, but only as surface finds. Hand-axes occur in the raised beaches of Portugal and northern Spain and there are some important sites in England in Sussex and Hampshire, near Chichester and Portchester in the so-called 30 m raised beach.[41] Another coastal site, this time on an island sea, is Yashtukh on the Black Sea coast.[42]

The use of caves and rock shelters is attested by various sites in Europe and Africa. It is possible that caves were used much more than the evidence suggests, for most caves are formed in relatively soft calcareous rocks by chemical action and water erosion. Such processes are usually continuous, and enough time has elapsed since the end of the Middle Pleistocene for cave systems of that time to have eroded away, and what remains of the sediments once within them to have collapsed into new hollows. This may explain the occasional, puzzling discovery of stone tools and faunal remains in the fillings of fissures in limestone rock. Orgnac, in Provence,[43] is an example of such a redeposition of rock shelter or cave sediments although, in this case, erosion and collapse were contemporary with the occupation and a valuable chronological sequence remains. However, some caves still exist and contain the deposits which accumulated during their occupation by hunting groups with or without hand-axes: Makapansgat and Montagu Cave in South Africa, Bambata Cave in Rhodesia, Oumm-Qatafa in Palestine, and Lazaret, Tautavel, Pech de l'Azé and others in southern France.

Open sites in areas far removed from fresh water are virtually unknown. Where they do exist, such as at Elandsfontein in the southern Cape, investigation has proved the existence of seasonal lakes (vleis) during the Late and Middle Pleistocene and it is more than likely that the stone industry is to be associated with them.[44] Similarly, there are sites such as Tihodaine in the central Sahara,[45] where hand-axes and cleavers are found among sand dunes in a now totally desiccated area. This could indicate periods of wetter climate, when some water would have been available in the Sahara, rendering movement possible from one water-hole to another. Many cleavers have come from near Jos, Nigeria,[46] on the southern fringes of the Sahara. Sites in the Sudan are associated with old water courses.

Sites in the high rainfall area of central Africa are rare, although there is an important one in the Congo on the River Pupa at Le Plateau des Biano.[47] There are thus few habitats which do not seem to have been explored by these hunting groups, although there was a definite preference for rivers and lakes.

There are also a few hand-axe sites that owe their position to the availability of a rich source of raw material. Such a site is Hangklip on the coast of Cape Province, South Africa, where a veritable hand-axe factory site exists at the foot of a mountain of good-quality siliceous quartzite.[48]

Food Supply

Where the broken bones of animals are found with hand-axe industries it is reasonable to assume that, for the most part, they constitute food debris. Even if this cannot be proved, it is certain that they represent the species that would have been available. At sites like Hoxne, Suffolk,[49] where the material is in a primary context, there can be no doubt of the association. Table 4.1 shows some of the animals represented at three Acheulian sites where it is almost certain they were hunted beasts butchered for food.

Table 4.1: Animals Found at Three Acheulian Sites, Mainly Representing Part of the Food Supply

X = present   XX = common   XXX = very common

	Hoxne, England	Swanscombe, England	Olorgesailie, Kenya
Horse: *Equus caballus*	XXX	XXX	
Equus oldowayensis			X
Aurochs: *Bos primigenius*	XX	XXX	
Buffalo: *Homoioceros sp.?*			X
Red deer: *Cervus elaphus*	XXX	XX	
Fallow deer: *Dama dama*		X	
Giant deer: *Megaloceros*	X		
Antelopes: *Tragelaphus* (Bushbuck, Kudu and others)			X
Taurotragus (Eland)			X
Rhinoceros: *Dicerorhinus kirchbergensis*	X	X	
White Rhinoceros: *Ceratotherium sirnium*			X
Giant pig: *Metridiochoerus*			X
Straight-tusked elephant: *Elephas antiquus*	X	XX	
Elephant: *Elephas recki*			X
Hippopotamus: *Hippopotamus gorgops*			X
Giraffe: *Giraffe camelopardalis*			X
Lion: *Panthera leo*		X	
Wolf: *Canis lupus*	X		
Hare: *Lepus sp.*			
Giant baboon: *Simopithecus*			X
Bird	X	X	
Fish	X		

Sources: for Hoxne, Wymer, 1974; for Swanscombe, Ovey, 1964; for Olorgesailie, Isaac, 1977.

There can be no doubt that big game was hunted successfully. Some of the carnivores, such as wolf and lion, may not have been hunted for food, but for their furs. Everything else would have made good eating except perhaps the giant baboon at the African site. Horse, ox and deer (in Europe) and antelope, pig and horse (in Africa) were the usual quarry. There is little evidence to give any clue to the hunting techniques which were used, although some of the wooden objects from Kalambo Falls, Rhodesia,[50] are thought to be clubs (Plate XV). These may have been suitable for despatching an injured beast but not for hunting one down. Wooden spears must have been used, although none has survived or yet been found, apart from a possible tip of one at Torralba, and another at Kalambo Falls. The spear from Clacton-on-Sea[51] is contemporary, but was found with a chopper-core industry. One from Lehringen[52] was found between the ribs of a straight-tusked elephant but is of Last Interglacial age and associated with a few unmodified flakes. Other, more sophisticated hunting methods may have been practised, such as the bolas, for groups of suitably sized spherical pebbles have been found on some African sites including Olorgesailie. If pits were dug as traps, none has been found. Elaborate traps may have been constructed from branches or, where possible, game may have been chased into places where it could not escape. The site of Wonderboompoort, near Pretoria in South Africa,[53] is within a gap of a mountain range and could have been used in this way. Similarly, many river and lake sites may have been adjacent to swamps into which game could be driven and hopefully retrieved.

Fish bones are known from a few sites but are rarely preserved. Even when they are it usually takes sophisticated excavation techniques to recover them. Sea-fish remains have been found in the coastal sites of Terra Amata and Lazaret in southern France, and freshwater fish at Orgnac in Provence and at Hoxne, Suffolk. Birds also occasionally occur. There is no evidence to show that shell-fish were part of the diet, although at most sites conditions would not be conducive to their preservation.

Vegetable foods must have been collected, but little could be expected to remain as archaeological evidence. The exception is Kalambo Falls; apart from pointed, wooden sticks, which may have been used for digging up root vegetables, seeds of edible fruits were found among the macrofloral remains and one of them, at least, appears to have been foreign to the district and thus presumably brought in by some food gatherer.

Domestic Activities and Equipment

There is proof that the specialised hunting groups of this period used fire.[54] What is so surprising is that the evidence is restricted to a very few sites. If the use of fire was widespread, plenty of evidence for it would be expected: charcoal, hearths, ash, burnt stones, reddened clay, darkened sand and calcined bones. Yet these things are normally absent, even at sites where actual living surfaces have been excavated, such as at Olorgesailie in Kenya. At Swanscombe, there is nothing but a few burnt flints and some specks of possible charcoal. Perhaps, of course, most of the rich hand-axe sites were just places where animals were butchered, and portions of dismembered carcasses were taken back to a home base elsewhere. If so, with rare exceptions, these sites have not been found. Alternatively, if they were living sites, the meat was eaten raw. Some of it may have been sun dried, like biltong, so that a reserve of food was always available.

There are a few caves where fire was used: the aptly named Cave of Hearths at Makapansgat, South Africa, the Montagu Cave in Cape Province, and the French caves at Lazaret, Mas des Caves and Pech de l'Azé. As will be seen below, some of these caves appear to have been modified by simple structures which warrant a description as dwellings, and the traces of fire come from genuine hearths. A dwelling with a central hearth implies a considerable social advance. This is how the excavators interpret the site at Terra Amata, at Nice in southern France[55] (Figure 31): a shelter made of branches with an internal hearth. However, as stated, this domestic scene does not seem to be borne out by the vast majority of sites of this period, where an occasional fragment or speck of charcoal is the only sign of fire, and even that may not be the result of human activity. This is particularly puzzling when it is recalled that the much earlier chopper-core site of Choukoutien in China showed that *Homo erectus* was using fire, and that large charred logs were found at Kalambo Falls.

Fire, of course, has several uses: heating, lighting, cooking and also as a weapon. The latter may be defensive, as in a cave to ward off undesirable carnivores or other dangerous animals, or offensive in the form of setting grassland or forest alight in order to drive out game. Or it could be used just to clear an area that was too overgrown for comfortable occupation. Whether the hunters of this period were able to manufacture fire or merely collected and conserved it from occasional natural conflagrations is unknown. The latter seems much more likely.

The earliest example of man's impact on the environment may be contained within a pollen diagram produced from the lake beds at Hoxne, Suffolk, for in the upper part of the early-temperate zone there is a series of kinks indicating that there was a temporary reduction in the forest, with a corresponding increase in open grassland. This coincides exactly with the level at which hunters began to occupy the edge of the lake, and specks of charcoal were found in the lake muds.[56] The inference is that the hunters had set light to the forest, intentionally or accidentally, on such a grand scale that the local vegetational succession was disrupted. This deforestation phase also occurs in the pollen diagram at Marks Tey, Essex, 60 km distant (Figure 2), where, although no archaeological site is known, a few hand-axes and some faunal remains discovered in the last century suggest that one exists. Either the hunters at Marks Tey were also setting light to the forest or, not inconceivably, one enormous fire spread over the whole distance. Alternatively, a minor climatic fluctuation within the interglacial may have been responsible for the deforestation, and the hunters were innocent of such destruction.

If food was cooked there is no definite proof of it: calcined bones are virtually unknown, although many splinters of burnt bone are reported from an Acheulian site at Jisr Banat Yaqub, Israel.[57] The bones from grilled meat suffer little or no change but, if grilling was a common practice, some bones were bound to have fallen into the fire and become unmistakably white, cracked and brittle. Yet some puzzling discoveries at Hoxne do suggest a cooking process, for, during the course of excavation, a few concentrations of smashed bones were found; usually a dozen or so pieces of backbone or skull fragments. Only human selection could account for this, and they formed such tight, closely packed groups of bones that it is possible they were originally within a bag of some sort, since perished. Water may have been added to the bag and, held over a fire, a thin stew created from otherwise non-nutritious pieces. This is rather fanciful but other explanations seem equally so. Some form of ceremonial or magical rite may be involved, for the largest concentration of many hundreds of minute pieces of bone has been shown to include the broken skulls of a deer, a horse and an ox — the three most important sources of food for the hunters.

Figure 31: An Acheulian Shelter
This reconstruction is based on evidence revealed by excavations at Terra Amata, Nice, France. The size is indicated by peripheral stones and the localised concentration of occupational litter, including a hearth. The hut was about 8 m long and 4 m wide. Pollen contained in human coprolites suggest it was occupied in late spring to early summer. It was situated on a beach, now 25 m above present sea level, and choppers, hand-axes and cleavers were made mainly from pebbles of the hard, local limestone. The hand-axes are rather crude pointed forms, made by hard hammerstone technique, for the raw material is not conducive to refined bar-hammer flaking. Bones of the following animals were recovered in association: wolf, pig, ibex, giant ox, red deer, rhinoceros, straight-tusked elephant, rabbit, small rodents, birds and turtle. The site is thought to date to a temperate phase about 450,000-380,000 years BP, mainly on this faunal evidence, although there is a thermoluminescent date from some burnt flint of 380,000 years.

earliest container ever found wooden bowl with round bottom

Stone tools must remain the best source of evidence for domestic activities, as they survive in great numbers where virtually everything else has perished. Until recently, common sense and the cautious use of ethnographic parallels were all that could be used to determine the use of various tool types. In rare cases, it is

lumps of red ochre painted as pencil.

now possible to be more objective and specific. Techniques have been developed for studying the edge damage and microwear on stone tools.[58] It can be demonstrated that the use of a tool in a particular manner on particular material imparts distinctive signs which can be identified by microscopic examination. Minute striations and edge chipping will differ in their form according to whether the tool was used for cutting, chopping or scraping, or if the worked material was meat, bone, wood or plant fibres. This technique can only be applied to tools made of very fine-grained rocks such as flint or obsidian, but an even more inhibiting factor for Palaeolithic tools is that they must be in pristine, mint condition, exactly as discarded by the ancient workmen. The vast majority of Palaeolithic flint tools are, as has been stressed, derived, that is, in a secondary position; natural agencies have generally eroded them from the surface of one deposit into the body of another. Once a flint has been subjected to such processes, it is obvious that all these microscopic wear traces will be destroyed.

At Hoxne wear traces were identified on 38 flints and related to specific activities. It is significant that the majority of the flints are not specialised tool types, but flakes apparently selected from the large numbers produced in the process of making hand-axes (Figure 32). Some may have been purposely struck from cores. The following activities are indicated by this study:

1. meat cutting/butchering;
2. hide scraping;
3. hide cutting;
4. bone boring;
5. wood chopping/adzing;
6. wood wedging;
7. wood whittling or planing;
8. wood scraping;
9. wood boring;
10. plant gathering/cutting.

This gives a vivid insight into the mode of life of these hunters and a selection of the actual tools can be seen in Figure 32. A few of the flakes had some slight secondary working, but the only specialised tools on which microwear traces could be found were:

1. cordate hand-axe:	meat cutting;
2. ovate hand-axe:	meat cutting;
3. 3 convex side scrapers:	hide scraping;
4. 1 end scraper:	hide cutting.

Some doubt has been expressed above on the functional use of hand-axes, but these two from Hoxne would certainly appear to be tools. However, it is still possible that some kind of rite or symbolism was involved. Meat cutting was also done by eight ordinary flakes.

The wood-working tools suggest an elaborate industry. The wedges show clear signs of damage, from pressure against the piece to be split at one end, and bruising and chipping at the other by the use of a soft hammer. Green oak of about 15 cm diameter, or even more, could be split quite easily by this

Figure 32: Microwear Analysis
Primary and finishing flakes from the Lower industry at Hoxne, Suffolk. Their functions
have been identified by study of the microwear imparted on them by their usage. The
dotted lines indicate the part of the edge of the flake that was actually used. Such studies
can only be made on material found in pristine, mint condition. (See Keeley and Newcomer,
1977)

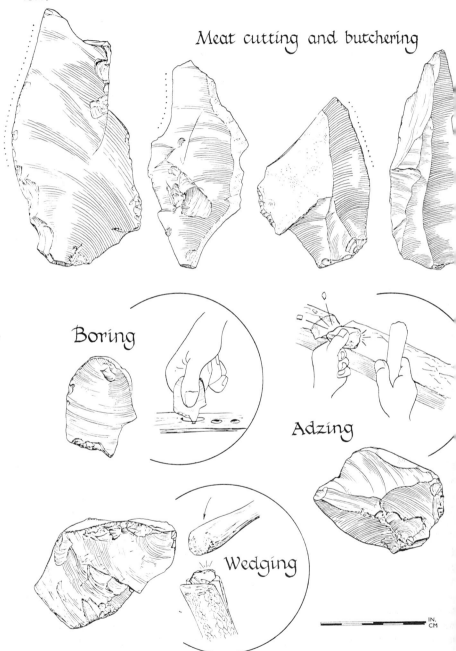

method, although it is difficult to know how it would be cut transversely in the first place. The construction of animal traps, spears and other equipment should have created no difficulties with this flint tool kit. It is to be hoped that a site in Europe will eventually be found like Kalambo Falls in Rhodesia, where wooden objects have been preserved. (Objects from the latter site are illustrated in Plate XV.)

The cutting of plant material for bedding is an obvious activity, although plants may have been cut for many other uses. Hides may have been used for constructing shelters or for making clothes or containers, but this must remain supposition for this period of the Palaeolithic until positive evidence is discovered. Leather will survive in exceptional conditions for long periods, although none has ever yet been discovered as old as this.

Structures

Figure 31 shows the reconstruction of a wooden hut at Terra Amata, dated to the period of the Mindel Glaciation. It is based on the presence of a hearth, the localised distribution of artifacts and natural stones, and shallow post holes in the sand. Although it is possible to dispute this reconstruction, there is nothing unreasonable in it. There is also some evidence that these specialised hunting groups of the later Palaeolithic modified the interiors of caves. At Lazaret, also at Nice in southern France, and of later Riss age, alignments of stones have been interpreted as marking the limits of dwelling spaces. There are similar alignments of dry stone walling associated with hut floors in the Grotte du Mas des Caves in southern France. At Lazaret, stems of grasses found inside one enclosure are interpreted as bedding. Domestic refuse was mainly outside, water channels had been dug to take the run-off (Figure 33), and it is further suggested by the excavator Professor Henry de Lumley, that skins draped over branches gave extra shelter to the occupants. This suggestion is based on the distribution of the foot bones which remained on the pelts. There was also an internal hearth. If this is the correct interpretation, it shows that these hunting groups had attained a much higher standard of social organisation than is normally accredited to them. The hut at Terra Amata was 8 m x 4 m (32 m²), and the tented area at Lazaret was 11 m x 3.5 m (38.5 m²).

At Latamne in northern Syria[59] there is an Acheulian site in a primary context which may be as early as the time of the Mindel Glaciation. The hand-axes are made by stone-hammer technique and there is the usual assortment of small, unspecialised flake tools. Limestone was used for some choppers and scrapers and, surprisingly for such an apparently early industry, a few flint blades had been struck from single platform cores. The most interesting aspect of the site is that associated with the concentration of stone artifacts in an area of about 19 x 12 m (228 m²) were numerous blocks of limestone lying in short lines, or in groups of three to five close together. Their presence is clearly the result of human activity but it is difficult to interpret them. Comparisons have been made with the spread of displaced stones found on the deserted camp sites of modern nomads, where the stones had been placed to hold down wind-breaks or tent covers. This might suggest a large, communal dwelling at Latamne, but there is a serious objection to this interpretation, for very little animal bone has been found. If this had been a living site, large numbers of fractured bones would be expected. This is not a case of lack of preservation, since those few bones which have been found are well preserved. An alternative, feasible explanation is that the blocks of stones formed a hide for the hunters in the open landscape. This would account for the numbers of stone tools and the lack of bone, for dismembered carcasses of animals would have been carried away to the living sites.

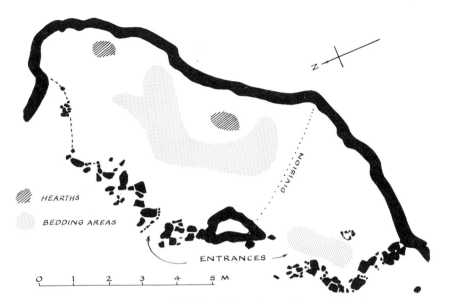

Figure 33: Plan of an Acheulian Dwelling within a Cave at Lazaret, Nice, France
The dwelling was excavated in the uppermost levels of 7 m of deposits which partly fill a large cave, close to the sea. It is associated with an Acheulian industry of mainly pointed hand-axes and numerous scrapers and other flake tools, dated to the end of the Riss Glaciation, c. 130,000 years ago.

The plan shows the rocks which were placed on the cave floor to delimit an area 11 m long and 3.50 m wide, close to the cave mouth and against its east wall. They may have secured a wooden framework for hide coverings, as protection from the cold winds blowing into the cave. The positions of the bedding areas are based on the distribution of small shells brought in with seaweed bedding material, and the foot bones of furry animals (wolf, lynx, fox, panther) remaining on pelts used as bed covers. The division is suggested by an accumulation of stone and bone litter across the dwelling, as if it had been banked against something. (After de Lumley and Boone, 1976)

Artificial arrangements of stones have also been reported from a hand-axe site at Hungsi, South India.[60] A line of granite boulders had been placed to complete the enclosure of an oval-shaped open space, 60 m², formed by natural clusters of boulders.

Another type of structure, now known from several Palaeolithic sites of this period, is the use of stones placed close together to form a floor or 'pavement'. These have been found on several of the occupational levels at Olorgesailie, with hand-axes mixed indiscriminately with pebbles and rock fragments. Stony rubble was also laid on the ground at Isimilia.[61] A similar spread of stones, 2 m x 1 m, was found within the flood plain silts of the upper part of the sequence at

Hoxne, Suffolk. At all these sites the ground surface was silt or clay and it seems likely that the stones had been put down to prevent a quagmire developing underfoot. Trunks of trees lay criss-crossed under part of the Kalambo Falls Acheulian site and it is possible that these were so placed intentionally for the same purpose.

Stone floors are also known from some cave sites. Caves can be very wet and muddy, as was the cave of La Baume Bonne in Provence during the Riss. Pebble floors had been constructed on at least four occasions. On one of them the stones were fairly closely packed with 185 to the square metre, but it is possible that some of the gaps were filled by limestone pebbles which have since dissolved away. At another French cave site, La Grotte d'Aldène, flattish slabs had been put down to form a neat pavement, and at Tautavel stones had been laid down, not so much for preventing damp, but to prevent sinking into the soft, sandy floor.

Within the cave of Pech de l'Azé in central France, some of the hearths were upon neatly paved areas of about one square metre, and other hearths were encircled by stones. Similarly, stones and earth surround one of the hearths at the Acheulian site at Orgnac, but the most elaborate Lower Palaeolithic hearth yet found is the one at Grotte de Rigabe in southern France, which was surrounded by dry stone walling 40 cm high.

Considering the sophistication of some of these structures it is surprising that more have not been found, but the number of primary context sites of this period that have been excavated in a suitable manner is extremely small. Pits are unknown.

Table 4.2 gives some details of the structures mentioned above.

Man in the Middle to Late Pleistocene

At the beginning of the Middle Pleistocene there was *Homo erectus*; at the time of the early part of the Last Glaciation there was *Homo sapiens*. Put in another way, Man with traits most conveniently described as *erectus* had evolved to Man with traits most resembling those of modern man, or *sapiens*. Although broadly true, this statement requires much qualification. The Man at the recent end, to judge by the fossil evidence, is still not exactly like ourselves, and is frequently very different. To differentiate him from the present population of *Homo sapiens sapiens*, he is entitled *Homo sapiens neanderthalensis*, or Neanderthal Man. The difficulty lies in defining Neanderthal Man, and physical anthropologists have discussed and argued this matter ever since the first skull was unearthed in the small cave of Neanderthal, near Düsseldorf, in 1856. Rather than become enmeshed in taxonomy and anatomical arguments, it seems best to consider one of the so-called 'Classic' Neanderthalers, such as the old man of La Chapelle (Plate XVIII).

A complete skeleton was found buried in the floor of a small cave at La Chapelle-aux-Saints, Corrèze, with a Mousterian flint industry and the bones of reindeer, woolly rhinoceros, horse and other animals. As can be seen from the illustration, the skull is large, with thick brow ridges, a receding forehead, a heavy chinless mandible and a rather pointed back to the skull. The limb bones were short and thick and some of the hand and foot bones stout. All these are

Table 4.2: Structures Associated with Specialised Hunting Groups

Site	Feature	Industry	Date
Lazaret, Alpes-Maritimes[a]	Stone alignments and hut floors with internal hearth	Acheulian	Riss
Latamne, Northern Syria[l]	Stone arrangements	Acheulian	Mindel or Mindel-Riss
Terra Amata, Alpes-maritimes, France[a]	Hut beside the sea with internal hearth	Acheulian	Mindel
Olorgesailie, Kenya[b]	Stone floor	Acheulian	Middle-Late Pleistocene
Hungsi, India[c]	Stone alignments	Acheulian	Middle-Late Pleistocene
Isimila, Tanzania[d]	Stone floor	Acheulian	Middle-Late Pleistocene
Hoxne, Suffolk[e]	Stone floor	Acheulian	Early Wolstonian
Pech de l'Azé, Dordogne[f]	Stone hearths	Acheulian	Riss
Orgnac III, Ardèche[g]	Hearth surrounded by stones and earth	Acheulian	Riss
Kalambo Falls, Rhodesia[h]	Wooden platform?	Acheulian	Late Pleistocene
Tautavel, Pyrénées-Orientales[j]	Stone floor	Tayacian	Riss
Grotte du Mas des Caves, Hérault[j]	Stone alignments and hut floors	Proto-Mousterian	Riss
Grotte d'Aldène, Hérault[j]	Pavement	Tayacian	Riss
Grotte de la Baume Bonne, Basses-Alpes[k]	Stone floors	Tayacian	Riss
Grotte de Rigabe, Var[k]	Hearth surrounded by dry stone wall	Pre-Mousterian	Riss

Sources: a. Lumley and Boone, 1976; b. Isaac, 1977; c. Paddayya, 1977; d. Howell, Cole and Kleindienst, 1962; e. Wymer, 1974; f. Guichard, 1976; g. Combier, 1967; h. Clark, 1962; j. Lumley, 1976c; k. Lumley, 1976b; l. Clark, 1969a.

features attributed to Neanderthal Man. Neanderthal and La Chapelle are only two of the numerous sites in Europe and elsewhere at which such human remains have been found, generally dating to the earlier half of the Last Glaciation. Not all these features, especially of the skull, are necessarily present on the many examples described as Neanderthal. There is a great range of variation within this group, and the matter is further complicated because virtually all of these features come into the range of variation in modern man, even if at the extremes. However, it would be rare to find a man of the twentieth century with a facial structure like the man of La Chapelle and, taken all together, a Neanderthal population would be very distinct from any modern one. The large, bony, chinless face of most of the Neanderthalers is reminiscent of the earlier *erectus*, and is the main difference between them and ourselves. Although stockier, the body of Neanderthal Man was less different, and past descriptions of his semi-erect, brutish aspects have been based on false interpretations or remains of arthritic individuals.

The association of Neanderthal Man with Mousterian industries, and the evolution of modern man, is the subject of the next chapter. Here, we are concerned briefly with the long interval of three or four hundred thousand years or more prior to his appearance. Table 4.3 gives some details of most of the human remains which fit into this period.

Table 4.3: Middle to Late Pleistocene Hominid Fossils

Site	Remains	Status and stone industry if known (see text)	Date
Europe			
Banolas, Spain	mandible	*Homo sapiens neanderthalensis* no industry	Riss-Würm or Würm
Biache-St Vaast, Pas de Calais	skull	*Homo sapiens* Acheulian	Riss
Bilzingsleben, East Germany	occipital and frontal fragments	*Homo erectus* chopper-core 'Tayacian'	Holstein
La Chaise, Charente i) La Grotte Bourgeois-Delaunay	mandible, skull fragments, teeth, femur, phalange, scapula	*Homo sapiens* cf. *erectus/ neanderthalensis* no industry	Riss-Würm
ii) Abri Suard	skull fragments, mandible, teeth	ditto, with Acheulian	Riss-Würm
Fontéchevade, Charente	skull fragments of two individuals	*Homo sapiens* cf. *neanderthalensis* Tayacian	Riss-Würm
Ganovce, Czechoslovakia	skull fragments, endocranial cast, mould of radius and fibula	*Homo sapiens* cf. *neanderthalensis* Micro-Mousterian	Riss-Würm
Grimaldi, Grotte du Prince, Italy	ilium	Acheulian	Riss
Krapina, Yugoslavia	remains of at least 13 individuals: skulls, teeth,	*Homo sapiens* cf. *neanderthalensis* Mousterian	Riss-Würm or Würm

Table 4.3: contd

Site	Remains	Status and stone industry if known (see text)	Date
	mandibles and post-cranial bones		
Lazaret, Alpes-Maritimes	2 teeth and infant parietal	Acheulian	Riss
Malarnaud, Ariège	mandible and vertebra	*Homo sapiens* cf. *neanderthalensis*	? Riss-Würm
Monsempren, Lot-et-Garonne	mandibles and skull fragments of 7 individuals	*Homo sapiens neanderthalensis* Tayacian-Microquian	? Riss-Würm
Montmaurin, Grotte de la Niche Haute-Garonne	mandible	*Homo sapiens* cf. *erectus/ neanderthalensis* Acheulian	Mindel or Mindel-Riss
Orgnac l'Aven, Ardèche	teeth (all imm. except 1 canine)	Acheulian	Riss
Petralona, Greece	skull	*Homo erectus* cf. *sapiens* chopper-core industry	Mindel-Riss or earlier
Quinzano, Verona, Italy	occipital	*Homo sapiens* cf. *neanderthalensis* ? Mousterian	Riss-Würm or Würm
La Rafette, Dordogne	occipital fragments		? Riss
Saccopastore, Italy	skull	*Homo sapiens neanderthalensis* no industry	Riss-Würm
Steinheim, Germany	skull	*Homo sapiens* cf. *neanderthalensis* no industry	Holstein or Saale
Swanscombe, Kent (Plate XVII)	skull excluding frontal	*Homo sapiens* cf. *neanderthalensis* Acheulian	Hoxnian or Wolstonian
Taubach, Germany	molar of child	*Homo sapiens neanderthalensis* Mousterian	Eemian
Tautavel, Caune de l'Arago, Pyrénées-Orientales (Plate XVI)	skull, 20 teeth, skull fragments, finger bones, 2 mandibles	*Homo sapiens* cf. *neanderthalensis* Tayacian	Saale
Terra Amata, Alpes-Maritimes	foot impression	Acheulian	Mindel or Mindel-Riss
Vergranne, Doubs	canine tooth		Mindel
Weimar-Ehringsdorf, Germany	parietal	*Homo sapiens neanderthalensis* Mousterian	Eemian
Asia			
Azykhskaya Peshchera, Azykh Cave, Azerbaidzhan, USSR	mandible	*Homo sapiens neanderthalensis*	Early Upper Pleistocene
Changyang, Hupei, China	maxilla and 3 teeth	*Homo erectus* cf. *sapiens*	Late Middle Pleistocene

Table 4.3: contd

Site	Remains	Status and stone industry if known (see text)	Date
Djebel Kafzeh Cave, Israel	skull fragments, teeth, mandibles and post-cranial bones of 5 individuals	*Homo sapiens sapiens* cf. *neanderthalensis* Lower Levalloisian	Riss-Würm
	skulls, mandibles and post-cranial bones of 4 individuals	*Homo sapiens sapiens* Levalloiso-Mousterian	Riss-Würm or early Würm
Mapa, Kwantung, China	skull	*Homo erectus* cf. *neanderthalensis* none known	Late Middle or early Late Pleistocene
Mugharet-es-Skhul, Mt Carmel, Israel	remains of 10 individuals	*Homo sapiens neanderthalensis* cf. *sapiens* Levalloiso-Mousterian	Riss-Würm or Würm
Mugharet-es-Tabun, Mt Carmel, Israel	remains of 7 individuals incl. near-complete female skeleton	*Homo sapiens neanderthalensis* cf. *sapiens* Levalloiso-Mousterian	Riss-Würm or Würm
	femur fragments and tooth	ditto with Acheulian	Riss-Würm
Mugharet-el-Zuttiyeh, Israel	skull	*Homo sapiens neanderthalensis* Levalloiso-Mousterian	Riss-Würm
Shuiyen Cave, Kwangsi, China	tooth		Mid-Late Pleistocene
Ting-ts'un, Shansi, China	3 teeth	chopper-core industry	Early Late Pleistocene
Africa			
Broken Hill, Zambia	skull, skull fragments, post-cranial bones of at least 3 individuals	*Homo sapiens neanderthalensis* African Middle Stone Age — proto-Stillbay	Late Pleistocene
Cova Negra, Spain	parietal	*Homo sapiens neanderthalensis*	Riss or Würm
Elandsfontein, Hopefield, South Africa	skull	*Homo sapiens neanderthalensis* Acheulian	Late Pleistocene
Eyasi, Tanzania	skull fragments	*Homo sapiens neanderthalensis* Levalloisian	Late Pleistocene
Ferme Bouassa, Morocco	remains of several individuals	*Homo sapiens* ? cf. *neanderthalensis* Acheulian	unknown
Jebel Ighoud, Morocco	2 skulls	*Homo sapiens neanderthalensis* Levalloiso-Mousterian	Pre-Soltanian or Soltanian
Kanjera, Kenya	skull fragments, 2 femora	*Homo sapiens* cf. *neanderthalensis* Acheulian	Middle Pleistocene

Table 4.3: contd

Site	Remains	Status and stone industry if known (see text)	Date
Klasies River Mouth, South Africa	4 mandible fragments, teeth, skull fragments	*Homo sapiens sapiens* cf. *neanderthalensis*	equivalent of Last Interglacial or early Last Glacial
Laetoli, Tanzania	skull	*Homo sapiens* cf. *sapiens*	Late Pleistocene
Makapansgat, Cave of Hearths, South Africa	mandible fragment	*Homo sapiens* cf. *neanderthalensis* Acheulian	Late Pleistocene
Rabat, Morocco	mandible fragment, skull fragments	*Homo sapiens* cf. *neanderthalensis* no industry	Riss
Sidi Abderrahman Morocco	mandible fragment	*Homo erectus* Acheulian	Tensiftian
Singa, Sudan	skull	Levalloisian or proto-Stillbay	Upper Pleistocene
Temara, Grotte des Contrebandiers, Morocco	mandible fragment	*Homo sapiens* cf. *neanderthalensis* Acheulian	Ouljian

In the table an attempt has been made to nominate the specific status of these discoveries, but it must be emphasised that this classification is not definitive. Many anthropologists would classify them differently. This divergence of opinion is perhaps less important when the nature of the problem is considered.

Three species of *Homo* can be distinguished: *Homo erectus*, *Homo sapiens neanderthalensis* and *Homo sapiens sapiens*. There are no objective definitions for any of them and, even if there were, the fragmentary nature of the remains as found would almost certainly prevent any general application of such definitions. All that can really be said is that certain characteristics are more likely to belong to one species than another; for instance, a mandible with a chin eminence is *sapiens sapiens* and a heavy supra-orbital ridge at the base of the frontal bone coupled with a large brain capacity is *sapiens neanderthalensis*. In many cases it is impossible to classify the remains as they do not fit neatly into any of the sub-specific categories, but seem intermediate, or slightly more like one than the other. This is particularly true of the period prior to the Last Glaciation, and some anthropologists have bypassed the dilemma by referring to all of them as pre-Neanderthalers. In the table, the status given is one which accords best with the generally accepted interpretation or description. Thus the Swanscombe skull (Plate XVII), although devoid of its frontal, morphologically has greater similarities with Neanderthal Man than modern man, so is classified as *Homo sapiens* cf. *neanderthalensis*, a category which includes several of the late Middle Pleistocene remains. Others have full *sapiens* or *neanderthalensis* status, but even this sometimes requires a further qualification where there seems some justification for distinguishing them from what is regarded as normal.

There are several ways of interpreting these human discoveries in terms of evolution. Many charts have been published on the family tree principle: the usual one shows *erectus* leading to *sapiens* with *neanderthalensis* going off on a side branch between the two; another has a unilinear *erectus* — *neanderthalensis* — *sapiens* sequence. The former sees Neanderthal Man as an aberrant offshoot from the main evolutionary progression, becoming extinct about 35,000 years ago. The latter accepts him as a stage in the evolution of modern man. The pre-Neanderthalers are not always linked to *erectus*, but sometimes with a hypothetical, as yet undiscovered, hominid of *sapiens* form. A third interpretation sees little merit in any of these schemes, and is comparable with the suggestions made in Chapter 2 on the subject of the evolution of the hominids from the hominoids. In other words, this evolution is a matter of inherited characteristics drawn from a common gene pool. The increase or decrease, development or extinction, spread or localisation, success or failure of particular characteristics are influenced by a multitude of factors. Culture is perhaps one of the most important factors, and this is shown by the archaeological evidence. It is not that particular stone industries are confined to particular human species or sub-species, but the gradual refinement and elaboration of equipment does broadly proceed with the evolution to modern man. As yet, only sensible guesses can be made as to how Man evolved in the Middle Pleistocene, but the mechanics are slowly being revealed.

The gradual trend, at least in Europe, Africa and the Near East, from about 400,000 years ago, was for the human skull to become larger, with the occipital becoming more rounded and brow ridges less prominent. This may have been through a reduction in the size of the jaw; large canines and massive molars were no longer an advantage for tearing up foodstuffs as stone tools did the job more efficiently. As jaws decreased in size, so the necessity for thick muscle attachments on the skull may have diminished and the skull changed shape accordingly. Whatever the reason, this happened, and is a non-*erectus* characteristic. It may be seen as a Neanderthal characteristic or, if accentuated, a *sapiens* characteristic. Similarly, the reduction of jaw size leading to the relatively gracile mandible of modern man, another *sapiens* characteristic or trait, can be seen by the end of the Last Interglacial at least. By the Late Pleistocene it seems that individuals were likely to possess either *sapiens*, *neanderthal* or even *erectus* traits in varying proportions. The range of variation within the population was probably greater than it is today, and it is significant that two sites so far distant from each other, and both dating to the end of the Last Interglacial, Mount Carmel and Klasies River Mouth, should both produce mandibles of *sapiens* and Neanderthal type.

Gradually, during the Last Glaciation, *sapiens* traits dominated. In the Far East *erectus* appears to have continued longer, with less change, but Neanderthal traits become apparent in Java and elsewhere about this time.

The pre-Neanderthalers were thus a varied population. There is considerable resemblance between the skulls of Steinheim, Swanscombe and Tautavel, all of late Middle Pleistocene to Late Pleistocene date. They still had prominent brow ridges and heavy jaws, but considerably lighter than those of their *erectus* predecessors, and they had much larger brains. Swanscombe Man made hand-axes almost to the exclusion of any other tool forms. Tautavel Man made them rarely. The industry of Steinheim Man is unknown, although one hand-axe comes from a probably contemporary deposit nearby. Neanderthal traits dominated by the beginning of the Last Glaciation, but the pace of change was increasing. This is the subject of the next chapter.

Notes

1. Newcomer, 1971.
2. M.D. Leakey, 1972.
3. Clark and Kurashina, 1979a, 1979b.
4. M.G. Leakey, Tobias, Martyn and R.E.F. Leakey, 1969.
5. Mason, 1962; Sampson, 1974.
6. M.D. Leakey, 1970a.
7. Robinson and Mason, 1962.
8. McBurney,.1960, pp. 99-101.
9. Ibid., pp. 114-21.
10. Bar-Yosef, 1975.
11. Avnimelech, 1967; Anati and Haas, 1967; Anati, Avnimelech, Haas and Meyerhof, 1973.
12. Chang, 1977.
13. Butzer, 1965; Howell, 1966; Biberson, 1968; Aguirre, 1969; Freeman, 1975.
14. Breuil, 1939; Bourdier, 1969.
15. Campbell and Sampson, 1971.
16. M.J. Bishop, 1975.
17. Roe, 1975.
18. R.A. Smith, 1911.
19. Agache, Bourdier and Petit, 1963.
20. Wymer, 1968, pp. 354-6.
21. Ibid., pp. 322-6.
22. Guichard, 1976.
23. Lumley, 1976c.
24. Lumley, 1976b.
25. Lumley, 1976c.
26. Behm-Blancke, 1960.
27. Wymer, 1968, pp. 202-7.
28. Lumley, 1976b.
29. Müller-Karpe, 1966.
30. Garrod and Bate, 1937.
31. Rust, 1950.
32. Garrod and Kirkbride, 1961.
33. Isaac, 1977.
34. M.D. Leakey, 1972.
35. Clark, 1959, pp. 126-7.
36. Chang, 1977.
37. Sankalia, 1969, 1971; Wainwright and Malik, 1967.
38. McBurney, 1960, pp. 103-6.
39. Clark, 1967a; Howell and Clark, 1963.
40. Clark, 1954.
41. Calkin, 1934; Apsimon, Gamble and Shackley, 1977.
42. Klein, 1966; Sulimirski, 1970.
43. Combier, 1967.
44. Singer and Wymer, 1968; Butzer, 1973.
45. McBurney, 1960, p. 110.
46. Bordes, 1968, p. 72.
47. Anciaux de Faveaux, 1962.
48. Sampson, 1962.
49. Wymer, 1974.
50. Clark, 1962, 1969b.
51. Oakley, Andrews, Keeley and Clark, 1977.

52. Movius, 1950.
53. Clark, 1959, p. 107.
54. Oakley, 1956.
55. Lumley and Boone, 1976.
56. West, 1956.
57. Clark, 1966b.
58. Semenov, 1964; Keeley and Newcomer, 1977; Keeley, 1977.
59. Clark, 1966b, 1967b, 1969.
60. Paddayya, 1977.
61. Howell, Cole and Kleindienst, 1962.

References

The archaeology of most of the sites mentioned in this chapter is dealt with in more detail in the general works already cited for Chapter 3. Similarly, the more important finds of fossil man are summarised in Michael Day's *Guide to Fossil Man* (1977) and the French discoveries in H. de Lumley (ed.), *La Préhistoire Française* (1976a). Particularly useful and readily available are J. Desmond Clark, *The Prehistory of Southern Africa* (1959), Sonia Cole, *The Prehistory of East Africa* (1954), C.B.M. McBurney, *The Stone Age of Northern Africa* (1960), W.F. Albright, *The Archaeology of Palestine* (1949), A.L. Mongait, *Archaeology in the U.S.S.R.* (1961) and Stuart Piggott, *Prehistoric India* (1950), all published by Penguin Books. Valuable surveys of most of the important European Lower Palaeolithic sites are in F. Clark Howell's paper in the *American Anthropologist* (Howell, 1966). Together with J.M. Coles and E.S. Higgs, *The Archaeology of Early Man* (1969), the reader should have no difficulty in obtaining further information or reference to the original sources. For convenience, however, some of the more relevant or accessible works of reference have been indicated in the notes above. See also the references to specific Acheulian sites appended to the distribution map, Figure 26.

Chapter 5

The Transition from Savagery to Barbarism: Mousterian and other Industries

Specialised hunting groups were savages. Subsistence, and hence population numbers, was dependent on a balance between the available food supply, over which they had no control, and an ability to exploit it. Yet, from this time, there are signs that human ingenuity was increasing the ability of hunting groups to exploit the food supply with much greater efficiency. The combination of fire and the use of natural shelters opened up new hunting grounds in regions hitherto avoided because of cold or wet climate; thrusting or throwing spears were superior weapons to stone missiles and standardisation of tool types implies a division of labour or some other social change. The implication is of larger hunting groups and more of them, spreading into new regions. Whether hunting groups by this time had developed much beyond extended family groups is doubtful, but possible. It might be more correct to refer to them as bands.

Hunting techniques must have continued to improve until, in a few favoured regions, our ancestors found themselves dominant in their own known world, relatively secure from predators and able to obtain sufficient food at will. They were on the verge of controlling the resources instead of adapting to an unquestioned fate, whether it was benign or malignant. By the first part of the Last Glaciation some human groups had achieved stability. Sites such as Combe Grenal in France, Jabrud in Palestine, Haua Fteah in North Africa, and Klasies River Mouth in South Africa, demonstrate an astonishing duration of occupation at the same place. They are all natural rock shelters or caves. Once settled, people at these places lived for tens of thousands of years in a manner that altered very little. Occupation of these favoured sites was not likely to have been permanent in the literal sense of constant habitation. It may have been seasonal or cyclical but it was certainly regular. There are few sterile layers indicating any long periods of non-occupation. The population must have increased but it could not exceed the food supply. The apparent stability of the economy could be the result of a conscious decision not to over-exploit the resources; if so, men were well past the threshold dividing us from other animals. The environment was coming under their control, or nearly so. Some form of selection may have been practised in hunting large game, some conscious restriction on numbers taken, so ensuring the perpetuation of herds. This is not to credit these savages with high reasoning powers or even a concept of cause and effect; it was more the ability to judge what was an advantage from trial and error. The significant point was that there must have been some realisation that a few fundamental requirements of life could be controlled: fire could be made, not just collected; stone could be shaped at will; the furs of dead animals could give the warmth of life; large game was available for the taking, subject to the hunter's restraint. If these matters could be commanded, or at least regulated, why not other things? The idea of adapting the environment to suit themselves, instead of the other way round, was inevitable. The servant had turned on the master and in the process fumbled for explanations. The unknown had been created and, with it, the physical fears and anxieties that seem peculiar to *Homo*. It is no coincidence that the first intentional human burials occur at this stage, that things are found which have no simple, functional explanation, and that the first weak expressions of decoration and art appear.

There are many more remains of people themselves from this period, mainly because of intentional burials and, possibly, a veneration for the bones of deceased persons. This is the time of Neanderthal Man, but it does not mean that one uniform species of man inhabited the whole earth, all with certain basic characteristics that warrant the name *Homo sapiens neanderthalensis*. These characteristics are supposed to include a high cranial capacity, sometimes exceeding that of modern man, massive brow ridges, and the occipital region of the skull projecting backwards in an angular contour. He had large nasal apertures, a heavy face with large upper jaws and a massive receding chin, teeth with big pulp cavities and fused roots, and flattened extremities to some of the postcranial long bones. Such would describe the famous finds at La Chapelle-aux-Saints, La Ferrassie or Neanderthal itself, but not all human remains of this period have all these characteristics, or even many of them. Some people had chins similar to our own, yet also had heavy brow ridges, as at Mugharet-es-Skhul, Mt Carmel. It was a matter of individuals inheriting numbers of characteristics that might be described as *erectus*, *neanderthal* or *sapiens* traits. Eventually, from about 35,000 years ago, *sapiens* traits became dominant.

The Neanderthal face does, in its heaviness, bear a close resemblance to *erectus* and also to the pre-Neanderthalers such as from Tautavel and Steinheim. The basic difference between *Homo sapiens neanderthalensis* and *Homo sapiens sapiens* is the relative lightness of our face. Our foreheads are more upright, the brow ridges drastically reduced to little more than slight bony swellings over the eyes, our noses narrower, the backs of our skulls rounded, and the jaw small but forward-jutting. One recent suggestion is that the lightening of the face caused a corresponding change in the structure of the thorax and larynx, allowing fully articulate speech. Certainly, at this cultural stage, speech would have had a great evolutionary advantage and might explain the reduction in facial size if this really was essential for its development. Also, it could suggest that only a very rudimentary form of communication existed beforehand. Another possibility is an increase in brain power through changes in the shape of the skull rather than in its capacity. This may have been especially true of the frontal regions. The retention of childlike features through a complex genetic mechanism may have contributed, for the skulls of *neanderthal* children are very similar to *sapiens*.

Whatever the reason, the archaeological record shows a marked increase in the complexity of life during this period and, by the time that advanced hunting communities existed, modern man was dominant. Some connection between this cultural evolution and cerebral development is implied. By 35,000 years ago, at least, people over most of the Old World had reached a physical and mental potential as high as that of modern man. As evolution must be a slow process in a population dispersed over half the globe, many people must have reached

Figure 34: Principal Discoveries of 'Neanderthal Man' or Allied Human Types in the Late Pleistocene

The sites shown are those thought to lie between the time range of the Last Interglacial and the first half of the Last Glaciation in the northern hemisphere, c. 130,000-40,000 years BP. The majority can be described as *Homo sapiens neanderthalensis* (e.g. Neanderthal, La Quina, La Chapelle, La Ferrassie). *Sapiens* traits are more dominant in some, such as at Mount Carmel, Florisbad and Klasies River Mouth. In Java, the Wadjak skull has affinities with the later Pleistocene population of Australia.

1. Neanderthal, Germany.
2. Spy and La Naulette, Belgium.
3. La Cotte de St Brelade, Jersey.
4. Arcy-sur-Cure, France.
5. Fontéchevade, France.
6. La Chapelle, France.
7. La Quina, France.
8. Le Moustier, La Ferrassie, Regourdou, Roc de Marsal, Combe Grenal, Pech de L'Azé, all Dordogne, France.
9. Hortus, France.
10. Les Peyrards, France.
11. Rigabe, France.
12. Banolas, Spain.
13. Cova Negra, Spain.
14. Pinar, Spain.
15. Gibraltar.
16. Jebel Ighoud, Morocco.
17. Ehringsdorf and Taubach, Germany.
18. Krapina, Yugoslavia.
19. Saccopastore, Italy.
20. Monte Circeo, Italy.
21. Kuk-Koba and Starosele, Crimea, USSR.
22. Mt Carmel: Es-Skhul and Et-Tabun, Israel.
23. Jebel Kafseh, Israel.
24. Amud, Israel.
25. Omo, Ethiopia.
26. Broken Hill, Zambia.
27. Border Cave, Natal.
28. Florisbad, Orange Free State.
29. Klasies River Mouth, Cape.
30. Shanidar, Iraq.
31. Teshik-Tash, Uzbekistan, USSR.
32. Ngandong, Java.
33. Wadjak, Java.
34. Haua Fteah, Cyrenaica.

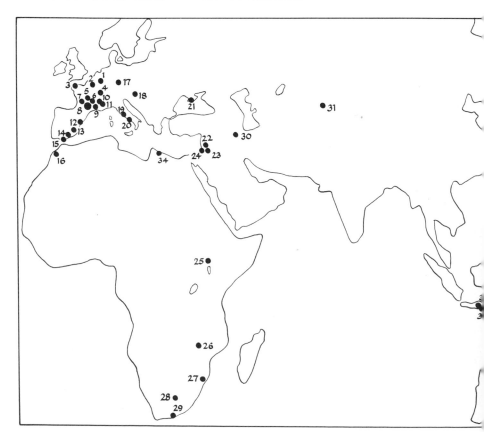

this stage earlier. In parts of the Far East, and perhaps elsewhere, change was slower, and *erectus-neanderthal*-like populations continued some thousands of years longer.

'Neanderthal Man' is used below in connection with the various remains of human activities during this transitional period, but it is not meant to imply the absence of *sapiens* traits.

Stone Industries

The Mousterian industry is usually associated with Neanderthal Man, yet it is an oversimplification to state that the Mousterian is the industry of Neanderthal Man. His remains have been found with other industries in Europe, Africa and the Near East, although these do share certain features in common.

The Mousterian is named after the type site at Le Moustier, Dordogne, France, where in the lower shelter were several levels, with the burial of a young man near the bottom, and an infant grave at a higher level.[1] The industry with the lower skeleton is regarded as typical Mousterian, in spite of some hand-axes occurring with it. Also untypical was the fact that the young man who had been buried, although estimated to be about 16 years old, and thus almost fully developed, did not have the well-developed brow ridges typical of Neanderthal Man! At other sites in France there are Mousterian industries of different types: some have numerous side scrapers, Levallois technique is used or not used, hand-axes are absent, rare or common, and the proportions of one tool form to another may vary. French archaeologists see these variations as particular traditions of the same basic industry. They recognise four main ones and regard them as partly contemporary with each other,[2] whereas some other archaeologists interpret the four types as a typological sequence.[3] Yet others see these variants of the Mousterian as nothing but differences due to their makers having been engaged on different activities (Figure 35).

The Mousterian is so well represented in France, together with remains of Neanderthal Man, that, important as they are, there is a tendency for other parts of the world to be overshadowed. It is unlikely that France was the main centre of advance at this time, although it may have been one of them during the latter part of the period. The same is true of the remainder of Europe. In Northern France[4] and Britain,[5] allied industries have been found in gravels and other sediments dating to the time of the Last Glaciation, or slightly earlier (Figure 37).

The hand-axe tradition persisted, with the Micoquian industry of France and rare finds of magnificently made plano-convex examples from sites such as Wolvercote in Oxford (Plate XIV). Mousterian of Acheulian tradition and also La Quina type has been recognised in Belgium, together with remains of Neanderthal Man. Surface finds in Germany, probably of this period, include some very thin leaf-shaped or foliate hand-axes, and these may be the origin of the leaf-shaped points ('Blattspitzen') of central and eastern Europe (Figure 38). The gradation from these fine, thin hand-axes to the bifacially flaked leaf points of the Eastern European Mousterian is so even that it is hard to know where to draw the line between them. The leaf points are assumed to have tipped heavy spears, so it is arguable that some of the thinner hand-axes may have done

Figure 35

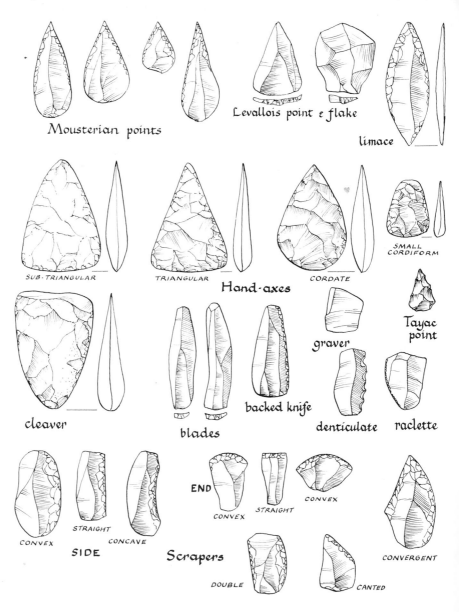

Mousterian points

Levallois point & flake

limace

SUB-TRIANGULAR

TRIANGULAR

Hand-axes

CORDATE

SMALL CORDIFORM

cleaver

blades

backed knife

graver

Tayac point

denticulate

raclette

SIDE

CONVEX

STRAIGHT

CONCAVE

END

CONVEX

STRAIGHT

CONVEX

Scrapers

DOUBLE

CANTED

CONVERGENT

Figure 35: Elements of the Mousterian Industries of France
Four main variants of the Mousterian are recognised in France, mainly on the basis of the presence, absence and differing proportions of certain tool types. Interpretations vary as to whether these variants represent human groups with different industrial traditions, living contemporaneously, or are part of a chronological succession with origins in the Acheulian evolving towards leptolithic industries of the Upper Palaeolithic. (See Bordes, 1961, 1968; Mellars, 1969, 1973)

1. *Typical Mousterian*

Levallois technique:	not common
Hand-axes:	rare
Scrapers:	numerous
Points:	well made
Backed knives:	rare
Denticulates:	uncommon
Blades:	absent

2. *Charentian or La Quina-Ferrassie Mousterian*

Levallois technique:	absent at La Quina, used at La Ferrassie
Hand-axes:	absent or rare
Scrapers:	very common
Points:	absent
Backed knives:	absent
Denticulates:	rare
Blades:	absent

3. *Denticulate Mousterian*

Levallois technique:	sometimes present
Hand-axes:	absent
Scrapers:	few
Points:	few or none
Backed knives:	absent
Denticulates:	very common
Blades:	absent

4. *Mousterian of Acheulian Tradition*

   Type A
Levallois technique:	absent
Hand-axes:	common
Scrapers:	common
Points:	common
Backed knives:	few
Denticulates:	common
Blades:	present

   Type B
Levallois technique:	absent
Hand-axes:	few
Scrapers:	few
Points:	few
Backed knives:	common
Denticulates:	common
Blades:	common

Also found in France, but restricted to the south, is a Mousterian containing cleavers of African-Spanish type, known as Vasconian, which is clearly derived from the Mousterian of the Pyrenees.

Figure 36: Mousterian Industries — France
1. Convex side scraper. Combe Grenal, Dordogne. Type: Quina (after Bordes, 1961). 2. Point.
3. Elongated point. Bouheben, Landes. Type: Typical (after Thibault, 1976). 4. Convex
side scraper. La Quina, Charente. Type: Quina (after Bordes, 1961). 5. Levallois point.
6. Point. Roc de Marsal, Dordogne. Type: Quina (after Guichard, 1976). 7.-8. Denticulates.
Arcy-sur-Cure, Yonne. Type: Denticulate (after Girard, 1976). 9. Sub-triangular or flat-
butted cordate hand-axe. Saint-Jacques-sur-Darnétal, Seine Maritime. Type: Acheulian
tradition (after Bordes, 1961). 10. Cordate hand-axe. La Plane, Dordogne. Type: Acheulian
tradition (after Guichard, 1976).

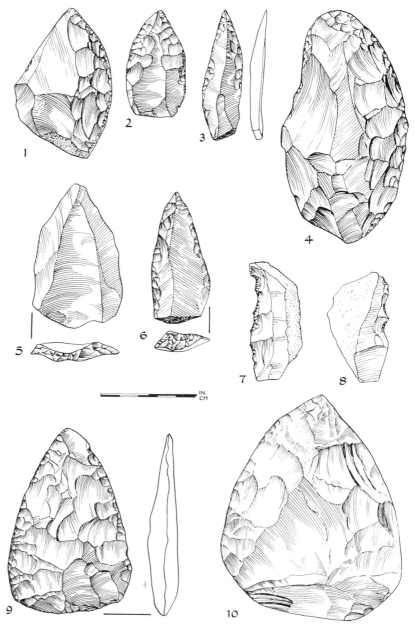

likewise. Levallois technique was used to varying degrees, and similar industries can be traced throughout Austria and Czechoslovakia to Poland,[6] across Hungary and the Balkans, into Greece, Western Russia and the Crimea[7] (see map, Figure 39).

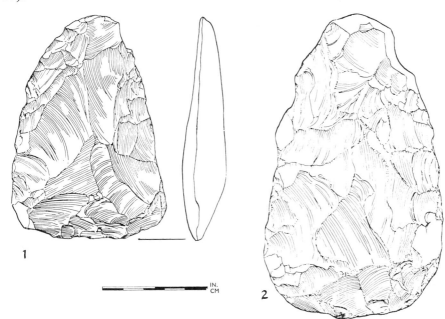

Figure 37: Mousterian of Acheulian Tradition Industry in Britain
A distinctive industry appears to have developed in Britain during the latter part of the Last Interglacial and into the Last Glaciation, characterised by small, thin sub-triangular hand-axes often, as in these examples, with flat butts. They are sometimes associated with Levallois flakes.
1. Brandon Down, Suffolk. 2. Sicklesmere, Suffolk.

The key sites in the Near East are Mount Carmel, Israel,[8] Jabrud in Syria,[9] Abu Sif Cave in Jordan[10] and the Abri Zumoffen at Adlun, in the Lebanon.[11] In this region the sequence is different from that of Europe.[12] Dating is not precise but, at about the time of the end of the Last Interglacial, there was a distinctive industry, Jabrudian, named after the great cave site in Syria. This industry contains a mixture of heavy scrapers of La Quina type made on thick flakes, hand-axes and Levallois flake-blades (Figure 40). At Jabrud it overlies an Acheulian industry and at Mount Carmel, in the cave of Et Tabun, it overlies Acheulian and a flake industry like the Tayacian. This sequence is not particularly different from that of western Europe, and the Jabrudian could be regarded as a regional variation of the Mousterian theme, but the sequence differs significantly in having a blade industry beneath or within the Jabrudian levels. At Jabrud itself it comes within the Jabrudian, as it does at Et Tabun, where it is above a Jabrudian with many scrapers and below one rich in hand-axes. At the Abri Zumoffen, this blade industry is on the floor of a 12 m beach, stratified beneath a Jabrudian industry. It is referred to as the Amudian industry after the Amud Cave at Lake Tiberias (see Figure 59). There is no

Figure 38: Mousterian Industries — Germany and Russia
The Mousterian of Germany and Eastern Europe is characterised by thin leaf-shaped points, known as 'Blattspitzen', some of which may have been used to tip spears.
1.-4. Mauern, Germany. 1.-3. Leaf points. 4. Side scraper (after Bohmers, 1951).
5.-7. Starosele, Crimea, Russia. 5.-6. Leaf points (after Müller-Karpe, 1966). 7. Leaf point with incipient tang (after Klein, 1969a).

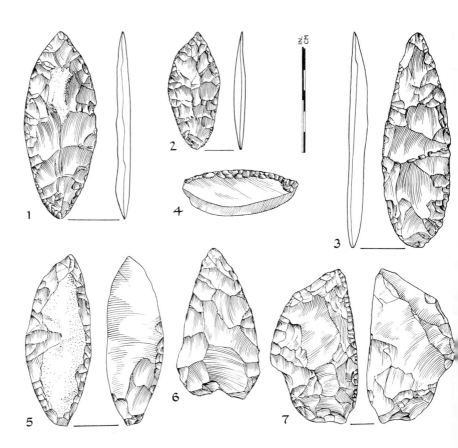

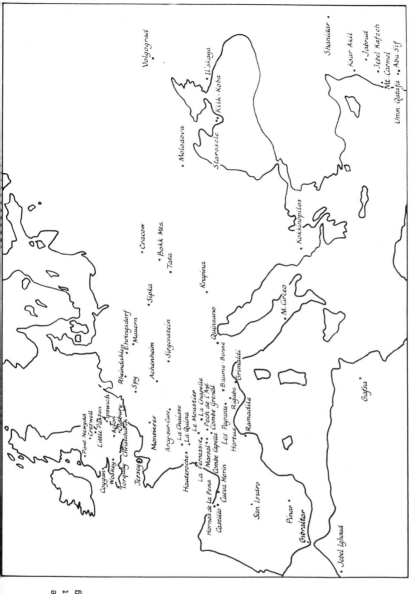

Figure 39: Map of Major Sites of Mousterian or Contemporary Industries in Europe, North Africa and the Near East

The majority of these sites date to the earlier half of the Last Glaciation or the preceding interglacial.

comparable blade industry in Europe at such an early date and the stratification at these sites in the Near East suggests that this industry is a separate cultural tradition from the Jabrudian. Such blade industries are, in the absence of other more satisfactory evidence, taken as the work of advanced hunting communities which are the proper subject of the next chapter, but here in the Near East they have been found beneath a typical 'transitional' industry. There can be little doubt of their early date. Above the Jabrudian at Et Tabun come several levels of Mousterian-like industries with much use of Levallois technique, generally referred to as Levalloiso-Mousterian, but they vary considerably from one level to another and they could be subdivided into variants as has been done in France. The lower levels at El Wad Cave, also at Mount Carmel, continue the succession from the upper part of Et Tabun, with further variations of the Mousterian theme. A special type of point, known as the Emiran point (see Figure 59), occurs in the lowest of these levels at El Wad,[13] blades are common in the next level and then a true blade industry comparable to the Aurignacian (see p. 186) of Europe. At the Abu Sif Cave there is also a Mousterian-like industry with plenty of blades. Typologically, it is difficult to refute the view that this true blade industry of the Near East actually evolved in the region, yet another true blade industry makes its appearance much earlier and disappears. Is it valid to regard this succession of stone industries in terms of human cultural evolution and population movement? It is best to look at the rest of the world first, and especially at Africa, before trying to answer such a question.

The distance from the southern Cape coast of Africa to the Mediterranean is about 4,800 miles, but this would not necessarily have prevented groups of hunters moving within a few generations from one end of the continent to the other. There is no geographical barrier of any consequence from the very south, through the Transvaal and Rhodesia into the great Rift Valley and so up to northern Kenya. The mountains of Ethiopia do create a barrier, even if it would not have been insurmountable, but it is the deserts of Sudan and Nubia that constitute the greatest obstruction to population movement. However, it is very likely that there were periods when changes in the climate were sufficient to transform these deserts into regions which were at least capable of supporting vegetation, and animal and human life. Such periods may have coincided with the times of maximum glaciation in the northern hemisphere, or have been the result of purely local factors. If the period coinciding with the first part of the Last Glaciation of the northern hemisphere, 80,000-70,000 years ago, was one of these, and communication between East and North East Africa was not difficult, the archaeology is easier to interpret.

The final Acheulian industry of South Africa is known as the Fauresmith, and Levallois technique was used frequently in this industry. It is the most likely origin of the stone industries which predominate in South Africa during the equivalent time of the Last Interglacial, from about 120,000-80,000 years. These industries are based on the production of flake-blades by Levallois technique and a variety of tools made from them, including scrapers, gravers and denticulates. Unifacial or bifacial leaf points are usually present. Within South Africa there are numerous local variants of industries of this type (Pietersburg in the Transvaal, Mossel Bay and Stillbay in the Cape, for example) which are otherwise grouped together as 'Middle Stone Age'. A key site for this period is Klasies River Mouth in the eastern Cape Province,[14] where a 22 m thickness of occupational deposits is associated with a complex of caves and rock shelters beside the Indian Ocean (Plate XIX). The lowest occupational layer rests on shingle of the 6-8 m raised beach of Last Interglacial age, and molluscan evidence indicates a progressive cooling of the climate up the long stratified sequence. The site was abandoned when the global fall in sea level of the Last Glaciation left it many miles inland because, as will be seen below, the occupants relied on marine resources for much of their food supply. Independent evidence suggests this was about 70,000 years ago, so the whole Klasies River Mouth sequence is considerably earlier than comparable industries in North Africa, the Near East and Europe. Once again, it looks as if Africa was the centre of human advance but, in due course, much of the world would catch up.

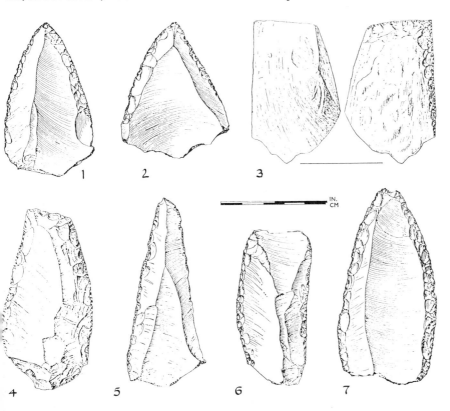

Figure 40: Jabrudian Industry
This industry, named after a cave site in Syria, appears to be a local variant of the Mousterian. It overlies levels with Acheulian and Tayacian industries, but is contemporary with a lepto-lithic blade industry, the Amudian.
1. Point. 2. Levallois point with secondary working. 3. Convergent straight scraper. 4. Double straight and convex scraper. 5. Backed knife. 6. Double convex and concave scraper. 7. Double convex scraper on Levallois flake-blade. (From Rust, 1950)

The Middle Stone Age industry at Klasies River Mouth can be divided strati-graphically into four stages (Figure 41). The most surprising thing in the whole sequence is that between stages 2 and 3 of the Middle Stone Age is about 2 m of

Figure 41: Middle Stone Age (MSA) Industry — South Africa
The artifacts figured are from Klasies River Mouth in the Eastern Cape, where a large, coastal cave complex was occupied with no major interruption for perhaps 40,000-50,000 years, during the equivalent of the Last Interglacial and well into the Last Glaciation. They are made of local quartzite, found in great abundance as beach cobbles. The industry, as are all MSA industries in southern Africa, is based on flake-blades made by Levallois technique.
1. Graver. 2.-3. Unifacial leaf points. 4. Rounded end scraper. 5. Denticulate. 6. Levallois point. 7.-8. Flake blades. 9. Pointed flake-blade with secondary working along edge near tip.

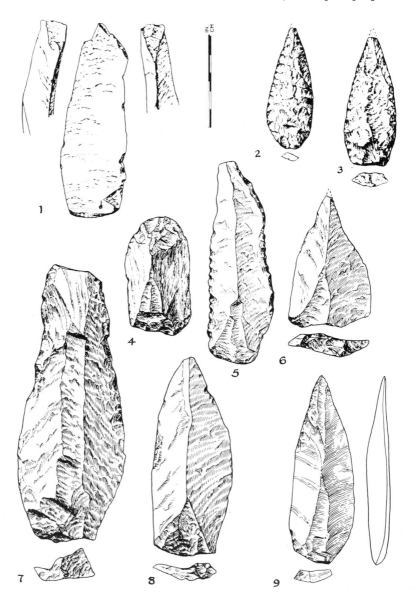

occupational levels containing a very different true blade industry, with an elaborate series of backed blades in the form of crescents, triangles and trapezes, often of microlithic size. Such an industry would seem to be the work of advanced hunting communities, and the suddenness with which they appear in this sequence shows clearly that it was intrusive and did not evolve in that place. It disappeared just as abruptly and the site was immediately reoccupied by people with a stage 3 Middle Stone Age industry.

This blade industry, wedged into the Klasies River Mouth Middle Stone Age sequence, is known from other sites in South Africa, and is referred to as Howieson's Poort after a site near Grahamstown. It also occurs at the Montagu Cave above the Acheulian levels, with radiocarbon dates which must be regarded as beyond the range of the technique. Middle Stone Age industries in the Border Cave, Natal, appear to go back even further than Klasies River Mouth, probably to the equivalent of the Riss Glaciation in Europe, c. 130,000 years ago.[15]

The Stillbay variant of the South African Middle Stone Age[16] contains elegant bifacial leaf points, generally made on fine-grained rocks such as silcrete or indurated shale. The more ubiquitous quartzite of the Table Mountain Sandstone series is brittle, and not very suitable for thin leaf points, so the Stillbay industry probably owes its character more to the availability of suitable rock than to anything else.

There is an uncanny similarity in the archaeological record between Klasies River Mouth and the Near East site of Mount Carmel. Both have a true blade industry wedged into the middle of a sequence of stone industries which, having clear origins in the Lower Palaeolithic, may be referred to as Mousterian-like or transitional. Similarly, in the basal levels of the great cave of Haua Fteah in Cyrenaica, North Africa,[17] is the same Amudian industry, beneath Levalloiso-Mousterian which, in turn, underlies another true blade industry, the Dabban (see Figure 60).

The vast intervening area between these two regions does not yield any information that might help to connect these broadly contemporary events at both ends of the African continent. Middle Stone Age variants, often referred to as Stillbay industries because of the fine leaf points generally found with them, occur throughout Rhodesia, Zambia, Kenya, Uganda and Somaliland. The Neanderthal-like skull from Broken Hill, Rhodesia, was associated with some Middle Stone Age artifacts. At Elmenteita and Little Gilgil, Kenya, there are magnificent leaf points made of the local shiny, black obsidian. The wide distribution of these Middle Stone Age industries in southern Africa, in almost every possible type of terrain, indicates considerable human activity during the time comparable to the Last Interglacial and Last Glaciation of Europe. The Howieson's Poort true blade industry, which is found at such an early date in South Africa, is in the same tradition as the Magosian industry of Uganda, also recognised in Tanzania and southwards to South Africa, where it is particularly well represented in the Cave of Hearths at Makapansgat, above Middle Stone Age layers. Its equivalent in Kenya is to be found in Gamble's Cave, Elmenteita.

The Magosian is also evident in the Porc Epic Cave, Dire Dawa, Ethiopia, stratified above a Middle Stone Age 'Stillbay' industry, so, apart from the Sudan, it can be said that Middle Stone Age and true blade 'Howieson's Poort' or 'Magosian'-type industrial traditions are found on the eastern side of Africa, from north to south. These are described more fully in the next chapter.

In western and more central parts of Africa, including much of the moist rain forest, human occupation at this period was not so intensive. In Angola and Zaire is found an industry, termed Sangoan,[18] which represents a different cultural tradition, with a greater emphasis on hand-axes of pick-like form rather than flake-blades, although the latter do occur, together with occasional leaf points. The same industry is found in the Zambezi Valley, in parts of South Africa and Botswana and, typologically, must have evolved from the final Acheulian industries of Fauresmith type. There seems to be a relationship between the main distribution of this industry and habitat, for it is found mainly in river valleys, low-lying country and tropical rain forest. The Sahara appears to have been an effective barrier to movement, for the Sangoan is not found in North Africa.

North Africa is of great interest as a possible corridor of movement from Egypt to Morocco and so to Spain. African-type Middle Stone Age is found in Egypt, in the 22-24 m raised beach of the Fayum[19] and could well be the source from which developed the so-called Levalloiso-Mousterian of Haua Fteah. There are leaf points and Levallois flakes in the Mughåret el 'Aliya Cave near Tangier,[20] but Mousterian industries, as found in France, Spain and Italy, are either absent or poorly developed along the North African coast. A typical Mousterian has been found at one cave in Morocco, at Djebel Irhoud,[21] but this seems more likely to be the result of influences from Spain.

Mention has been made of the Eastern Mousterian of the Crimea. Further east into Asia there is the site of Teshik Tash, a cave in the mountains of Uzbekistan, only 60 miles from the border of Afghanistan. An elaborate child burial, described below, was accompanied by such a Mousterian-type industry, with a blade element. This Eastern Mousterian is found as far east as Lake Balkash, approaching the Chinese border. Beyond this there appears little or no contact with hunting groups of India, China and the Far East. In these regions, the transition to advanced hunting communities was less rapid, and both specialised and unspecialised hunting groups continued with little change, unaware of the developments elsewhere in the world that were destined to undermine all the ingrained customs of savages.

Habitat

Almost every type of habitat was exploited, from as high as 1370 OD up in the Alps[22] to the lowlands of river valleys. Living sites were inland or coastal and within climatic zones varying from subtropical to periglacial. Humid, tropical zones and thick forest were mainly avoided. The ability to live in such a range of habitats was little more than a continuation of the adaptability of specialised hunting groups, but there was now a much greater use of natural shelters. Where a food supply seemed secure, hunters sought out rock shelters and caves for their habitation. In the colder regions there was an obvious advantage in the protection from frost, wind and rain, but the main reason which applied everywhere was the adoption of a less nomadic form of existence. There can be no other explanation for the accumulations of discarded bones and artifacts, spreads of ash and charcoal, disturbed soil and other litter beneath many rock shelters or in cave mouths; accumulations that sometimes became metres thick before they were sealed by sterile layers indicating an interval of non-occupation, probably quite thin and followed by yet more accumulations of occupational deposits (Plate XIX). Such archaeological layers do not result from casual, intermittent bivouacing, but from semi-permanent or permanent dwelling on the one site.

There may have been seasonal movements from site to site, temporary abandonments for many different reasons, but generation after generation of hunters and their families were using some sites in favoured areas. The 'home base' in many instances had become a genuine 'home', with some of the occupants probably in residence at all times. Hunters of game still had to make their forays, which may have lasted days, and other groups had to make excursions for gathering vegetable foods and fruits, suitable raw material for stone tools and other requirements. Settlement of this form, if it were to work successfully, needed a much more complex division of labour, and it suggests a larger population to which the term 'band' can reasonably be applied, with its implications of organisation. Some form of leadership would have been essential.

It is not often that archaeology can produce any tangible evidence for such things, but an insight into hunting organisation is strongly inferred from a study of animal bones from two South African Middle Stone Age sites. At Klasies River Mouth, a large settlement site, there are many limb bones of the two most favoured game animals, eland and buffalo, and few vertebrae, whereas Duinefontein,[23] which is an open-air site, contained relatively few limb bones of the same animals and many vertebrae. Presumably the latter site was a hunting camp, the animals had been butchered on the spot and the best cuts, including the legs, had been carried away to some settlement site.

Open-air sites of this period are not so common as those in caves and rock shelters, possibly because the former are mainly temporary camps, which have relatively small numbers of artifacts and bones left on them, and they are not so likely to be preserved beneath any natural or artificial deposit, or be discovered by archaeologists. A few are known in France: as at Fontmaure[24] with a Mousterian of Acheulian tradition. There are occasional surface finds of industries probably belonging to this period, especially in Germany, and there are many well-stratified industries of Levalloisian flakes and hand-axes in the loess of northern France, a few in the Thames Valley 'brickearths', and also derived artifacts in low-lying terrace gravels as at Montières in the Somme Valley.[25]

It is also in this period that there is the first definite evidence of the exploitation of marine resources. This is shown by two important cave sites at opposite ends of the African continent: Haua Fteah and the Klasies River Mouth site. At the latter, in the lowest occupational layer on the 6-8 m raised beach, Middle Stone Age stage 1, sea shells are intermingled with the animal bones. This is so throughout the very long sequence at this site. The occupants collected winkles, mussels, turbo shells, clams and limpets. A large land gastropod, *Achatina zebra*, was also included. Bones of penguin and dolphin show that these animals were also caught, and also many bones of the black-backed gull occur throughout. Fish bones are rare, and restricted to the jaws, cleithrum and vertebrae of fairly large fish which may have been scavenged off the beach. Similar evidence comes from the rather later occupational levels of Haua Fteah.

Dwellings

Emphasis has been put on the several sites of this period which indicate a much more settled existence than had previously been enjoyed by hunting groups in the Palaeolithic period. Caves and rock shelters were used over long periods of time yet, in spite of this, there is no evidence to show that any of them in Africa and the Near East had ever been modified. Extensive and careful excavation at various sites has failed to disclose any post holes, stone pavements or alignments or other structures. This is not the case in Europe, where a few constructions have been found, ranging from simple settings of stones to the remains of actual walls. This could be explained by the greater inducement provided by an inhospitable climate to improve on natural shelters, or the greater sophistication of the hunting groups in the later part of this transition to barbarism.

The only structures in Africa which can be related to a Middle Stone Age industry are a group of small curved or semicircular stone settings at Orangia,[26] an open site in South Africa. Dolerite cobbles and boulders had been roughly set on the ground, mainly facing east. Eight distinct sets were placed close together, probably to form the foundations for wind-breaks of woven branches. Stone artifacts were concentrated much more in the northern group, but it must be doubted whether this justifies the interpretation of that as having been the activity area, while the possibility that the southern area was consequently reserved for sleeping must also be doubted. The site is regarded as a temporary camp by the excavator, although the total absence of bone and charcoal is puzzling, especially as soil conditions seem suitable for their preservation. Perhaps these are the remains of hides rather than dwellings.

At Cueva Morin in northern Spain[27] there are the remains of a collapsed dry stone wall in one of the Mousterian levels that may have formed a partial barrier across a narrow constriction just inside the cave mouth, but no hearth was associated with it. A dry stone wall was also found in the cave of Pech de l'Azé, Dordogne.[28] More elaborate was a semicircular 'wall' of intertwined reindeer antlers in the cave of Roc en Paille, Maine-et-Loire,[29] 3 m across at the base and about 0.70 m high. Within the cave of La Baume des Peyrards,[30] a line of stones had been placed to delimit the area against one wall, 11.5 m x 7 m. A series of hearths was inside this structure and Mousterian artifacts were found around them, and not outside. Some paving slabs at La Ferrassie, also in France, appear to be associated with a burial and are described below (p. 169).

There are two sites which can be interpreted as the remains of constructed dwellings: Cracow in Poland,[31] and Molodova in the USSR. Three circles of mammoth bones were found at Cracow, covered by loess, and this is of especial interest as it will be seen in the next chapter that similar huts were made from mammoth bones and tusks by later people. Mammoth bones and tusks had also been used to make the dwelling at Molodova[32] (Figure 42). They formed a circle of about 7 m diameter, with a tumble of additional bones on the east side possibly connected with an entrance. There was no central post hole, but a logical reconstruction would be one or more internal posts supporting a roof of skins held down by the heavy bones. There need have been no more reason to insert any central posts in holes than with a modern tent. The position of the fire had been changed on several occasions, as had probably the bones and skins when the latter flapped about too much. The northern side was kept free of

Figure 42: Plan and Reconstruction of a Mousterian Dwelling at Molodova, Russia
This site, Molodova I, is on the River Dniester, about 240 km north west of Odessa. In the fourth archaeological level, associated with a Mousterian industry, was a rough oval ring 10 m in diameter of mammoth bones and tusks, enclosing 15 hearth areas (shaded on the plan). The bones probably weighed down mammoth skin hides laid over a framework of branches. The position of the fire had obviously been changed on several occasions, as had the bones and skins when the latter flapped about too much. The entrance was on the east side (top of the plan). Animal remains included woolly mammoth, woolly rhinoceros, giant ox or bison, moose, reindeer, brown bear, wolf and hare.

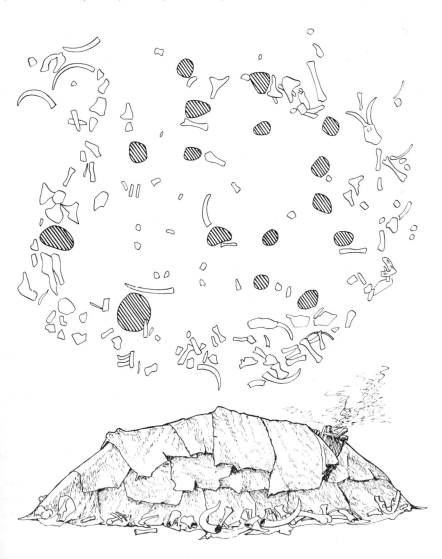

hearths, so this was likely to have been the sleeping area.

Also reminiscent of some of the dwellings of later hunters is a shallow, oval pit that had been dug into Last Interglacial loess at Rheindahlen, Germany.[33] It measures 3.70 m x 2.90 m, and is about 0.50 m deep. On each side were two holes for posts which may have supported skins to make a roof. Numerous flints were outside the structure and, although no hearths were found, burnt flints proved the use of fire. This primitive shelter is dated to the beginning of the Last Glaciation. The industry is of Mousterian type with a concentration on flake-blade production from prepared cores, but not by Levallois technique.

One of the several Mousterian sites in the Caucasus Mountains, Il'Skaya,[34] contained a stone setting 5 m in diameter with a hearth but, otherwise, little more is known of the open-air dwellings of this period. Central Europe, under periglacial conditions, cannot have been a hospitable region, yet Mousterian hunters seem to have braved the elements on their forays. When hunting, they could not have carried with them anything suitable for erecting shelters, and certainly not heavy skins. Mobility was the foremost consideration and if the chase was long, and one or more nights had to be spent on the tundra, they just had to make the best of it. Such a bivouacing site may be represented by the site at Salzgitter-Lebenstedt in Germany,[35] where a rich Eastern Mousterian industry with leaf points was associated with a natural gully, 12 m x 8 m. Pollen analysis at this site shows that the climate was sub-arctic, with a few pine trees in a bleak, grassy tundra. Bones of reindeer, mammoth, bison and horse may indicate butchering on the site in preparation for carrying the meat back home, plus some eating at the camp. Their equipment included pointed hand-axes, some points made on mammoth ribs, a small barbed bone point and a club of reindeer antler.

There is some evidence for seasonal occupation of the cave at Hortus, France,[36] about 30 km west of Nîmes. This site is approached along a narrow ledge with a drop of 260 m to the bottom of the valley. Behind the low entrance is a narrow, steep-sided passage and a similar-shaped side-gallery. Up to 7 m of occupational deposits indicate a long series of visits to the cave by Neanderthal hunters, divided into four main phases. Goats were one of the sources of food and, as these animals have a restricted breeding season, the proportions of adults to juveniles will vary throughout the year. Thus, as only adult goats were found in Phase 2, the hunters were only living in the cave at the end of winter. This suggests, of course, that there was a selective element in the hunt, and that young goats were not killed. However, in Phase 4, there is good evidence that the cave was not used in the summer, for there are a number of bat bones, including juveniles, in the deposits. Bats would not have been living in the cave during their breeding season if humans were present.

Varying numbers of stone artifacts and bones within the several levels at Hortus have been interpreted as showing that only brief visits to the cave were made in the first two phases. Afterwards it was used more frequently. In the final phase there were temporary camps near the entrance. The bones of carnivores such as lion, panther and lynx emphasise the dangers of using caves for temporary occupation, and fires, found deep in the interior, may have been lit for protection as much as illumination.

By now, fire was commonly used, and the hearth, with its social implications, may have become the symbol of the home. Sometimes properly constructed hearths are found, such as the circle of stones around the fireplace at Arcy-sur-Cure, France.[37] At Ramandils,[38] also in France, the fire was within a series of very large stones, up to a metre long. One of the most elaborate hearths was found at La Grotte de Hauteroche, Charente,[39] where two layers of limestone slabs surrounded a shallow pit, only 30 cm in diameter. The only indication of fire making is a charred piece of birch wood from the Krapina Cave in Yugoslavia,[40] thought to be a fire 'twirl'. Such hearths may indicate a more permanent settlement, with particular areas restricted to certain activities.

In spite of an obvious ability to dig (e.g. the Hauteroche scooped-out hearth and, more impressive, the Rheindahlen dwelling hollow), simple pits are very rare in association with dwelling sites of this period. At Klasies River Mouth, in the near total excavation of the largest cave in the complex, not a single pit had been dug. Some of the layers were somewhat jumbled, as if they had been disturbed to a depth of a few centimetres, perhaps to scrape loose soil over something offensive, but at no time had anyone thought it necessary to dig a hole. About the only site where a pit has been recorded, other than those associated with something like a burial or ritual activity, is Combe Grenal, France.[41] No purpose for the Combe Grenal pit could be detected.

Drinking water would not have been any problem at most of the cave and rock shelter sites, for these usually owe their origin to river erosion, and rivers generally flow close to them. Whether the hunters had among their equipment anything which could be used to carry or store water can only be guessed, but skins and bladders are obvious means of making such containers. Fragments of ostrich egg shell at Klasies River Mouth may be the remains of complete, perforated shells used to hold water, as commonly used over much of Africa by Later Stone Age people and modern bushmen.

We can also only guess at the hygienic habits of people at this cultural stage, but there is no reason to think that they allowed their dwelling places to become fetid dens. Constant defecation inside a cave, or the tolerance of heaps of rotting organic food waste, are likely to have left some trace in the soil. Such organic material, in association with clay and damp, tends to form a distinctive blue mineral called vivianite, and this has never been recorded at any of the sites.

Hunting and Food Supply

One of the most significant aspects of this transitional period is the appearance of stone projectile points, absent in the stone industries of the specialised hunting groups of Chapter 4. Levallois pointed flake-blades, the thinner Mousterian points, unifacial and bifacial leaf points are all expressions of the same need to increase the weight and penetration of wooden spears. Some of these points exhibit thinning of the butt and slight notches on the edges, suggesting they were hafted in split ends and tied on. An almost universal change in hunting tactics may be inferred, although it is difficult to think what it was. In spite of the lack of identifiable projectile points in the earlier hunting groups, elephants, hippos, rhinos and other big game animals had been killed. Perhaps other methods than spearing had been used, for it is not easy to believe that wooden spears would be very effective against a charging straight-tusked elephant. The use of stone-tipped spears, acutely pointed and razor sharp, deployed in unison by a well-controlled hunting group, must have increased the hunters' chances of success. A Levallois point was actually found in contact with the skeleton of a mammoth at Hounslow in the Thames Valley. Moreover, a wooden spear was found embedded in the ribs of a straight-tusked elephant at Lehringen in Saxony,[42] on a Levalloiso-Mousterian site.

The stone structures at Orangia may have been hides, and it is probable that all manner of ingenious traps and techniques were used. Hunters adapted to the fauna of the region they were exploiting and, as stated, there is good reason to think that, at some of the important sites in South Africa and the Near East, some conscious conservation may have been practised. Otherwise, it would seem certain that the whole ecology of a region would have been disturbed and occupation at one place for a long period of time made impossible. Such restraint is the logical step in the direction of the advanced hunting communities that were to evolve.

The faunal lists from some selected sites (Table 5.1) indicate the species of large and small mammals that have been identified, excluding micro-mammals such as rodents, which are unlikely to owe their presence to hunting activities. Not all of them, especially carnivores, would have been part of the food supply.

Table 5.1: Examples of Faunal Remains Associated with Mousterian and Allied Industries

---

La Grotte de l'Hortus, Hérault, France[a]

Goat (*Capra ibex*)	Rhinoceros	Lynx
Red deer (*Cervus elaphus*)	Horse	Panther
Bos or bison	Cave bear	Rabbit
Cave lion	Wolf	

Molodova, USSR[b] (level associated with dwellings)

Woolly mammoth	*Bos* or bison	Brown bear
Woolly rhinoceros	Moose	Wolf
Horse	Reindeer	Hare

Weimar-Ehringsdorf, Germany[c]

Straight-tusked elephant	Pig	Badger
Giant ox (*Bos*)	Elk	Otter
Bison	Hare	Pine marten
Merck's rhinoceros	Hyaena	Cave lion
Horse	Brown bear	Cat
Giant deer	Cave bear	Lynx
Red deer	Wolf	Beaver
Fallow deer	Fox	

Sirgenstein, Germany[d]

Woolly mammoth	Horse	Bison
Woolly rhinoceros	Reindeer	Cave bear

La Cotte de St Brelade, Jersey[e]

Woolly rhinoceros	Rabbit	Wolf
Red deer	Straight-tusked elephant	Birds including: geese,
Reindeer	Steppe mammoth	moorhens, dipper,
Horse	Giant deer	grouse, ptarmigan,
Ox	*Bos*	kestrel
Fox	Hyaena	

Table 5.1: contd

Le Moustier, Dordogne, France[f]		
Woolly rhinoceros	*Bos* or bison	Reindeer
Horse	Red deer	Goat

Mount Carmel, Israel[g] (layers Ec and Ed of excavators)

Jabrudian of Et Tabun:

Hippopotamus	Gazelle	Steppe rhinoceros
Pig	Ox	Elephant
Persian fallow deer	Horse	Crocodile
Goat	Wild ass	

Levalloiso-Mousterian of Et Tabun: (layers C and D of excavators)

Hedgehog	Goat	Wild ass
Hyaena	Warthog	Ox
Jackal	Leopard	Gazelle
Fox	Small bear	Hyrax
Polecat	Porcupine	Crocodile
Pig	Hippopotamus	Persian fallow deer
Roe deer	Hartebeest	Steppe rhinoceros
Red deer	Horse	

Klasies River Mouth, Cape Province, South Africa[h]

Middle Stone Age Stage 2:

African elephant	Vaalribbok	Clawless otter
Black rhinoceros	Southern reedbuck	Genet
Hippopotamus	Mountain reedbuck	Egyptian mongoose
Giant buffalo	Blue antelope	Brown hyaena
Cape buffalo	Bastard hartebeest	Wildcat
Warthog	Porcupine	Caracal
Bushpig	Mole rat	Leopard
Quagga	Rock hyrax	Cape hare
Grysbok	Chacma baboon	Cape fur seal
Oribi	Honey badger	Elephant seal
Wildebeest	Springbok	Bushbuck
Kudu	Eland	Dolphin
Whale		

Sources: a. Lumley, 1972; b. Coles and Higgs, 1969, pp. 327, 337, 351-5; c. Soergel, 1926; d. Osborn, 1924, pp. 201-2; e. Marett, 1916; f. Osborn, 1924; g. Garrod and Bate, 1937; h. Wymer and Singer, in press.

Many more examples could be given in Table 5.1, but these suffice to demonstrate the great range of animals involved. This has to be considered against a background of different climates, geographical regions and preferences of the hunters.

In Europe, during the first part of the Last Glaciation, woolly mammoth, woolly rhinoceros, horse and deer were the favourite game animals, together with giant ox, bison and reindeer, although the latter tended to be more sensitive to changing climates and thus was not always available. In southern Africa, buffalo and the many species of antelope constituted the favourite meat food.

The rarity of certain animals, such as bushpigs and warthogs as Klasies River Mouth, may reflect the danger of hunting these beasts. At the same site, the hippopotamus is represented mainly by the large incisor teeth, so this animal may not have been hunted at all but the teeth scavenged as prized objects from chance finds of carcasses or skeletons.

Large birds were caught, for their bones have been identified at several French Mousterian sites. Excluding falcons and owls, which would be expected within caves, and are likely to occur in any level, some bird remains are restricted to levels of human occupation. The clearest example is at Hortus, where numbers of partridges and pigeons were found. Plenty of black-backed gulls appear to have been eaten at Klasies River Mouth, but virtually no other birds. These large gulls congregate on beaches and can be approached quite close, so a well-aimed missile would secure one.

Freshwater fish remains have been found at a few sites of this period, such as in the cave of La Naulette in Belgium.[43] In La Grotte du Salpêtre de Pompignan, only 8 km distant from Hortus, several fish bones were found in Mousterian levels:[44] eel, trout, carp, tench and laveret. Only a few fish vertebrae and some jaws of musselcracker were found in the Middle Stone Age levels of Klasies River Mouth, and the inference is that the hunters were not fishermen, but picked up anything they might find on the beach. The presence of fair numbers of seals and dolphins at the latter site begs the question of how they were caught. The odd whale may have been stranded, but it seems unlikely that the seals and dolphins can be accounted for in this way. Dolphins come close to shore and it is feasible that a strong swimmer armed with a spear could get one. Seals generally live on islands, but colonies may have existed on nearby beaches. There is no need to imply any form of marine craft.

Mention has already been made of the evidence for the exploitation of marine resources at Haua Fteah and Klasies River Mouth. Many other coastal sites must exist where the collecting of shellfish was an important part of the food economy, but very favourable circumstances are required for the preservation of this evidence.

Vegetable foods in the form of edible roots, fruits and nuts can be assumed to have been an important part of the diet, as with all hunting groups of all periods, provided they are available. As yet there is no concrete archaeological evidence for this activity, let alone any knowledge of what was collected. This also applies to other periods of the Palaeolithic, apart from a few rare instances such as the seeds from Kalambo Falls, hazelnuts at Taubach and hackberries at Orgnac. Pollen analysis is unlikely to help, unless flowers were collected, but microanalysis of occupational soils may eventually produce some information.

Human Burials and Other Cults

Modern society takes the disposal of the dead so much for granted that the lack of any such provision seems unthinkable, yet the earliest known human burials in the world are those in Europe, Asia and Africa in the earlier part of the Last Glaciation. Prior to this, for two million years or more, dead people suffered the same fate as dead animals. It is often asked why more remains of fossil man are not found, or what happened in a human group when someone died. The former question is easy to answer: human remains are not likely to be preserved unless there has been an intentional burial or collection of remains. Both occurred during this transitional period from savagery to barbarism and there is a corresponding increase in the number of fossil discoveries. As to what happened in the absence of any purposeful disposal of the body by other members of the hunting group, speculation must suffice. Carnivores, bacterial and chemical action soon reduce an animal corpse on the surface to a few bones, and these will disappear in time, dependent on the soil conditions. Some carnivores, of course, eat bones.

It is impossible to gauge what effect death had on the early hunting groups. An unquestioning acceptance does not imply callous indifference; death was part of the complex, never-ending cycle from generation to generation. Such an event might precipitate the move to another home base or camp or, in more settled groups, the carriage of the body to some obscure place not too far away where nature could perform its task unseen.

The advent of intentional burial marks a significant change in attitude and it cannot be coincidental that it occurs when the archaeological evidence shows a considerable advance in the economy of the hunting groups. Conscious attempts to understand, and therefore control, the environment raised a thousand questions. At this early stage, little could have been comprehended. Death was a major puzzle and we can do no more than guess what prompted the idea of burial, or why occasional objects were placed with the corpse. Nor do we know, as there are so few examples known of this practice, why some people were selected for burial and others were not. Of the 47 individuals listed in the table below, 16 are children, and there are more males than females.

Table 5.2: Neanderthal and Related Burials

Site	Type of grave	Industry	Local chronology and estimated date
La Chapelle-aux-Saints, Corrèze, France[a] Adult male	rectangular grave 1.45m long, 0.30m deep; with grave goods	Mousterian (Quina-Ferrassie)	Würm II c.50,000
Le Moustier, Dordogne, France[b] Adolescent male	unknown; with grave goods	Mousterian (Typical)	Würm I or II c.80,000-60,000
Infant	pit 50cm wide, 40cm deep	Mousterian (?Typical)	Würm I or II c.80,000-50,000
La Ferrassie, Dordogne, France[c] (Figure 43) 8 associated burials: 1 adult male, 1 adult female, 4 small children, 1 new-born infant and 1 foetus	shallow pits and low mounds; some grave goods	Mousterian (Quina-Ferrassie)	Würm II c.50,000
Combe Grenal, Dordogne, France[d] Infant	in shallow mound pit with stones placed over the body	Mousterian (Quina-Ferrassie)	Würm II ? 50,000

Table 5.2: contd

Site	Type of grave	Industry	Local chronology and estimated date
Regourdou, Dordogne, France[d]			
Adult	beneath cairn on pavement of stones	Mousterian	Würm I c.80,000
Roc de Marsal, Dordogne, France[e]			
Child of 3 years	shallow grave	Mousterian (Typical)	Würm I-II c.70,000
La Quina, Charente, France[f]			
Adult female	unknown	Mousterian (Quina-Ferrassie)	Würm II c.60,000
Orneau Cave, Spy, Belgium[g]			
2 adult males	shallow graves	Mousterian (Quina-Ferrassie)	Würm II c.60,000
Neanderthal, Germany[h]			
Adult male	unknown	unknown	probably Würm II c.60,000
Et Tabun, Mt Carmel, Israel[j]			
Adult female	on surface of broken and burnt animal bones	Levalloiso-Mousterian	Würm I-II c.75,000
Es Skhul, Mt Carmel, Israel[k]			
5 adult males, 2 adult females, 3 children	shallow graves	Levalloiso-Mousterian	Würm I-II c.65,000
Shanidar, Iraq[l]			
7 adults	killed and buried by rock fall	Eastern Mousterian	Würm II c.70,000
Jebel Kafzeh, Israel[m]			
1 adult	contracted, on right side	Levalloiso-Mousterian	Last Interglacial or Würm
2 adults	contracted burial	with a leptolithic element	
2 infants usually regarded as *Homo sapiens sapiens* but with some Neanderthal affinities	flexed burial all within occupational layers		
Amud Cave, Israel[n]			
1 adult male *Homo sapiens neanderthalensis* but with *sapiens* affinities	contracted burial within occupational layers	Levalloiso-Mousterian or Amudian	?Würm II-III or earlier

Table 5.2: contd

Site	Type of grave	Industry	Local chronology and estimated date
Starosele, Crimea, USSR[p]			
1-2-year-old child	within occupational debris; with grave goods	Eastern Mousterian	Last Glaciation ? 50,000
Teshik-Tash, Uzbekistan, USSR[q]			
8-9-year-old boy	encircled by goat horns	Eastern Mousterian	Last Glaciation ? 60,000
Kiik-Koba, Crimea, USSR[r]			
Adult and child	shallow graves	?Eastern Mousterian	Last Glaciation ? 60,000
Broken Hill, Zambia[s]			
Adult male and other remains	unknown ?accidental	Middle Stone Age	Late Pleistocene c.80,000
Border Cave, Natal, South Africa[t]			
Infant	shallow grave with *Conus* shell	Middle Stone Age	Late Pleistocene c.80,000

Sources: a. Bouyssonie and Bardon, 1909; b. Hauser, 1909; c. Bergounioux, 1958; d. Vandermeersch, 1976a; e. Heim, 1976; f. Vandermeersch, 1976b; g. Twiesselman, 1958; h. Day, 1977. pp. 51-4; j. Day, 1977, pp. 82-8; k. Day, 1977, pp. 89-95; l. Solecki, 1953, 1963, 1972; m. Day, 1977, pp. 96-102; n. Day, 1977, pp. 103-8; p. Mongait, 1961, p. 85; q. Okladnikov, 1953; r. Mongait, 1961, p. 85; s. Singer, 1958; t. Beaumont and Boshier, 1972, Beaumont, 1973.

The young man buried at Le Moustier was said to have had worked flints alongside him, and the remains of a charred ox skull. Another small oval grave at the same site contained the remains of a new-born child accompanied by flint tools. The grave was covered by three blocks of stone. An even more unusual burial in France was found at Regourdou. The skeleton of an adult was found inside the cave, laid on a flat bed of stones and covered by a veritable cairn of other stones, surmounted by sand and ash. Mixed with the covering stones were many cores, flakes and scrapers, and animal bones, mainly of bear and deer. Nearby, the body of a brown bear had been placed in a dug grave, but the significance of this will be considered below in connection with other aspects of a possible 'bear cult'.

No grave goods are reported from the two adult burials in the cave at Spy, Belgium, and the skeleton from Neanderthal itself was dug out long before its importance was realised, so little is known of the discovery. As most of the skeleton appears to have been found it is included with the list of burials, but whether it came from a grave or not is unknown.

The burials from Mount Carmel have been the subject of much controversy ever since they were found, especially the relative ages of Et Tabun and Es Skhul. At one time it was thought that the burials from both these sites, only a few metres from each other, were contemporary and, as the Tabun burial was of a woman with very marked Neanderthal characteristics, and the Skhul people had a mixture of Neanderthal and *sapiens* characteristics, there had been an interbreeding population of the two sub-species. The problem is altered by the present interpretation of a long time interval between the two groups of at least 10,000 years, and possibly 25,000 years. The ten burials in the cave of Es Skhul were also considered to be a kind of cemetery, but it is now thought that they are not all contemporary and could be separated by an unknown amount of time. There is no particular direction in which the graves have been aligned. The bodies are all more or less flexed and the only certain instance of anything being placed with them is a bear's head within the arms of Burial V. The ox skull near Burial IX is probably a later intrusion, and the flint scraper near Burial IV accidental. One of the men at Es Skhul had died from a severe wound; a wooden spear appears to have been thrust completely through the head of his femur. Was this a hunting accident or deliberate murder?

The skeletons from the great cave at Shanidar, Iraq, may have been accidentally entombed by a rock fall. Particularly important as an insight into the social life of these people was the presence of a cripple, a man whose right arm and shoulder were deformed; at some time, the arm had been amputated below the elbow. He had clearly suffered from an arthritic condition from birth and yet he did not die until he was about 40 years old. His survival can only be explained by the supposition that other members of the hunting group supported him.

The most interesting of the few burials of this period from the USSR is that of a young boy about nine years old from a small cave in the mountainous region of Uzbekistan, known as Teshik-Tash, which means 'the rock with a hole in it'. The child had been placed in a shallow grave and his head surrounded by five or six pairs of goats' horns (the Siberian ibex, *Capra sibirica*) stuck upside down into the earth to form a kind of crown. The skeleton was poorly preserved, partly due to the activities of hyaenas. This cave is at about 1,500 m above sea level, in a dangerous rocky terrain, still frequented by numerous goats. These hunters may have based their economy on this animal and developed a cult relationship with it; hence the placing of the horns around the dead boy. Fatal mishaps must often have happened in such a district. Remains of other animals were also found in the cave: horse, deer, leopard, brown bear and birds. The Mousterian industry contains a blade element.

There does not seem to be anything comparable to this rite of human burial in Africa during the same period. Nothing of this nature was found at Klasies River Mouth in spite of large-scale excavations of several caves and rock shelters although, as stated, this site mainly covers a period rather earlier than the Neanderthal burials of Europe and Asia. Broken Hill, Zambia, is included in the table as it is possible that at least one complete skeleton was present, and perhaps more, but mining operations precluded any controlled examination. Several individuals may have been buried in this cave as, apart from the skull of 'Rhodesian Man', there were cranial fragments of one or two others and isolated post-cranial bones of three individuals.

If burials are exceedingly rare discoveries of this period, isolated fragments of human skeletons are not. A multitude of sites in Europe, Asia and Africa have yielded odd bones, from complete skulls or mandibles to broken pieces of various parts of the body. As these remains are generally in useful archaeological contexts they provide a valuable source of information for the student of human evolution. This brief survey is more concerned with the reasons for their presence in levels of otherwise purely occupational debris. Skulls and upper and lower jawbones predominate over other parts of the skeleton and this cannot be mere chance.

Some examples from well-known sites are listed in Table 5.3.

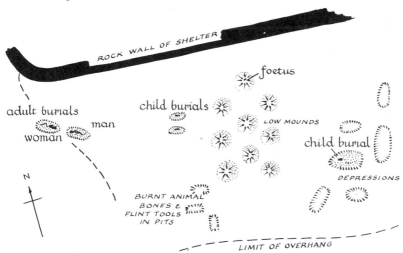

Figure 43: Plan of Mousterian Human Burials at La Ferrassie, Dordogne, France
The majority of the known Mousterian burial sites are in France and the most elaborate is the one found at La Ferrassie, a rock shelter close to Les Eyzies. Six burials were found at the same level and are seen as one complex, even as the equivalent of a family vault. The man was in a shallow, sub-rectangular grave and the skeleton was completely preserved but for the hands and right foot. Three flattish stones had been placed around the head, and pieces of animal bones laid on his body, some with scratches on them. Many worked flints are recorded as being with the burial, and a quartz hammerstone. The woman was in a similar grave. Both bodies were in a flexed position, the woman so tightly that the body may have been bound before burial, in fact before *rigor mortis* had set in. One of the children in the pair of graves was three to five years old and had been partly covered by a limestone slab with a cup-shaped depression carved on its lower face, surrounded by smaller cup-marks in groups of two or four. Such artificial carving is unique for this period. The head of this child was missing, but whether this was intentional dismemberment prior to burial or the result of later carnivore activity is not known. Nearby, a foetus of seven to eight months had been placed under a small mound of soil, accompanied by two finely made scrapers and a Mousterian point. The separate child burial was surrounded by five other depressions. Seven more small mounds, some stone 'paving' and three rectangular pits containing animal bones and worked flints completed this 'cemetery'.
(After Bouyssonie in Bergounioux, 1958)

Table 5.3: Sites with Isolated Human Bones

SKULLS
Europe
France: Hortus (fragments of 3)
                                 Pech de l'Azé (2-year-old child)
Belgium: Engis (child)
Spain: Cova Negra
                                 Gibraltar (5-year-old child)
Italy: Monte Circeo (adult)
Greece: Petralona (adult)
                                 Saccopastore (2 skulls)
Israel: Mugharet-el-Zuttiyeh
Yugoslavia: Krapina (c. 20 individuals)

Africa
Morocco: Jebel Ighoud
Tanzania: Eyasi
South Africa: Florisbad (*sapiens*)
                                 Klasies River Mouth (fragments)
Sudan: Singa

Asia
Java: Ngandong (11 skulls including one child)

MANDIBLES
Europe
France: Malarnaud
                                 Combe Grenal (6-8-year-old child)
                                 Hortus (17 individuals)
Belgium: La Naulette
Czechoslovakia: Ochoz
                                 Sipka (child)
Spain: Banolas
Italy: Monte Circeo

Africa
Morocco: Temara
Cyrenaica: Haua Fteah (2: 1 female and 1 youth)
Ethiopia: Porc Epic, Dire Dawa
South Africa: Klasies River Mouth (4 individuals)

TEETH ONLY
Europe
Channel Islands: La Cotte de St Brelade
Germany: Taubach

(Full bibliographic references can be found in the British Museum *Catalogues of Fossil Hominids* (Oakley and Campbell, 1967, and Oakley *et al.* (eds), 1971) or in M.H. Day, *Guide to Fossil Man* (1977).)

Post-cranial bones are less common. At Bisitun, Iran,[45] there are some long bones and nothing else. There were two limb bones with the Ngandong skulls. In Europe, at the sites of Hortus and Krapina which have produced the largest number of human bones of this period, various parts of the body are represented. At Hortus, scattered through several archaeological layers, were, apart from the numerous mandibles, maxillae and skulls listed above, the following:

femur	2
humerus	3
radius	1
clavicle	1
atlas	1
iliac	1
phalanges (hand)	13
phalanges (foot)	3

This impressive total of bones from Hortus has been analysed to show that a minimum number of 20 individuals is represented, and a maximum of 36. Forty per cent of the people were between 15 and 30 years old, and 20 per cent were over 50 years old. Certain parts of the skeleton preserve better than others, but differential preservation cannot account for the lack of 480 vertebrae and 1,000 hand bones, to take the minimum figure for the number of individuals! The only possible conclusion is that human selection has been responsible. Either most, if not all, of the bones had been brought into the cave from some source of human bones, or whole bodies had been brought in and, when reduced to skeletons, all the bones excluding those found were removed from the cave. The former seems more likely, in which case some cult involving human bones is inferred. If cannibalism was being practised at Hortus there was no question of it being a matter of survival, for the human bones are found mixed indiscriminately with animal bones, indicating a plentiful food supply. There is nothing to prove cannibalism, or disprove it, though it is perhaps supported by the fact that the long bones were broken in the same manner as the other kitchen refuse.

However, there can be little doubt that the large numbers of human bones found at the rock shelter of Krapina are the result of cannibalistic feasts. More than 500 fragments of human bones were found from every part of the skeleton, belonging to at least ten individuals, both children and adults. In one archaeological layer there were the remains of a large fire in which were found almost nothing but human skulls, broken and burnt. Deposits of ash, charcoal and other burnt human bones show that such feasts took place on many occasions. Long bones were found, as at Hortus, split for their entire length, presumably for the extraction of marrow.

Further evidence of this practice comes from a cave at Monte Circeo, Italy,[46] where a human skull and the mandible of another individual had been placed within the centre of a small circle of stones. The skull was upside down and the foramen magnum had been cut away and enlarged artificially, in the same manner as was done by the Melanesian head hunters in historical times, for the extraction of the brain. The stone industry at this site was a kind of Mousterian termed Pontian, made on small pebbles.

Similar mutilation of the base of human skulls is found on two of those from

Ngandong in Java. One of the two leg bones, which were with the skulls, was broken at both ends; the other was nearly complete.

Scratch marks on some of these human remains, especially at Krapina, may result from the use of sharp flints in cutting away flesh. The case for cannibalism by Neanderthal Man seems proven, but whether it was common practice is another matter. The selection of particular bones such as skulls and jawbones at so many sites, in Europe, Africa and Asia, does point to some almost universal cult at this time, not necessarily involving cannibalism.

A few other discoveries can be interpreted as attempts by these hunting groups to control objects and events by means we should describe as magical. In the mountainous regions of Europe, where caves could be found, the greatest enemy was the cave bear (*Ursus spelaeus*) and, to a lesser extent, the brown bear. Whole colonies of these beasts inhabited the larger cave complexes. At Rouffignac in France, the deepest part of the cave, nearly a kilometre from the entrance, abounds with the hollowed-out nests of cave bears. Their claw marks can still be seen on the soft walls, 3-4 metres from the ground. Many dramas, often tragic, must have preceded the occupation of caves already inhabited by bears and it is not surprising that the animal was frequently foremost in the minds of the hunters.

Several sites have features which suggest some form of bear cult.[47] The most spectacular is Regourdou in France, found beside the cairn burial described above. A trench had been dug, 1.5 m long, 0.60 m deep, in which was buried the body of a brown bear, covered over by a very large stone weighing 850 kg. It would appear to be contemporary and connected with the cairn burial, but constructed first. Bear bones had also been intentionally placed in heaps elsewhere in the cave. At Drachenloch, Switzerland, a stone cist had been built to house a stack of bear skulls and there were piles of sorted long bones placed along the walls of the cave. In another heap, a leg bone had been forced through a skull which was resting on two other long bones of two different bears. Ten bear skulls had been laid on a natural platform at the Petershohle Cave in Bavaria and at Wildenmannlisloch, also in Germany, 310 canine teeth of bears had been amassed. At Les Furtins in France six bear skulls had been placed on limestone slabs, two others put nearby, and a bundle of long bones set on a slab against the cave wall. A rather different arrangement was found in a cave at Veternica, Yugoslavia, where some bear bones had been placed in a crevice before blocking it with stones. Regular alignments of bear bones were found in another French cave at Isturitz in the Pyrenees. Finally, many of the caves in the USSR, inhabited by hunters with Eastern Mousterian stone industries, have very large numbers of bear bones. What Neanderthal Man hoped to achieve by all this is obviously unknown, but it is clear that he had beliefs in powers he did not understand. Belief in magic may explain the occasional discovery of human occupation of this period in inaccessible or uncomfortable places. At Arcy-sur-Cure, for example, hunters had apparently squatted deep inside the cave in a small area which was the only dry place, in complete darkness and without a fire. Conversely, certain places may have been forbidden by a taboo of some sort. Such might explain a small cave among the complex at Klasies River Mouth in South Africa, which was unoccupied. Admittedly, it was very damp and contained numerous calcitic formations, but the almost total absence of stone tools or bones within it is puzzling. It was easily accessible and immediately beside the wide cave mouth which had the greatest amount of evidence for occupation. As the normal litter accumulated, the opening to this small cave become blocked and it was to remain so until excavated. When eventually reopened, the only sign of human activity was a pathway smashed through some stalagmites towards the rear, and a few bones and stones that had been thrown in.

Other Activities

Some of the specialised tool forms of this transitional period, such as gravers, point to the fashioning of materials like bone, antler and wood, yet very little has survived to confirm it. The only site where wooden implements have been recorded is Florisbad in the Orange Free State,[48] where a human skull was found in a spring deposit, beneath peat, associated with a Middle Stone Age stone industry. These wooden pieces are described as throwing sticks. The Florisbad skull is of great interest as, although it has Neanderthal features, it differs from the Broken Hill skull considerably; it has a wider brain case and a flatter, broader forehead with less prominent brow ridges. In these respects it is thus more *sapiens*-like.

Wood is so rarely preserved that the lack of such objects elsewhere is not unexpected, but the paucity of evidence for working bone is difficult to explain. Remains of animal bones have been found at nearly all of the rock shelter and cave dwellings sites, and many have been broken and split. Some bear the marks of sharp cutting tools, but this is very different from the actual use of bone as a medium for making tools and weapons. Nevertheless, about three or four sites have produced a few bone artifacts which show that it was sometimes used. Most puzzling is the tip of a well-fashioned point from Combe Grenal, and a barbed point from the German open-air site of Salzgitter-Lebenstedt.[49] Both are so much more sophisticated than anything else that is known of this age and, in Europe at least, such bone weapons do not feature as normal equipment until about 30,000 years BC. They are so unusual that it would be easier to believe that they are intrusive from more recent archaeological levels. The same Lebenstedt site also produced 10 mammoth ribs which had been pointed, and a club of reindeer antler. From Tata, Hungary,[50] a piece of mammoth ivory had been shaped into a roughly oval plaque and coloured red. Presumably it had some symbolic value. No worked bone has been found save one rib fragment in the Klasies River Mouth Cave, South Africa, that has a few serrations cut into one edge. Bone and antler may have been used occasionally, but there is no real bone industry until the development of later advanced hunting communities.

There is no direct evidence that clothes were made and worn by people at this stage, although it seems reasonable to assume that they were, at least by those members of hunting groups living in Europe during the colder phases of the Last Glacial period. The occupation of such an area would have been impossible without protective clothing, and the large numbers of small scrapers found in all stone industries of this period may reflect the preparation of animal skins and furs for this purpose. The occurrence of animals such as beaver, fox, cat and rabbit, as well as the larger carnivores, in the faunal lists from dwelling sites may have been the result of purposeful selection for the attractive pelts. In Asia and Africa, the necessity for clothing was not as great, but garments may still have been worn at times, for decoration as much as anything else. In the Die Kelders Cave, South Africa,[51] detailed analysis of the bones found in the Middle Stone Age layers revealed the existence of large numbers of mole rats with relatively few foot bones preserved. The inference is that the feet were removed with the skins. These may have been made into attractive capes, headgear, leggings or other garments; thus it may not be fanciful to picture some of these hunting people looking quite ornate and colourful at times.

Most groups throughout the world seemed to be concerned with decoration, for natural pigments, usually red ochre, are found in many of the occupational layers. Whether this was used to paint objects or themselves is unknown; the latter is more likely. Red ochre occurs as lumps of iron oxide or forms of haematite in various geological formations. It is quite common in the Table Mountain Sandstone series of South Africa and lumps were found throughout all the Middle Stone Age levels at Klasies River Mouth. Some of the lumps had facets on them from where they had been rubbed against whatever was to be coloured. One large, rare piece of fine, soft ochre had been bevelled and used like a crayon. When the ochre is crushed and mixed with animal fats, a real paint can be made. In Europe, limestone blocks at the French sites of Pech de l'Azé and Le Moustier have been identified as grinding stones. Black pigments were also made from manganese oxide. There is no evidence whatsoever that hunters at this stage were artists, in the sense of painting pictures, but the use of ochre seems to have assumed a surprising importance and led to actual open cast mining of ochre at Lion Cave, Ngwenya, Swaziland.[52] Middle Stone Age levels overlay mined bedrock from which it is calculated that at least 1,200 tons of pigment had been removed. The ochre is, technically, a specularite-rich haematite, ideally suited for use as red pigment, but mining on this scale during the Middle Stone Age is astonishing. However, it is not unique, for there is a European equivalent in Switzerland. Here, at a site known as Löwenburg farm in Bern Canton,[53] another open cast mine existed; people with a Mousterian industry had dug into the slope of a hill in order to extract good-quality flint. The bed-rock is Upper Kimmeridgian limestone, which contains nodules and slabs of a flint-like siliceous stone. Quartzite pebbles had been used to smash up the limestone and antlers as picks to prize out the unweathered flint. The earliest known ochre mine in Europe is at the Lovas Caves,[54] near Lake Balaton, Hungary, where haematite and limonite had been dug out of the dolomitic limestone. Bone picks and shovels were used by the miners, but the stone industry found associated with the mining belongs more to the beginning of the advanced hunting communities than to the transitional period.

Many other natural objects, such as birds' feathers, may have been used for decoration. One form of personal adornment that is absent throughout is the perforated bead or pendant. There is nothing to suggest that necklaces, head bands or anything similar were made or worn. Sometimes there is a suggestion that attractive pebbles had been purposely collected. Lines are scratched on pebbles from Isturitz in France and Tata in Hungary,[55] and other scratched lines on bones may have been more than just doodling with a sharp flake. A shaped, limestone 'amulet' from the last site does have a distinct cross engraved across one face. Apart from the cup-shaped depressions cut into the stone slabs over the La Ferrassie grave, already mentioned, sculpture and pictorial representations did not yet exist, but the base was being laid for them.

Notes

1. Osborn, 1924.
2. Bordes and de Sonneville-Bordes, 1970; Bordes, 1973.
3. Mellars, 1969.
4. Tuffreau, 1971.
5. Mellars, 1974.
6. Koslowski, 1972.
7. Kernd'l, 1963; Klein, 1969a.
8. Garrod and Bate, 1937.
9. Rust, 1950; Waechter, 1952.
10. Bordes, 1968, p. 128.
11. Garrod and Kirkbride, 1961.
12. Howell, 1959.
13. Garrod, 1955a.
14. Wymer and Singer, in press.
15. Beaumont and Vogel, 1972.
16. Cooke, 1966.
17. McBurney, 1967.
18. G.H. Cole, 1967.
19. McBurney, 1960, pp. 79, 146.
20. Ibid., p. 184.
21. Bordes, 1968, p. 121.
22. Osborn, 1924, p. 200.
23. Inskeep, 1976; Klein, 1976a.
24. Gruet, 1976.
25. Bourdier, 1969.
26. Sampson, 1968.
27. Freeman and Echegaray, 1970.
28. Bordes, 1954, 1955.
29. Lumley, 1976d, p. 653.
30. Ibid., pp. 645-654.
31. Koslowski and Kubiak, 1972.
32. Coles and Higgs, 1969, pp. 327, 337, 351-5.
33. Bosinski and Brunnacker, 1966.
34. Coles and Higgs, 1969, p. 329.
35. Ibid., p. 306.
36. Lumley, 1972.
37. Girard, 1976, 1978.
38. Lumley and Boone, 1976, pp. 651-2.
39. Ibid., p. 653.
40. Oakley, 1956.
41. Bordes, 1968, Figures 49-50.
42. Movius, 1950.
43. Dupont, 1866.
44. Lumley, 1972, p. 612.
45. Coon, 1951.
46. Blanc, 1958.
47. Bergounioux, 1958, pp. 164-5.
48. Sampson, 1974.
49. Coles and Higgs, 1969, p. 306.
50. Bordes, 1968, p. 110.
51. Klein, 1975.
52. Dart and Beaumont, 1969.

53. Schmid, 1969.
54. Meszáros and Vértes, 1955.
55. Vértes, 1964.

References

For general works see the references for Chapters 3 and 4. Specific publications on Mousterian industries or Neanderthal Man are almost entirely confined to reports and papers in the proceedings or journals of numerous learned societies, several of which appear in the notes to this chapter. One exception is a recent publication by M.L. Shackley, *Neanderthal Man* (1980). A valuable collection of papers by specialists appears in G.H.R. von Koenigswald (ed.), *Neanderthal Centenary 1856-1956* (1958).

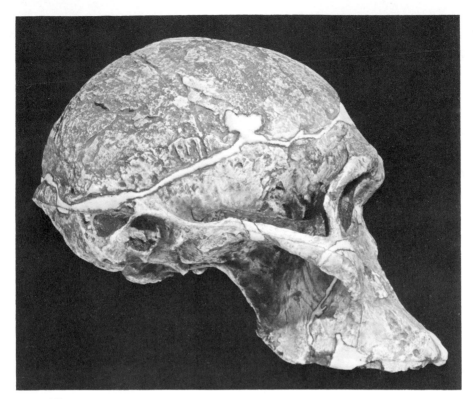

⊢——⊣ cm

Plate I. Skull of *Australopithecus africanus*, Sterkfontein, South Africa (Photograph: reproduced by courtesy of the Trustees of the British Museum (Natural History))

Plate II. Skull of *Australopithecus robustus*, Swartkrans, South Africa (Photograph: reproduced by courtesy of the Trustees of the British Museum (Natural History))

Plate III. Mandible of *Homo habilis*
(H7), Olduvai Gorge, Tanzania
(Photograph: reproduced by
courtesy of the Trustees of the
British Museum (Natural History))

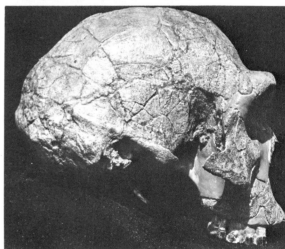

⊢⊣cm

Plate IV. Skull, right lateral view, of *Homo s.
indet*. (cf. *erectus*) (KNM-ER 3733) Koobi
Fora, Lake Turkana, Kenya. Found below
Koobi Fora Tuff (Photograph: National
Museums of Kenya)

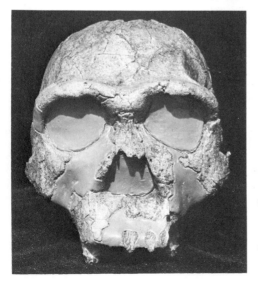

⊢⊣cm

Plate V. Skull, frontal view, of *Homo sp.
indet*. (cf. *erectus*) (KNM-ER 3733) Koobi
Fora, Lake Turkana, Kenya (Photograph:
National Museums of Kenya)

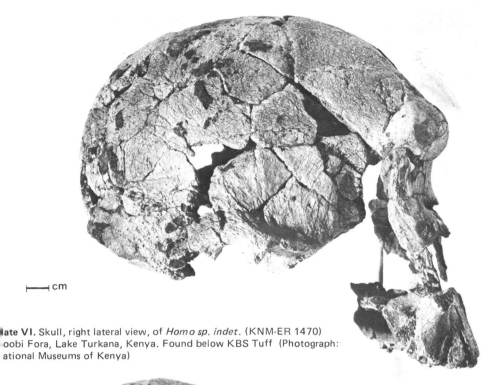

├───┤ cm

Plate VI. Skull, right lateral view, of *Homo sp. indet*. (KNM-ER 1470)
Koobi Fora, Lake Turkana, Kenya. Found below KBS Tuff (Photograph:
National Museums of Kenya)

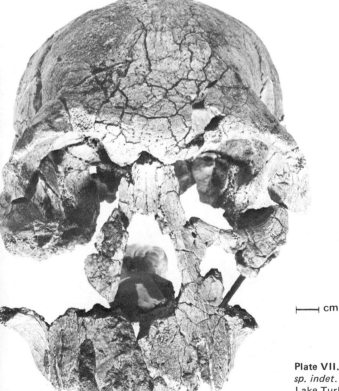

├───┤ cm

Plate VII. Skull, frontal view, of *Homo
sp. indet*. (KNM-ER 1470) Koobi Fora,
Lake Turkana, Kenya (Photograph:
National Museums of Kenya)

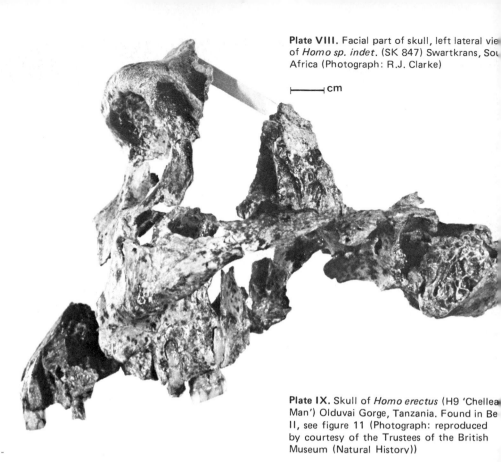

Plate VIII. Facial part of skull, left lateral view of *Homo sp. indet.* (SK 847) Swartkrans, South Africa (Photograph: R.J. Clarke)

⊢———⊣ cm

Plate IX. Skull of *Homo erectus* (H9 'Chellean Man') Olduvai Gorge, Tanzania. Found in Bed II, see figure 11 (Photograph: reproduced by courtesy of the Trustees of the British Museum (Natural History))

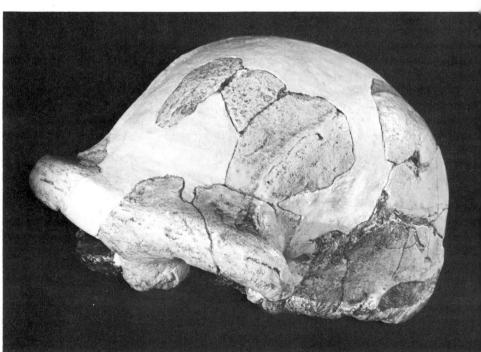

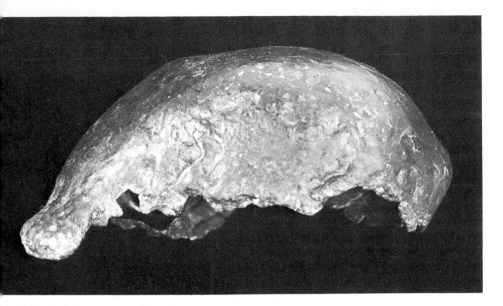

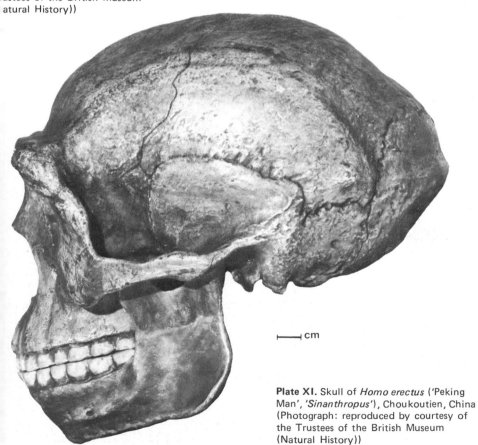

├────┤ cm

Plate XII. Wooden spear of Clactonian Industry, Clacton-on-Sea, England (Photograph: reproduced by courtesy of the Trustees of the British Museum (Natural History))

Plate XIII. Giant hand-axe. Acheulian Industry, Furze Platt, Maidenhead, England (Photograph: reproduced by courtesy of the Trustees of the British Museum (Natural History))

⊢———⊣ c

⊢—⊣ cm

Plate XIV. Large, finely made plano-convex hand-axe. Acheulian Industry, Wolvercote, Oxford, England (Photograph: Pitt River Museum, Oxford)

Plate XV. Wooden implements of Acheulian Industry from Kalambo Falls, Rhodesia (a) club (b) trimmed stakes (Photograph: J.D. Clark)

a

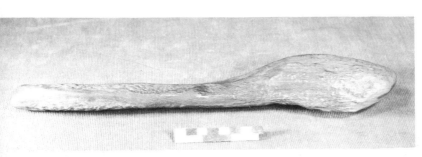

b

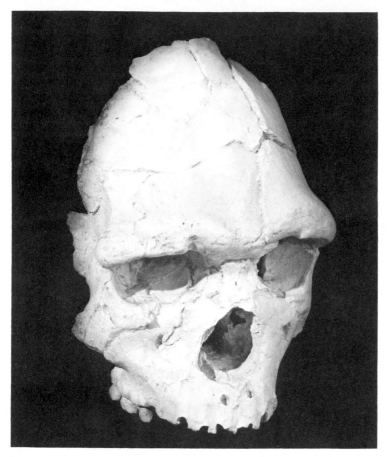

Plate XVI. Skull of *Homo sapiens pre-Neanderthal* from Arago Cava, Tautavel, France (Photograph: reproduced by courtesy of the Trustees of the British Museum (Natural History))

Plate XVII. Two views of *Homo sapiens pre-Neanderthal* from Swanscombe, England (Photograph: reproduced by courtesy of the Trustees of the British Museum (Natural History))

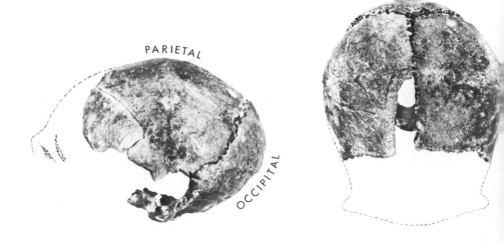

PARIETAL

OCCIPITAL

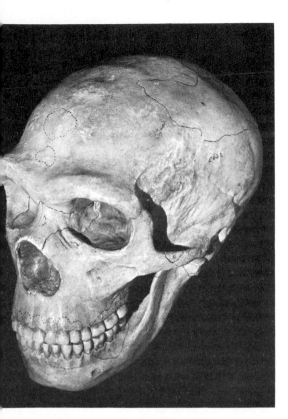

Plate XIX. Section through occupational deposits within a coastal cave on the Tzitzikama Coast, Klasies River Mouth, South Africa. The light band half way down the sequence is wind-blown sand that accumulated when the sea retreated during the equivalent of the Last Glaciation. The deposits below are of African Middle Stone Age and rest on a marine gravel 6-8m above present sea-level. The deposits above the sand are of Later Stone Age, *c*.1000-3000 BC

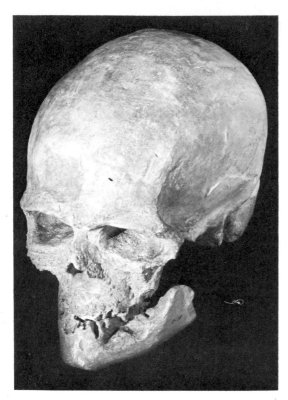

Plate XX. Skull of *Homo sapiens sapiens*, Cro Magnon, France (Photograph: reproduced by courtesy of the Trustees of the British Museum (Natural History))

Plate XXI. Large superbly made leaf point of Solutrian Industry, Volgu, France (Photograph: reproduced by courtesy of the Trustees of the British Museum)

⊢——⊣ cm

Advanced Hunting Communities of the Upper Palaeolithic: Distribution and Industries

If the Mousterian industries of Europe and the Near East are to be equated with Neanderthal Man, it can be said that the Upper Palaeolithic is likewise equated with Modern Man. As with most generalisations, neither statement is entirely true, but certainly they are broadly correct. There may be a few discoveries of Modern Man with Mousterian-like industries (e.g. Jebel Kafzeh) and, conversely, Neanderthal Man with Upper Palaeolithic industries (e.g. Wadi Amud), but generally the equations hold firm. Similarly, it is fair to state that there was a gradual typological evolution from the Mousterian and allied stone industries of Africa and Asia, to the blade-based leptolithic industries of the Upper Palaeolithic. However, this was not a simple, uniform, continuous development in one part of the world which spread outwards to form one harmonious culture, any more than human culture has progressed in such a manner during the last few thousand years of its history. Rates of change have differed widely from one region to another. There has been a complex interplay of invention, imitation, migration, possible extinction, success and failure. Nor has the rise of advanced hunting communities been restricted to any one type of geographical region or particular climate; from the southern tip of Africa to the periglacial lands of Europe and Asia, the hunting bands of the Late Pleistocene period formed themselves into highly organised communities. Some were more advanced than others, some advanced hardly at all, but, as a species, it is clear that advancement was only progessing in one direction. There is an impression that human groups were passing a threshold beyond which there would be an inevitable trend to civilisation. However, this was not to be evident until after 8500 BC, when glacial ice would retreat in the northern hemisphere for the last time.

The term 'Upper Palaeolithic' is used here in the cultural sense. Leptolithic is sometimes used as an alternative, for it means 'light stone' and this accurately describes one of the fundamental aspects of the stone-working technology of the period. The production of thin blades of flint or other fine stone from carefully prepared cores was, apart from anything else, a more economical use of the raw material. It meant that a far greater length of useful cutting edge could be obtained from a given quantity of stone, and the delicate blades could be fashioned into the numerous specialised forms that were required. Bone and antler were now frequently used for making weapons, tools and other objects, often with great skill.

Painting and sculpture flourished in a few regions, prompted by magic, decoration or sheer artistic expression. Personal ornaments such as necklaces and beaded head-dresses appear. On a more material plane, elaborate dwellings were constructed with the aid of skins, poles, large bones and stones. Improved hunting techniques and consciously practised conservation brought in sufficient food to ensure a security which, if not total, allowed expansion. The wealth of archaeological sites of this period in certain favoured regions, such as France, reflects an increasing population. This implies larger communities and all the organisation and leadership required to maintain them and, equally important, the movement of people. Even in the areas with the most favourable natural resources, communities could not expand beyond certain limits. If they became too large, groups would have to leave and form other communities elsewhere. Successful hunters need many hundreds of square miles for themselves, but the world would still have seemed of infinite size. The necessity to impinge on the territories of other hunting communities probably did not exist, although particularly favoured spots may have been coveted and consequently have been the cause of inter-community squabbles. If they did fight, there is no convincing archaeological evidence for it. Expansion was natural and inevitable. It is not surprising that this is the time when hunters first reached the continents of America and Australia.

At this stage of human development, archaeologists, in their attempts to discover the manner in which hunting groups and communities progressed, become more and more involved in the actual processes of cultural evolution. In some regions, such as France and much of central Europe, there are a great number of sites, each with numerous levels of occupation superimposed on each other. The relative dating of one level to another is a simple matter of stratigraphy which can rarely be disputed, and the typology of particular stone industries warrants comparisons between one site and another. Correlations made on this basis may be corroborated by similarities of fauna (by analysis of associated bones, shells, micro-fauna, etc.), climate (deduced from the faunal remains, vegetational evidence from pollen analysis, or soil properties and geological processes) or by absolute dates obtained by the radiocarbon method. It is extremely fortunate that the latter part of this period comes within the dating range of radiocarbon although, as has been stated in an earlier chapter, dates of over 20,000 years should not be accepted uncritically, and dates of over 30,000 years may often indicate little more than minimum dates. However, where a succession of radiocarbon-dated samples comes from one site and increases in order with the stratigraphy, that succession may be accepted with greater confidence. The precise relationship between radiocarbon years and solar or calendar years is still not known beyond about 5000 BC, but there is every reason to think that radiocarbon years are generally a little less than solar years. Thus, when radiocarbon dates are quoted, with their identifying suffix bc or bp, the real date is probably a thousand years or so older. Assuming that radiocarbon years are consistent, this is of little consequence, and still makes radiocarbon dating the most powerful chronometric tool available, at least back to 30,000 years ago or a little more.

The wealth of information that has been obtained in some regions allows very detailed comparisons to be made from one site to another. Detailed analyses of stone industries in one local succession may show a gradual typological evolution, suggesting internal developments. Alternatively, the sudden appearance of a stone industry with little or no connection with the typology of those industries stratified beneath it suggests an external replacement. Sometimes, an industry in one region may be so similar to that in another many hundreds of miles away that a movement of population is suggested. Others may argue that any suc

imilarities result not from population movement but from independent evolu-
ion along the same lines, in other words convergence. It is usually very difficult,
f not impossible, to conclude whether some ideas, such as the use of microlithic-
acked blades as barbs for spears in combination with prepared poison, were the
esult of independent evolution or of imitation: in archaeological terms, con-
ergence or diffusion. Sometimes one would apply, sometimes the other, depen-
lent on chance, opportunity and necessity. Such developments occurred against
a background of migration, isolation, natural disasters, disease and all the other
agaries inseparable from complex human communities. Archaeology will never
be able to sort all this out, but it can give remarkably clear illustrations of
arious episodes at different times and in different places. When placed in a time
cale, and considered regionally, the general pattern of the prehistory of this
inal stage of the Palaeolithic period becomes discernible.

In climatic terms the period under consideration is equivalent to the latter
art of the Last Glaciation of the northern hemisphere, the Devensian Stage of
3ritain, the beginning of which is estimated at about 70,000-80,000 years.
Geological deposits of the Last Glaciation are widespread and result from
numerous oscillations of climate: a series of interstadials within the glacial stage.
Eight interstadial periods have been recognised in the Netherlands Weichselian
Stage and placed in a dated sequence on the basis of radiocarbon, extrapolation
and stratigraphy.[1] This would seem to be the most reliable and complete framework available, and is used here. Correlations with other parts of Europe, particularly France and Britain, are not straightforward, but the probable ones are
shown in Figure 44.

Almost every country in the world that was inhabited during the Late
Pleistocene has its own series of names to describe the sequence of the stone
ndustries that have been found. This is inevitable as a safeguard to prevent the
confusion that previously existed when the terminology of the French Upper
Palaeolithic industries was applied to industries elsewhere, but it does introduce
a host of terms which are difficult to remember or relate to each other. The
ypology of these industries has become, particularly in France where they are
o well represented, a complex subject. It would be impossible in this survey to
eview all the evidence and arguments that have absorbed archaeologists for over
a century, but some details of the various Upper Palaeolithic stone and bone
ndustries that have been recognised in different regions of the world are given
below in the next section. They constitute the solid core of our understanding
of this formative period, on which can be put all the additional information that
assists interpretations of economies, environments, modes of life and, to a very
imited extent, thoughts and beliefs.

First, however, it is necessary to consider the beginnings of Upper Palaeolithic
culture. This cannot have involved any sudden change, except where migration
was involved, and it has already been seen in the last chapter how the activities
of hunting groups in the earlier part of the Late Pleistocene were evolving
owards it. No hard line can be drawn between the culture of the 'transitional'
groups, so well represented by the Mousterian of Europe and the Middle Stone
Age of Africa, and the Upper Palaeolithic. All the elements are there and, where
n one region the stone industries appear to evolve into true leptolithic indus-
ries, it would seem that it is a straightforward case of local development in
esponse to increased hunting efficiency, larger numbers of people and a gradual

Figure 44: Time Scale for the Last Glacial Stage in Europe

The most complete sequence of geological deposits for this stage is found in the Netherlands. Eight interstadials have been recognised, although the most recent two are sites actually in Denmark, as shown in the left-hand column. The climatic curve in the same column is based on pollen analyses of organic deposits and radiocarbon dating, and on reasoned extrapolation. The curve indicates estimated mean July temperature, increasing from $0°C$ on the left edge of the column to $20°C$ on the right.

British interstadials have been recognised by pollen analyses and beetle faunas (Coope, 1975). There are two radiocarbon dates for the Upton Warren Interstadial: $41,900 \pm 800$ bp (GRO-1245) and $41,500 \pm 1200$ bp (GRO-595). Correlations with the Netherlands sequence is uncertain, but Chelford has been correlated with the Brørup Interstadial.

(Netherlands succession after van der Hammen *et al.*, 1967, and Waterbolk, 1972.)

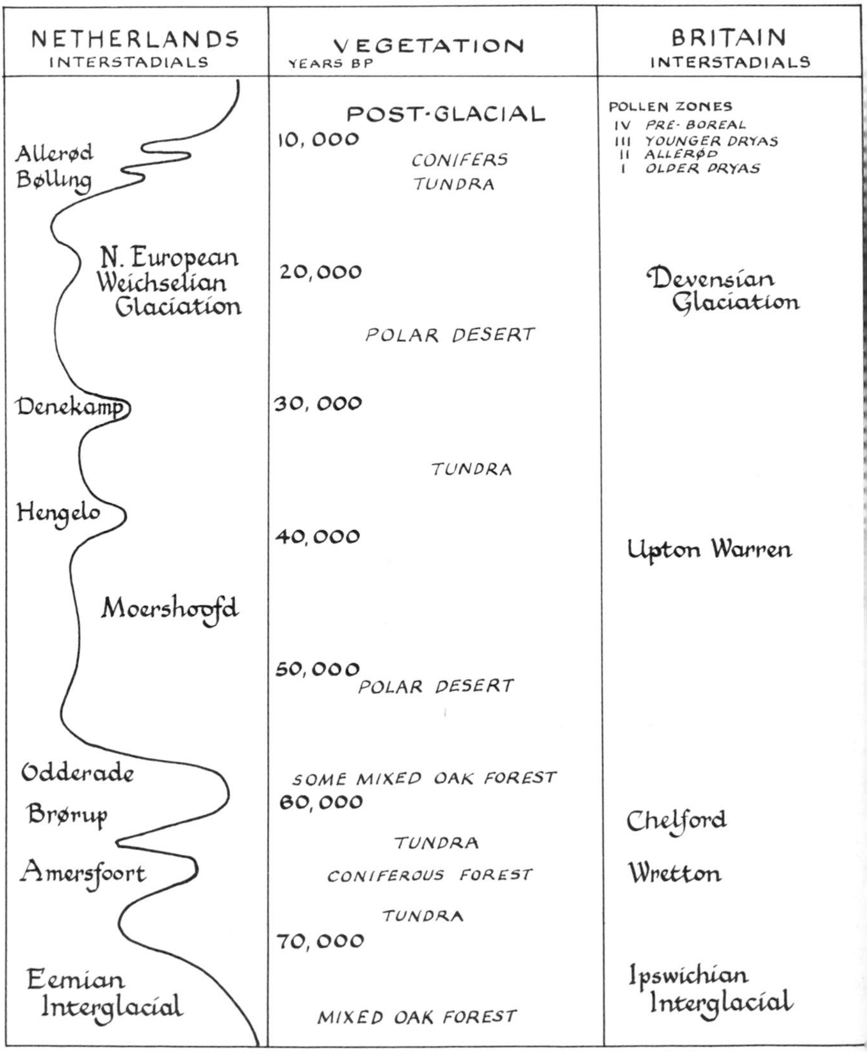

NETHERLANDS INTERSTADIALS	VEGETATION YEARS BP	BRITAIN INTERSTADIALS
Allerød Bølling	POST·GLACIAL 10,000 CONIFERS TUNDRA	POLLEN ZONES IV PRE-BOREAL III YOUNGER DRYAS II ALLERØD I OLDER DRYAS
N. European Weichselian Glaciation	20,000 POLAR DESERT	Devensian Glaciation
Denekamp	30,000 TUNDRA	
Hengelo	40,000	Upton Warren
Moershoofd	50,000 POLAR DESERT	
Odderade Brørup	SOME MIXED OAK FOREST 60,000 TUNDRA	Chelford
Amersfoort	CONIFEROUS FOREST TUNDRA 70,000	Wretton
Eemian Interglacial	MIXED OAK FOREST	Ipswichian Interglacial

awareness of the power to control and dominate. If this is really what happened, there is no need to invoke a spread of ideas by migration or diffusion; specialised hunting groups could have gradually evolved into the elaborate hunting communities of the Upper Palaeolithic wherever conditions were favourable.

The archaeological record tends to support this convergence theory for in several areas of the world it is possible to see a connection between the earliest leptolithic industries and the industries that immediately precede them. The Perigordian of France evolves from the Mousterian of Acheulian tradition, the Szeletian of central Europe from the specialised Mousterian of that region, as does the earliest Upper Palaeolithic industry in the USSR at Kostienki. The Aurignacian of the Near East probably derives from the Amudian which, in turn, has its roots in Africa. The Aterian of North Africa has its origins in central African industries, and the Upper Palaeolithic of Siberia has affinities with the Mousterian-type industries of China. The archaeological record is far from complete but it would seem that these regions were the most important centres of advancement. However, these developments were certainly not contemporary, so that for the first half of this period, at least, different cultural stages existed together in the world. What contact, if any, there was between them is unknown. In the latter part of the period, from about 35,000 years ago, there was a greater degree of cultural uniformity in the world, although it was far from complete and in some regions, such as South East Asia, Lower Palaeolithic economies continued to prevail.

The Upper Palaeolithic, as a period and not a culture, terminates with the final retreat of glacial ice in the northern hemisphere, about 8500 BC. By conventional definition, anything after this date is Mesolithic until the advent of farming communities and ultimately urban civilisation. The break is only an archaeological convenience, although it does coincide with several changes in certain parts of the world, particularly in Europe and the Near East. These changes mainly reflect the response by the advanced hunting communities to the opening up of vast hunting grounds on the tundra and scrub in the wake of the retreating ice. This was particularly evident in North West Europe, commencing about 12,000 BC. In the British sequence this period of 12,000-8500BC is referred to as Late Glacial, and comprises three pollen zones, (I-III), still included within the Devensian Stage (see Table 1.2). The middle zone (II), known as the Allerød Interstadial, was relatively mild, but was followed by about 500 years of intensely cold climate. To some extent there was a breakdown of the economies which had produced the most tangible evidence of cultural advance, such as that associated with the Magdalenian of France and Spain. Populations moved and much was lost. The semi-permanent occupation of caves and rock shelters became difficult or impossible. Art declined and disappeared. However, the same disruption may have been a major factor in bringing about the first food-producing economies in the Near and Middle East. This Late Glacial period covers the Late Upper Palaeolithic, much of which is transitional to the Mesolithic and cannot be dealt with here in much detail, but some of the sites and stone industries are mentioned below.

It is a matter of importance to know when and where was the earliest manifestation of the Upper Palaeolithic. This has to be assessed, rightly or wrongly, on the first appearance of a true blade-based or leptolithic stone industry. In western Europe this was about 35,000 years ago, and perhaps a little earlier in central Europe and western Russia. In the previous chapter it was seen that in the Near East and North Africa there is a blade industry, termed the Amudian, which is much earlier. At Jabrud, it underlies 14 layers of Mousterian, and it also occurs beneath the Jabrudian at Et Tabun, Mount Carmel. In the Abri Zumoffen in the Lebanon, the same industry is found immediately above a 12-13 m raised beach dating to the Last Interglacial. Even if this industry is not of Last Interglacial date, it cannot be much more recent than the beginning of the Last Glacial phase, about 70,000 years ago.

There is another very advanced leptolithic industry in southern Africa which also dates to about this time: the Howieson's Poort. There are many conflicting dates for this industry, mainly based on radiocarbon samples, but at Klasies River Mouth it appears in the succession there at about the time of the climatic deterioration, equivalent to the beginning of the Last Glaciation in the northern hemisphere. The industry is clearly intrusive at Klasies River Mouth, wedged between two stages of the Middle Stone Age, and certainly did not evolve from them. The same industry at the Montagu Cave in the Cape has very early radio-carbon dates, indicating that it is likely to be considerably earlier than them. Not enough is known of the similar industries in Uganda, Tanzania and elsewhere in East Africa to assess whether they are contemporary or not, but the evidence of the Amudian in the Lebanon and the Howieson's Poort of Klasies River Mouth warrants the conclusion that the first appearance of the Upper Palaeolithic was in Africa.

Distribution and Typology of Stone and Bone Industries of the Upper Palaeolithic

Europe

France. The typology and classification of the French Upper Palaeolithic are complex and, although there can be no doubt about the main industrial divisions, the identification of numbered sub-stages may be questionable. This is critical when correlations inferring contemporaneity are based on nothing but typology, although the typologies are the result of detailed analyses involving not only distinctive tool types,[2] but also the combinations or proportions of one class of tool to another.[3] Some archaeologists prefer a less rigid system, and use the terms lower, middle and upper instead of stage numbers. A detailed radiocarbon chronology may eventually replace the present typological scheme but, in the meantime, the stage numbers do make a useful working model, they are commonly used by archaeologists, and both radiocarbon and stratigraphy support their relative sequence. For this reason, broad outlines of the classification system are given. Also, the stone industries of this period in France have been studied in greater detail than anywhere else in the world, and the descriptions of the tool types can in many instances be applied to industries elsewhere.
PERIGORDIAN (Figure 46)
This industry is thought to have evolved from the local Mousterian of Acheulian tradition,[4] for it is found immediately above such an industry at La Ferrassie, and there are transitional industries at Arcy-sur-Cure between the Mousterian and Perigordian. Subdivided into various stages (I-VI), the earliest level is often referred to as Châtelperronian,[6] and the distinctive curved-backed knife of this

Figure 45: Map of Upper Palaeolithic Sites in South West France and Northern Spain
Many hundreds of sites exist in this region, mainly beneath rock shelters or in cave mouths. Some of the more important and those mentioned in the text are shown on this map. Stars indicate caves with particularly fine paintings or engravings of the period.

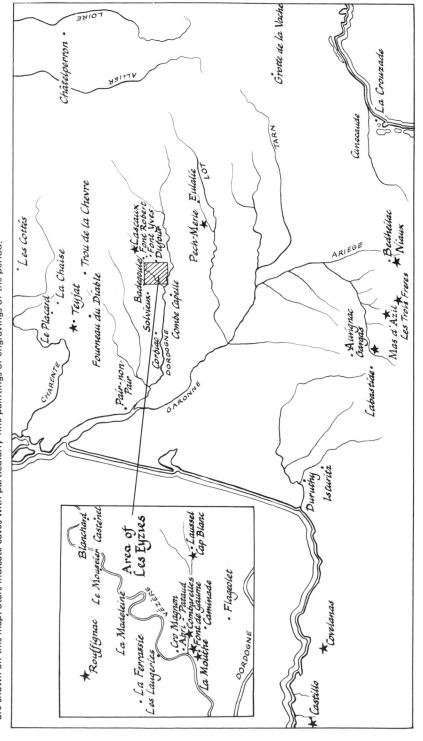

stage as a Châtelperronian point. Several Mousterian features, such as Levallois flakes and scrapers on flakes, occur in Perigordian I.

The Perigordian was mainly restricted to central France, particularly the Perigord region of the Dordogne.[7] It is found in the foothills of the Pyrenees but not in Provence. Most French archaeologists regard this industrial tradition as mainly contemporary with another termed the Aurignacian (see below). The early phase is well represented, but Stage II is only known from Les Cottés and La Ferrassie and may be Aurignacian. Stage III has, since the original classification, been found at the Abri Pataud in Les Eyzies,[8] stratified above Stage V, so it has been renamed Perigordian VI.

The final stages (IV and V) are well represented and are sometimes termed Gravettian,[9] as the industry includes many straight-backed blades (Gravette knives or points). In Stage V there is a distinctive tanged point, known as a Font Robert point, and a type of graver made on a small flake known as a 'Noailles burin'. The latter occurs in a sub-stage, Vc.

Bone working was not much developed until the final stage, but simple points and awls were made at all stages.

Table 6.1: Representative Perigordian Sites (see Figure 46)

Stage I:	Châtelperron
'Châtelperronian'	La Ferrassie (layer E)
	Les Cottés
	Trou de la Chèvre
	Roc de Combe Capelle (layers 8 and 10 with Aurignacian in between)
	Gargas
	Arcy-sur-Cure
Stage II	La Ferrassie (layer Ei)
	Les Cottés (layer G)
Stage III (renamed VI)	
Stage IV:	
'Gravettian'	Abri Pataud (layer 5)
Stage V:	Roc de Combe Capelle
'Gravettian'	Flageolet I (layers 4-7)
	Crouzade (layer 7)
	Font Robert
	Abri Pataud (layer 4)
Stage VI:	Laugerie Haute (layer B)
	Abri Pataud (layer 3)
	Corbiac
	Roc de Combe Capelle
	Flageolet I

PROTO-MAGDALENIAN

This industry is found at two sites in Les Eyzies, Dordogne: at Laugerie Haute and the Abri Pataud. At the latter site it occurs in level 2, above Perigordian

Figure 46: Upper Palaeolithic of France: 1. Perigordian Industries
1. Abri Audi point, Abri Audi, Les Eyzies, ?Proto-Perigordian ass. with typical Mousterian.
2.-7. Châtelperron points, Châtelperron, Allier, Stage I. 8. Obliquely blunted blade,
Châtelperron, Allier, Stage I. 9. Microlithic-backed blade, Châtelperron, Allier, Stage I.
10.-11. Obliquely blunted blades, Châtelperron, Allier, Stage VI. 12.-13. Bevelled-based
bone points, Laugerie Haute Est, layer B, Stage VI. 14.-15. Backed micro-blades, Laugerie
Haute Est, layer B, Stage VI. 16. End scraper, La Ferrassie, layer E, Stage II. 17. Double
angle graver, La Ferrassie, layer E, Stages I-II. 18. Small angle graver ('burin de Noailles'),
Petit-Puyrousseau, Stage V. 19.-21. Gravette points, La Gravette, Stage V. 22.-24. Font
Robert tanged points, La Ferrassie, layer J, Stage V. 25. Double-ended end scraper and
dihedral graver, Laugerie Haute Est, Proto-Magdalenian.
(All after Sonneville-Bordes, 1960, except 1 after Goury, 1948; 2-3 after Delporte, 1976;
4-9 after Lacaille, 1947; 19-21 after Lacorre, 1960. See also Lynch, 1966)

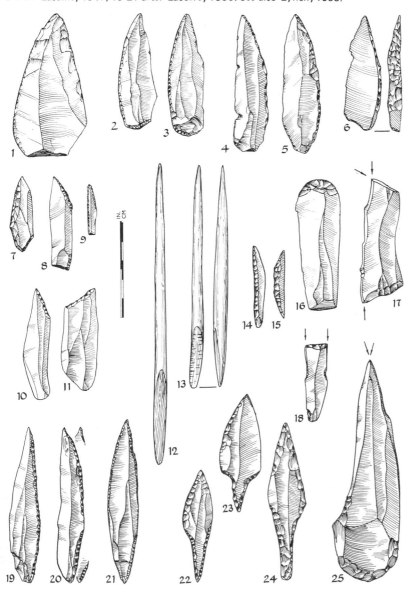

VI.[10] Gravette points have become rare and the industry is characterised by large, superbly struck flint blades, often retouched into elegant end scrapers, gravers, borers and other tools. Microlithic-backed blades, sometimes denticulated, occur, and bone working is more important.

Some archaeologists prefer to see this industry as a final Perigordian (Stage VII). Typologically it appears to be this, and also transitional to later Magdalenian industries.

AURIGNACIAN (Figure 47)

The differences between the stone and bone tools of the Aurignacian and the Perigordian seem to warrant the distinction that French archaeologists make between them. Radiocarbon dating and stratigraphy confirm that they are contemporary and the interpretation is that the Aurignacian represents a separate industrial tradition that had its origins outside France. The blade element is more pronounced and the retouch is characteristically shallow; nosed scrapers are much more common and there is an absence of both Châtelperronian and Gravette points. However, it is in the bonework that the greatest distinction lies, for it is highly developed and sophisticated. Split-based bone points are found in the first stage, but give way later to flattened or bevelled points with rounded or lozenge-shaped cross-sections.

Five stages of the Aurignacian are recognised (I-V), each with its distinctive range of tools. The Aurignacian is found in most of the country. However, there is very little in the north and it is mainly in central and southern France.

Table 6.2: Representative Aurignacian sites

Stage I	La Ferrassie (layer F)
	Aurignac
	Abri Blanchard
	Laussel
	La Comba del Bouïtou (lower level)
	Abri Caminade
	Abri Castanet
Stage II	La Ferrassie (layer 6)
	Abri Blanchard
	La Comba del Bouïtou (upper level)
	Dufour
	Abri Pataud (level 7)
Stage III	La Ferrassie (layer H(i))
	Abri Pataud (level 6)
	Flageolet I
Stage IV	La Ferrassie (layer H (ii))
	Abri Pataud (level 6)
Stage V	Font Yves
	Laugerie Haute

Figure 47: Upper Palaeolithic of France: 2. Aurignacian Industries
1. Split-based bone point, Gorge d'Enfer, Les Eyzies, Stage I. 2. Bevelled-based bone point,
La Ferrassie, layer F, Stage I. 3. Biconical bone point with round section, La Ferrassie,
layer H, Stage III. 4. Simple bone point with bevelled base, Laugerie Haute Ouest, layer D,
Stage V. 5. Dihedral graver, La Ferrassie, layer H, Stage IV. 6. Busked graver, La Ferrassie,
layer H, Stage IV. 7.-9. Dufour bladelets, Font Yves, Stages Early I-II. 10.-12. Font Yves
points, Font Yves, Stages Early I-II. 13. Double-ended angle graver, La Ferrassie, layer H,
Stage IV. 14. End scraper, La Ferrassie, layer F, Stage I. 15. Borer, La Ferrassie, layer F,
Stage I. 16. Strangulated scraper, La Ferrassie, layer F, Stage I. 17. Nosed scraper, Abri
Castanet, Stage I. 18. Carinated scraper, Abri Castanet, Stage I.
(All after Sonneville-Bordes, 1960, except 1 after R.A. Smith, 1926. See also Peyrony,
1934)

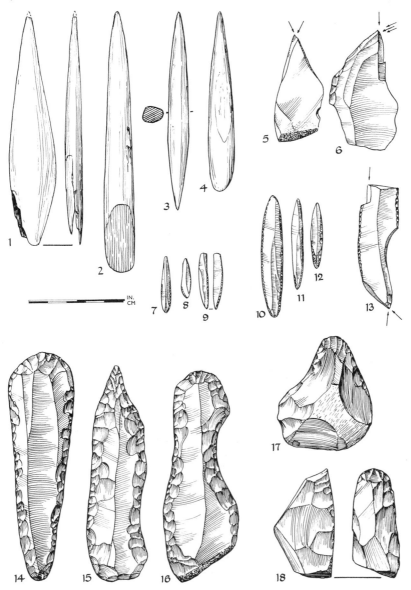

Figure 48: Upper Palaeolithic of France: 3. Solutrian Industries
1.-2. Unifacial points ('Pointe à face plane'), Laugerie Haute Ouest, layer H, Early Stage.
3. Small leaf point, Pech de la Boissière, Late Stage. 4. Unifacial point, Laugerie Haute
Ouest, layer G, Proto-Solutrian. 5. Bifacial leaf point, Fourneau du Diable, Late Stage.
6. Bone pin or needle, Laugerie Haute Ouest, layer H, Late Stage. 7. Bevelled-based bone
point, Les Jean-Blanc, Late Stage. 8. Biconical bone point, Fourneau du Diable, Late Stage.
9. Borer, Laugerie Haute Est, layer H, Late Stage. 10. Large bifacial leaf point, Pech de la
Boissière, Late Stage. 11. Willow leaf point, Fourneau du Diable, Late Stage. 12. Shouldered
point ('Pointe à cran'), Pech de la Boissière, Late Stage. 13. Shouldered point, Badegoule,
Late Stage. 14. End scraper, Fourneau du Diable, Late Stage.
(All after Sonneville-Bordes, 1960. See also P.E.L. Smith, 1966)

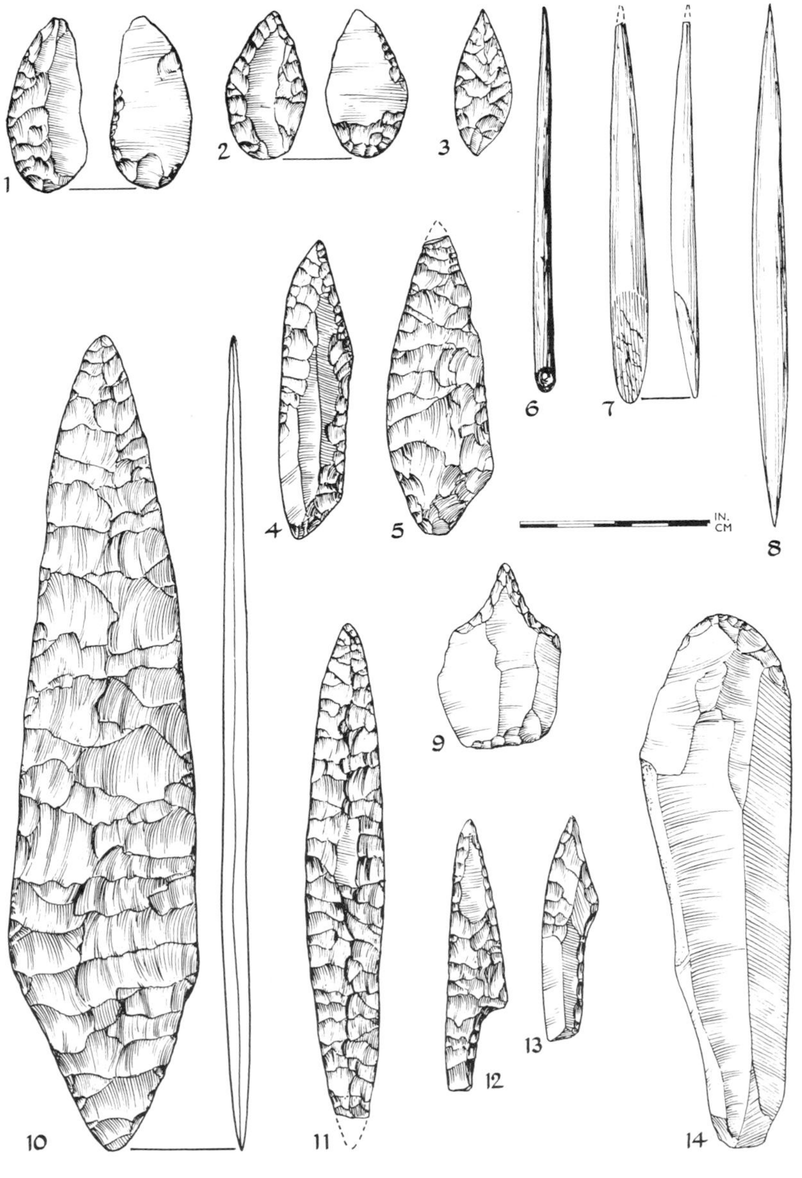

SOLUTRIAN (Figure 48)

This industry represents the highest achievement of flint craftsmanship in the whole of the Palaeolithic period, only to be equalled by much later Neolithic industries in Egypt and Denmark and, more recently, by some South American pre-Columbian work. The characteristic piece is a finely flaked, bifacial leaf point (French: *feuilles de laurier* — laurel leaves), sometimes so perfectly made that it could more rightly be regarded as an art object (Plate XXI) than a functional tool or weapon. It has been demonstrated that some of the partly made flint leaf points were subjected to an elaborate heat treatment to facilitate the precision of the final flaking.[11] There are other forms of stone points which indicate progressive technological development through time. The bone industry is less significant, but eyed needles appear in the final stages.

The origin and fate of this industry is a major problem in French Upper Palaeolithic archaeology:[12] it appears suddenly after the Proto-Magdalenian, from which it could not have evolved, and disappears about 2,000 years later just as abruptly. It has been suggested that it may have been derived from an earlier Spanish Solutrian having African origins but there is no Early Solutrian on the French side of the Pyrenees and there are typological reasons against this suggestion. Similarly, it does not seem to be related to the central European industries deriving from the Mousterian with leaf-shaped points ('Blattspitzen'). The interpretation favoured at present is that it evolved from a local French Mousterian industry that had survived somewhere in spite of the presence of Perigordians and Aurignacians. If so, no such industry has yet been discovered, and what it means in terms of human activity is a mystery.

Table 6.3: Representative Solutrian Sites

Proto-Solutrian	Laugerie Haute
	Badegoule
	Grotte de la Salpêtrière
Early Solutrian	Laugerie Haute
	Grotte de la Salpêtrière
	Isturitz
Middle Solutrian	Grotte de la Salpêtrière
	Isturitz
Late Solutrian	Solutré
	Laugerie Haute
	Fourneau du Diable
	Lespugue
	Grotte de la Salpêtrière (evolves into Salpêtrien)
	St Eulalie
	Mas d'Azil
	La Crouzade
	Le Placard

Figure 49: Upper Palaeolithic of France: 4. Magdalenian Industries
1. End scraper, La Madeleine, Stage IV. 2. Double end scraper, La Madeleine, Stage IV.
3.-4. Shouldered points, Duruthy, Stage VI. 5. Star-shaped multiple borer, Duruthy, Stage
VI. 6. Double borer, Laugerie Basse, Stage IV. 7.-8. Denticulated, backed micro-blades,
Duruthy, Stage VI. 9. Shouldered point on micro-blade, Duruthy, Stage VI. 10.-11. Triangular
microliths, Maurens, Stage VI. 12. Micro-burin, Maurens, Stage VI. 13.-21. Microliths,
Duruthy, Stage VI. 22. Teyjat point, Teyjat, Late Stage. 23. Backed angle graver, La
Madeleine, Stage IV. 24. Parrot-beaked graver, Abri Daufaure, Late Stage. 25. Double end
scraper and obliquely backed angle graver, Les Martres-de-Veyres, Late Stage. 26. Raclette
(small, irregularly shaped steeply backed flakes), Laugerie Haute, Stage I. 27. Dihedral
graver, Maurens, Stage VI. 28. Dihedral graver, La Madeleine, Stage IV.
(1-2, 23, 28 after Capitan and Peyrony, 1928; 3-5, 7-9, 14-21 after Arambourou, 1976;
6, 24 after Goury, 1948; 10-13, 27 after Lenoir, 1976; 22 after Bordes, 1968; 25 after
Delporte, 1976; 26 after Sonneville-Bordes, 1960)

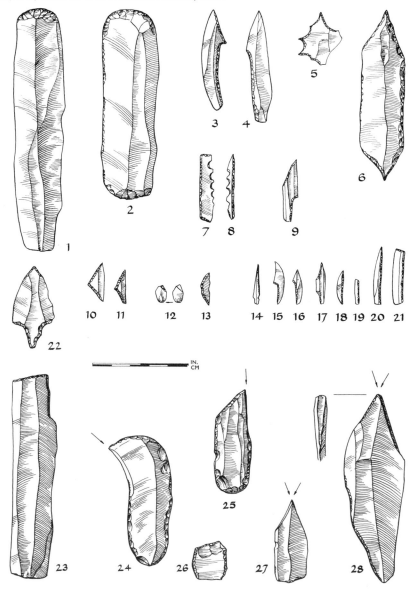

Figure 50: Magdalenian Bone and Antler Industry
Spear and harpoon heads were mainly made from reindeer antler. Blanks were obtained by the groove and splinter technique: parallel incisions were made with a flint graver along the main beam of an antler at the required width until the spongy tissue inside the antler was penetrated. It was then possible to prise out a suitable splinter for carving into various tools and weapons. Cutting could be made easier by first soaking the antler.

1. Simple point. 2.-4. Bevelled-based points. 5.-10. Uniserial barbed points. 11.-13. Biserial barbed points. 14. Awl. 15.-16. Needles. 17. Polisher or burnisher. 18. Polisher or pestle. 19.-20. Flat uniserial barbed points.

All from La Madeleine, Dordogne, France (after Capitan and Peyrony, 1928) except 2, 3, 9 and 13 from Kesslerloch, Switzerland (after Merk, 1876); 4 from Canecaude, Aude, France (after Sacchi, 1976); 19-20 from Grotte des Eglises, Ussat, Ariège (after Clottes, 1976). See Figure 77 for further examples of Magdalenian bone and antler work.

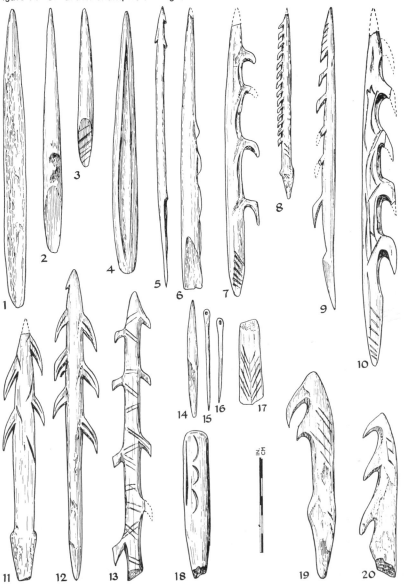

MAGDALENIAN (Figures 49 and 50)

The origins of this industry are probably in both the Perigordian and the Aurignacian, but not necessarily in France. Central European and Spanish influences are evident. It is best known in its later stages when bone working reached a very high standard. The spear thrower, a mechanical device for increasing the thrust of a spear, appears, and, at the same time, intricate barbed points of bone and antler. There is a progressive development from one row of simple barbs to deeper more angular ones and, eventually, a double row of barbs. These weapons would have tipped wooden spears and, when there is an obvious intentional thickening at the base, or a perforation, a socket and attached cord (as on a true harpoon) are indicated. Tridents may have been fishing spears. Needles are now common, as are elaborately decorated 'bâtons de commandement', which may have been spear straighteners or purely cult objects, or both.

The flint industry varies; where good-quality flint is plentiful, as in central France, especially the Perigord region, the technique was good.[13] Long blades were skilfully struck from large blade cores and either used as they were or fashioned into elegant scrapers, gravers or borers. However, where flint was less easy to obtain, such as in the Pyrenees, the quality declined. There seems to have been little attempt to seek out suitable material, although the uniformity of earlier industries suggests this was done, almost implying a specialised activity of flint prospecting, and even trade. During the Magdalenian there was a steady increase in the use of microlithic-backed blades and an evolution of geometric microliths.

In some areas of France, archaeologists have found it difficult to fit certain Magdalenian-like industries into the accepted framework and have given them different names, such as the Rhodanian of the Jura and Alpes du Nord,[14] and the Badegoulian of the South West Paris Basin.[15] The latter appears to have been influenced by the Solutrian.

The final Magdalenian of the South West Paris Basin is of great interest as, at sites such as Pincevent[16] and La Pierre aux Fées, it includes a very distinctive small, asymmetrically pointed boring tool ('Zinken') which is characteristic of Hamburgian sites in North West Germany, dated to Zone I of the Late Glacial.

Table 6.4: Representative Magdalenian Sites

Early Magdalenian	Cassegros	
	Isturitz	
	Beauregard	
	Laugerie Haute	
Late Magdalenian	La Madeleine	Grotte de la Vache
	Grotte de l'Adaouste	Grotte du Mas d'Azil
	Abri de Chinchon	Labastide
	Grotte de la Salpêtrière	Isturitz
	La Crouzade (layer 5)	Duruthy
	St Eulalie	Pincevent

AZILIAN

The Magdalenian persists into the Late Glacial period, when it is replaced by the Azilian and other so-called Epi-Palaeolithic industries. In Southern France the

Azilian may well be the industry of dispersed Magdalenian communities; the flint and bone industry is far less rich and refined. The blade element is poor by comparison with the earlier Upper Palaeolithic industries, and there is a concentration on microlithic types and very small scrapers. The bone industry is restricted mainly to rather crude, flattish barbed points. The type site is Mas d'Azil, Ariège.[17]

In Provence and Languedoc there are industries of this period that are not truly Azilian, and they have been given a host of special terms (Languedocian, Volorguian, Castelnovian, Montadian, Bouverian). Similarly, in the South West Paris Basin there is the Beaugencian, with numerous microliths.

This must have been a period of considerable population movement and this is emphasised by the lack of uniformity in the flint industries.

Table 6.5: French Upper Palaeolithic Industries (see Figures 46-50 and their captions)

Industry	Main characteristics	Development	Distribution	Time range bc
Perigordian	Many backed blades; thick scrapers, strangulated blades; some end scrapers, gravers, denticulates and truncated blades. Simple bone points.	Pointed curved-backed blades (Châtelperron points) in Stage I; pointed straight-backed blades (Gravette points) in final stages. Levallois technique and Mousterian forms present at first, but disappear. Font Robert points and 'Noailles burins' in Stage V. Bone working more important in Stage VI.	Mainly central France. Early Perigordian is found in the Paris Basin but not in the Pyrenees or Provence.	33,000-20,000
Aurignacian	Blade technique is highly developed; many retouched and truncated blades, and thick-nosed scrapers. Backed blades and gravers less common. Dufour micro-blades and microlithic-backed blades at most levels. A rich bone industry including perforated antler bars (bâtons de commandement),	Split-based bone points only in Stage I. Less retouched blades in later stages but more gravers. Busked gravers in Stage II. Font Yves points in early stages. Round-sectioned biconical bone points in	Found mainly in central France and Pyrenees, also in Paris Basin and Loire. In Languedoc but rare in Provence.	30,000-20,000

Table 6.5: contd

Industry	Main characteristics	Development	Distribution	Time range bc
	various types of simple points, awls, spatulae and polishers.	Stage IV.		
Solutrian	Highly refined flint working with considerable use of shallow 'pressure' flaking. Small and large leaf points. Also unifacial simple or shouldered points ('pointe à cran'). Scrapers and gravers on elegant blades. Bone working less important than in Aurignacian.	Unifacial points in early stages is superceded by bifacial leaf points of middle and late stages. Shoulder points (willow leaves) in late stage. Bone working increases in late stage and includes first known eyed needles.	Early Solutrian is only known from central France and South West Paris Basin. Late Solutrian has a much wider distribution in Loire, Charente and the Pyrenees. It is not known in Provence.	19,000-17,000
Magdalenian	Blade industry, refined or poor depending on type of flint available. Blades often unretouched. Many microlithic-backed blades, gravers, scrapers and borers. Fine bone and antler industry, including harpoons or barbed points, tridents, various simple points, awls, needles, polishers, 'bâtons de commandement'. First spear throwers.	'Raclettes' distinctive of early stage. Microlithic element increases. First harpoons in late stage (IV). Single rows of barbs on harpoons of Stage V, double in Stage VI. 'Parrot-beaked' gravers and Teyjat or Font Brunel points in late stage.	Widely distributed in central and southern France, particularly in the Dordogne and Pyrenees. Only Late Magdalenian is found in the north. Early Magdalenian is not present in the Pyrenees, and rare in Languedoc.	15,000-9,500
Azilian	Less refined industry. Small blades and flakes. Diminutive 'thumbnail' scrapers. Microlithic-backed blades. Bone used for little more than flat, barbed antler points, some perforated (harpoons).	Harpoons become progressively smaller and cruder.	Mainly in Pyrenean region region but present in Provence, the Perigord, Loire and Auvergne. Not found in North France.	9,500-9,000

Table 6.6: Typology of French Upper Palaeolithic Industries

	Perigordian					(Ex III) or Proto-Magdalenian VI	Perigordian VII	Aurignacian				Proto-Solutrian	Solutrian					Magdalenian					
													Early		Middle	Late		Early		Middle		Late	
	I	II	III	IV	V	VI	VII	II	III	IV	V		I	II	III	IV	V	I	II	III	IV	V	VI
Weapons																							
Tanged/shouldered points					●																		▲
Leaf points: unifacial						▲						▲		▲	▲	▲	●						
bifacial				▲	▲										▲	▲	▲						▲
Mousterian points[a]	●	●	▲																				
Châtelperron points[a]	●	●			● ●		▲																▲
Gravette points[a]				●	▲	●	▲	▲		▲							▲					▲	▲
Microlithic-backed blades	▲		▲	▲	▲	▲	▲	▲	▲	▲	▲			▲	●	●		▲	▲	●	●	▲	●
Bone points: split-based	▲	▲		▲	▲	▲	▲	▲	▲	●	▲							▲ ▲	▲ ▲	▲ ▲	▲ ▲	▲ ▲	▲ ▲
simple based									●	▲	▲ ▲							▲ ▲	▲ ▲	▲ ▲	▲ ▲	▲ ▲	▲ ▲
bevelled								●	●													▲	▲
uniserial barbed								▲											▲	▲	▲	▲	▲
biserial barbed																					▲		
barbed															▲			▲				▲	▲
Spear thrower	▲																	▲					
Domestic or industrial																							
Levallois flakes	●	▲	▲	▲	▲	▲ ●		▲ ●	▲ ●	▲ ●	▲ ●	▲ ●	▲ ●	▲ ●	▲ ●	▲ ●	▲ ●	▲ ●	▲ ●	▲ ▲	▲ ▲	▲ ●	▲ ●
Scrapers: flake	▲ ▲	▲ ▲	▲ ▲	▲ ▲	▲ ▲	▲	●	●	●	●	●	▲	▲	▲	▲	▲	▲	● ▲	▲	▲	▲	▲	▲
blade	▲	▲	▲	▲	▲	●	●	●	●	●	▲	▲	▲	▲	▲	▲	▲	▲ ● ▲	▲	▲	▲	▲	▲
nosed								▲	●		▲	▲	▲	▲	▲	▲	▲	▲ ▲ ▲ ▲	▲	▲	△	▲	▲
Blades: backed, truncated or otherwise modified	●	●	●	●	●	●												● ● ● ▲	▲	▲	●	●	●
Denticulates	▲	▲	▲	▲	▲	▲	▲	▲			▲	▲	▲	▲	▲	▲		▲	▲	▲			
Strangulated blades								▲										▲					
'Raclettes'																							
Gravers	● ▲	● ▲	● ▲	● ▲	● ▲	● ▲	● ▲	● ▲	● ▲	● ▲	● ▲	▲ ▲	▲ ▲	▲ ▲	● ▲	● ▲	▲ ▲	● ● ▲	● ▲	● ▲	● ▲	● ▲	● ▲
Bone awls	▲ ▲	▲ ▲	▲ ▲	▲ ▲	▲ ▲	▲ ▲	▲ ▲	▲ ▲	▲ ▲	▲ ▲	▲ ▲	▲ ▲	▲ ▲	▲ ▲	▲ ▲	▲ ▲	▲ ▲	▲ ▲	▲	▲ ▲	▲	▲	▲
Bone polishers	▲	▲	▲	▲	▲	▲	▲	▲	▲	▲	▲	▲	▲	▲	▲	▲	▲	▲	▲	▲	▲	▲	▲
Bone perforated 'bâtons'							▲	▲										▲					
Bone 'wands'																	▲						
Bone needles																		● ● ▲ ▲	▲	▲ ▲	▲ ▲	▲	▲ ▲

Note:
a. These could equally have been used as knives.

Symbols
▲ usually present
● abundant or particularly distinctive

The absence of a symbol does not preclude an occasional presence of the artifact class, nor the use of a symbol its inevitable inclusion in the assemblage of every site of the stage indicated.

Table 6.7: Selected Radiocarbon Dates for the French Upper Palaeolithic
The dates are quoted with their standard deviation and their laboratory reference number, in years bc (i.e. radiocarbon years bp minus 1950). (Laboratories: GrN = Groningen; Ly = Lyon; Gif = Gif-sur-Yvette.)

Perigordian

I	Les Cottés, St Pierre de Maille	31,350 ± 500	(GrN − 4333)
I	Grotte du Renne, Arcy-sur-Cure	31,910 ± 250	(GrN − 1742)
IV	Abri Pataud, Les Eyzies	26,200 ± 225	(GrN − 4634)
IV	Abri Pataud, Les Eyzies	19,830 ± 215	(GrN − 4631)
V	Abri Pataud, Les Eyzies	25,110 ± 370	(GrN − 4280)
Late	Les Vignes, St Martin sous Montaign	19,150 ± 1300	(Ly − 310)
Late	Solutré	21,250 ± 650	(Ly − 561)

Aurignacian

Early	Abri Pataud, Les Eyzies	31,350 ± 760	(GrN − 4610)
Early	Abri Pataud, Les Eyzies	27,350 ± 450	(GrN − 3105)
Early	La Caminade, Caneda	27,150 ± 300	(GrN − 1491)
Early	La Rochette, St Leon sur Vézère	26,910 ± 300	(GrN − 4530)
II	Grotte du Renne, Arcy-sur-Cure	28,850 ± 250	(GrN − 1717)
III	La Ferrassie	26,870 ± 1500	(Gif − 2427)
Late	La Salpêtrière, Remoulins	18,680 ± 770	(Ly − 942)

Proto-Magdalenian

	Abri Pataud, Les Eyzies	18,590 ± 140	(GrN − 2081)
	Abri Pataud, Les Eyzies	19,430 ± 340	(GrN − 4231)

Solutrian

Early	Laugerie Haute	18,800 ± 150	(GrN − 4573)
Early	Grotte Oullins, La Bastide de Virac	17,760 ± 400	(Ly − 799)
Middle	Laugerie Haute	17,790 ± 140	(GrN − 4495)
Middle	La Salpêtrière, Remoulins	18,250 ± 600	(Ly − 940)
Late	Laugerie Haute	17,650 ± 140	(GrN − 4442)
Late	Laugerie Haute	18,500 ± 240	(GrN − 4441)

Magdalenian

Early	Vilhonneur, La Rochefoucauld	10,940 ± 140	(GrN − 4677)
Early	Lassac, Sallèles-Cabardes	14,800 ± 250	(Gif − 2981)
Mid-Late	Le Flageolet 2, Bezenac	10,920 ± 390	(Ly − 916)
Mid-Late	Le Flageolet 2, Bezenac	12,160 ± 690	(Ly − 917)
V	La Gare de Couze, Lalinde	10,480 ± 320	(Ly − 975)
IV	La Madeleine, Tursac	11,490 ± 300	(Ly − 922)
V	La Madeleine, Tursac	11,120 ± 190	(Ly − 921)
V	La Madeleine, Tursac	10,800 ± 240	(Ly − 920)
VI	La Madeleine, Tursac	10,690 ± 260	(Ly − 919)

Azilian

	Le Saut de Loup, St Remèze	9,550 ± 380	(Ly − 320)
	Le Pont d'Ambon, Bourdeille	8,440 ± 190	(Gif − 3368)
	Le Pont d'Ambon, Bourdeille	7,880 ± 180	(Gif − 2570)

Spain and Portugal. There are rich Upper Palaeolithic sites in northern Spain along the Cantabrian mountain range which faces the Atlantic. Many are within the numerous caves in the Cretaceous and Carboniferous limestone hills, famous for their well-preserved paintings. Few have been excavated but there are some complex sequences proving occupation for long periods. The industries discovered have been compared to their French counterparts, and the similarities are so great that this is justified. The Late Magdalenian is particularly well represented and it seems to have flourished in the region, for much of the cave art is of this time, and there are finely decorated objects of bone and antler. The best-stratified site is at Puente Viesgo in the province of Santander, at the mouth of the cave of El Castillo.[18] This site is also important for the presence of Acheulian and Mousterian industries, which are at the bottom of the great thickness of occupational deposits that accumulated. Above the latest Mousterian is an Aurignacian industry followed by Late Perigordian with Gravette points. There is one level of Early Solutrian, then Middle and Late Magdalenian levels with Azilian on top.

Only one site in Spain has yielded the earliest Perigordian: the Cave of Reclau-Viver in Catalonia, east of the main distribution. The industry is succeeded by typical Aurignacian, a Late Perigordian with Gravette points, and Solutrian. Few Upper Palaeolithic sites are known from other parts of Spain, although one of the most important is considerably further south down the Mediterranean coast at Parpallo, Valencia.[19] Here, the Solutrian is found between Late Perigordian and several Magdalenian levels. It is also known in Cantabria at Tito Bustillo Cave,[20] and there are several isolated discoveries, such as apparent Magdalenian in the cave at Nerja in Andalusia. Little is known of the Upper Palaeolithic in Portugal. Further sites may well come to light in the future, but it is unlikely that the general pattern will be very much altered.

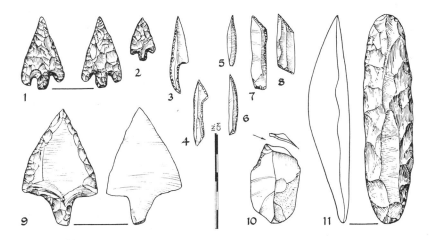

Figure 51: Upper Palaeolithic Industries of Spain and Africa
Spanish Solutrian, Parpallo (after Pericot Garcia, 1942): 1.-2. Barbed and tanged arrowheads. 3.-4. Shouldered points.
Oranian, Sidi Mansur (after McBurney, 1960): 5.-8. Microlithic-backed blades.
Aterian, Oued Djebbana, Libya (after Tixier, 1961): 9. Tanged point.
Dabban, Hagfet ed Dabba (after McBurney, 1967): 10. Transverse graver.
Lupemban, Mbalambala, Angola (after Clark, 1963): 11. Pick.

Although the majority of these industries have considerable similarities with the French, and can be regarded as part of a large region of local development, the same is not necessarily true of the Spanish Solutrian. This has a few very distinctive features that are absent in France: in particular the presence of different forms of bifacial leaf points and of small barbed and tanged points that look like arrowheads. The leaf points sometimes have concave bases, or are asymmetrical, and there are shouldered points of unusual type (Figure 51). There is no clue to the evolution of these unusual forms; the barbed and tanged projectile points are certainly very similar to those in the transitional Aterian industry which survived to this time in North Africa, but the remainder of the industry is entirely different.

Italy and Sicily. A famous and important group of caves and rock shelters is situated beside the Mediterranean at Grimaldi, just on the Italian side of the border with France. The steep limestone cliff is indented with caves and over-hangs and is known as Balzi Rossi.[21] The southward-facing situation and specta-cular view have attracted hunters since the cliff was formed in the Late Pleistocene. Most of the archaeological levels revealed by excavation within the various caves have produced evidence of Last Interglacial fauna and Mousterian industries. These caves are more famous for their Upper Palaeolithic burials and Venus figurines than for the flint industries found within them. At least three stages of the Upper Palaeolithic are represented, by comparison with the French classification. There are split-based bone points in the lower Upper Palaeolithic levels of La Grotte des Enfants, and Dufour bladelets (see Figure 47) in the Mochi shelter, so advanced hunters in the Aurignacian I and II tradition were certainly there. The upper occupational levels of both these sites yield what has been termed a Mediterranean facies of Gravettian, i.e. Late Perigordian. There are Gravette points and characteristic Noailles burins (see Figure 46). A similar industry is found at sites in the Arno Valley, east of Pisa, where there are many Gravette points of microlithic size and also unifacial leaf points.

The French system of classification did not seem very appropriate when the industry at the Fossellone Cave was first discovered. This is at Monte Circeo in the province of Lazio, 100 km south of Rome. The industry was originally called Circean, but it has been demonstrated that its unusual aspect is the result of small beach pebbles being the only raw material available. It is really a typical early Aurignacian industry, with nosed scrapers, gravers and other normal forms, but diminutive on account of the material. The presence of split-based bone points confirms the identification. However, at Romanelli, near Lecce on the tip of Italy's heel, there is a cave with an industry that bears little resemblance to anything in the French sequence, but is probably contemporary with the Magdalenian. It contains many microliths, small semi-shouldered points, thumb-nail scrapers and well-made bone points. Some Mousterian forms and unifacial leaf-shaped blades may be an admixture from an earlier industry. It is termed Romanellian, and must be a local development.

The distribution of Upper Palaeolithic industries in Italy, especially in the later period, may be more extensive than is now known. Several sites are reported from Sicily, where cave art has also been discovered.

Britain and the Low Countries. The maximum southward extent of the last glacial ice sheet was between about 25,000 and 13,000 years BC. It covered almost the whole of highland Britain north of the Bristol Channel, including Ireland, and a further tongue of ice impinged against the east coast as far south as Hunstanton in Norfolk. At this time all of Denmark was beneath ice which reached almost as far as the mouth of the River Elbe. The Low Countries, the Midlands of Britain, East Anglia and the south were thus actually free of ice, but even in the short glacial summers conditions would have been harsh and uninviting. The barren landscape supported few animals so there was little to induce hunters to brave such inhospitable regions. However, during the preceding interstadial, the Denekamp, and in Zone II of the Late Glacial (Figure 44), milder conditions allowed a spread of vegetation which attracted herds of animals: mammoth and woolly rhinoceros are typical of the Denekamp; reindeer, giant deer, horse and elk of the Allerød. Hunters followed these herds and most of the known sites are probably temporary camps. The sea level was very low in the Late Glacial period, more than 100 m below its present level, so communication between France, Britain and the Low Countries was devoid of any sea barriers.

Compared to France and Spain, the Upper Palaeolithic sites of North West Europe are very sparse, as might be expected if they merely represent the temporary camps of hunters making rare forays into the region. However, many undiscovered sites must exist along the banks of major rivers in their estuarine regions, now deeply buried beneath sediment that has accumulated since the post-glacial rise in sea level. The absence of rich sites makes it difficult to compare the flint industries with those so well known in France or elsewhere, but it would seem that there were incursions from both France and central Europe. In Britain, there is a fairly clear division between a small series of earlier Upper Palaeolithic sites, and another series of later ones. The latter are certainly of Late Glacial age, and the former are probably of the Denekamp Interstadial (Figure 44), so an interval of 10,000-15,000 years may separate them. This would correspond well with the time when the country was mainly under ice.

The British Early Upper Palaeolithic contains a few examples of unifacial or partly bifacial leaf points, reminiscent of some European 'Blattspitzen'. French influence is strongly suggested by the discovery of busked burins in Kent's Cavern and a cave in North Wales, Ffynnon Beuno. The latter site is of particular interest as, in the nearby cave of Cae Gwyn, an archaeological horizon is covered by over 3 m of boulder clay. Busked burins are characteristic of Aurignacian, Stage II, radiocarbon dated in France to about 28,000 years BC, which predates the main glacial advance.

Most of the sites are within small caves on the fringes of the highland zone, but there are a few discoveries of leaf points and other flint tools within gravels deposited during the latter part of the Devensian, such as in the Ipswich area. Dating is difficult, but it is not impossible that these leaf points are a natural development from a local Mousterian-like industry as found in the same gravels. A human burial in the Paviland Cave of the Gower Peninsula is probably to be associated with an Early Upper Palaeolithic industry, although the radiocarbon date is too young. However, a date now obtained from an animal bone in the cave is exactly in keeping with what might have been expected.

The British Later Upper Palaeolithic is much better represented, both at caves and at open sites (Figure 52). When sites can be dated, they belong to the mild Allerød period (Late Glacial zone II) or more recent. Wandering hunters still seem to be responsible for most of the sites. A fine, biserial barbed bone point of Final Magdalenian type comes from Aveline's Hole in the Mendips. Another comes from Kent's Cavern, Devon, and there are a few distinctive

Figure 52: Map of British Upper Palaeolithic Sites
The majority of known British Upper Palaeolithic sites are in caves, shown by solid symbols. Open sites are indicated by open symbols.

Earlier Upper Palaeolithic sites at Wookey include the Badger Hole and Hyaena Den, at Cheddar the Soldier's Hole, and at Creswell Crags Pin Hole and Robin Hood's Cave. Later Upper Palaeolithic sites at Cheddar include Gough's Cave (the richest site in Britain), Soldier's Hole and the Sun Hole, at Creswell Mother Grundy's Parlour, Pin Hole and Robin Hood's Cave, and in the Derbyshire and Staffordshire Peak District Dowel Cave, Fox Hole, Elder Bush Cave, Ossum's Cave and Thor's Fissure. The Earlier sites at Ipswich are at Bramford Road and Constantine Road.

By definition, sites more recent than Pollen Zone III (Younger Dryas) are termed Mesolithic. Some of the Later Upper Palaeolithic sites may well extend into Zone IV (Pre-Boreal) so are really beyond the Palaeolithic period.

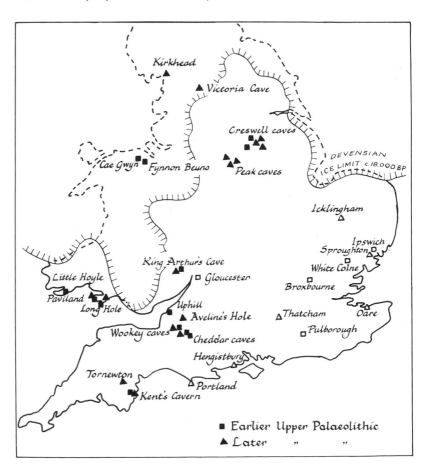

pieces of worked bone from Creswell Crags, Derbyshire, Gough's Cave, Cheddar, and Cathole Cave, Gower Peninsula. There are clear signs of movement from North West Germany, or at least some connections, for there are shouldered points as found in the Hamburgian industry at Mother Grundy's Parlour, Creswell Crags, and a characteristic 'Zinken' from Gough's Cave, Cheddar. An open site at Hengistbury Head, Dorset, has its best parallels with the later Ahrensburgian industry of the Netherlands and North West Germany. Other barbed bone and antler points have been found in a Zone II deposit at Poulton-le-Fylde, Lancashire, associated with an elk skeleton, and in Zone III gravels at Sproughton, near Ipswich. Occasional surface finds of tanged points probably date to the very end of the Palaeolithic period in Britain, but the most interesting stone industry is the Creswellian, as found in several of the caves at Creswell Crags, and others in the Mendip Hills, the Gower Peninsula and the Peak District of Derbyshire. It is also known from Kent's Cavern, King Arthur's Cave in Herefordshire and as far north as Kirkhead Cave in North Lancashire. This Creswellian industry contains backed blades of unusual form, obliquely truncated to form points at one or both ends (Figure 53). A form of this industry in the Cheddar caves has sometimes been termed Cheddarian. It contains 'Cheddar points' and more end scrapers than at Creswell Crags, but there seems little to justify its being more than a local variant or development. There is nothing quite like the Creswellian in the rest of North West Europe except for the so-called Tjonger Group of industries in the Netherlands. These are mainly more recent and continue into the Early Mesolithic period, so the inference is that they derive from the British Creswellian, which is best regarded as a local British Later Upper Palaeolithic tradition.

The evidence from Holland and Belgium for the Upper Palaeolithic is not so different from the British evidence, which is not surprising in the absence of the North Sea, for it was virtually the same geographical region. It is mainly restricted to cave sites in Belgium in the provinces of Manur and Liege.[22] At several of the caves (e.g. Goyet, the Trou Magrite at Pont à Lesse, and the Cave du Docteur near Huccorgne) there are two periods represented in separate levels. The lower contains an industry which is likened to the Aurignacian or Gravettian (i.e. Perigordian), and the upper to the Magdalenian. Diagnostic pieces such as split-based bone points, Gravette points and 'bâtons de commandement' in the lower, and biserial barbed bone points and art objects in the upper, seem to justify these correlations. Particularly convincing as a pointer to the direction of the movement of these hunting communities in the upper levels is the presence of pierced fossil shell ornaments, which can only have come from the Champagne or Paris region of France. Whether this bipartite division of the Upper Palaeolithic in Belgium corresponds to the British Early and Later Upper Palaeolithic, in the sense of having a long period of no human habitation between them, as a result of the proximity of ice sheets during the maximum of the glaciation, cannot be proved, but seems likely.

During the Late Glacial period, in the cold Zone I, it would seem that communities with a Magdalenian-type industry occupied Belgium, while those with a Hamburgian industry were in Holland. However, at least one site in Belgium, Bois St Macaire, near Mons, indicates a Hamburgian (see pp. 207-8) influence on the Later Upper Palaeolithic industry there. In the milder Zone II, the Tjonger Group appears in North Belgium and the Netherlands, originating, as mentioned

Figure 53: British Upper Palaeolithic Material

1.-8. Earlier Upper Palaeolithic. 9.-17. Later Upper Palaeolithic.
1. Bone spatulate tool, Paviland Cave. 2. Part of decorated bone rod, Pin Hole Cave. 3. Base of double bevelled bone point with decoration, Pin Hole Cave. 4. Bifacial leaf point, Kent's Cavern. 5. Tanged point, Pin Hole Cave. 6. Partly bifacial leaf point, Bramford Road Pit, Ipswich. 7. Simple bone point with perforation at base, Little Hoyle. 8. Busked graver ('Burin busque'), Ffynnon Beuno Cave. 9. Part of biserial barbed point of antler, Kent's Cavern. 10. Bone needle, Kent's Cavern. 11. Flat biserial barbed point of red deer antler, Victoria Cave. 12.-13. Uniserial barbed points of antler, Kent's Cavern. 14. Cheddar point, Aveline's Hole. 15. Shouldered point, Hengistbury Head. 16. Hooked point or 'Zinken', Kent's Cavern. 17. Perforated antler ('Bâton de commandement'), Gough's Cave.
(All after J.B. Campbell, 1977, except 4 after J. Evans, 1897)

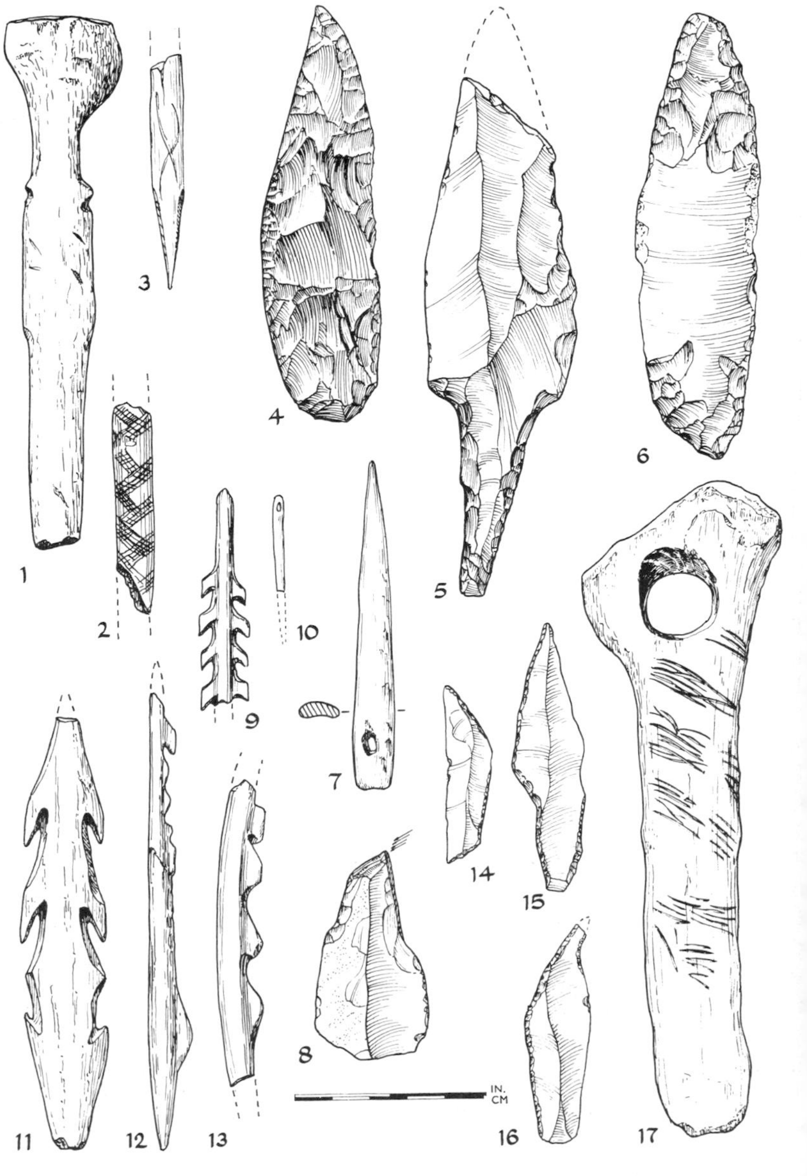

above, probably from the Creswellian of Britain. Finally, in the cold Zone III, there is the Ahrensburgian industry which developed from the Hamburgian (see Table 6.8).

Table 6.8: Selected Radiocarbon Dates for the British Upper Palaeolithic

Early Upper Palaeolithic			
Paviland Cave, Gower	*Bos* bone	25,650 ± 1300 bc	(BM — 1367)
Paviland Cave, Gower	Leg bone of human burial	16,510 ± 340 bc	(BM — 374)
Kent's Cavern, Devon	Bone associated with	26,210 ± 435 bc	(GrN — 6201)
	leaf point and	26,770 ± 450 bc	(GrN — 6202)
Later Upper Palaeolithic			
Kent's Cavern, Devon	Bone associated with	12,325 ± 120 bc	(GrN — 6203)
	uniserial barbed point and	10,230 ± 100 bc	(GrN — 6204)
Robin Hood's Cave,	Bone associated with	8,440 ± 90 bc	(BM — 603)
Creswell Crags, Derbyshire	Creswellian industry and	8,640 ± 90 bc	(BM — 604)

Central and Eastern Europe. French terminology has been applied to the major leptolithic industries; in some respects it is justified, in others it is misleading. As a compromise, the practice of using the qualifying adjective 'Eastern' prevents confusion and is used here. However, the first two industries described below have no French counterparts and have names derived from their type sites in Hungary and Poland. Both could be regarded as transitional between a local Mousterian-type industry and a leptolithic industry. As they appear partly to overlap in time with the latter they are included in this chapter.

SZELETIAN

The type site is the Szeletha Cave in the Bükk Mountains of Hungary. The industry includes numerous 'blattspitzen',[23] i.e. bifacial leaf points, in all three of the levels that have been distinguished (Figure 54). Those in the lowest level are more like very thin hand-axes, but are contemporary with a few split-based bone points regarded as diagnostic of Aurignacian industries. There are Mousterian-like side scrapers and the upper level contains backed and flat retouched blades. The industry is radiocarbon dated to about 29,000 BC at Istállóskö.[24]

Leaf points occur at some other sites in this part of Europe in association with Eastern Aurignacian industries (Istállóskö, Hungary; and Nova Dedina and Predmost, Czechoslovakia). It is therefore difficult to decide whether a Szeletian industry has adopted leptolithic techniques, or vice versa.

JERZMANOVICIAN

The industry from the Nietoperzowa Cave at Jerzmanovice, Poland,[25] also includes leaf points, some bifacial, but others only partly so, made on blades (Figure 54). It underlies later leptolithic industries and some early radiocarbon dates allow it to qualify as a transitional industry. Similar leaf points occur at several other sites across eastern Europe into Russia, and are more likely to reflect just one method of making thin pointed, leaf-shaped stones for knives or spearpoints, rather than a particular industrial tradition.

EASTERN AURIGNACIAN

The validity of separating Eastern Aurignacian and Eastern Gravettian industries on such delicate typological distinctions as the inclusion of backed blades, as

Figure 54: Upper Palaeolithic Industries of Eastern Europe

1.-2. Kostienki shouldered points, Willendorf I, Eastern Gravettian. 3. Kostienki shouldered
points, Willendorf II, Eastern Gravettian. 4. Unifacial leaf point, Nietoperzowa Cave
Jerzmanovice, Jerzmanovician. 5.-6. Krems points, Krems, Eastern Aurignacian. 7. Eight
microliths, Willendorf II, Eastern Gravettian. 8. End scraper, Willendorf I, Eastern
Aurignacian. 9. Oblique angle graver, Willendorf I, Eastern Aurignacian. 10. Szeletian point
Troubsko, near Brno, Szeletian. 11.-12. Nosed scrapers, Willendorf II, Eastern Aurignacian
13. Mladec bone point, Istállóskö, Eastern Aurignacian. 14. Split-based bone point
Istállóskö, Eastern Aurignacian. 15. Bone point with rudimentary barb, Willendorf II
Eastern Gravettian. 16. Jerzmanovician unifacial leaf point, Nietoperzowa Cave
Jerzmanovician.
(1-3, 7-9, 11-12, 15 after Felgenhauer, 1959; 4, 16 after Chmielewski, 1961; 5-6 after
Schwabedissen, 1954; 13-14 after Vértes, 1955. See also Valoch, 1968)

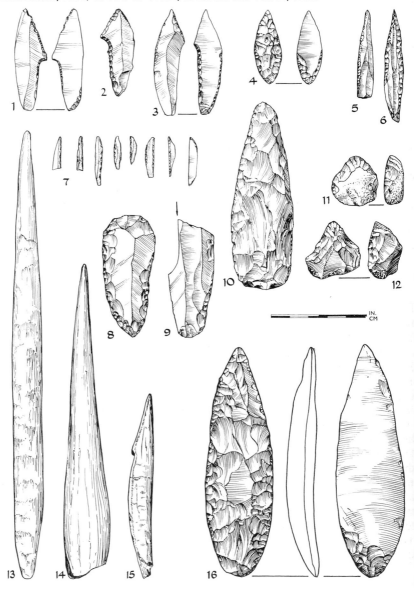

against flat retouched blades, is questionable. However, where there are long sequences at one site, such as Willendorf in Austria,[26] Aurignacian-type industries do underlie Gravettian-like ones. This site is on the left bank of the Danube, and nine separate archaeological horizons are stratified within Last Glaciation loessic sediments which cap the river deposits. The upper five are Eastern Gravettian, the lower four Eastern Aurignacian. The fauna indicates that the climate was full periglacial at the top of the sequence, after a period of less cold conditions. The lower industries have backed blades, nosed scrapers, gravers and, at one level, a type of flint point made on a small blade, known as a Krems point (Figure 54) after another Eastern Aurignacian site not far from Willendorf. The bone industry is poor, and mainly confined to simple points made on split long bones. There is not very much of these industries that is distinctive, and their identification depends to a great extent on the lack of the classical Eastern Gravettian forms, as represented at the top of the Willendorf sequence, and on their stratigraphical position below it. This, coupled with their earlier dates, when known, does justify the distinction between the Eastern Aurignacian and the Eastern Gravettian.

Industries of this type have been found across much of Europe from Vogelherd in Württemberg, Germany, to Roumania and Yugoslavia. The split-based bone points which are the characteristic feature of the earliest Aurignacian in France occur at several sites: Vogelherd in Germany, Istállóskö in Hungary, Mokriskajama in Yugoslavia, the Pest Caves and Morowitza in Roumania, and Bacho Kiro in Bulgaria. Actual migration seems rather more likely than convergence to account for this. There is another form of bone point that is found at some Eastern Aurignacian sites and not at French sites: large, flattish lozenge-shaped points termed Mladec points after a site in Czechoslovakia (Figure 54). These are found at Istállóskö in a level dated to 28,760 ± 600 bc. This level is stratified above the earlier levels previously mentioned as characterised by split-based bone points. Mladec points also occur in the cave at Baia de Fier, Roumania.

The site of Barca, Czechoslovakia, is probably early Eastern Aurignacian. There are leaf points with the industry at Nova Dedina, also in Czechoslovakia, and the industry was also present in the lower levels at Predmost. It occurs in Poland at Gora Pulawska and Piekary II, and at Mokriskajama and Potočka Zijacka in Yugoslavia. The latter site is in a cave at the great altitude of about 2,000 m, and the numerous broken skulls of cave bears associated with the industry imply a fierce struggle for occupation of the cave. Apart from those already mentioned, a few other sites occur in Roumania, such as Temmata-Dubka, which has small flint points similar to the Font Yves points of France.

The location of these sites is shown in Figure 55.

EASTERN GRAVETTIAN

These industries have a wide distribution from Germany to Greece and span a similar time range to their counterparts in France, except that the earliest dates are more recent: about 30,000 BC instead of 33,000. This could imply an eastwards migration from western Europe, rather as the earlier dates in central and eastern Europe for the Eastern Aurignacian could imply a westwards migration towards France. This cannot be demonstrated; more important is the cultural uniformity during this period over most of Europe, from the Atlantic Ocean to the Russian steppes.

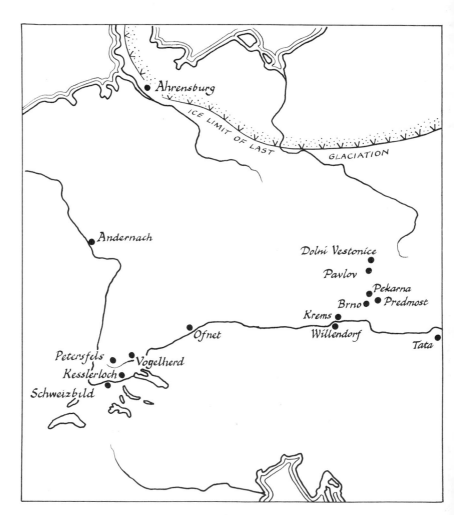

Figure 55: Map of Some Principal Upper Palaeolithic Sites in Central Europe
N.b. Only Ahrensburg is a Late Glacial site and, at the time of its occupation by reindeer hunters with a Hamburgian industry, c. 8500 BC, the ice had retreated to southern Sweden and Norway.

The industry is best represented in Austria and Czechoslovakia, usually at sites on the loess-covered slopes of hills above rivers or marshes. The uppermost level at Willendorf is regarded as the classic Eastern Gravettian industry, with backed blades and points, gravers and microliths. There are bone points, one with the suggestion of a barb, and a few distinctive shouldered Kostienki points of flint (Figure 54). This is also the level which has produced the famous female statuette, the 'Venus of Willendorf'. Virtually the same industry is found at Dolni Vestonice in Czechoslovakia, which also had an elaborate bone industry of points, awls, needles, knives, mammoth rib lanceheads and a form of shovel made from the flat parts of reindeer antlers. Venus figurines of clay were associated, as were dwelling structures. Human burials, other dwelling structures and immense accumulations of mammoth bone have been found with Eastern Gravettian industries at such rich sites as Pavlov, Predmost and Brno in the same country.

The resemblance of this industry to the Late Perigordian of France is remarkable, but whether the presence of curved-backed 'Châtelperronian' knives at Ofnet and Ranis in Germany implies it is the same Early Perigordian industry is questionable.

The leptolithic industries of Greece, exemplified by those in the caves of Kastritsa and Asprochaliko, have affinities with the Eastern Gravettian. Some of the more important sites are shown on the distribution map (Figure 55).

EASTERN MAGDALENIAN

The Late Magdalenian industries found in Germany and Switzerland have all the characteristics of those in France, and there can be little doubt that they represent the northern and eastern movement of populations towards the close of the Last Glaciation. Some of the sites are dated to Zone I (i.e. Older Dryas of the Late Glacial pollen zones). There is a rich site at Gonnersdorf in the Rhine Valley. Andernach, also in Germany, is typical Late Magdalenian with uniserial and biserial barbed points, bevelled bone points and needles. It is in loess conveniently sealed beneath pumice that accumulated during minor volcanic activity during Zone II (Allerød). It is probably contemporary with the Hamburgian, as may be Petersfels, a cave site near Lake Constance. The latter site includes perforated 'bâtons'. Two famous Swiss sites are also in this area: Kesslerloch[27] and Schweizersbild. The former is a cave in the Canton of Schaffhausen, and also contained a Late Magdalenian industry with some fine 'bâtons de commandement' decorated with engravings of horses and a rich bone industry including uniserial and biserial barbed points, needles, polishers, awls, simple bevelled points and various perforated pendants. Schweizersbild is a rock shelter only seven kilometres to the west of the former site. Magdalenian is the only Upper Palaeolithic industry found in Switzerland.

Further east, in the Pekarna Cave near Brno, Czechoslovakia, the stone industry less resembles its French counterparts, but the bone industry is similar, with needles, 'bâtons' and a triple barbed harpoon. In the same country are open sites, at which hunters lived in the same type of semi-underground dwellings (known as 'zemlyankas') as the earlier Eastern Gravettians. There appears to have been some mingling of both traditions, and this could be true of the industry in the Maszycka Cave in Poland. Yet further east, as will be seen in the account on Russian sites, contemporary industries may have Magdalenian affinities, but it is misleading to use the French terminology.

LATE GLACIAL INDUSTRIES

The great dispersal of advanced hunting communities in Europe in the Late Glacial period, with the opening up of new hunting grounds, the proliferation of vast migrating herds of reindeer and the virtual or complete extinction of the mammoth, produced radical changes in life style and economy. North West Europe and much of eastern Europe witnessed the formation of various new stone industries, all with their roots in Late Upper Palaeolithic traditions, and all meeting similar demands albeit in different ways. Barbed bone points were favoured by some for hunting, others concentrated on furnishing their spears and arrows with razor-sharp flint points and barbs. Hence there was greater microlith production. Tanged flint points were inserted into light throwing spears. All these techniques had been used for hundreds of generations, but the gradual evolution by necessity towards reindeer hunting was now complete there was little left to hunt in this region of the world other than the fleet reindeer, and the typology of the weapons reflects this fact.

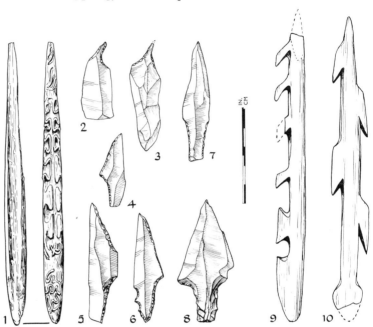

Figure 56: Late Glacial Industries in North West Europe
1. Decorated bone, Ahrensburg (Hamburgian). 2.-3. 'Zinken', Ahrensburg (Hamburgian). 4.-5. Shouldered points, Ahrensburg (Hamburgian). 6. Tanged point, Ahrensburg (Ahrensburgian). 7. Tanged point, Bromme. 8. Tanged point, Lyngby. 9. Universal barbed antler point, Meiendorf (Hamburgian). 10. Biserial barbed antler point, Stellmoor (Ahrensburgian).
(1-6 after Rust, 1958; 7-8 after Mathiassen, 1948; 9-10 after Clark, 1975)

In North West Germany was the Hamburgian, typified by the sites of Late Glacial Zone I age at Meiendorf[28] and Stellmoor[29] (lower level) with characteristic shouldered flint points and beak-like boring tools ('Zinken') (Figure 56). This industry extended into the milder Zone II period, but by Zone III it had developed into the Ahrensburgian (Stellmoor, upper level), with tanged points, microliths, barbed points of antler and axes made of antler (Figure 56).[30] The industry can be traced eastwards to Prussia and Poland, where a Swiderian industry with tanged points and simple microliths is centred on the river valleys of the Vistula and Bug. Further subdivisions include the Tarnovian, Masovian and the Pludian industries, ranging from and through all the Late Glacial Zones. They all have tanged points, but the Masovian also has leaf points. In Denmark, uninhabitable throughout the latter half of the Last Glaciation, hunters were setting up camps around Late Glacial lakes at Bromme and Lyngby n Jutland and Bro in Funen. Axes or picks made of reindeer antler at Lyngby oreshadow the hafted flint axes of the Later Mesolithic period.

Table 6.9: Selected Radiocarbon Dates for some Central European Upper Palaeolithic Sites

Jerzmanovician			
Nietoperzowa Cave, Poland		36,550 ± 126 bc	(GrN — 2181)
Eastern Aurignacian			
Willendorf, Austria	basal industry	28,360 ± 250 bc	
	level with Krems points	29,890 ± 250 bc	
	Upper Aurignacian or transitional industry	30,050 ± 300 bc	
N.b. the radiocarbon dates decrease in reverse order to the stratigraphy — GrN and H)			
Istállóskö 2	Aurignacian II	28,950 ± 600 bc	(GrN — 1935)
Eastern Gravettian			
Dolni Vestonice, Czechoslovakia		23,820 ± 180 bc	(GrN — 1286)
Pavlov, Czechoslovakia		22,970 ± 160 bc	(GrN — 1325)
Asprochaliko, Greece		24,150 ± 900 bc	(I — 1965)

Laboratories: GrN = Groningen; H = Heidelberg; I = Isotopes Inc.)

USSR (West of the Ural Mountains). More than two hundred Upper Palaeolithic sites are known in European Russia, mainly in the valleys of the great rivers which flow to the Black Sea or Sea of Azov. They extend northwards along the west side of the Ural Mountains in an area which was generally free of ice during the Last Glaciation (Valdai Glaciation of USSR). The richness of these sites is only equalled by those of France and a few in eastern and central Europe. There is a direct connection with the latter, for they are linked across the great European Plain, but there is a marked contrast with the French sites, not so much in the typology of the flint and bone industries, as in the environments these advanced hunting communities had to cope with. France is an example of their development in a highly favoured region abounding in natural shelters; European Russia is the complementary example of equally successful adaptation to a bleak, open landscape devoid of all natural shelter.

The artificial shelters or dwellings which were constructed are the subject of the first section of Chapter 7 below, and the effects such differences in habitat may have had on the economy and population movement are considered. Contacts across wide areas between peoples with different economies and traditions cannot be regarded as impossible. The Magdalenian could, for instance, have originated in central Europe and spread by an actual process of migration. Similarly, the Gravettian probably originated outside France, but whether in terms of the diffusion of ideas or by the actual migration of hunting communities, the major force which controlled typology was the manner in which these people adapted to the rigorous existence on the steppe-tundra of Russia. The species of animals hunted, the hunting methods, the raw material available for making clothes and domestic objects, would all have influenced the types of artifacts they made. Such things changed not just by time, but by locality as well. From an inherited tradition of technology, which we conveniently term 'leptolithic', custom and necessity interplayed to produce distinctive kits of tools. It is no coincidence that the greatest similarities to levels I to VI at Molodova V are with the Magdalenian and later Hamburgian of western Europe, for these were all communities with a hunting economy based on the reindeer. In spite of this, flint and bone industries of Russia have usually been referred to by Soviet archaeologists as local variants of the leptolithic traditions of France. Hence, the presence of leaf points = Solutrian, straight-backed blades = Gravettian, female figurines = Aurignacian, etc.

It has already been seen that the practice of using French terminology has drawbacks in describing the central and eastern European industries. The drawbacks increase with distance and it seems unwise to use French terms for the USSR industries. The alternative could be a classification in terms of early, middle and late Russian Upper Palaeolithic, but this implies a time or cultural sequence or both. The great variety of Russian Upper Palaeolithic industries defies, at present, any demonstrable technological succession, so there would be difficulties in using such subdivisions in anything but a temporal sense. The only satisfactory method is to take a few important sites which illustrate some of the developments in the region.

MOLODOVA V

This is one of the richest sites[31] in Western Russia, on the banks on the River Dniester. Eleven archaeological horizons within a body of loams and loess-like loams yield leptolithic industries, spanning a period of 20,000 years or more. Some of the major aspects of the stratigraphy are shown diagrammatically in Table 6.10. The Mousterian industry and dwelling found below the leptolithic industries have already been mentioned in the previous chapter, and are separated from them by a sterile zone which could represent several tens of thousands of years. Although there are obviously considerable time gaps between each leptolithic cultural level, there is nothing to dismiss the idea that they are a series of points in a long local succession.

The lowest Upper Palaeolithic level (X, see Table 6.10) contains an unusual tanged point with a very rounded point. The richest level is VII with a radiocarbon date of 21,750 ± 320 bc, contemporary with dates obtained for the Late Perigordian (Gravettian) of France. Levels I to III, are of Late Glacial age and are contemporary with the Magdalenian of France and eastern Europe.

There is a magnificent industry of bone and ivory throughout this sequence, including a few art objects such as a stylised mammoth statuette in level VIII and a human statuette in III. Particularly unusual are a series of lengths of mammoth rib that have been slotted as if to take some inset flint blades (Figure 57, no. 14).

Mammoth remains do not occur above level III and it is significant that there is an antler axe in the topmost level, for this is the time when such tools appeared in North West Europe.

KOSTIENKI-BORCHEVO

Over twenty individual sites have been investigated on the right bank of the River Don around three small villages: Kostienki, Alexsandrovka and Borchevo (alternative spellings: Kostenki, Borshevo), with only about 8 km between the furthest apart. The various archaeological levels are within loess-like loams and colluvial (i.e. slope wash) sediments on the low terraces of the river, at 15-20 m and 8-10 m above its present level (Figure 58).

Radiocarbon dates, quoted below, suggest a time span of 21,000-9,200

Figure 57: Upper Palaeolithic Industries of Russia

1.-3. Kostienki shouldered points, Kostienki I, level I. 4. Tanged bifacial leaf point, Molodova V, level X. 5. Part-bifacial leaf point, Telmanskaya, level I. 6. End scraper, Molodova V, level III. 7. Kostienki knife, Kostienki I, level I. 8. Unifacial leaf point, Molodova V, level X. 9. Mattock of mammoth tusk, Kostienki I, level I. 10. Axe-head, Kostienki I, level I. 11. Shouldered point, Molodova V, level VII. 12. Gravette point, Kostienki IV, level II. 13. Biserial bone harpoon, Molodova V, level Ia. 14. Slotted mammoth rib, Molodova V, level II.

(1-3, 5, 7, 12 after Klein, 1969a, and Efimenko, 1958; 4, 6, 8-9, 11, 13-14 after Coles and Higgs, 1969, and Chernysh, 1961; 10 after Semenov, 1964)

One of the best sequences is that from Molodova V, as shown in Table 6.10.

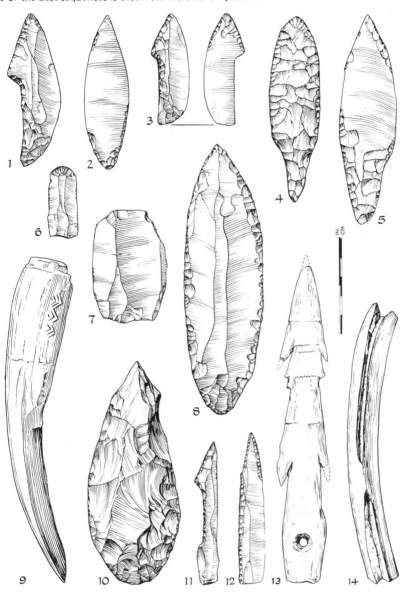

years BC. The lowermost industries, in spite of the relatively recent age, have Mousterian affinities, but so does one near the top of the sequence! Possible influence from a local, or intrusive, Mousterian survival cannot be discounted for the earlier group, but would be unlikely for the latter. In any case, there is a normal leptolithic industry at the same level as the earlier 'Mousterian'. The natural stratigraphy allows a good correlation of one site with another, and some of the important sites are shown in Figure 58. There is some doubt about the validity of the two humic layers, which could reflect on the date of the lowest leptolithic industry. Both humic layers may derive from the erosion of one earlier soil horizon.

Table 6.10: The Succession at Molodova V

Stratigraphy	Climate	Level	Aspects of Industry	Features	14 C Date bc
Chernozem soil					
	Late	I	antler axe		
	Glacial	I	biserial harpoon	traces of hut	$8,640 \pm 230$
		II	slotted mammoth ribs	hearths and	$9,850 \pm 200$
				hut	$9,950 \pm 230$
Loess-like loams		III	stylised human figurines	post holes and hearths	$11,740 \pm 540$
		IV	groove and splinter antler technique slotted mammoth ribs 'parrot-beaked' gravers	numerous hearths	
		V		numerous hearths	
		VI	slotted mammoth ribs	oval hut 7 x 4 m	
		VII	small shouldered points, tanged points in rich industry of blade cores, gravers, end scrapers, retouched blades, backed blades, awls, etc. perforated antler batons,		$21,750 \pm 320$
	Warmer		one with anthropomorphic engraving		
		VIII	mammoth statuette	18 hearths	
Palaeosol		IX	pestles, grindstones and ochre		
		X	bifacial tanged point sterile		
Palaeosol		XI		hearths	
	Warmer	XII		hut	
		XIIa		hearths	
Pebble beds of Last Interglacial Terrace					

The wealth of the stone industries is equalled by other important finds: magnificent remains of bone working, art objects including many Venus figurines, structural remains of dwellings and human burials. Some of the aspects of the flint industries are recorded in Figure 57 and Table 6.11.

Most of the usual range of leptolithic tool forms occur at various levels in varying proportions. The similarity of the Kostienki points to those at Willendorf in Austria does suggest some contact, but Jerzmanovician points could just as easily have evolved independently. Of especial interest is a flint axe-head, which is the earliest known example of a hafted axe in the world (Figure 57, no. 10). Microwear on the cutting edge has characteristic curved striations indicative of the tool being used in a haft.[32] It comes from Kostienki I, level I.[33]

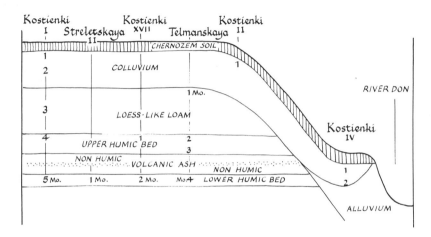

Figure 58: Diagram of Stratigraphy and Stone Industries in the Kostienki-Borchevo Complex of Sites
The numbers in the vertical columns are the level numbers for the individual sites named above them. Mo. beside the level number indicates a Mousterian industry. All other industries are of leptolithic type, but note the presence of a Mousterian industry (on grounds of typology) at the top of the loess-like loam at Telmanskaya.

There is a great diversity of stone and bone material within this sequence, as can be seen in Table 6.11.

Microwear studies have also demonstrated that the asymmetric Kostienki-Willendorf points were not necessarily projectile points but knives, the majority of the use being on the tip, and the shouldered part acting as a part to grip. Gravers would normally be inserted into handles to allow greater pressure to be exerted. Some microlithic points from Kostienki had been used as drills or awls, as micro-striations on the tip were circular along the line of movement. Micro-wear also demonstrated that numerous flakes had been used for meat cutting. Such studies are an important reminder that the names given to stone tools for the convenience of classification are not necessarily descriptive of their use. However, leaf points are generally regarded as projectile points, and it is consoling to know that, among the broken ones at Kostienki, stumps outnumber points. The latter were presumably lost in the chase.

Table 6.11: Sequence and Typology of Stone Industries at Kostienki-Borchevo

Stratigraphy (see Figure 58)	Levallois flakes	Mousterian points	Hollow-based leaf points	Bifacial leaf points	Jerzmanovice points	Kostienki-Willendorf points	Gravette points	Side scrapers	End scrapers	Nosed scrapers	Kostienki knives	Gravers	Retouched blades	Backed blades	Micro-backed blades
1. *Within colluvial deposits*															
Kostienki I – level I				X	X	X			X	X		X	X	X	X
Kostienki II – level I									X			X	X	X	
Kostienki IV – level I				X					X	X			X	X	X
Kostienki IV – level II							X			X			X	X	X
2. *At top of loess-like loam*															
Telmanskaya – level I	X	X		X	X			X				X	X		
3. *Within loess-like loam*															
Kostienki I – level III						X	X	X	X	X	X			X	X
4. *In Upper Humic Bed*															
Telmanskaya – level II									X	X			X	X	X
Telmanskaya – level III												X	X		
5. *In Lower Humic Bed*															
Kostienki I – level V	X	X	X					X	X	X			X	X	
Streletskaya II – level I		X						X	X					X	
Kostienki XVII – level II									X		X	X	X		

Table 6.12: Radiocarbon Dates of Kostienki-Borchevo Sites

Kostienki XIX		charred bone	12,070 ± 60 bc	(GIN – 86)
Kostienki II	level I	mammoth bone	10,050 ± 200 bc	(GIN – 93)
Kostienki I	level I	charred bone	9,850 ± 500 bc	(GIN – 107)
Kostienki XVII	level II	lower humic bed	18,150 ± 200 bc	(GIN – 78)
Kostienki XVII	level I	upper humic bed	18,050 ± 350 bc	(GIN – 77)
Kostienki XII		upper humic bed	21,110 ± 300 bc	(GIN – 89)

(GIN = Geological Institute Laboratory)

OTHER SITES

Many of the Russian sites are important for their remains of dwellings, which are described in the next chapter. Some other sites are listed here because they add to the pattern of distribution or are of special interest.

1. Babin, banks of the River Dneister: three occupational levels; leptolithic industries, the middle one with bifacial leaf points.

2. Byzovaia: an open site almost within the arctic circle at 65°N – the most northerly site known in Russia and the only one associated with the polar bear; few flint tools found but probably Late Glacial.

3. Podlouzhie, Byelorussia: the earliest Upper Palaeolithic site of this region, with Kostienki shouldered points. Probably equivalent in time to the warmer interval preceding the maximum of the Last Glaciation.

4. Radomishl, Ukraine: Mousterian and leptolithic forms are mixed at this site so it is regarded as a possible transitional industry.

5. Siuren, Crimea: a rock shelter with several levels of occupation. The upper layers have backed bladelets, Gravette-like points and gravers, and also a few Mousterian-type tools. Dufour bladelets and small Font Yves-type points are in the middle and lower layers, but any connection with their French counterparts is questionable. The upper part of the sequence is probably Late Glacial.

6. Soungir, near Vladimir, north east of Moscow at nearly 65°N: the industry here is remarkably similar to the Mousterian-like industry with hollow-based points at Kostienki, level V. It has been dated to 12,000 BC but this seems too recent.

LATE GLACIAL INDUSTRIES

These have already been mentioned as occurring in the upper levels at Kostienki and Molodova V. Several others exist and are characterised by the presence of reindeer but no mammoth. The industries include microlithic points and small scrapers, a tendency reminiscent of the Magdalenian-Azilian evolution in France. At Borcheroll, in the Kostienki group of sites, such an industry overlies a similar one *with* mammoth.

The disappearance or human extinction of the mammoth at this time may have coincided with a concentration in some areas on bison hunting. At Amyrocievkaya on the lower reaches of the Don, one of several sites in this region and along the northern shores of the sea of Azov, there is a ravine with great numbers of bison bones associated with a Last Glacial industry. It is estimated that about 1,000 beasts had been slaughtered.

Asia

The Near East

AMUDIAN (Figure 59)

This is the earliest leptolithic industry known in either Europe or Asia and has already been mentioned in the previous chapter because it is contemporary with transitional industries in the Near East. It may date to the beginning of the Last Glacial stage, and is separated from the later leptolithic industries described below by a long period of time. At Jabrud it is covered by 14 levels of Mousterian. The Amudian contains numerous backed blades and small, triangular unifacial points although it also contains pebble chopper-cores and small hand-axes. The type site is the Amud Cave beside Lake Tiberias but it is best represented at Adlum, Lebanon, in the Abri Zumoffen, where it lies on deposits of a 12-13 m raised beach and is covered by Jabrudian levels. It was formerly called Pre-Aurignacian.

ANTELIAN and ATLITIAN (or Near East Aurignacian)

There are rich leptolithic industries throughout the Levant, as revealed by excavations at such sites as El Wad at Mount Carmel, Abou Halka, Ksar' Akil and Rock Shelter no. 3 at Jabrud. The succession is complex and seems to vary from site to site. Six stages have been recognised, the first four of which would correspond with what was originally referred to as Aurignacian because of the general resemblance of the industries to the classic French ones. Of these four stages, the first two are now known as Lower Antelian, and the other two, as Upper Antelian.

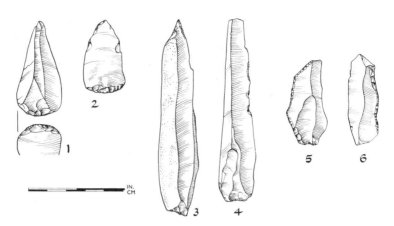

Figure 59: Earliest Leptolithic Industries of the Near East
1.-2. Emiran points, as found in the Lower Antelian industry of the Near East. They are small, Levallois pointed flake-blades with the butt trimmed from both sides. 1. Mugharet el Emirah. 2. Mount Carmel.
3.-6. Amudian industry. One of the earliest leptolithic industries in the world, possibly dating back to the end of the Last Interglacial. 3.-4. Haua Fteah, Cyrenaica. 5.-6. Abri Zumoffen, Lebanon.

Table 6.13: Stages of the Antelian Industry

Stage 1	A leptolithic industry with backed blades, scrapers and gravers, but also containing Mousterian-like points and scrapers and a distinctive piece termed an Emiran point (Figure 59). This is a Levallois pointed flake-blade with a bifacially trimmed butt.
Stage 2	Stratigraphically separated from the previous stage. Similar industry but no Emiran points and a few Mousterian elements.
Stage 3	Mousterian forms decrease even further. Numerous end scrapers and small backed blades resembling Font Yves points.
Stage 4	This industry bears the greatest resemblance to the Aurignacian of France, with nosed scrapers, busked gravers, truncated and backed blades. As in the previous stage, the bone industry is not well developed but there are some biconical points.
Stage 5	(Atlitian) Best represented at El Wad, overlying the previous stage. It contains high proportions of steep scrapers and gravers.

The major problem with this succession is really one of archaeological interpretation. These leptolithic industries are found within sediments that accumulated on uneven cave floors composed of the eroded occupational soils of earlier Mousterian levels. Further erosion took place during wet periods associated with the later industries, so it cannot be ruled out that some of the archaeological levels, or parts of them, were mixed by natural agencies, apart from any human disturbance. Thus, many of the Mousterian forms that occur in Stages 1 to 3 may not be part of those industries at all, but derived from earlier deposits.

There is an important site at Ksar' Akil in the Lebanon which has partly bifacial leaf points in the lowest levels and a Magdalenian-like industry at the top. Stage 4, Upper Antelian, is beneath a layer with a radiocarbon date of 26,500 ± 380 bc. At Abou Halka, also in the Lebanon, there are Emiran points in the bottom level but no other indication of Levallois technique, yet the latter occurs in the layer above it.

KEBARAN (Stage 6)

There are Late Upper Palaeolithic industries in this region which probably correspond in time to the Late Glacial industries of Europe. They have large numbers of small, backed blades and microliths. Variants have been termed the Skiftian and Nebekian. There can be little doubt that these industries developed into that of the Mesolithic Natufians in the Judean Desert who were on the fringe of domestication, agriculture and urbanisation.

The Middle East

BARADOSTIAN

Leptolithic industries in the Middle East are only known from the Zagros Mountains of Iraq and Iran, where water is plentiful and there are several natural rock shelters and caves. Although Mousterian industries occur in the same area there is no evidence for any continuity, nor are there any signs of the earlier Amudian blade industry of the Near East. Neither are Emiran points found. In spite of this, radiocarbon dates place the Baradostian between about 36,000 and 25,000 bc, but the early dates may be unreliable.

The richest sites are in the Khorramabad Valley of Luristan, Iran, at the caves of Yafteh, Gar Arjenah and Pa Sangar. There are gravers, side, end and nosed scrapers, backed bladelets and a distinctive 'Arjenah point', a small leaf-shaped point with flat retouching from both edges resembling a Font Yves or Krems point. There is little bonework, and there are no art objects, but a few pebble pounders and grinders were found, some of which had been used for crushing ochre pigment. At these sites it is possible that there was a continuation through until the later Zarzian industry, the latter being a natural evolutionary development from the Baradostian. Also, at Wawasi and Ghar-i-Khar near Kermanshah, the industry may have continued to exist in the region after the latest radiocarbon dates.

The origin of the industry is thought more likely to have been in the Caucasus region of Russia than in the Near East. Much further to the east, in Afghanistan, is a leptolithic industry with five radiocarbon dates all earlier than 32,000 bc. This is at the cave of Kara Kama, 14 km north of Haiback, where at least four archaeological levels have been identified. The lowest, on the cave bed-rock, contained only a few flakes, but within layers of loess above was an industry with flakes, blades and bladelets, several nosed scrapers and a few bone awls.

No gravers were found. A Mesolithic industry occurred at the top of the sequence. As with the Baradostian, this industry probably had its origins in Russia.

ZARZIAN

The type site is the Zarzi Cave in Iraq, where the industry occurs in a layer 1.5 m thick. At Shanidar Cave, Iraq, and at Wawasi, Ghar-i-Khar and Pa Sangar in Iran, it overlies the Baradostian. Radiocarbon dates extend back to about 10,000 bc but the industry could be earlier. It contains geometric microliths, micro-burins, gravers, end scrapers, distinctive notched blades, and a few shouldered points and bone awls. The rich Mesolithic sites around the Caspian shores at the Ali Tappeh, Belt and Hotu Caves have industries of similar type.

Table 6.14: Selected Radiocarbon Dates of Baradostian and Zarzian Industries

Baradostian				
Yafteh Cave	40,000 BP	(SI	—	335)
Yafteh Cave	32,850 ± 2,900 bc	(GX	—	711)
Yafteh Cave	27,460 ± 1,150 bc	(SI	—	332)
Shanidar Cave	33,490 ± 600 bc	(GrN	—	2016)
Shanidar Cave	31,350 ± 1,000 bc	(W	—	650)
Zarzian				
Shanidar Cave	10,050 ± 400 bc	(W	—	179)

(Laboratories: GrN = Groningen, GX = Geochron, SI and W = Smithsonian Institute)

The Far East and Siberia. The Late Pleistocene archaeology of India, China and the rest of the Far East is very different from that of Europe, Africa and the Near and Middle East. It was noted in the last chapter that earlier stone-working traditions persisted when, elsewhere, transitional industries developed. In Europe and Africa the evidence suggests movements of people, the spread of new ideas and the gradual formation in most areas of advanced hunting communities with leptolithic stone industries designed to meet new demands in weapons and hunting equipment. Change varied in pace and intensity from one region to another. In the Far East the pattern appears to have been a steadier continuity and uniformity. Contact with the rest of the world was minimal and population movements restricted for the most part to within the sub-continental peninsula. Basic chopper-core traditions sufficed, although Levallois technique was sometimes used, occasionally with sophisticated results. This was more likely to have been independent invention (i.e. convergence) than a borrowed idea, but it never seems to have caused any fundamental changes. Blades were produced at times but no true leptolithic industry developed. Only in the northernmost area of Mongolia is there any more definite sign of a diffusion of ideas from the technologically advanced west.

Industries found in the Ordos Desert, sometimes called Ordosian, contain Mousterian forms and true blade forms,[34] but the latter must relate to the very late Upper Palaeolithic of Siberia which will be described briefly below. Only at the very end of the Pleistocene, in the equivalent of Late Glacial times, did leptolithic industries spread to any extent into the Far East and they never seem to have expanded as they did in so many other regions, with all their manifestations of progress towards larger communities with relatively stable economies. One, if not the main, reason for such a difference could have been the lack of necessity for change: the Far East was less affected by climatic changes during the Last Glaciation, and simple hunting groups with chopper-core industries were coping with their environment quite successfully. The adoption of new hunting techniques such as poison-tipped barbed spears was doubtless welcomed, but the economy was not radically altered; they only meant, presumably, an easier method of obtaining the same animals. The economy was not based on vast herds of migrating beasts. In the tropical regions roots, fruits and vegetables probably supplied the bulk of the food.

In the absence of sealed sites and radiocarbon dates it is not often possible to know whether the first leptolithic industries in the Far East are very Late Pleistocene or post-Pleistocene, and hence Mesolithic by definition. This applies particularly to India, where such industries occur at numerous sites in Kashmir, Potwar, Narmada River basin, Bihar and Chittoor district. At Singhbhum, Bihar, an industry with gravers overlies a flake industry described as Late Soan or Indian Middle Stone Age. Three stratified layers, all with leptolithic industries, occur in deposits of the Belan river in Allahabad district. The lowest is mixed with 'Middle Stone Age', and the top contains microliths. This site is thought to show a local evolution. Bone points and harpoons have been found in Kashmir and in the Billa Surgam Cave, Kurnool, but could be Mesolithic.

In Java, there is the famous site at Ngandong where eleven human skulls were found. The dating is broadly Late Pleistocene and the industry associated is a rather undiagnostic one of small flakes and blades of chalcedony, some worked as scrapers or borers.[35] Spines of sting-ray tails may have been used as barbs in the same manner as microliths, and some deer antlers could have been picks. If a biserial barbed bone point is really associated, a very late date, if not post-glacial, is inferred. This has important implications because of the nature of the skulls for, although classified as *Homo sapiens*, they have strong supra-orbital ridges and features that are reminiscent of *erectus* or *neanderthalensis*. However, there is no reason for implying that the lack of leptolithic industries is a result of the absence of true *sapiens*, because in not too distant Borneo, in the cave of Niah, a skull of *Homo sapiens sapiens* has been found in a level radiocarbon dated to about 38,000 bc, associated with pebble tools and large flakes.

Leptolithic industries reached Japan about 11,000-10,000 bc on the basis of radiocarbon dating. At Shirataki, Hokkaido, there is a stratified sequence in sediments of the Yubetsu River.[36] There are retouched blades and gravers made on obsidian and some large leaf points. At Iawjaku, large blades and partly polished bifacial tools occur at a level radiocarbon dated to earlier than 11,000 bc. Such industries may be the earliest in Japan, although a few surface finds of coarse flakes and pick-like forms may be even earlier. There are also a few possible flakes from river deposits at Torigasiki and Tamatsukuri-Miyagaki, and a few others from near Izumo in terrace gravels containing volcanic ash radiocarbon dated to 28,650 ± 3,600 bc and 15,050 ± 400 bc.

In China, microlithic industries occur in the loess that was deposited at the very end of the Last Glaciation. An industry at Sjara-osso-gol in the southern Ordos Desert is contained within lake sediments associated with woolly rhinoceros and mammoth. It is non-leptolithic although the artifacts are small, including unifacial points and scrapers. In spite of its late date it could be described as a transitional industry. Similarly, the industry from the upper cave at Choukoutien is only composed of chipped pebbles and flakes of quartzite and chert, with some scrapers and knives, yet is Late or even post-Pleistocene in date. The presence of a long bone needle, beads of bone, tooth, shell and bone, some painted red, is more in keeping with a later date.

SIBERIAN UPPER PALAEOLITHIC

The large area of central Siberia around Lake Baikal and in the valleys of the great rivers Lena, Angara and Yenesei has produced numbers of rich Upper Palaeolithic sites. Although little is yet known of the earlier episodes, this must rank as one of the more important centres in the world for this period. There are several indications of connections with the Russian sites west of the Ural Mountains: subterranean dwellings, mammoth bone structures and a rich bone industry including female figurines and animal statuettes.[37] Most of the known sites are of late date, probably extending into Late Glacial times, but others are deep in loess with the archaeological horizons sometimes distorted by ice wedges. Few sites are above Latitude 61 but undiscovered sites could exist there as the area has been submerged since the Last Glaciation.

The great interest of the stone industries is their combination of true leptolithic and Mousterian traditions. It is possible that there was both a local development from the latter and an influence from the west for the former. One of the most famous sites is Malta, west of Lake Baikal on the River Belava, a tributary of the Angara. The industry, at a depth of about 1 m in loess, is basically Mousterian, with tortoise cores and Mousterian points, but also blades, scrapers, gravers and leaf points. Bonework included needles, points, awls, figurines and two rare antler handles, one with a retouched flint blade inserted, probably to serve as a chisel. A similar industry was found at Buret, also in the Angara Basin.

Several sites have also been found between the Altai Mountains and Lake Baikal, well represented by the cave at Ust' Kanskaya, probably of Late Glacial age. The industry includes Levallois flakes, discoidal cores, Mousterian points, side scrapers, large blades, a few gravers and some crude bifacial leaf points, also bone points and pendants.

The site of Afontara Gora on the Yenesei has yielded a similar industry with the addition of end scrapers, small backed bladelets and microliths, with bone needles, awls and ground points.

North Africa

ATERIAN

The sequence of stone industries from Egypt to Morocco, along the Mediterranean coast and its hinterland, is markedly different from that on the European side. This suggests that contact, if any, was minimal. The stone industries have their origins within the African continent or are apparently intrusive from the Near East. The Aterian is found mainly north and east of the Atlas Mountains, from Tunisia to Morocco, but it also extends across much of what is now the Sahara Desert and as far east as the Nile. It is not a leptolithic blade industry and really belongs with what have been described in the previous chapter as transitional industries. The survival of earlier Palaeolithic traditions is shown by the continued use of Levallois technique, so that the industry contains numerous miniature discoid and other prepared cores, and flake-blades with faceted striking platforms. The characteristic piece, however, is a tanged point; these are sometimes so small that they may have been arrowheads.[38] The majority would presumably have tipped spears; they have distinctive wide tangs and rather obtuse points (Figure 51). There are also bifacial leaf points, various flake tools and even an occasional small hand-axe.

The type site of the Aterian is Bir El Ater in southern Tunisia, where the industry is found within alluvium. Three phases of the industry have been identified in excavations at the cave of Taforalt in Oran. An Early Aterian is found at a coastal site in Morocco, Dar es Soltan, within a red loam containing a fauna reminiscent of the earlier part of the Late Pleistocene, and the radiocarbon date suggests an age greater than 30,000 years. The industry may extend even further back in time than this and, in the other direction, it may have continued in parts of North Africa until the equivalent of post-glacial times. In stratified contexts, leptolithic industries lie above the Aterian, but these spread slowly and, in North West Africa, only began partly to replace the Aterian from about 16,000 BC. Its distribution across the Sahara to its southern limits must have coincided with the wetter conditions of the final part of the Late Pleistocene, probably equivalent to the time of maximum glaciation in Europe.

The Aterian has affinities with the Lupemban industry of central Africa which is another survival of earlier stone-working techniques. It is contemporary with it, and both the Aterian and the Lupemban have their roots in the Sangoan with its Acheulian traditions. The typology indicates an apparently unbroken evolution from the end of the Middle Pleistocene, but there was no evolution of leptolithic industries in this sequence and it can be inferred that there was no corresponding cultural evolution of the hunting groups.

DABBAN

The type site of this true, early leptolithic industry is the cave of Hagfet ed Dabba in Cyrenaica, about 20 km inland from the coast. Two phases are represented there, and in the lower one there are backed blades and a very distinctive form of graver (Figure 51, no. 10) which is also known from the Lower Antelian Upper Palaeolithic industry of Palestine. This could indicate a likely place of origin for the community which settled in this cave. The later phase contains a greater number of scrapers.

Only 60 km distant from this site is the great coastal cave of Haua Fteah.[39] Large-scale excavations and detailed analyses of the material have produced the most important and detailed sequences of industries known from any site in North Africa, and it has already been mentioned in connection with transitional industries and a very early blade industry known as the Amudian. Figure 60 shows the main succession of industries at Haua Fteah, with assessments of dating based on radiocarbon and rates of sediment accumulation, together with the mean annual temperatures calculated from oxygen isotope analysis of shells. The gradual rise in temperature in the upper half of the sequence coincides with a drastic decrease in the numbers of large animals such as horses, wild cattle and antelopes, while goats correspondingly increase. The section shows the long succession of archaeological levels with a Dabban industry, ranging from about 38,000 to 12,000 years BC.

The Dabban has the usual leptolithic tool forms: backed blades, scrapers, gravers of normal type and a microlithic element. The specialised 'Emiran-type'

Figure 60: Diagram of the Sequence at Haua Fteah

At least 12 m of occupational deposits fill the great cave of Haua Fteah in Cyrenaica, representing the richest and most complete succession for the latter part of the Late Pleistocene in North Africa. The lowest industry, the Amudian, contains true blades and is the earliest leptolithic industry of the region, possibly in the world.

The climate is deduced from oxygen isotope analyses of marine shells found in the deposits. The temperature curve appears to reflect the climatic changes of the Last Glaciation, although at such a southern latitude there were no harsh, cold periods. Mammalian faunas vary in proportion through the sequence: large bovids and gazelles were far more abundant during the warmer, drier periods.

(After McBurney, 1967)

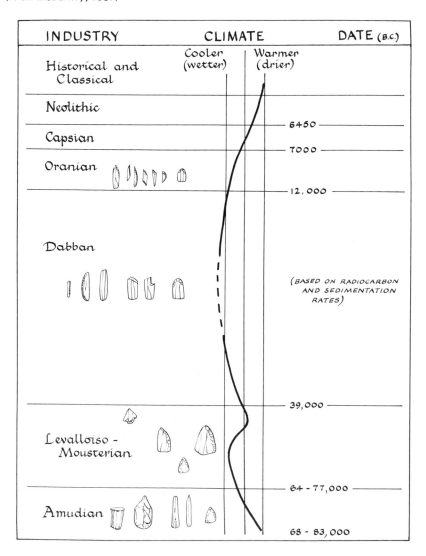

transverse gravers are restricted to the lowest levels, where there are many backed blades but few gravers and scrapers; whereas in the upper levels there are many more scrapers and, surprisingly, fewer microliths. Bone tools are present throughout, but the industry is not very well developed.

ORANIAN

This is a microlithic blade industry that belongs to the final stages of the Upper Palaeolithic of North West Africa, partly contemporary with Aterian survivals, and continuing into the Mesolithic period. Radiocarbon dates suggest it may have arrived in the region about 16,000 years BC. At Haua Fteah it overlies the Dabban at about 12,000 BC and there is a date of about 10,000 BC from the Taforalt Cave. It is the first known leptolithic industry in the Maghreb and is well represented in the upper silts of Sidi Mansur, near Gafsa, in Tunisia, where there are many backed blades of microlithic form, including oblique points, crescents, trapezes and other geometric forms (Figure 51). Micro-burin technique was practised, an ingenious method of snapping off the thick, irregular bulbous ends of micro-blades in order to produce microliths. The bone industry was mainly restricted to simple awls and projectile points. The type site is La Mouilla, Oran, hence the name, although the industry is sometimes referred to as 'Ibero-Maurusian'.

SEBILIAN

The uppermost silts of the Nile Valley in the region of Kom Omo are up to 6 m thick and contain numerous stone artifacts of the very Late Pleistocene. The presence of small Levallois cores and flake-blades indicates the long survival of this technique in Egypt. Various distinctive assemblages have been recognised and given names and one of them, the Sebilian, has been considered a local leptolithic development from surviving Levallois-type industries. Other influences seem more likely, as it contains many microlithic forms. However, it seems to cover a range of time of about 14,000 to 9000 BC and thus be contemporary with the Oranian. Another microlithic industry, the Sebekian, is radiocarbon dated to earlier than 12,050 BC, but others, the Silsilian and Menchian, are more likely to be of the Early Mesolithic period.

Southern Africa

HOWIESON'S POORT INDUSTRY

This industry could be regarded as a variant of the Magosian but it is known by this name in South Africa. It has already been mentioned in the previous chapter because, although it is a true leptolithic industry, it has been found wedged into the sequence of a transitional Middle Stone Age industry. Radiocarbon dating and stratigraphical evidence convincingly put the Howieson's Poort in Cape Province back to 70,000 years or more, perhaps even to the equivalent of the end of the Last Interglacial period. If radiocarbon samples from the type site are not contaminated, then the industry had a very long existence until about 17,000 bc. It is earlier than any other leptolithic industry in the world apart from the Amudian of the Near East and North Africa, with which it could be contemporary. At Klasies River Mouth, Eastern Cape, the Howieson's Poort is found beneath one of the shelters, stratified above a long succession of Middle Stone Age industries, in black and white ashy layers about 1.5 m thick. These, in turn, are covered by sandier levels with further Middle Stone Age non-leptolithic industries. There is no evidence to indicate any significant interval of time between these different industries, either below or above the Howieson's Poort. Nor is there any indication that the Middle Stone Age evolved into the Howieson's Poort, or that the latter had any influence on the later Middle Stone Age above. It seems to be a clear example of intrusion and departure by people with greatly contrasting industrial traditions and it is tantalising not to know anything of the dramatic scenes that may have ensued because of it.

The origin of this industry may have been in South Africa, although obviously not at the site above, for at the Border Cave in Natal it has been claimed that a similar industry (referred to as Epi-Pietersburg) actually evolved from the underlying Middle Stone Age. The industry overlies an Acheulian one at Montagu Cave, but there was probably a long time interval between them. At Skildergat Cave, Fish Hoek, and in the Cave of Hearths, Makapansgat, it is found above a 'Stillbay' Middle Stone Age.

Although so early, the industry contains nearly all the tool types and techniques found in leptolithic industries (Figure 61). Blades and bladelets, struck from small prismatic cores, were fashioned into scrapers and gravers, but the main feature of the industry is the number of small backed blades of crescentic or trapezoidal form, sometimes of microlithic dimensions. Micro-burin technique was known. Strangulated bladelets, notched flakes and various semi-specialised forms occur. At the type site there are numerous small triangular bifacial points but these do not occur at Klasies River Mouth nor at the Montagu Cave. At the latter site there are also flake-blades and partly retouched points of Middle Stone Age type. Such differences do little to dispel the homogeneity of the industry which contrasts so greatly with the transitional Middle Stone Age with which it must have long been contemporary.

Table 6.15: Selected Radiocarbon Dates for Howieson's Poort Industries in South Africa

Montagu Cave	43,950 ± 2,100 bc	(GrN	—	4728)
	21,250 ± 180 bc	(GrN	—	4726)
Howieson's Poort	16,790 ± 320 bc	(I	—	1844)
Rose Cottage Cave, Ladybrand	>48,250 bc	(Pta	—	213)
	>42,500 bc	(Pta	—	214)
Klasies River Mouth	>30,050 bc	(GX	—	1376)
	>33,050 bc	(GX	—	1380)
	>36,180 bc	(GX	—	0983)

(Laboratories: GrN = Groningen, I = Isotopes Inc., Pta = Pretoria, GX = Geochron.)
N.b. The high dates are probably best regarded as minimum dates.

MAGOSIAN

This term has been used to cover a number of industries found between the Cape and Somaliland, including the Howieson's Poort noted above. The elements in common (blades and bladelets, crescents and trapezes often microlithic, scrapers, gravers, etc.) seem to justify some such term under which these widespread industries can be grouped, but many of the occurrences are undated and this term may be blanketing a more complex sequence. It may also be suggesting a uniformity over much of Africa which never really existed but, conversely, there

Figure 61: Howieson's Poort Industry, Klasies River Mouth, South Africa
This is one of the earliest leptolithic industries in the world, dating back to about 70,000
years or more, many thousands of years before anything similar in Europe. It was contemporary with Middle Stone Age (MSA) industries in the same part of Africa which concentrated on heavy flake-blades produced by Levallois technique.
1.-4., 14. Trapezes. 5., 15. Triangles. 6.-13. Crescents. 16.-19. Obliquely blunted blades.
20.-23. Aberrant, notched forms of backed blades. 24. Micro-burin. 25. Small bifacial tool,
possibly a wedge. 26. Distinctive form of 'outil écaillé', also possibly used as a wedge.
27.-28. Micro-gravers. 29.-33. Blades. 34.-35. Blades with hollows (34 — strangulated scraper).
36. Rounded end scraper.
(After Wymer and Singer, in press)

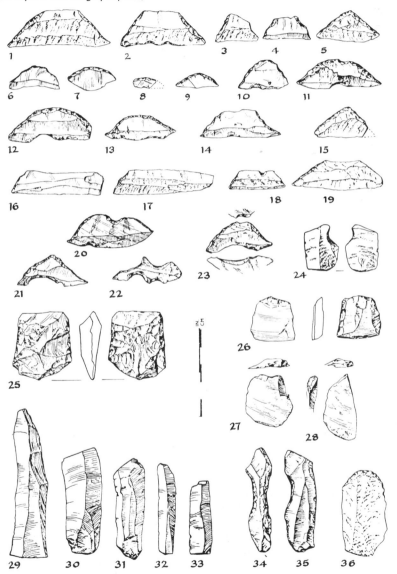

could have been a high degree of cultural uniformity. The similarities of the industries at sites so far apart as Porc Epic in Somaliland, Pomongwe, Sawmills and Khami in Rhodesia, and the Howieson's Poort of the Cape cannot be overlooked, yet radiocarbon dates are conflicting. The Magosian levels at Pomongwe Cave are radiocarbon dated to as recent as 13,850 ± 200 bc (SR — 11). Similar industries are known from Kenya and Tanzania, although the type site is Magosi in Uganda, about 250 km north of Mount Elgon. At this site it overlies a type of Middle Stone Age industry known as 'Stillbay'. There can be little doubt that Magosian industries originated in Africa from Middle Stone Age traditions, but whether this happended in one or more areas, or at the same time or at very different times, is not known. It is also unknown whether it penetrated north of the Sahara and Sudan Deserts or had any influence on developments in the Near East and North Africa. However, the very early dates for its South African equivalent, the Howieson's Poort, make this a strong possibility. Certainly, Africa can claim to have as early an expression of leptolithic traditions as anywhere else in the world, if not the earliest.

ROBBERG INDUSTRY

This is named after the Robberg Peninsula which juts into Plettenberg Bay in Cape Province. Several coastal caves exist, and the Nelson Bay Cave has produced some of the only evidence for post-Middle Stone Age non-Magosian industries in the whole of South Africa.[40] Although Magosian industries appear to have developed from Middle Stone Age ones, it is clear that this did not happen everywhere, and the latter tradition persisted. For how long is not known, and it may be very significant that where any such later Middle Stone Age industry is found, such as at Klasies River Mouth, there is generally a hiatus between it and succeeding Later Stone Age industries. At Nelson Bay Cave the hiatus probably represents a time gap of 10,000-15,000 years. At Klasies River Mouth it may have been 50,000 years. Only at Border Cave in Natal and Boomplaas Cave in the Cape does a Later Stone Age industry appear to occur directly after the Middle Stone Age, and there is little or no sign of any connection or continuity between them. The name Robberg industry has been given to these Later Stone Age industries which predate the Smithfield and Wilton Later Stone Age industries of South Africa. They seem to bridge the gap between them and the Middle Stone Age, from perhaps 40,000 to 12,000 years ago. Compared to the preceding and probably contemporary Magosian industries, the Robberg is an impoverished one, mainly of flakes and scrapers, but with a leptolithic element.

Very little is known of this period in South Africa or further north. Nothing seems to have taken the place of the highly successful Middle Stone Age economy, and the continent was no longer in the centre of advancement. One reason may have been the dependence on marine sources of food. The recession of the coastline in the latter part of the Last Glaciation could have gradually destroyed the economy.

Australia

There were no leptolithic industries in the whole of this continent prior to the world-wide amelioration of climate after about 8500 BC, i.e. the equivalent of the end of the Last Glaciation in the northern hemisphere and a convenient point to close the Palaeolithic, in the temporal sense if not a cultural one.

Neothermal is perhaps a better term to describe the post-glacial period, which continues to the present day, as it does not imply in these southern latitudes the previous existence of ice sheets.

The prehistory of Australia is probably the best example in the world of the survival of human hunting groups with economies and traditions that may have changed very little from a long way back in the Palaeolithic period. The continent was first occupied about 40,000 years ago, presumably when the sea level was low enough to allow a relatively easy passage from Indonesia. This is a time which accords well with population movements on a grand scale, in terms of distance if not of numbers, and it must reflect the outer ripples of developments in the western world, including much of Africa. With some minor differences, which could be regarded as local idiosyncrasies, these earliest stone industries in Australia can be classified as chopper-core industries. There is much less emphasis on the chopper element and more on the use of simple flakes, modified or not into unspecialised tool forms. These continued well into neothermal times and, in Tasmania, into historical times. The Australian and Tasmanian aborigines must be classified as *Homo sapiens sapiens*, even if they possessed some traits more reminiscent of *erectus*.

The earliest dates for human occupation in the continent are based not on archaeological material but on a veritable cemetery at Lake Mungo in New South Wales.[41] Radiocarbon indicates an age of about 32,000 years for the first burials, and a later date of about 25,000 years for an actual human cremation, the earliest known example in the world of this method of disposal of the dead. The individuals were of modern type, unlike those in a later series of burials at Kow Swamp, described below. The earliest radiocarbon dates for archaeological sites come from flakes and rock shelters in the north, particularly at Malanganerr, Arnhem Land. In the lower, unstratified sands beneath the shelter is an industry of simple cores, flakes and unspecialised modified pieces conveniently described as scrapers. Radiocarbon dates are:

20,950 ± 1000 bc (ANU – 77b)
20,750 ± 700 bc (GaK – 628)
17,650 ± 700 bc (GaK – 729)
16,050 ± 400 bc (ANU – 19)

In spite of the simple industry there is one form of specialised tool that also occurs which, in some respects, is more advanced than contemporary industries elsewhere in the world: a ground edge axe (Figure 62). These are made of fine-grained volcanic rocks with a cutting edge produced by laborious grinding of two edges. They also have shallow grooves pecked or ground on them to facilitate hafting. Similar artifacts are known from the eastern highlands of New Guinea, and they also occur at a few other Australian sites with early radiocarbon dates, e.g. Nawamoyn (with flakes and core tools): 19,500 ± 380 bc (ANU – 51).

A similar time range is represented by the Oenpelli site at the northern extremity of the continent, which also has ground edge axes. As these tools have not yet been found on more recent radiocarbon-dated sites it seems that their presence may indicate a particular migration into the continent by hunting groups familiar with their manufacture and use, the art of which was gradually lost.

Figure 62: The Earliest Industries of Australia

1. Grooved and ground edge axe of hornfels, Malangangerr, Northern Territory, a site radiocarbon dated to 16,000-18,000 BC.
2. Small, thick scraper, Green Gully, Keilor, Victoria (radiocarbon date: 15,350 ± 700 bc (V-73)).
3. Grooved and ground edge axe of prophyritic dolerite, Nawamoyn, Northern Territory (radiocarbon date: 19,500 ± 380 bc (ANU-51)).
4. Horsehoof core, Kenniff Cave, Queensland (radiocarbon date: 10,600 ± 110 bc (NPL-10)). The axes of fine-grained rock are the earliest known examples in the world of the technique of producing a sharp edge by grinding. Surprisingly, this innovation was not developed for such axes do not occur in later Australian industries. The technique was not used again until the post-glacial period in the Mesolithic industries of some European countries.

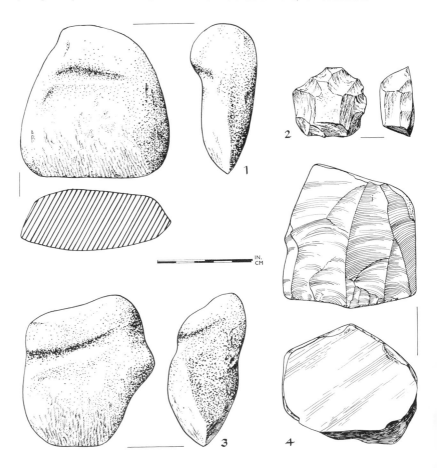

A few artifacts in the silts which contained a human skull at Keilor, Victoria, are about 2 m above a radiocarbon sample giving a date of 18,000 ± 500 bc (NZ – 207), but such silts can accumulate very rapidly and the artifacts and skull may not be much younger. At Green Gully, also at Keilor,[42] there is another radiocarbon date of 15,350 ± 700 bc (V – 73) associated with a flake industry with large side scrapers and other worked flakes. Other radiocarbon dates from Noola and Lake Menindee, New South Wales, and Kenniff Cave, Queensland, range between 17,000 and 10,000 bc. There is thus good evidence for the Late Pleistocene occupation of Australia by unspecialised hunting groups, although in some respects they could be regarded as 'transitional'.

America

PALAEO-INDIAN INDUSTRIES

The characteristic products of Palaeo-Indian industries are various forms of elegant bifacially flaked points (Figure 63). These have been found in a few contexts radiocarbon dated to about 10,000 BC, and have been regarded as the earliest definite evidence for the human occupation of the New World. There are three reasons for doubting that this is so; and concluding that the American continent was discovered several thousands of years earlier:

1. earlier radiocarbon dates have been obtained from isolated finds of stone tools or human remains;
2. the sites dated to about 10,000 bc are far south in New Mexico;
3. the ice barrier between the New and Old Worlds may not have been removed before about 6500 bc.

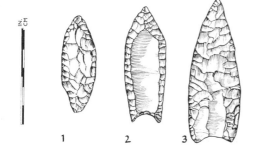

Figure 63: Palaeo-Indian Leaf Points of America
1. Clovis point, Dent, Colorado.
2. Folsom point, Lindenmeir, Colorado.
3. Sandia point, Sandia, New Mexico.
(1-2 after Heinzelin de Braucourt, 1962, and Lorenzo, 1958; 3 after Coles and Higgs, 1969, and Willey, 1966)

There can be little doubt that the migration route from Asia was overland, and this could only be across what is now the Bering Straits or along the Aleutian Islands at a time of low sea level. The world-wide drop in sea level at the maximum of the Last Glaciation would have produced a land passage but, at the same time, created an impregnable barrier of ice across Alaska. This barrier was the result of two major ice sheets, the Cordilleran ice sheet of the United States and the

Keewatin ice sheet of Canada. These are known to have coalesced, but are thought to have melted sufficiently by about 10,000 BC for an ice-free corridor to form between them. This would have allowed migration from Asia, but it does not explain how sites immediately appear in New Mexico with distinctive projectile points. If the ice corridor was not open until very much later, as geologists now consider, the only explanation is that hunters arrived in America prior to the formation of this impassable ice sheet. This may not have been before 23,000 BC, although it has been suggested that Beringia was possibly too swampy after 33,000 BC to permit migration. However, a date of about 25,000-20,000 is feasible, and would fit well with the earliest Siberian Upper Palaeolithic. This would imply that hunting communities which reached America at about this time would be cut off from Asia until well into post-glacial times, and their stone industries could be expected to develop independently. The early Siberian Upper Palaeolithic (see above) contained both Mousterian and lepto-lithic elements, and a strong tradition of leaf points. This is exactly how the Palaeo-Indian industries could be described and it is unlikely to be a coincidence.

The earliest radiocarbon date for a site with projectile points is Fort Rock, Oregon: 11,250 ± 720 bc. If the earlier chronology is correct there is no difficulty in accepting this. It also explains the distribution of hunters down the west coast of South America as far as Patagonia to the very southern tip at Tierra del Fuego, with several sites radiocarbon dated to about 10,000 BC and earlier. The puzzle is why sites have not been discovered with much earlier dates. Early dates do exist for some of the sites, but the association between the dated samples and the industries is usually suspect. At Hueyatlaco in Mexico, unifacial leaf points and flakes associated with horse, camel and mastodon underlay other levels with bifacial tools and points. Shells, thought to be associated, gave a radiocarbon date of 19,900 ± 850 bc. Similarly, at Tlapacoya near Mexico City, a stone blade was found beneath a fallen tree and dated to 21,000 ± 950 bc. A hearth found in a beach deposit gave a date of 22,050 ± 4000 bc. A human skull from Los Angeles is dated to about 20,000 BC and there is the strange discovery of the remains of an infant of about one year old at a site in Alberta, beneath 9 m of till at a depth of 18 m.[43] Unfortunately, the bones were too small to use for radiocarbon dating.

At Ranco le Brea, Los Angeles, there are famous tar pits containing huge quantities of bones from animals trapped within them. These appear to extend back in time through much of the Late Pleistocene. Excavations are in progress and, although only a few stone tools and a woman's skull have yet been found in the uppermost levels, radiocarbon dated to 7050 ± 80 bc,[44] earlier archaeological material may be discovered.

The earliest assemblages which can be considered as industries are the Llano Complex, of Texas and New Mexico. At the Sandia Cave in New Mexico, distinctive Sandia points (Figure 63) are found stratified with an extinct fauna including mammoth, mastodon, camel, horse and bison, below other occupational levels with Folsom points, still containing mammoth. Folsom points also occur stratified above Clovis points at Blackwater Draw, New Mexico. Clovis points are particularly distinctive and have been found over most of North and Central America.

There is considerable variation from site to site, but Palaeo-Indian industries generally consist of flakes and blades, side and end scrapers, rare gravers, choppers and grinding stones, apart from various types of points. The bone industry was simple, mainly restricted to awls and points, and there are no art objects. It is particularly significant that small-backed blades and microliths are not part of the equipment, whereas these tend to dominate all the later leptolithic industries of the Old World.

The Palaeo-Indian period represents a remarkable phase in human history: the opening up of a vast continent by advanced hunting communities. The manner in which these spread with rapidity from one end to the other reflects the energy and organisation of these peoples.

Notes

1. Hammen, Maarleveld, Vogel and Zagwijn, 1967; Waterbolk, 1972.
2. Movius, David, Bricker and Clay, 1968.
3. Bordes, 1950.
4. Mellars, 1973.
5. Peyrony, 1934.
6. Lacaille, 1947.
7. Lynch, 1966.
8. Movius, 1975, 1977.
9. Lacorre, 1960.
10. Movius, 1975.
11. Robins, Seeley, McNeil and Symons, 1978.
12. P.E.L. Smith, 1966.
13. Capitan and Peyrony, 1928.
14. Desbrosse, 1976.
15. Schmider, 1971; Delporte, 1976.
16. Leroi-Gourhan, Brézillon and Schmider, 1976.
17. Simonnet, 1976.
18. Obermeier, 1924.
19. Garcia, 1942.
20. Moure-Romanillo and Cano-Herrera, 1979.
21. Cardini, 1930.
22. Otte, 1977.
23. Freund, 1952.
24. Vértes, 1955.
25. Chmielewski, 1961.
26. Felgenhauer, 1959.
27. Merk, 1876.
28. Rust, 1937.
29. Rust, 1943.
30. Rust, 1958.
31. Chernysh, 1961.
32. Semenov, 1964.
33. Efimenko, 1958.
34. Chang, 1977.
35. Movius, 1949.
36. Serizawa and Ikawa, 1960.
37. Coles and Higgs, 1969, pp. 341-8; Mongait, 1961, p. 98.
38. Tixier, 1961.
39. McBurney, 1967.
40. Klein, 1974.
41. Barbetti and Allen, 1972.
42. Gill, 1966.
43. Bryan, 1969, p. 344.
44. Oakley, Campbell and Molleson, 1975.

References

The later chapters of most of the general works mentioned in the bibliographies for Chapters 3-5 contain details and references for this period, although surprisingly there is no one book devoted just to this period in all its aspects. Summaries of the French sites, with original references, are given by regions in H. de Lumley (ed.), *La Préhistoire Française*, vol. 2 (1976). The French sites of the Périgord region are superbly documented in great detail in two large volumes by D. de Sonneville-Bordes, *Le Paléolithique Supérieur en Périgord* (1960), although numerous fresh discoveries have been made since their publication. Reports on individual sites in Europe, USSR, the Near East, Africa and elsewhere are contained in a multitude of monographs or articles within the proceedings of learned societies, usually in the language of the country concerned. The majority of the sites are described in the books or papers listed below, but references to some of the more significant aspects are indicated by numbers in the text. There is also an exhaustive bibliography of the European Upper Palaeolithic by Schmider (1975). The subject of Upper Palaeolithic art, however, is dealt with comprehensively by many publications, ranging from large, expensive, finely produced volumes by authorities, to numbers of humbler but good and readable books. In the former category, all in English editions, are: H. Breuil, *Four Hundred Centuries of Cave Art* (1952), P. Graziozi, *Palaeolithic Art* (1960) and A. Leroi-Gourhan, *The Art of Prehistoric Man in Western Europe* (1967). A detailed survey of the possible interpretations of Palaeolithic art is provided by P. Ucko and A. Rosenfeld in their *Palaeolithic Cave Art* (1967). A. and G. Sieveking, *The Caves of France and Northern Spain* (1962) is an indispensable guide if visiting those sites, and something of the thrill of discovery and the mystery of many of the sites is conveyed by N. Casteret in his *Ten Years Under the Earth* (1952). A. Sieveking's *The Cave Artists* (1979) is an excellent recent survey, well illustrated and authoritative.

Listed below are some references mainly to general surveys of regions, in which details can be found of most of the Upper Palaeolithic sites mentioned in this chapter. Coles and Higgs (1969) also includes many of them.

France:	Lumley, 1976a; Bourdier, 1967.
Spain:	Obermeier, 1924.
Germany:	Schwabedissen, 1954.
Central and Eastern Europe:	Chmielewski, 1961; Valoch, 1968.
Denmark:	Becker, 1971.
Russia:	Sulimirski, 1970; Klein, 1969b; Kernd'l, 1963; Boriskovsky, 1958; Ranov, 1974; Mongait, 1961.
Near East:	Howell, 1959; Garrod, 1955a; Garrod and Kirkbride, 1961.
Iran:	Hole and Flannery, 1967; P.E.L. Smith, 1971.
India:	Murty, 1969; Ghosh, 1969.
Afghanistan:	Allchin and Hammond (eds), 1978.
China:	Chang, 1977.
Southern Africa:	Sampson, 1974; Mason, 1962; Clark, 1959.
Northern Africa:	Alimen, 1957; McBurney, 1960; Thompson, 1946.
Australia:	Allchin, 1957; Mulvaney, 1975.
America:	Willey, 1966; Bryan, 1969; Lorenzo, 1958.
Britain:	Bonsall, 1977; Campbell, 1977; Mellars, 1974.

Chapter 7

Advanced Hunting Communities of the Upper Palaeolithic:
Activities and Way of Life

Dwellings

The evidence for artificially constructed dwellings in the Upper Palaeolithic is restricted to those latitudes in the northern hemisphere where, during much of the latter part of the Last Glaciation, shelter was essential for survival. In France and Spain there were regions with a multitude of natural caves and rock shelters which afforded protection from the elements. The archaeological deposits that accumulated beneath testify to the use that was made of them. In some cases the natural features were improved upon by such modifications as stone flooring, low dividing walls, wind-breaks or even small tented structures. The disposition of hearths and distribution of domestic litter within an archaeological level inside a cave or beneath a rock shelter can tell much of the mode of life of the past occupants. Elsewhere, in regions without caves or rock shelters, something had to be made. Such open sites are frequently represented by nothing but a spread of discarded flints and animal bones, perhaps with the trace of one or more hearths. When the horizontal pattern of the discarded litter forms a rough circle, or it stops along definite lines suggesting former obstructions, a wall of some sort can be inferred. In most cases there is nothing left to indicate what kind of structure may have existed, and this is hardly surprising when the flimsy and perishable nature of a skin or reed-covered tent is considered. Even a fairly large, modern tent can be moved from site to site and it is unlikely that the most skilful excavator could find any traces of its former presence. The average tent peg only penetrates the topsoil which, under natural conditions alone, is subject to perpetual disturbance by worms, the weather and vegetation. When stake or post holes are discovered by archaeologists it can be concluded that they belonged to a fairly substantial structure. Fortunately, bones and stones were often used to weigh down the bottom edges of tent coverings and, although the latter may have perished or been purposefully carried away, these weights may remain as a ghost outline. Stone or cobble pavements may have a regular shape, which could correspond to the interior of a covered area but, in the absence of any other evidence, it cannot generally be proved that they were covered at all.

As noted below, there is good evidence for simple tents, particularly on the loess plains of Europe across to the Ukraine and Siberia, and for much more elaborate structures, involving the digging of large hollows and the utilisation of mammoth bones for walling or framework construction. Interlocking reindeer antlers were also employed for framing. The use of wood must have been extensive, but nothing has survived except a few post holes. When tundra conditions prevailed, as they clearly did during much of the time when central Europe and Russia were inhabited during the Upper Palaeolithic, suitable timber may not have been readily available for building; or what there was could be put to better use as fuel. This may explain the preference shown by the hunters in Russia for mammoth bones as constructional material, although there may have been a cult reason as well. Vast numbers of mammoth bones occur on some of these sites, and it seems that this was the result not just of butchery, but of intentional collecting. It has been shown by chemical analysis at one of the Kostienki sites that the mammoth bones at one particular level are of very different ages. Such sites are not 'kill' sites but accumulations of bones and tusks brought back to camp by hunters in the course of their expeditions, presumably from the skeletons of mammoths that had been killed in the past.

Most of the features of Upper Palaeolithic dwellings are known to a lesser degree in earlier transitional industries, especially the Mousterian. However, some of the Mousterian sites could possibly have been contemporary with the earliest leptolithic industries and the principle of diffusion might explain the similarities. Conversely, the hut at Molodova V (p. 159) is well stratified beneath the leptolithic industries, and the evidence from sites such as Hortus (p. 160) shows that these earlier hunting groups were capable of quite sophisticated constructions. As with the technological transition from Mousterian-type industries in various regions to leptolithic ones, so there was continuity in other things.

As explained above, little is known of the various modifications that were made to natural caves and rock shelters in France. They are confined to a few stone settings, pavements, post holes and one remarkable hut. The latter is in the entrance of La Grotte du Renne, Arcy-sur-Cure, Yonne,[1] and consists of 11 post holes enclosing an area of about 10 square metres, with a large hearth near the entrance and a smaller one inside (Figure 64). Big and small stones had formed a low enclosing wall and perhaps a partial paved area. The post holes should perhaps be termed tusk holes, for mammoth tusks had been inserted, presumably to help carry the roof covering. This formed the dwelling of people with a Perigordian I 'Châtelperronian' industry. The tusk holes had been dug into earlier Mousterian levels.

The only stone pavement beneath a rock shelter is at Flageolet II.[2] At the adjacent site of Flageolet I, small blocks of limestone had been placed to form walls up to 30 cm high and enclose an area about 3 x 2 m. This feature was associated with a Late Perigordian industry. Similar piled blocks of stone, under the rock shelter of Fourneau du Diable,[3] appear to have been the foundation of a rectangular hut 14 x 7 m, with three post holes on one side (Figure 64). Incorporated into the structure were two stones bearing sculptures in the form of oxen. The industry was Late Solutrian. Post holes are known from the cave at Duruthy and the shelter of La Salpêtrière.

As would be expected, remains of hearths are common in the occupational levels of this period in caves or beneath rock shelters. They vary in form from small, isolated examples a metre or less in diameter, sometimes surrounded by stones, to more elaborate ones in basin-like depressions dug in the floor. Other sites have extensive layers of ash and charcoal, suggesting large-scale bonfire-type arrangements. Differences in hearth construction, or in their position or relation to other hearths, may reflect social habits. Especially interesting in this respect was the discovery in the Late Perigordian levels at the Abri Pataud of a series of hearths, spaced fairly evenly in a line along the back of the rock shelter

Figure 64: Upper Palaeolithic Structures in French Caves

Fourneau du Diable, Bourdeilles, Dordogne. A rectangle of low walls surrounded a block, propped up by three stones, on which three fine low relief sculptures of wild oxen had been carved. Nearby was another smaller sculptured stone and another that had been painted. Three post holes suggest a central ridge to support some roof covering at the opposite end of this 'sanctuary'. They were in Late Solutrian levels. Post holes are also known from the cave at Duruthy and the shelter of La Salpêtrière.

Grotte Du Renne, Arcy-sur-Cure, Yonne. Post holes, paving slabs, occupational debris and hearths mark the position of this shelter, erected in early Perigordian (Châtelperron) times, within one of the many caves at this site. Uprights of mammoth tusks and long bones had been inserted in the post holes which had been dug into the Mousterian levels immediately below the floor.

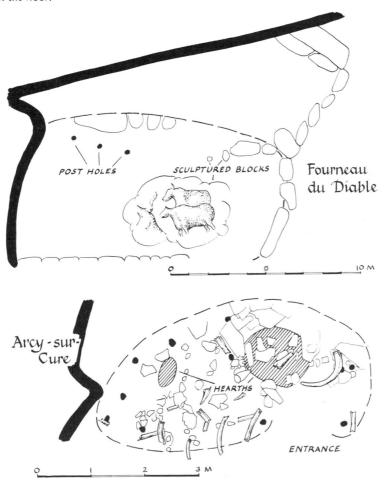

wall.[4] They appear to be contemporary and suggest a division of the dwelling area, possibly into family units. Similar evidence for such social divisions comes, as will be seen below, from Upper Palaeolithic dwellings in Russia.

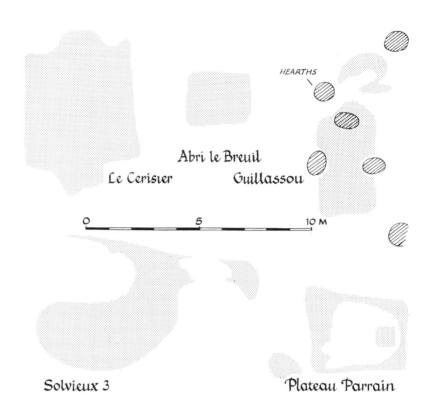

Figure 65: Open-air Dwelling Sites of the Upper Palaeolithic in the Valley of the Isle, Dordogne, France
Shading of the plans indicates the areas with the greatest concentrations of cobbles, probably corresponding to hut floors. Rectangular patterns may be dwelling floors, although all indications of walling or roofing have disappeared. At Solvieux there is a great spread of cobbling at least 48 m long.
   The apses each end of the Le Cerisier pavement are puzzling. Flint tools and working debris were found outside this structure, whereas at Plateau Parrain they were inside. A circular setting of stones exists outside the rectangle at Guillassou.
   All these sites are associated with Magdalenian industries, although Solvieux is multi-period and has some stone settings dated to the Late Perigordian and earlier.
   (All plans to the same scale)

The hunting communities of the French Upper Palaeolithic did not restrict their dwelling places to caves and rock shelters, as was once thought. Recent excavation has shown that open sites existed, probably in even greater numbers. A particular group has been investigated in the valley of the Isle in the Perigord,[5] not far from many of the famous cave sites. Nearly all of them are associated with cobbled areas or pavements. They vary in shape (Figure 65) from near-rectangular at Guillassou, Le Breuil and Le Cerisier to vast areas, the shape and extent of which are less easy to determine, as at Solvieux. The smaller, regularly shaped areas of cobbling were probably hut floors, but it is not possible to be certain of this. At Plateau Parrain stones had been used to delimit a rectangular area, which may have been the foundation of a dwelling structure. Inside, at one end and touching the 'wall', was a paved area about one metre square. Outside was a small circular structure. The purpose of the stone cobbling was presumably to maintain a relatively dry surface, either for a hut interior or for an outside working area. The apses at each end of the Le Cerisier pavement are puzzling. Flint tools and working debris were found mainly inside this structure, whereas at Plateau Parrain they were outside. A circular setting of stones also exists outside the rectangle at Guillassou. All these sites in the valley of the Isle are associated with Magdalenian industries, although Solvieux is multi-period and has some stone settings dated to the Late Perigordian and earlier.

A few other open sites in France are associated with a Magdalenian industry. At Etiolles, Essonne,[6] two roughly circular settings of flints and blocks of limestone, 5 and 6 m diameter, are close together. Traces of fire are within each of them, and one contains numerous flints, including some massive cores and blades up to 30 cm long. Flint working seems a particularly important aspect of this site for, close outside these two circular stone settings, were two separate piles of flint cores and flakes. At Saint-Mars-la-Brière, Sarthe,[7] a pile of stones is interpreted as the fallen wall of a dwelling, for domestic litter stops on one side of it, indicating the existence of some obstruction. Similar careful, detailed recording of archaeological material has enabled the plan to be reconstructed of a dwelling at Pincevent,[8] 60 km south of Paris (Figure 66). On the basis of the distribution of flints, bones and ochre, and the position of three hearths and piles of stones, the dwelling is thought to have been a tented structure, subdivided into three roughly circular parts.

At Corbiac,[9] in the valley of the Dordogne, there is an earlier Late Perigordian site, with a series of post holes possibly outlining two oblong huts. An associated pit contained flaking debris. Apart from this example, small pits are unknown from French Palaeolithic sites (excluding dug-out hearths) yet at contemporary sites in Russia they are a common feature, and are considered to have been used for various purposes, such as baking or storage.

Apart from some Late Glacial structures near Hamburg, there is a dearth of sites eastwards in Europe until one reaches Czechoslovakia or East Germany. At Ostraya-Petřkovice in Moravia,[10] three bowl-shaped hollows appear to be sunken dwellings ('Zemlyanka'). There were no post holes, but a converging branch framework could have been erected without them to make a tepee-like tent. There was a rich Eastern Gravettian industry at this site and of particular interest was the use of coal as fuel. Coal outcrops locally and is known to have been used at a few other Upper Palaeolithic sites, including Kesslerloch in Switzerland. Another semi-underground dwelling at Predmost[11] is mentioned below in connection with a burial that had been placed within it. The Predmost *Zemlyanka* was deep in loess above a layer containing the remains of hundreds of mammoths. The actual pit was 4 x 2.5 m and 5 m deep and surrounded by mammoth bones, presumably used to weigh down the roof covering. Numerous similar huts have been found at Pavlov, oval, circular or five-sided. Some carbonised timbers may have been part of roof structures or walls. At least two huts are known from the rich site of Dolni Vestonice,[12] famous for its female figurines (see Figure 71). One, 15 x 9 m, like Predmost had a burial placed on one side of it. It had stones around the edge, 5 hearths and a flint knapping floor in the centre. A second hut, 80 m distant, had been built by partially digging out the side of a slope and using the clay and limestone to make a wall on the downward side (Figure 67). At Revnice, near Prague, an occupational area of this period had been paved with stones.

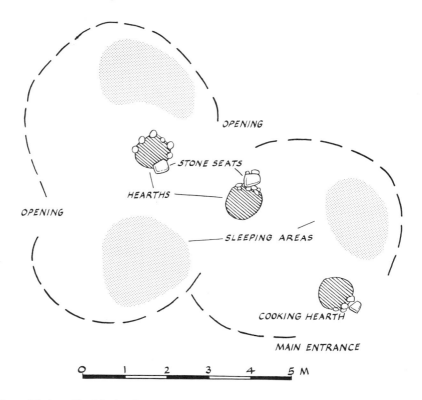

Figure 66: Late Magdalenian Dwelling at Pincevent, Seine-et-Marne, France
The reconstructed plan is based on the results of methodical archaeological excavation. The dwelling is thought to have been a tented structure, subdivided into three roughly circular parts. The limits of the dwelling area are defined by the distribution of flint artifacts around the hearths, which were mainly prevented from scattering beyond the line shown on the plan, presumably by the obstruction of animal skins or some other form of walling. Openings are identified by spreads of flint and other litter beyond their limits. Areas with relatively little of such litter are considered sleeping areas. The hearth by the main entrance is thought to be the cooking fire as a charred reindeer foot was found in the ashes, and its siting by the entrance a sensible one. A spread of red ochre exists over the floor of the dwelling, suggesting that it may have been extensively used for colouring skins, body decoration, ornamenting wooden artifacts or painting pictures on bark.

Some of the richest evidence for Upper Palaeolithic dwellings comes from a number of sites in Russia, particularly along the valleys of the Dniester, Dnieper, Desna and Don in the Ukraine. Broadly, they can be divided into two kinds: small round houses, and larger elongated structures with multiple hearths. The

Figure 67: Plan and Reconstruction of Upper Palaeolithic Hut at Dolni Vestonice, Czechoslovakia

The hut was built by partially digging out a slope on the south side of a slight rise and using clay and limestone fragments to build a low wall in front and around it. A few shallow post holes (solid black on the plan) were cut in the surrounding clay and stone wall, with large stones as packing set around the posts which had been inserted. Several large mammoth bones were found, mainly on the south side. The entrance was to the east, with steps cut down to the hollow. In the centre of the hut was a hearth (hachured on the plan) surrounded by a low, vaulted structure made of the same firmly packed clay and stones used to make the wall. This has been interpreted as a kiln in which figurines and statuettes of clay were fired, such as the famous Venus figurine of Dolni Vestonice (Figure 71). Associated with the kiln were 2,200 pellets of baked clay, some of which were fragments of broken or unfinished animal statuettes.

The associated flint industry is Eastern Gravettian, radiocarbon dated to about 23,000 bc. This is the earliest known example in the world of the technique of firing clay, but it was never developed and no other use of it is known until the Neolithic period.

The whole circular area was presumably covered by hides, weighted down by bones, branches and earth, as shown in the semi-diagrammatic section of the suggested reconstruction.

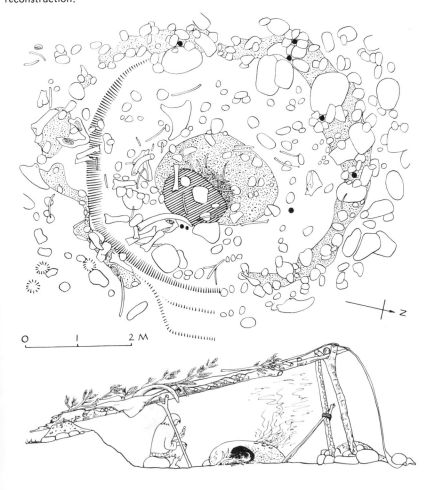

former were usually of the sunken 'Zemlyanka' type. Both usually employed mammoth tusks and bones, sometimes to such an extent that they are referred to as mammoth bone houses. Roof coverings were presumably large hides, sewn together. On the near-treeless tundra it is unlikely that anything else would have been available, but branches, stones, turves and soil may all have been used whenever possible or suitable. Particularly well-preserved and recorded long houses are at Pushkari and Kostienki I and IV.[13] Pushkari, on the Desna (Figure 68), was a shallow, oval depression 12 x 4 m with three hearths in a line along its major axis. Near the hearths were about thirty other holes dug into the floor, about 10 cm wide and deep, filled with red earth, flints, ashes and bones, and interpreted as storage pits. The sides of the dug-out depression were nearly vertical, except for parts on each side which may have coincided with entrance areas. Four mammoth jaws were found set vertically near the margins and were probably connected with the original roofing framework, as were numerous tusks found inside the living area, where they fell when the structure eventually collapsed.

Kostienki I[14] was a complex structure. It was not necessarily all of one period, but one definite feature was a line of nine hearths along the major axis spaced at 2 m intervals. There was also one other hearth at least within the dwelling, but not on the central line (Figure 69). Around the margin of this long house were 16 large pits, 1-2 m diameter, four of which were interpreted as living or sleeping areas as they were connected to the main dwelling by steps cut in the clay. The largest of the four habitation chambers had many mammoth tusks and bones on its floor, resulting from the collapse of the roofing framework. A complete musk ox skull may once have capped the roof as a trophy or emblem. The other pits are interpreted as storage pits; they contained mammoth bones put there as meat reserves or as fuel, for certain bones had a combustible content. Various other pits and depressions had been dug in the floor of the main dwelling area and appear to have been storage places for flint tools, female figurines, animal statuettes and other objects. Some may have been post holes. In one place mammoth long bones had been stuck vertically in the ground and their articular ends used as anvils. A large, oval depression in one corner, 8 x 6 m, may have been an earlier 'Zemlyanka', or an additional part of the long house. The remains of another long house were partly exposed by excavation only 5 m away.

Two other well-preserved long houses were found at another site in this archaeologically rich region, Kostienki IV, of about the same age as the one at Kostienki I but on a lower terrace, closer to the river. The first (a) was 34 x 5.5 m, dug out to a depth of 0.4 m, and divided by low, transverse earthen ridges into three compartments, 14, 9 and 11 m long (Figure 69). As at Kostienki I, numerous small pits had been dug into the floor; four may have been post holes. Some pits contained much red ochre and numerous remains of hares, especially paw bones, and may have been connected with the process of tanning and colouring hare skins for clothing. Kostienki IV (b) was a smaller long house, measuring 23 x 5.5 m, about 50 m north of its neighbour. It was devoid of earth ridges, but also had nine hearths in a row down the middle (Figure 69). At a slightly later date, two round sunken huts had been built above the first long house, actually cutting into it.

The methodical arrangements of the hearths at both Pushkari and Kostienki

Figure 68: Plan and Reconstruction of Upper Palaeolithic Dwelling at Pushkari, USSR
The dwelling consisted of a shallow, oval depression 12 x 4 m. The plan shows the mammoth bones, mainly tusks and ribs, that were found within it. They were probably connected with the roofing framework or with weighing down the hides which may have been used to cover a timber framework, as suggested in the reconstruction. The solid black areas on the plan are hearths.

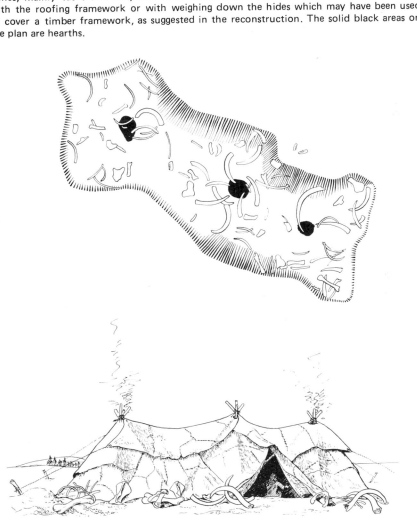

Figure 69: Plans of Upper Palaeolithic Dwellings at Kostienki, USSR

Three structures have been discovered at the rich Upper Palaeolithic site of Kostienki in the Ukraine of Soviet Russia, conforming to a long-house pattern with a central line of hearths. In each case there are nine hearths along the central line and at Kostienki IVa there is a suggestion of a tripartite division within the dwelling by two low banks of earth between the three sets of three hearths.

Kostienki I is a large, complex structure, not necessarily all of one period. A large pit with its own hearth in the north east corner may have been an earlier 'Zemlyanka' later incorporated into the long house. There were many internal pits. The major ones are shown and those lettered A-D have been interpreted as habitation pits as opposed to storage pits. If the spread of archaeological material and pits really does represent the covered area, it is very difficult to know how a width of about 16 m was spanned. More likely, the proportions of the tented area were like Kostienki IVa and IVb, with the major pits outside. Habitation pits could have been separately covered by a framework independent of the main structure.

Kostienki IVa and IVb were probably constructed in the same manner as the long house at Pushkari (Figure 68), by linking three tepee-like conical frameworks of branches covered with skins and weighed down by large bones and tusks. As at Kostienki I, numerous small pits had been dug into the floor; four may have been post holes. Some pits contained much red ochre and numerous remains of hares, especially paw bones, and may have been connected with the process of tanning and colouring hare skins for clothing.

Charred bone from Kostienki I gives a radiocarbon date of 12,070 ± 60 bc. The long houses of Kostienki IV are on the terrace below Kostienki I (see section, Figure 58) and may be a little more recent.

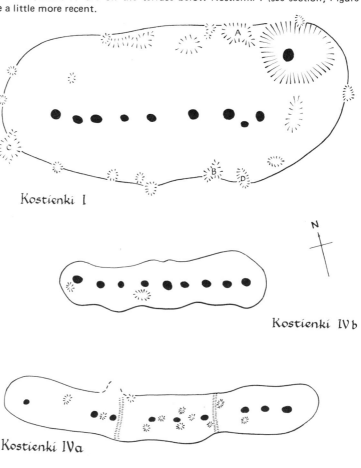

Kostienki I

Kostienki IVb

N

Kostienki IVa

0   5   10 M.

● HEARTHS

⁂ PITS

leave little doubt that the community was strictly organised into separate units. Family units seem the most likely, but other social distinctions of age, sex or duty may have taken precedence over family ties. The hearth arrangements are reminiscent of the line of hearths spaced along the back of the shelter wall at the Abri Pataud in France, noted above. It may also be more than a coincidence that the division of these long houses appears to be in multiples of three. Far away in France, again, at the later site of Pincevent, there seems to have been a threefold division of the dwelling area. Also, at Yudinovo on a tributary of the Desna, was found a long house of mammoth bones construction, 17 x 10 m, divided into six sections, one of which had a large hearth 2 m diameter, thought to have been for heating. The floor had been dug out to a depth of more than 0.5 m and, at ground level, walls had been carefully constructed around the cavity of horizontally placed bones, or set vertically by being pushed through perforated shoulder blades or supported by skulls.

At Timonovka, also on the Desna, were six long houses of a completely different type. These were truly subterranean houses, being rectangular pits 2.5-3 m deep. They varied from 6 to 12 m in length and from 3 to 4 m in width. The walls had been dug vertically and revetted with timber, traces of which were found by the excavators. Sloping ramps, a metre wide, gave entrance to them and, as wood was available for the walls, it can perhaps be assumed that the roof consisted of branches laid horizontally over the pit, with earth spread on top. Hearths were only found in two of them, and the unheated ones were probably only for storage and not for habitation. The six houses formed three pairs, a heated one having an unheated one beside it in each case. There were also some pits and hearths outside the sunken houses, and the areas of flint working were associated with the unheated ones. Domestic equipment, such as bone needles, was found in those with hearths. Again, it may be significant that there were three open hearths.

Round or oval tented structures are much more common and are being found in increasing numbers in Russia, especially in the Ukraine. They are generally 3-6 m in diameter and have their floors dug half a metre or so into the ground. It is quite possible that some of these shallow depressions are merely the result of periodical scraping out of the soiled interior but, generally, the hollow would seem to have been intended to give additional protection from cold winds, and also to simplify the roof construction. Particularly good examples of this type of dwelling come from Molodova, on a terrace of the River Dniester (Figure 70). At Molodova V, in level 6 with radiocarbon dates of about 11,000 bc, an irregular oblong area was delineated by 64 stake holes, interpreted as marking the positions of large pegs to hold down the roof covering. The area contained a large central hearth and five small pits. A spread of reindeer antlers marks the position of another dwelling at the same site, in a higher level and possibly 1,000 years more recent. They may have formed part of an interlocking framework. In this case there were two hearths immediately outside. Another good example in the same region was found at Telmanskaya, in the upper level. This consisted of a rounded depression about 5 m in diameter, 0.5-0.7 m deep, with near-vertical sides except for a sloping ramp on the west side. There was a central hearth, but most of the occupational debris was outside the entrance.

A somewhat different type of structure is represented by a great accumulation of mammoth bones at another site in the Kostienki-Borchevo region,

Figure 70

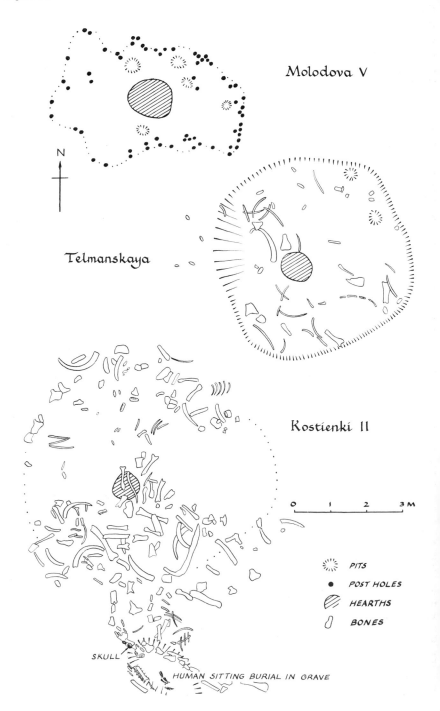

Kostienki II (Figure 70). They occurred in an oval area 8 x 6.5 m, and formed a thickness of more than half a metre. At least 28 mammoths had contributed to the 2,000 and more bones. This accumulation appears to be a collapsed structure, for it overlay a typical 'Zemlyanka' floor with a central hearth and occupational litter. The sitting burial described below was found at the southern end and formed part of the same structure, the north wall of bones being common to the dwelling site and the burial chamber.

Another collapsed mammoth bone structure found at Mezhirich comprised 385 mammoth bones. Mandibles and long bones had fallen gently inwards, showing that they had been placed upright on the ground against the tent covering. Mammoth tusks, more in the centre, would have been part of the roofing framework. This was a small dwelling, 3 m in diameter, with a central hearth and two others outside. Five 'Zemlyankas' were found at Eliseevichi on the Desna, associated with an area demarcated by a number of mammoth skulls, with a shallow corridor leading to it bordered by mammoth pelvic bones and shoulder blades.

Many other similar sites have been found in the Ukraine, and also much further east in Siberia, at Malta and Buret on the Angara River.[15] A sunken house at Malta, measuring 14 x 3 m, was walled with stone slabs and animal bones, with three hearths in separate compartments, if the mammoth tusks between them really represent fallen partitions. Inside was a rhinoceros skull beneath which had been placed many ivory objects. There was also a typical round house 5 m in diameter with a central hearth. Interlocking reindeer antlers had been used for the roof framework of a 'Zemlyanka' at Buret.

The custom of digging out the floor of a dwelling, sometimes to a considerable depth, obviously necessitated digging implements. At both Eliseevichi and Pushkari large mattocks were used, made from mammoth ribs or tusks. The

Figure 70: Plans of Some Russian Upper Palaeolithic Dwellings

Molodova V. 64 stake holes delineate a roughly oblong area containing a central hearth and five small pits. Skins were probably laid over a framework of branches and pegged down by wooden stakes. Radiocarbon dated to about 11,000 bc. A spread of reindeer antlers marks the position of another dwelling at the same site, in a higher level and possibly 1,000 years more recent. They may have formed part of an interlocking framework. In this case there were two hearths immediately outside.

Telmanskaya. A rounded artificially dug depression about 5 m in diameter and 0.5-0.7 m deep, with a central hearth. The entrance was probably on the west side, as elsewhere the sides of this 'Zemlyanka' were near-vertical. Also, most of the occupational litter was outside the depression, on the west side. A low, earthen wall surrounded the depression and the roof probably rested upon it. Large mammoth tusks and rib bones found inside may have fallen from part of the roof framework.

Kostienki II. Large numbers of mammoth bones cover an area about 7 m in diameter. There were over 2,000 bones, including about 100 ribs and 40 tusks. Long bones on the margin of the oval had been set vertically into the ground. There was a central hearth and most of the larger bones are thought to have fallen on to the floor of the dwelling when the roofing framework eventually collapsed.

At the south end was a narrow, oval grave lined with mammoth bones. This contained a human burial. The lower part of the body was found in the centre of the grave, but the skull and upper part were scattered to the north west, suggesting that the body had been buried in a sitting position with the upper part uncovered.

The dotted line indicates the original area of the dwelling. The blank areas on the east and west sides result from mutilation of the site by non-archaeological diggings.

regularity of the edge wear makes it seem very likely that these tools were attached to shafts. Bone shoulder blades could have been used as shovels and spoil carried away in baskets or skin containers. However such houses were constructed, there is a strong impression of communal activity and organisation. It is impossible to estimate population figures or the size of individual encampments, but it does look as if there were substantial numbers in each community, possibly to be measured in hundreds but not in thousands, spread out in small collections of tented dwellings, or among a few nearby rock shelters or caves. Liaison between communities in different areas may have been necessary, in order to regulate hunting activities. The migrations and movements of such animals as the reindeer and the mammoth would have had a profound effect upon the stability of a community, and there can be little doubt that notions of territory would have manifested themselves. Some communities may have moved seasonally from region to region, while others operated from one place for generations. Some of the smaller 'Zemlyankas' may be little more than temporary camps of travelling hunters, but the groups of long houses and the thick accumulations of occupational debris under some rock shelters imply an element of stability and security.

Clothing and Personal Ornament

When human groups began to move into northern latitudes, some form of protective clothing was essential for comfort or survival. Hunting groups with Mousterian industries are known to have lived almost on the edge of periglacial areas, yet nothing has survived to indicate what kind of clothing they must have had. Probably it was rudimentary: little more than a skin or fur wrapped round the shoulders, secured by a couple of thongs pushed through holes. There is no lack of flint tools by which the skins could have been cut, scraped, skived and perforated; but the garments themselves could hardly be expected to survive, so the lack of evidence is to be expected. However, there is positive proof that clothes were worn by people of the advanced hunting communities in Europe and Asia, although not necessarily at all times. Hunters may have been naked when in the chase, for ease of movement. Also, some clothing may have been regarded more as personal decoration than as protection.

The best source of information is from a few of the human statuettes — the so-called Venus figurines as they are almost all female — to be described in the final section of this chapter. Without exception, all those from Europe, including western Russia, are naked, but this is clearly the manifestation of some cult and does not imply that females did not normally wear clothes (Figure 71). Some of the Kostienki statuettes have girdles round their waists, and others have chest bands (Figure 71, nos 6-7) but there is nothing that could possibly be interpreted as a garment, except perhaps what might be a skirt on the rear of the Venus of Lespugue (Figure 71, no. 2). However, a few statuettes from the Upper Palaeolithic sites of Siberia at Malta and Buret make up for this deficiency and the one from the latter site clearly shows a quite elaborately fashioned one-piece combination suit with a hood (Figure 72). Male figurines are unknown apart from a rather featureless, broken one from Brno, but a bas-relief sculpture of a hunter from a rock shelter at Laussel, France, has a belt round his waist and,

Figure 71: Venus Figurines
1. Dolni Vestonice, Czechoslovakia (baked clay). 2. Lespugue, Haute Garonne, France (mammoth ivory). 3. Willendorf, Austria (limestone). 4. Sireuil, Dordogne, France (calcite). 5. Balzi Rossi, Italy. 6.-7. Kostienki I (layer I), USSR (mammoth ivory). (1, 3, 6, 7 half-scale, others approximately same scale)

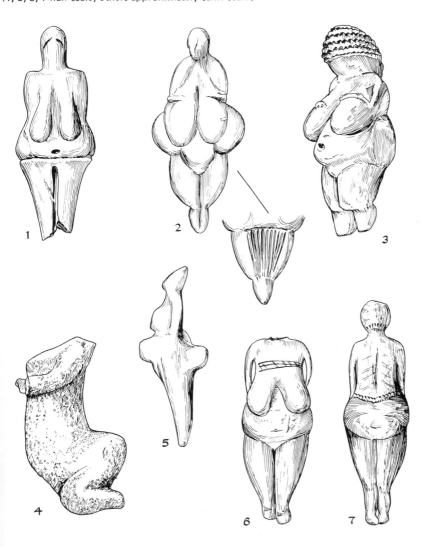

Figure 72: Clothing and Personal Ornament in the Upper Palaeolithic
1. Bone pendant, or possibly a 'Bull-roarer', i.e. spun at speed on an attached line so as to produce a loud, strange, whirring noise. Grotte de la Roche, Dordogne (Magdalenian). 2. Fragments of an ivory bracelet. Paviland Cave, Glamorgan (British Earlier Upper Palaeolithic). 3. Perforated flat bone disc, with engraving of *Bos*, possibly a button. Laugerie Basse, Dordogne (Magdalenian). 4. Necklace (reconstructed) of fish vertebrae and sea shells. Balzi Rossi, Italy ('Gravettian'). 5. Perforated bone pin, possibly a clothes fastening. Kostienki IV, level I, USSR. 6. Bone statuette of a hooded figure. Buret, Siberia. 7.-9. Grooved bear's tooth and two perforated land snails. Typical of most stages of French Upper Palaeolithic. 10. Small bone pendant. Cro-Magnon, Dordogne (Aurignacian). 11. Typical perforated shells for necklaces. Cro-Magnon, Dordogne (Aurignacian). 12.-13. Ivory beads. Abri Blanchard, Dordogne (Aurignacian). 14. Ivory bead. Kostienki IV, level I, USSR. 15. Stylised bone statuette, possibly based on hooded figures such as 6. Kostienki II, USSR.
(All approximately half-scale)

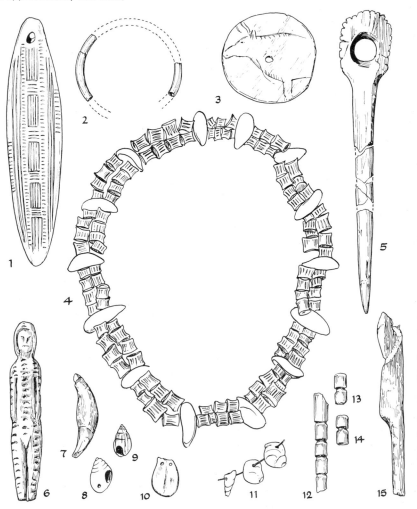

as his penis is not shown, it can be assumed that he is wearing trousers. An engraving on bone from Montastruc, Bruniquel, France, depicts a man with what must be a series of buttons up his front (see Figure 73).

The earliest needles are associated with the Solutrian of France, and they are commonly found in later Magdalenian sites and contemporary ones in Russia. The delicate nature of some of the needles suggests they were used for the intricate sewing of garments rather than for fixing hides together for tent coverings, for which larger examples would have served better. Bone points with knobs at one end may have been used as dress fastenings. Some perforated discs of bone and stone were probably buttons, as on the Montastruc figure. Decorated examples come from Laugerie Basse (Figure 72) and a few other French sites. Some grooved bone pieces from the triple burial at La Barma Grande, Balzi Rossi, Italy, may have been toggles.

The burial of an adult man at Soungir, USSR, is noted in the next section. The numerous beads found with the skeleton were in rows, round the forehead, across the chest and down the legs. They were probably sewn on to the skin clothes in which the man was buried; those on the head may have decorated the front of the hood of an anorak type of garment across which other rows of beads had been sewn. Trousers are indicated by the beads found along the entire length of the legs. Perforated carnivore canine teeth were also associated, so this man must have been buried in all his finery.

Beads and pendants are ubiquitous at this period, fashioned out of a multitude of objects or materials: bone, ivory, stone, amber, teeth, shells, fossils and fish vertebrae. When series of these are found around the wrist or neck it seems reasonable to accept them as bracelets or necklaces, but they could also, like the Soungir burial, have been sewn on to skin clothing. They have also been found near elbows, knees and ankles, and the same could apply. Occasionally, human or animal statuettes are perforated as if for suspension round the neck, as are a hooded woman statuette from Malta, Siberia, and a bear figurine from Isturitz in the Pyrenees. Personal decoration of this kind was not restricted to groups with leptolithic industries, for the burials in the upper cave at Choukoutien were accompanied by over a hundred pierced animal teeth, and also pebbles and sea shells. Perforations could have been made by using small, backed pointed blades as drills, and wear marks characteristic of such use have been identified on some specimens from Kostienki.

Elsewhere in the world, in sunnier climates where clothing was not necessary, there is a corresponding lack of obvious personal ornaments such as beads and pendants, so it would seem that there may be a relation between the two. There was, however, a great demand for red ochre and this was probably used for body decoration. It may also have been used to decorate spears and other artifacts or to make pigments suitable for rock painting. Red ochre is common in Magosian and Howieson's Poort occupational levels in Africa, yet there are no rock paintings which can be related. Whatever the motive, it is astonishing to discover that haematite was actually being quarried in the Lion Cavern, Ngwenya, Swaziland[16] before 20,000 BC and possibly, to judge from radiocarbon dates and Middle Stone Age tools found at the site, as far back as 40,000 years or more. Equally surprising is the existence of a similar pigment quarry in the Lovas Caves,[17] near Lake Balaton, Hungary. This was also for haematite and, as noted in Chapter 5, it has been dated to the time of the Szeletian industry, as a leaf point of that type was associated. There were also bone picks and shovels, and hollow long bones in which the precious crushed ochre had apparently been stored. Such intensive effort to obtain this material can only show that it was of great significance to nearly all the known types of communities of this period. It might be described as Upper Palaeolithic 'gold', but it is doubtful that any concepts of trade or personal wealth had been acquired.

Burials

In spite of the great contrast between the leptolithic industries and the preceding transitional ones, and in spite of all the evidence for a more organised and sophisticated society, customs for the disposal of the dead show little or no change. Intentional burial in shallow graves is still known, but rare, and isolated human skulls or other parts of the skeleton continue to occur unceremoniously mixed with occupational litter. Some burials were also strewn with red ochre prior to being covered. In western Europe, particularly France, all the known burials are within caves or beneath rock shelters. None is known from an open site, and this could imply that there was a matter of differential preservation, and that burials are only known from the caves and shelters because conditions were suitable for their preservation there. Elsewhere, it could be argued, inhumation may have been a common practice but nothing has survived. If this were not the case, it would have to be accepted that only a very few individuals were buried, possibly for their status or for some special reason. On the present evidence this does seem the more likely alternative, especially as there is corroborative evidence from the Upper Palaeolithic sites in Czechoslovakia and Russia. Here are no rock shelters and caves, but the living sites have been gently covered by wind-blown loess or fine fluviatile sediments. The significant point is that human burials in this region are all associated with dwelling sites, in some cases actually within abandoned sunken houses or beneath them. Any large-scale disposal of the dead in special areas unconnected with dwelling sites would, by now, have been discovered, for there are numerous commercial diggings in the loess. The conclusion is that there is a direct connection between intentional burials and living places, the reason for which is contained in the now unfathomable thoughts of these people.

Table 7.1: Major Upper Palaeolithic Burials

Site	Human remains	Position of body if known	Features	Industry
Cro-Magnon, Les Eyzies, France	3 adult males, 1 adult female,		sealed beneath occupational soils	Aurignacian
Combe-Capelle, France	1 adult male	contracted	sealed beneath occupational soil; ?flints as grave goods and necklace of shells	Aurignacian
Le Figuier, France	1 child	flexed		Solutrian

Site	Human remains	Position of body if known	Features	Industry
Cap Blanc, France	1 adult female	contracted		Magdalenian
La Chancelade, France	1 adult male	flexed		Magdalenian
Laugerie Basse, France	1 adult male	contracted		Magdalenian
Bruniquel, France	1 adult female	flexed		Magdalenian
La Madeleine, France	1 child	extended		Magdalenian
St Germain, France	1 adult female	contracted with arms above head		Magdalenian
Les Hoteaux, France	1 adult	contracted		Magdalenian
Balzi Rossi, Grotte du Cavillon, Italy	1 adult male	contracted on left side	strewn with red ochre; bone dagger by forehead and 2 flint knives by neck; shell ornaments	Gravettian
Balzi Rossi, Grotte de la Barma Grande, Italy	1 adult male, 1 young female, 1 young male	all extended face down or on left side	triple burial strewn with ochre; shell, teeth and bone ornaments; flint knives in left hands of adult male and female	Gravettian
	1 adult	extended face down or on left side	covered by stone slabs; shell ornaments	Gravettian
	1 adult		laid on hot fire	Gravettian
	1 young male	face down	no grave goods	Gravettian
Balzi Rossi, La Grotte des Enfants, Italy	2 infants		laid on sea shells beside each other	Gravettian
	1 adult male	on back	head on an ochre-covered slab; shell ornaments	Aurignacian
	1 young male, 1 adult female	male contracted, female flexed	double burial; head of youth protected by two upright stones with another laid across; shell bracelet and head ornaments; strewn with ochre	Aurignacian
Balzi Rossi, Arene Candide, Italy	1 youth		flint blade in right hand; shell ornaments; antler discs on arms; protective slabs; strewn with ochre	?

Table 7.1: contd

Site	Human remains	Position of body if known	Features	Industry
Paviland Cave, Wales	1 adult male	extended	strewn with ochre; bone tools by side	Early British Upper Palaeolithic
Gough's Cave, Cheddar, England	1 adult male		?washed into cave naturally	Creswellian
Zlaty Kun Cave, Czechoslovakia	2 adults			Szeletian
Brno, Czechoslovakia	1 adult male		under heap of mammoth tusks and rhinoceros bones; shell necklace; bone and ivory discs	Eastern Aurignacian
Dolni Vestonice, Czechoslovakia	1 adult female		burial on edge of sunken dwelling; covered by 2 mammoth shoulder blades; grave goods; strewn with red ochre	Eastern Gravettian
Pavlov, Czechoslovakia	1 adult			Eastern Gravettian
Predmost, Czechoslovakia	6 individuals and collective burial of 14 or more adults and children		covered by stones or mammoth shoulder blades in abandoned sunken dwelling; some ornaments but no grave goods	Eastern Gravettian
Kostienki II, USSR	1 adult male	sitting position, flexed	covered by a construction of mammoth bones; beside dwelling	Latest Kostienki Upper Palaeolithic
Kostienki XV, USSR	1 child		covered by mammoth shoulder blades; grave goods	Kostienki Upper Palaeolithic
Kostienki XVII, USSR	1 adult	contracted	covered by mammoth bones and broken tusks	Kostienki Upper Palaeolithic
Gorodtsovskaya, USSR	1 child	contracted in sitting position	oval grave 1.2 x 0.80 m, 0.43 m deep; grave goods and ornaments	Kostienki Upper Palaeolithic
Markina Gora, USSR	1 adult male	flexed, on left side	oval grave 1.0 x 0.40 m, 0.48 m deep; no grave goods; strewn with red ochre	Kostienki Upper Palaeolithic
Soungir, USSR	2 burials, 1 only a head	extended	oval grave strewn with hot coals; grave goods and many beads and bone ornaments	Kostienki Upper Palaeolithic

Table 7.1: contd

Site	Human remains	Position of body if known	Features	Industry
Malta, USSR	1 child		under dwelling strewn with red ochre; grave goods and ornaments	Siberian Upper Palaeolithic
Ksar 'Akil, Lebanon	1 child		surface burial	Antelian
Choukoutien, Upper Cave, China	1 adult male, 2 adult females		? in shallow graves strewn with ochre; with ornaments	non-leptolithic
Lake Mungo, Australia			cremation.	^{14}C date, c. 25,000 bc

It can be seen from the list in Table 7.1 that the inclusion of grave goods was uncommon practice. As shallow graves were generally dug through contemporary or slightly earlier occupational deposits, the backfilled material is bound to contain artifacts from them, and thus archaeologists always have difficulty in assessing whether apparently associated objects are purposely placed with the body or are accidentally derived. It is very rare to have such definite associations as at Balzi Rossi, where flint knives were actually gripped by the deceased. Sympathetic magic might explain the covering of graves with mammoth bones by mammoth hunters, or the placing of bodies on shells by coastal dwellers. There are two instances of cremation-like rites, as far apart as Italy and Russia. In both cases bodies had been placed on, or covered by, the hot coals and ashes of fires. The only evidence for real cremation comes from Lake Mungo, Australia. Other evidence for different burial customs in Australia is at Kow Swamp,[18] where a veritable cemetery was discovered of over 40 burials. Radiocarbon dating places this in the post-glacial or Mesolithic period, c.6000 BC, but it could perpetuate earlier traditions.

Where known, burials were extended, contracted or flexed, the latter implying some binding of the legs against the chest shortly after the time of death. Some burials are on the right side, some on the left, and there is no sign of any preferred orientation. Thus it is not possible to discern any form of rite connected with the positions of the bodies. Nor is there any explanation for the occasional multiple burial.

Several burials are accompanied by bone, shell or ivory beads or other personal ornaments. Although technically grave goods, these objects give valuable information on the clothing or personal appearance of the people of this period, and so were considered in a little more detail in the previous section of this chapter.

The famous discovery at Cro-Magnon, by the hotel of that name at Les Eyzies in the Dordogne, France, has given its name to the type of man associated with leptolithic industries across most of Europe and North Africa, and into Asia (Plate XX). He can be classified, unequivocally, as *Homo sapiens sapiens*. The face was broad with prominent cheek bones, the nose narrow, the forehead high and the chin strong and prominent. Generally, Cro-Magnon people were tall, one of the men from the site itself being nearly 2 m in height. Not all human discoveries of the Upper Palaeolithic fit this description. Racial characteristics have been claimed for various discoveries, particularly at Predmost, La Chancelade in France, and Grimaldi, referred to here as Balzi Rossi. The Chancelade remains are thought to have affinities with modern Eskimos, and the double burial from La Grotte des Enfants, Balzi Rossi, with the Negro race. Anthropologists prefer not to give a separate nomenclature for the minor physical differences involved, but it would seem that this was the period when the present major races of mankind were evolving. In the Far East, *neanderthal* or even *erectus* traits appear to have survived even into post-glacial times.

Art and Other Aspects of Upper Palaeolithic Life

Upper Palaeolithic art is a big subject, and in this archaeological survey it is only possible to consider briefly its different forms, age, distribution and what it may tell us of the mode of life at the time. The term 'art' has to be stretched to include everything from the crudest finger-squiggles on soft clay to polychrome paintings which can excite our admiration irrespective of their antiquity. The art falls into two very broad categories: parietal art (i.e. on walls) and mobile art (i.e. movable objects). The former may consist of engravings or paintings, the latter may be functional or non-functional, although sometimes it is difficult to know whether it is one or the other. Archaeologists and art historians have argued for years over the meaning of it all; was the art magical, was it decoration, or was it sheer self-expression? Most likely it was all three, being different things at different times. There can be no general rule, and the only hope of discerning anything of the motives must be by considering the circumstances and associations of individual discoveries.

Cave art of definite Upper Palaeolithic age is restricted almost entirely to France and Spain, especially in the Perigord, Pyrenees and Cantabrian Mountains. Some of the rock paintings and engravings in other parts of the world may be contemporary, but, when they can be dated at all, are post-Palaeolithic with some rare exceptions mentioned below. There is great difficulty in dating parietal art, and the vast majority of examples are of course, undatable, like any other artifact found on the surface. There can be no stratigraphical dating unless a painting or engraving is buried beneath archaeological deposits, and only engravings are likely to survive such burial. Such discoveries have been made, but they are very rare. One example was the engraved head of a horse at Laugerie Haute, but the Magdalenian levels which cover it only give a minimum date. Sometimes, as at La Ferrassie, slabs of limestone bearing paint have fallen from the shelter wall and become incorporated in the occupational deposits. At Le Roc de Sers, parts of the famous frieze of stone animal sculptures had similarly fallen into a datable context. Minimum dates are also given by occupational deposits which block the entrance to a decorated cave, as at La Mouthe and Marsoulas. Mobile art has a much more extensive distribution and is found well beyond the region of parietal art, especially in association with the Upper Palaeolithic sites of central and eastern Europe, Russia and Siberia.

Generally, such objects are found in occupational deposits and can be firmly dated. Sometimes, as at Altamira in northern Spain, engravings found on pieces of bone within known archaeological levels, in this case Magdalenian, were identical in form and style to engravings on the cave wall at El Castillo and thus almost certain to be contemporary (Figure 73, nos 8-9).

The only European cave art outside the main centres that has a firm claim to be of Upper Palaeolithic age is in the Kapova Cave of the southern Ural Mountains. This consists of paintings in yellow, red, brown and black of mammoth, horse and rhinoceros and, as mammoth did not survive into the post-glacial period, the paintings must be earlier. In the southern hemisphere, seven fragments of stone slabs bearing paintings of animals come from an occupational layer within the Apollo 11 Cave in South West Africa, radiocarbon dated between 23,000 and 28,000 years BC.[19] No other site in Africa has parietal or mobile art that has been dated to the Palaeolithic period, but this discovery suggests that many of the fine paintings in the caves and rock shelters of South Africa and elsewhere may really be this old. Paintings in the Nullabor Plain of South Australia are also thought to be earlier than 10,000 years.

Although the dating of parietal art is, in most cases, problematical, mobile art is found in France and Spain associated with all the major stone industries. Bone carving and ornamentation seems to have reached a zenith in stages 4 and 5 of the Magdalenian. Bas reliefs of animals and human figures are more typical of the Solutrian, Venus figurines of the Late Perigordian, and sexual symbols of the Aurignacian. The earliest examples of art in France date to about 30,000 BC. Some ivory animal statuettes of mammoth, horse, panther, bear and bison come from Vogelherd in South Germany and may be as old. The famous Venus of Willendorf (Figure 71) came from a level dated to about 27,000 BC.

For painting, pigments were ground on stone or bone palettes and probably applied with a form of brush or even with the fingers. Some negative hand impressions were executed by blowing liquid paint over an outstretched hand used as a stencil. Positive impressions were more easily made by dipping the hand in a pool of paint and dabbing it against the rock wall. Many of the hand impressions appear to show mutilated or missing fingers. Flint gravers would have been ideal tools for incising the lines of rock engravings. Some pieces of soft red ochre have smoothed ends and were obviously used as crayons (Figure 74). Lamps, for work done in the complete darkness of the inner recesses of caves, were hollowed-out pieces of softish rock such as sandstone or limestone containing animal fat, with a wick of some suitable vegetable matter dipped into it. Such simple, open lamps give a surprisingly good light. Those from Lascaux and La Mouthe were made with considerable care (Figure 74). The use of such lamps in pitch darkness may explain why so many engravings are superimposed one on top of the other for, if the lamp remains in one position, it is often impossible to see anything else but the line one is actually engraving. Similarly, the source of light may amplify certain natural contours of the rock, and the artists were quick to spot which ones would enhance the intended painting of an animal and, at times, give uncanny three-dimensional effect, accentuated by slight movement of the lamp. That is why many wall paintings are best seen by torchlight or acetylene lamp, for they simulate the original conditions. Electric lighting is dull and lifeless by comparison.

Provided the surfaces were suitable much parietal art may have been executed

Figure 73: Upper Palaeolithic Engravings
1. Horses, on bone: an impressionistic composition. Lespugue, Haute-Garonne (Late Magdalenian). 2. Giant ox, on wall of stalagmite in the cave of Teyjat, Dordogne (Late Magdalenian: broken blocks of other engravings once on the wall found in the occupational deposits below). 3. Mammoth, on wall of Les Combarelles, Dordogne (Magdalenian). 4. Bison, on wall of shelter at La Grèze, Dordogne (Magdalenian or Solutrian). 5. Reindeer, on bone. Limeuil, Dordogne (Magdalenian). 6. Salmon, in bas-relief on roof of a small cave, Grotte du Poisson, at Les Eyzies, Dordogne (probably Perigordian). 7. Woman: part of a series of incised lines ('macaronis') drawn with fingers on the soft clay of the roof of the cave of Pech-Merle, Dordogne (considered Aurignacian). 8. Deer hind, on wall of the cave of Castillo, Santander, Spain (Magdalenian). 9. Head of hind, on bone, found in Early Magdalenian occupational deposits at Altamira Cave, Santander, Spain. Note the similarity in style to 8. 10. Human figure, on bone, apparently wearing a garment secured by buttons. Cave of Montastruc, Bruniquel, Dordogne (Late Magdalenian).

Figure 74: Upper Palaeolithic Artists' Equipment
1. Bone paint-tube. La Grotte des Cottés, Vienne. 2. Reconstruction of engraving tool, set with resin into a wooden handle. 3. Stone plaque and pebble pestle for grinding pigment. Kostienki IV, USSR. 4. Limestone lamp. La Mouthe, Dordogne. 5. Mammoth rib, used as palette. Kostienki I, USSR. 6. Red ochre crayon. Abri Blanchard, Dordogne.

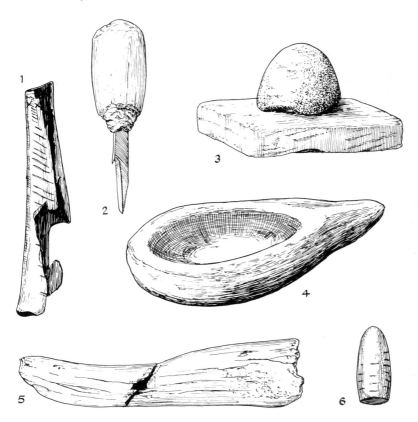

fairly close to cave entrances, where at least some light would penetrate, but, with the exception of a few engravings, if they did once exist then they have not survived. This is not surprising, as chemical dissolution and other natural erosion of the rock surface would be expected in places subject to damp, sunlight, frost and vegetation. However, it is tempting to imagine many of the rock shelters and cave entrances adorned with colourful paintings. Some support for the idea is given by occasional discoveries, as at Bagillou, of pieces of fallen rock wall bearing traces of paint found within occupational levels. Such painting may have been purely decorative, but when paintings, engravings and signs of other activities are found deep inside caves, often in places of very difficult access and total darkness, they can hardly have been prompted by such simple motives. The case for a magical element is strong, and many anthropologists would see virtually all Upper Palaeolithic art as an expression of the hunters' fears, desires and thoughts. Certainly, somewhere in the multitude of known paintings, engravings, symbols and patterns is contained something of their concept of the world about them. It was a vastly different world from ours and it could never be explained by what we like to call rationalism. Ritual and magic must have dominated and were probably essential for the co-ordination of the community. This is epitomised by dramatic discoveries in two caves in the Pyrenees: Montespan and Tuc d'Audoubert. At both places, within galleries over 100 m from the entrances and difficult to approach, are the remains of animals sculptured in clay. Some of those at Montespan are punctured with holes, presumably caused by spears thrown in some hunting ritual. There are thirty representations of animals in this gallery, either fully sculptured or in low relief, moulded out of soft cave earth. Round the walls are many engravings cut into the rock. None of the animal statues is very well modelled; the most famous is a headless bear, nearly a metre long. A real bear's skull was found between the forelegs of this statue and appears to have originally been attached to the body by a wooden peg. A bear skin may have been draped over the statue to increase the lifelike aspect of the animal, into which spears were thrown. At Tuc d'Audoubert were found two excellently modelled clay bisons, but these had not been mutilated by ritual 'killing'. Within the same gallery as these bison is a low alcove with traces of what has been interpreted as an initiation ceremony for children attaining puberty. The clay floor has a series of heel impressions forming a semicircle and is associated with a number of clay phalli.

Many other examples could be cited of engravings and paintings that appear to have a magical element. Less obvious, but of equal importance, are the positioning and grouping of them. Detailed analyses of French sites strongly suggest that this is by no means random, and it is not chance that has determined the grouping of certain types of animals together, however haphazard it may appear. Some archaeologists consider that it is the expression of the male and female principle. Certainly, the people of these advanced hunting communities were much concerned with sexuality and fertility, for simple, engraved representations of genitalia, mainly female, are frequently found, and the Venus figurines are pregnant, as also are many of the animals depicted. Particularly fascinating are the grid-like patterns of lines and dots that are painted in several caves, especially in those of northern Spain, referred to as tectiforms. What they symbolise or signify can only be guessed, but examples are shown in Figure 75, including some of the simple designs painted on pebbles, peculiar to the Azilian

Figure 75: Upper Palaeolithic Painted or Engraved Symbols
1. Hand impression on wall of cave. Pech-Merle, Dordogne. 2.-3. Mutilated hand impressions. Gargas, Hautes-Pyrénées. 4.-6. Tectiforms painted in red. Font-de-Gaume, Dordogne. 7.-10. Tectiforms painted in red. Castillo Cave, Spain. 11. Tectiform painted in black. Castillo, Spain. 12. Tectiform painted in red. Altamira, Spain. 13. Club sign painted in black. Pindal, Spain. 14. Hand sign painted in black. Santian, Spain. 15. Engraving. Altamira, Spain. 16. 'Basket' painted in red. Cantal, Lot. 17. Vulva, engraved on stone slab. La Ferrassie, Dordogne. 18.-20. Azilian painted pebbles. Mas d'Azil, Ariège. 21.-25. Tectiforms painted in red or black. Lascaux, Dordogne.
The chequered squares of 21 are black, red and yellow. The basket-like tectiform of 25 is the central piece of a composition with two ibexes.

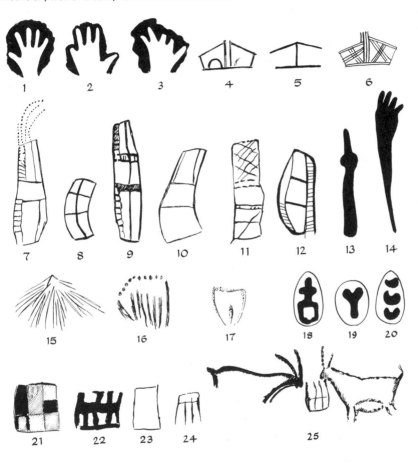

Figure 76

of France and Solutrian of Spain.

Occasionally, cave paintings form an obvious composition, in contrast to the apparent individual nature of most representations (Figure 76). One of the best is a line of deer heads painted above a natural ledge in the great cave of Lascaux, giving a wonderful impression of a swimming herd. Compositions are also evident on some engravings, such as the moving herd of deer on an engraving from Teyjat, Dordogne, a remarkable example of early impressionism. The artist, in these instances, may have been attempting to recreate a scene from his memory. A few paintings and rough engravings are also known involving stylised human figures which could be interpreted as depicting actual incidents. One of the most readily understandable is the scene painted in a lower gallery at Lascaux, showing a speared bison with its entrails hanging out. The wounded bison has apparently turned on the hunter, who lies stretched out before the animal. His penis is shown, so this supports the idea that hunters were often naked during the chase. Beside him is what looks like a bird on a stick, almost certainly a decorated spear thrower that he has dropped. Spear throwers (see below) have actually been found at Laugerie Basse and Les Trois Frères with their hooks in the form of a bird. In the background a rhinoceros is retreating and defecating.

The rarity of the human figure in Upper Palaeolithic parietal art contrasts with its common use in the much more representational art of later post-Palaeolithic hunters in Africa and Australia. A few examples are known, as at Pech Merle (Figure 73, no. 7), where a female figure has been traced in outline by finger or stick on the soft, decalcified limestone of the roof. Such tracings are usually nothing more than series of squiggles and lines, more akin to doodling than to art. They are aptly called 'macaronis'. When a human figure is drawn more carefully, there is none of the detail and skill shown in the animal paintings and engravings. It is not unreasonable to assume that there was some form of taboo on the representation of the human form, and that this was respected by the more proficient artists. This may have been relaxed for the painting of the strange, masked 'sorcerers' in the cave at Les Trois Frères (see Figure 78, no. 6) and Altamira or the engravings at Teyjat and Combarelles. Also, at Cougnac and Pech Merle are outline paintings of human figures with spears embedded in them, suggesting that murder or punishment was not unknown.

The most interesting human portrayals are the small statuettes known as Venus figurines (Figure 71), ranging from the naturalistic through various forms

Figure 76: Upper Palaeolithic Cave Paintings
1. Reindeer. Black and brown, polychrome. Lascaux, Dordogne. 2. Cow and horse. Black and red, polychrome. Lascaux, Dordogne. 3. Bison. Black and red, polychrome. Altamira, Spain. 4. Deer. Black outline. Chimeneas, Monte Castillo, Spain. 5. Horse. Black outline. Niaux, Ariège. 6. Speared human figure. Black outline. Cougnac, Lot. 7. Speared human figure. Red outline. Pech-Merle, Dordogne. 8. Mammoth. Black outline. Pech-Merle, Lot. 9. Elephant. Red outline. Pindal, Spain.
With few exceptions, Upper Palaeolithic representational parietal art is restricted to animals, mainly bison, horse and deer. Human figures are very rare, and are never portrayed in the same detail as many of the animals. Possibly a taboo existed, but this may have been relaxed for the painting of the strange, masked 'sorcerers' in the cave at Les Trois Frères and Altamira or the engravings at Teyjat and Combarelles. Also, at Cougnac and Pech-Merle are outline paintings of human figures with spears embedded in them, suggesting that murder or punishment was not unknown.

of stylisation to the almost unrecognisable. The majority are of pregnant women with their sexual characteristics exaggerated. By our modern standards, some are grotesque, others are beautiful; some have clearly been made incompetently, while others have had much skill and care lavished upon them. Their distribution is mainly in central Europe and western Russia, but they have been found in France and Italy. Where they can be dated, the majority belong to periods with Late Perigordian (particularly Vc with 'Noailles burins') and Eastern Gravettian leptolithic industries. Later forms are usually more stylised, as are the most easterly group known in the Siberian Upper Palaeolithic. Only at Brassempouy, France, is the modelling of a head done in such a fashion that it could be regarded as the likeness of a particular person. In all other instances the features of the face are rudimentary or non-existent. The figurines are generally only a few centimetres high; the Venus of Willendorf is, for instance, just under 11 cm. They are made from many different materials, but usually from a softish rock such as limestone or sandstone, or of bone or ivory. Some were very likely made of wood, but these have not survived. One from Savignano in Italy is made of serpentine rock, and the Venus of Sireuil, France, of stalagmite. The most surprising material used was that for the Venus of Dolni Vestonice, for this statuette has been finely modelled in a mixture of clay and wood ash and fired hard.

The Dolni Vestonice Venus is the oldest example of pottery in the world, and an actual kiln has been identified at this site, contained within the second hut noted in the first section of this chapter. The hearth of this hut was surrounded by a vaulted structure built of clay and limestone grit, 40 cm above the hearth floor, and showed signs of intense heating. The sooty layer above the hearth floor contained over 2,000 pellets of baked clay, waste products in the modelling and firing of human and animal statuettes of terracotta. Most of the pellets were shapeless, but some showed traces of modelling and fingerprints. These included many broken or unfinished animal figures. Pottery figurines are not known from any other Upper Palaeolithic site, and this invention of ceramic techniques was a flash which failed to ignite any need or response in the community and probably died with its inventor. There is no further evidence for pottery until the post-glacial period.

Bone objects were frequently made with great skill, and decorated with animal or geometric designs, either by engraving or by modelling in the round. Functional objects such as spear throwers were ideal for displaying imagination, and the hook at the end of this Magdalenian invention was carved in many different forms (Figure 77). Horses' heads were fashionable on one type, and the bird at the top of the spear thrower shown in the hunting scene at Lascaux has already been mentioned. A superb, complete example from Mas d'Azil can only be interpreted as an Upper Palaeolithic joke, for it depicts a young ibex as though it were standing on a rock, with its head turned to observe the bizarre spectacle of two birds perched on its own defecations! Even more astonishing is the discovery of the broken ends of two more spear throwers at Bedeilhac and Saint Michel d'Arudy, also in the French Pyrenees, with the same design in a somewhat degenerated form. The joke, or whatever it meant, was popular!

A puzzling type of worked deer antler is the so-called 'bâton de commandement', comprising the beam of an antler with a wide hole drilled or cut in the flattish fork between two truncated tines. Decorated and undecorated examples

Figure 77: Upper Palaeolithic Decorated Bone Objects and Sculpture
1. Spear thrower. Mas d'Azil, Ariège. ($^1/_3$) 2. Spear thrower. Le Placard, Charente. (c.$^1/_3$)
3. 'Wand'. Isturitz, Basse-Pyrénées. (c.$^1/_3$) 4. 'Bâton de commandement': either a shaft
straightener or some form of mace or insignia. Pekarna Cave, Czechoslovakia. (c.½)
5. 'Bâton de commandement'. Grotte de Lacave, Lot. (c.½) 6. Detail of hook of spear
thrower, carved as a mammoth. Canecaude, Aude. (½) 7. 'Amulet' of bone in the shape of
a horse's head. Grotte de la Vache, Ariège. (c.$^1/_3$) 8. Bone inscribed with dots and lines,
possibly some form of notation or a calendar. Gorge d'Enfer, Les Eyzies, Dordogne. (c.½)
9. Bear statuette carved from limestone. Anosovka, USSR (½) 10. Bone 'knife'. Predmost,
Czechoslovakia. (c.½)
All Magdalenian except 8 and 10 which are Aurignacian.

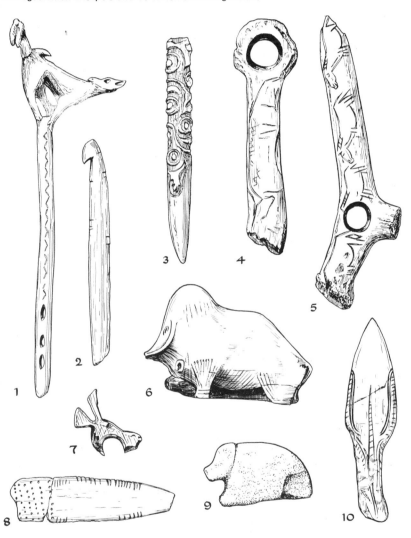

are known throughout the whole of the Upper Palaeolithic period in France, although it is those associated with the Magdalenian industry which are decorated (Figure 77). They have been interpreted as either some form of mace or insignia, hence 'bâtons de commandement', or as functional tools for straightening spear shafts, on the basis of their resemblance to recent Eskimo tools for this purpose. The tool is used by placing a wooden spear shaft through the hole and, where appropriate, twisting the handle so as to bend the wood. It gives a very delicate control over the pressure that is applied. If these perforated 'bâtons' have to be relegated to the role of tools, this cannot be the case with some elaborately decorated lengths of bone or ivory. These really may have been ceremonial wands. Richly decorated examples come from the Magdalenian levels at Isturitz and Saint Michel d'Arudy (Figure 77).

There is a multitude of different tools and other objects made of bone and ivory in the Upper Palaeolithic of Europe, Russia and Siberia: pins, spatulae, plaques, knives, daggers, fish hooks, fork-shaped pieces, handles, etc. (some typical examples are illustrated in Figure 77). The working of bone and antler involved many techniques. One of the most difficult operations was the production of a suitable blank, usually in the form of a flat length approximating to the shape of the piece to be made. This could be done by smashing bones with stone hammers until they splintered and then selecting a suitable piece. A more refined and controlled method was the groove and splinter technique, in which deep, parallel cuts were made with a flint graver through the hard bone until the soft, internal cancellous part was reached. The intervening splinter could then be prised up and taken out. By the time of the Magdalenian industry this technique was applied to antler so as to obtain blanks for the specialised barbed points. Controlled snapping of bone was achieved by preliminary grooving with a sharp flake, and final shaping was done by cutting, sawing, whittling, scraping and drilling. Mammoth tusk ivory was treated in a similar manner on Eastern Gravettian and Russian sites, with long strips removed by preliminary grooving. Percussion flaking was also used for the initial shaping of larger pieces. Ivory is best split when dried out, but bone and antler are very hard and difficult to work in this state. Antler, fresh from the animal, is relatively soft and resilient, but both bone and antler can be temporarily softened for ease of working by long soaking in water. It is claimed that a small diadem of ivory from Malta, Siberia, had been steamed into shape by first soaking, then placing in a wet skin on a fire.

Another aspect of Upper Palaeolithic art is the beauty of some of the flint-work; the regularity and symmetry of many flint blades represent an attainment of skill that justifies the term 'art'. An accidental discovery of a cache of 14 Solutrian laurel leaf points was made at Volgu, Saône-et-Loire in 1873. They are the most elegant flints ever fashioned in the whole of the Palaeolithic, only equalled by some of the work of Neolithic Egypt and Denmark. They are very thin and one, 0.35 m long, is made of superb-quality brown-coloured flint (Plate XXI). Red ochre is said to have been associated, and this hoard may have been a votive offering, although there is nothing else in this period to suggest such a custom. Also, from Etiolles in France, was a flint blade 0.60 m long, and this must have been made more as a *tour de force* than for the fulfilment of any useful need.

Many perforated bones have been found which are regarded as whistles and flutes (Figure 78). Perforated toe bones of deer, which would certainly have made effective whistles, are known from many sites and were possibly of great importance in directing combined hunting operations. Hollow long bones with lines of holes can only be flutes, but, unfortunately, not a single complete specimen has ever been found so it is not possible to know how they sounded or what scale interval was used. One from Molodova was made of elk horn and had six holes. There is a perforated long bone of hare from Kent's Cavern, and other flutes are known from Le Placard, Pair-non-Pair, Dolni Vestonice, Istállóskö and Pekarna. Some support for the idea of Upper Palaeolithic music comes from the engraving of a 'sorcerer' at Les Trois Frères, for there is an object in his mouth which might be a flute. The tonal qualities of stretched animal gut may well have been discovered, and the concept of rhythm could have been ingrained from much further back in time. 'Bull-roarers' are flat, elongated oval pieces of bone with a perforation at one end for the attachment of a line. When spun round at speed they emit a loud and strange whirring noise. They have been found at several sites and may come into this category of music.

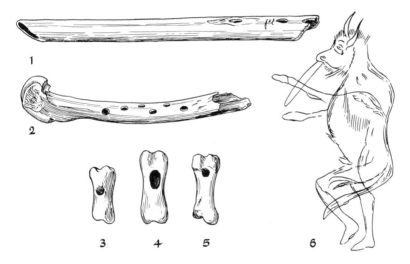

Figure 78: Upper Palaeolithic Music
1. Flute. Pair-non-Pair, Gironde. 2. Perforated leg bone of hare. Kent's Cavern, England. 3.-5. Perforated toe bones of deer, probably used as whistles. 3. Pekarna Cave, Czechoslovakia. 4. La Madeleine. 5. Bruniquel. 6. Engraving of a man clad in a bison's skin in the cave of Les Trois Frères, apparently playing a flute or bow-shaped instrument and dancing. A retreating deer and bison are part of the same composition.
People at this time may have discovered the tonal qualities of stretched animal gut, and the concept of rhythm could have been ingrained from much further back in time.

Curiosity seems responsible for the occasional presence in caves or other occupied sites of fossil shells, unusual stones, pieces of amber and various oddments foreign to the district, but certain bones with series of engraved marks and lines suggest that curiosity was leading to serious methodical attempts to comprehend the world. A careful, microscopic study of these notched bones has enabled marks on many of them to be placed into sets or series that appear to have been executed on single, specific occasions. It has been found possible to identify, for instance, marks cut by different tools. Statistical and arithmetical analyses of the results favour the idea of some form of notation, and this may have been of lunar observations. If these marked bones and tectiforms really are attempts to symbolise ideas by concrete signs, men of this period had already made the intellectual advance that was to lead to writing and numeration. It could be significant that examples of these 'calendars' are found in such contexts as the earliest Upper Palaeolithic industries in France (such as the Abri Blanchard), in the Perigordian at Isturitz, the Spanish Solutrian at Parpallo, and the Eastern Gravettian of Moravia. They are not restricted to the final stages of the Upper Palaeolithic.

Notes

1. Leroi-Gourhan, 1976, p. 661.
2. Rigaud, 1976, p. 1269.
3. Leroi-Gourhan, 1976, p. 656.
4. Movius, 1966.
5. Sackett and Gaussen, 1976.
6. Leroi-Gourhan, 1976, p. 659.
7. Ibid., p. 662.
8. Leroi-Gourhan and Brezillon, 1972.
9. Leroi-Gourhan, 1976, p. 659.
10. Klima, 1954.
11. Müller-Karpe, 1966.
12. Klima, 1954.
13. Klein, 1969b.
14. Grigor'ev, 1967.
15. Mongait, 1961, p. 98.
16. Dart and Beaumont, 1969.
17. Meszáros and Vértes, 1955.
18. Thorne and Macumber, 1972.
19. Wendt, 1976.

References

The publications noted for Chapter 6 apply equally to Chapter 7. Below are some references particularly relevant to this chapter.

Dwellings

France:	Leroi-Gourhan, 1976; Movius, 1966.
Czechoslovakia:	Klima, 1954.
Poland:	Kozlowski *et al.*, 1974.
USSR:	Childe, 1950; Klein, 1969b.

Upper Palaeolithic Human Discoveries

General:	Bordes, 1972.
France:	Lumley, 1976.
Europe:	Oakley, Campbell and Molleson, 1971.
Africa:	Oakley and Campbell, 1967.
Asia:	Oakley, Campbell and Molleson, 1975.
Australia:	Oakley, Campbell and Molleson, 1975; Mulvaney and Golson, 1971; Thorne, 1971; Barbetti and Allen, 1972.

America: Oakley, Campbell and Molleson, 1975; Bryan, 1969.
Britain: Molleson, 1976.

Art

General, descriptive: Powell, 1966; Kuhn, 1958, 1966; Laming, 1959;
                                  Sieveking, 1979.
Venus figurines: Graziozi, 1960.
Spear throwers: Garrod, 1955b.
Bone discs: Sieveking, 1971.
Notched bone calendars: Marshack, 1971, 1972, 1979.

Epilogue

The Upper Palaeolithic peoples in western Europe, from the Atlantic coast to the Ukraine, between about 33,000 and 9,000 BC, had achieved the most efficient and organised communities known in the world at that time. This is if achievement is measured in terms of economic stability, growth of population, territorial expansion, technical advance and invention. These are all material things which archaeology can, to a limited extent, discern from the evidence. As has been seen, in comparison with earlier periods, there is a wealth of knowledge for the Upper Palaeolithic. Is it possible to see how the economic successes of some of these people enabled arable and pastoral farming to flourish only a few thousand years after the last retreat of the glaciers in the northern hemisphere? What happened, between 8000 and 6000 BC, to create a completely new economy and eventually destroy almost all trace of the old hunting societies? Why did it not happen first in the region that was most advanced?

This period, by definition from about 8500 BC to the advent of farming communities, is known as the Mesolithic. It is not the concern of this general survey of the Palaeolithic to consider how farming communities became established, or the momentous changes that occurred as a result. This is a vast subject that has absorbed the attentions of numerous eminent archaeologists. However, it would be inappropriate to conclude this survey of the Palaeolithic age without some comment on the gradual disappearance of hunting economies.

It is irrefutable that the earliest Neolithic farming economies of the 7th millenium BC are found in western Asia and parts of the Balkans and the Mediterranean. In middle America they do not occur until about 2500 BC, and then on a more restricted level. In the Old World they spread outwards and, in this respect, it was clearly a matter of the diffusion of ideas or people, or both. However, some domestication of animals and the cultivation of certain plants and fruits were probably achieved independently by hunting groups in various parts of the world, merely to supplement the food obtained by hunting and gathering. Only when a community became *more* dependent for their food supply on cultivated crops and domestic animals than on the food obtained by hunting and gathering, can it be said to have achieved a true Neolithic economy. When a community became totally dependent on cultivated crops and domesticated animals, it can be said to have had a full Neolithic economy. Between such a full Neolithic economy, and hunting and gathering, was a countless variety of intermediate stages, many of which survived into historical time.

Mesolithic people were still motivated by traditions they had inherited from the advanced hunting communities of the Upper Palaeolithic. In many parts of the world they would have been oblivious of the great changes taking place elsewhere. In some places farmers and hunters would clash, but there is no archaeological evidence of any physical conflict. The world was still a large place, and the hunter-gatherers had little problem in finding alternative hunting grounds. Some adopted the new ideas.

To return to the questions, especially the one as to the problem of why the most advanced societies of the Upper Palaeolithic in Europe did not develop into the first farming communities, it is necessary to consider the state of the world at about 9000-8000 BC. The major retreat of glacial ice and a relatively rapid amelioration of the climate had drastic effects upon the populations of what are now the temperate zones of the northern hemisphere. Vast tracts of open grazing land were becoming forest, and herds of animals slowly migrated northwards to find feeding grounds. Reindeer, and later red deer, left central Europe and Russia. Aurochs and horse followed in smaller numbers. Mammoth and woolly rhinoceros were now extinct.

Similar migrations of animals must have taken place at other times in the Upper Palaeolithic, during the milder interstadial periods. These had occurred with no apparent serious disruption of the way of life. Although this amelioration of the climate may have been more marked, it cannot be the sole reason for the breakdown of the well-established Magdalenian communities, with their semi-permanent camps, advanced technology and refined art. Late Glacial and then Mesolithic communities had adapted to a more shifting, nomadic existence.

One of the reasons for this change to the nomadic life is likely to have been over-specialisation. It has been seen in the last two chapters that the Magdalenians in particular based their economy on the hunting of reindeer. In order to do this so successfully it seems certain that they practised some form of conscious conservation, culling the herds selectively. Light, flint-tipped throwing spears and bows and arrows would allow the accuracy of aim required for such systematic killing. As the herds migrated northwards the hunters did not attempt to change their economy and remain where they were, not because such change was impossible but because there was no apparent reason for it. One generation followed the customs and traditions of the previous one. Deer hunting dominated all other economic activities, and the latter must have contributed less and less as the hunters migrated into harsher habitats. Seasonal mobility became essential and the pattern for Mesolithic people's lives. The dog was domesticated to aid in the hunt, landscapes were burnt to encourage the growth of herbage for the deer, ivy was collected possibly as bait, or even as feedstuff for captured animals. This was the threshold of animal domestication, but it never developed. In western Asia, however, Mesolithic people with a Natufian industry went one stage further. Their economy was similar in that it depended on hunting gazelles and goats, but wild grasses were collected extensively in order to supplement the diet. Such grasses, the ancestors of cultivated wheat and barley, must have been collected by earlier hunter-gatherers in this region, but it was the combination of efficient, controlled gazelle hunting with the abundance of such grasses, at a time of very favourable climate, that probably allowed more permanent occupation of sites. It was but a short step to the intentional planting of the seed and the domestication of goats. Such humble activities were probably regarded as insignificant by the hunting section of the community. It was unlikely that anyone could have foreseen the inevitable consequences of such action: the eventual creation of static societies with a large surplus of food.

Figure 79: Tentative Time Chart of Palaeolithic Industries

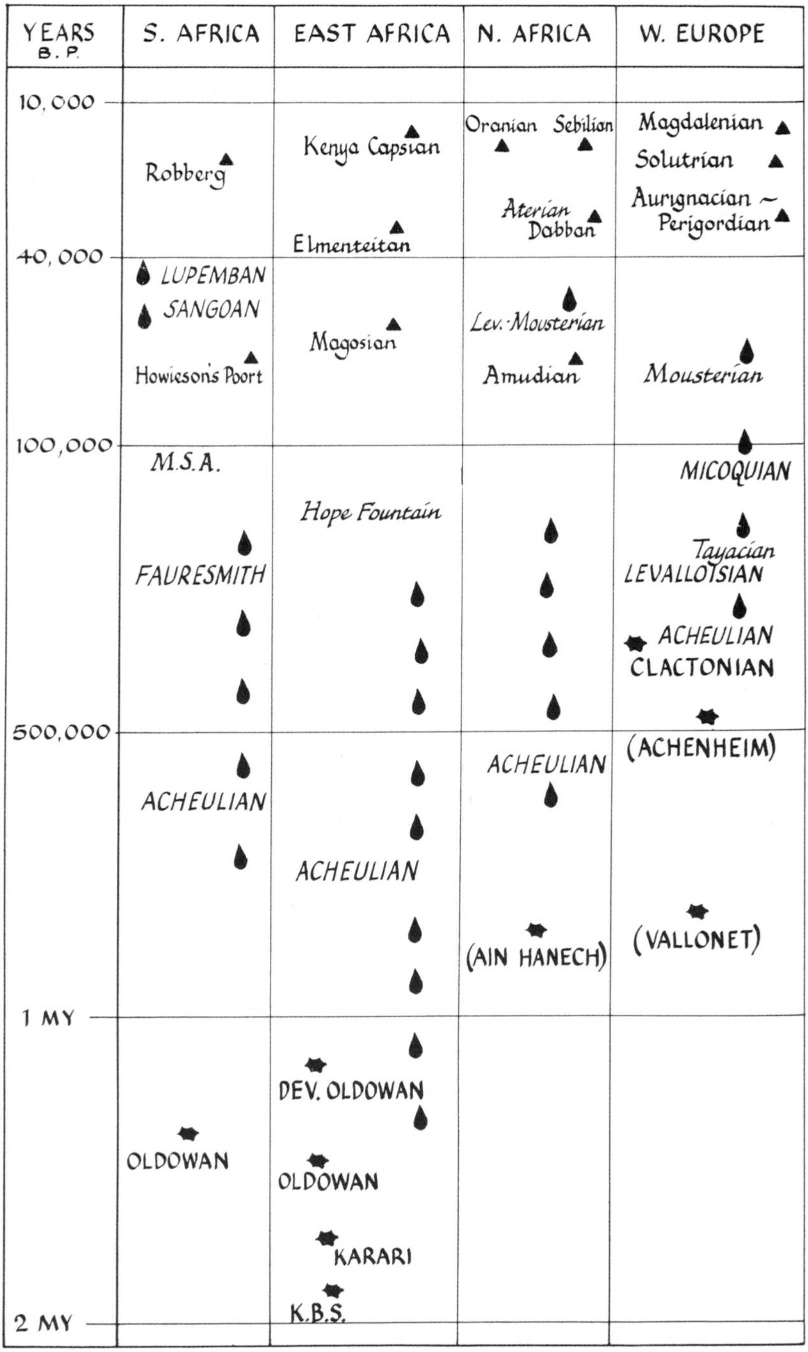

YEARS B.P.	S. AFRICA	EAST AFRICA	N. AFRICA	W. EUROPE
10,000	Robberg ▲	Kenya Capsian ▲	Oranian ▲ Sebilian ▲	Magdalenian ▲ Solutrian ▲ Aurignacian ～ ▲ Perigordian
		Elmenteitan ▲	Aterian ▲ Dabban	
40,000	● LUPEMBAN ● SANGOAN Howieson's Poort ▲	Magosian ▲	Lev. Mousterian ● Amudian ▲	Mousterian ●
100,000	M.S.A.	Hope Fountain	●	MICOQUIAN ●
	FAURESMITH ● ● ●	● ● ● ●	● ● ●	Tayacian LEVALLOISIAN ● ● ACHEULIAN CLACTONIAN ✱
500,000	● ACHEULIAN ● ●	● ● ● ACHEULIAN	ACHEULIAN ●	(ACHENHEIM)
		● ● (AIN HANECH) ✱		(VALLONET) ✱
1 MY	✱ OLDOWAN	● ✱ DEV. OLDOWAN ●		
		✱ OLDOWAN ✱ KARARI ✱ K.B.S.		
2 MY				

Figure 79: contd

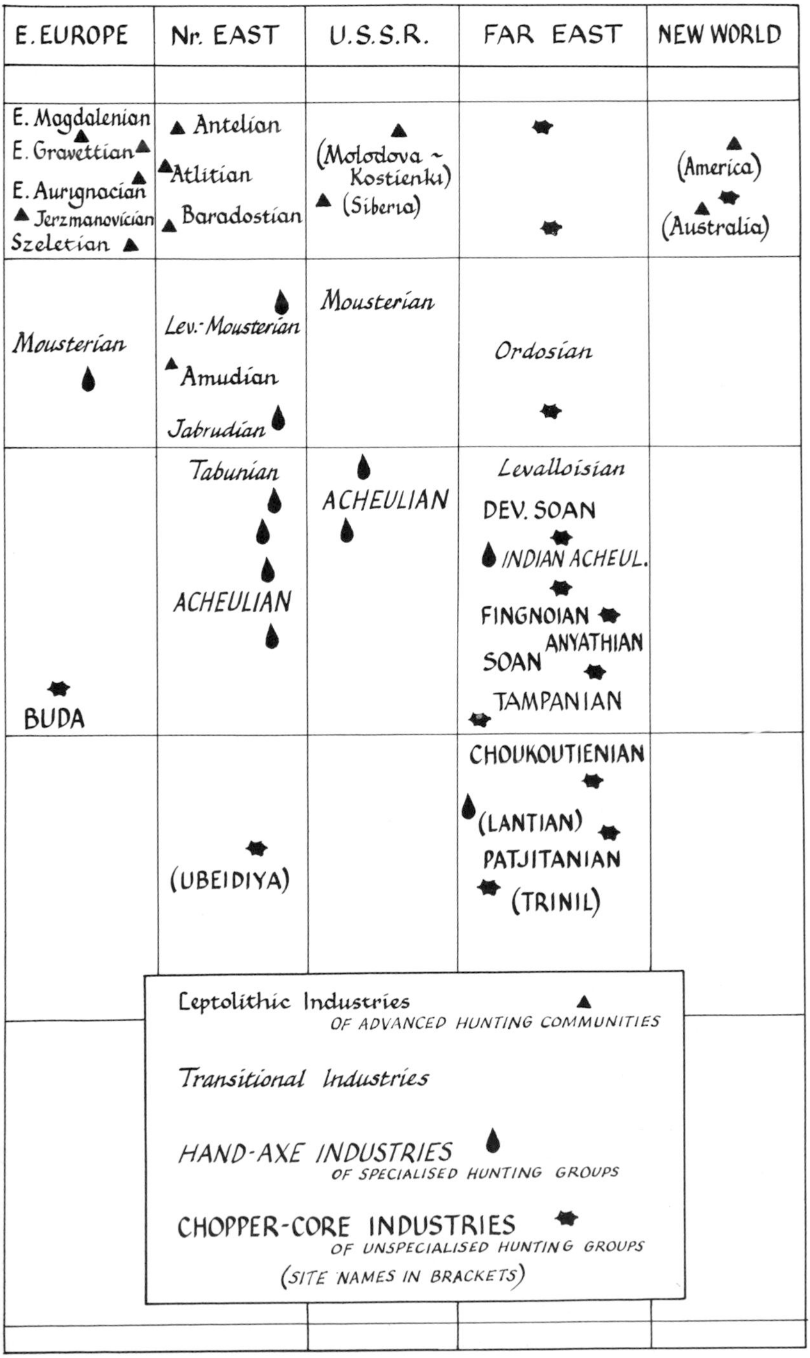

E. EUROPE	Nr. EAST	U.S.S.R.	FAR EAST	NEW WORLD
E. Magdalenian E. Gravettian ▲ E. Aurignacian ▲ ▲ Jerzmanovician Szeletian ▲	▲ Antelian ▲ Atlitian ▲ Baradostian	▲ (Molodova ~ Kostienki) ▲ (Siberia)	✶ ✶	▲ (America) ▲ ✶ (Australia)
Mousterian ◗	◗ Lev.-Mousterian ▲ Amudian Jabrudian ◗	Mousterian	Ordosian ✶	
✶ BUDA	Tabunian ◗ ◗ ◗ ACHEULIAN ◗	◗ ACHEULIAN ◗	Levalloisian DEV. SOAN ✶ ◗ INDIAN ACHEUL. ✶ FINGNOIAN ✶ ANYATHIAN SOAN ✶ TAMPANIAN	
	(UBEIDIYA) ✶		CHOUKOUTIENIAN ✶ ◗ (LANTIAN) ✶ PATJITANIAN ✶ (TRINIL)	

Leptolithic Industries   ▲
OF ADVANCED HUNTING COMMUNITIES

Transitional Industries

HAND-AXE INDUSTRIES   ◗
OF SPECIALISED HUNTING GROUPS

CHOPPER-CORE INDUSTRIES   ✶
OF UNSPECIALISED HUNTING GROUPS

(SITE NAMES IN BRACKETS)

These developments in Europe and western Asia tend to overshadow what was happening in the rest of the world. It has been seen that by now people had spread over all of the Old World, and much of the New. It is important not to forget that most of these people, probably the major part of the population of the earth, were at a far lower stage of economic and social development than the Euro-Asian Upper Palaeolithic. Parts of West Africa, South East Asia, Polynesia and Australia were not far removed from a lifestyle of savagery rather than barbarism in the sense of the terms as used here. The rich, advanced hunting communities of southern Africa appear to have degenerated or gone elsewhere. Shell middens on the African coasts give the impression of people with a precarious, lowly economy. Only in East and northern Africa are occupied rock shelters and cave mouths with evidence for a much less nomadic existence. Small, shifting hunting groups coping with their environments with varying degrees of success or failure populated China, India and much of the Far East. It is impossible to generalise or identify the factors which combined to produce success or failure in one place or another; they are too numerous or unknown. It is not even easy to assess what is failure or what is success. Starvation and death are certainly failure, but the measurement of success is a philosophical matter. What is certain is that, at the end of the Palaeolithic age, the levels of economies and social organisation throughout the world varied greatly. It is also apparent that from the earliest beginnings of humanity almost two million years ago there has always been a bewildering range of variation in physical make-up, cultural level, economies and technologies. There has never been one time when a uniform pattern of behaviour has been present in a world inhabited by the same sub-species of *Homo*. The closest to a uniform culture throughout the world was probably during the period of the specialised hunting groups, when hand-axes appear to symbolise it, but this may be more apparent than real.

It is difficult to deny that this ability to adapt and change in almost every environment is the advantage which places Man at the top of the evolutionary tree. If advancement is seen as a development towards modern society, then it is clear that it has not happened along a continuous line. Palaeolithic archaeology demonstrates that advancement by one group reaches a certain point beyond which it is seemingly inhibited from progressing or is unable to adapt successfully to changing circumstances. The 'torch' of advancement then transfers to another population group, where it burns even brighter. This seems particularly true of the Upper Palaeolithic, and the progressive nations of the present world might do well to ponder on it.

Bibliography

Agache, R., Bourdier, F. and Petit, R. (1963) 'Le Quaternaire de la Basse Somme: Tentative de Synthèse', *Bull. Soc. Géol. de France*, serie 7, *5*, 422-42

Aguirre, E. (1969) 'Torralba y Ambrona', *Zeltiberica*, Soria, *31*, 7-19

—, Basabe, J.M. and Torres, y T. (1976) 'Los Fósiles Humanos de Atapuerca (Burgos): Nota Preliminar', *Zephyrvs*, 26-27, 489-511

Aigner, J. and Laughlin, W.S. (1973) 'The Dating of Lantian Man and his Significance for Analysing Trends in Human Evolution', *American J. Phys. Anthropol.*, *39* (1), 97-109

Aitken, M.J. (1974) *Physics and Archaeology*, Clarendon Press, Oxford

Albright, W.F. (1949) *The Archaeology of Palestine*, Penguin Books

Alimen, H. (1957) *The Prehistory of Africa*, Hutchinson, London

Allchin, B. (1957) 'Australian Stone Industries. Past and Present', *J. R. Anthropol. Inst.*, *87*, 115-36

— and Allchin, R. (1968) *The Birth of Indian Civilization: India and Pakistan Before 500 BC*, Penguin Books

Allchin, F.R. and Hammond, N. (eds) (1978) *The Archaeology of Afghanistan*, Academic Press, London, New York

Anati, E., Avnimclech, M., Haas, N. and Meyerhof, E. (1973) 'Hazorea 1', *Archivi*, *5*, *Edizioni de Centro Camuno di Studi Preistorici*

— and Haas, N. (1967) 'The Hazorea Pleistocene Site: a Preliminary Report', *Man*, *2* (3), 454-6, Plates 4-8

Anciaux de Faveaux, Dom Adalbert (1962) 'Travaux d'Approche pour une Synthèse Climatique, Stratigraphique et Archaéologique des Plateaux des Biano', *Proc. 4th. Pan-Afr. Congr. Prehist.*

Apsimon, A., Gamble, C. and Shackley, M. (1977) 'Pleistocene Raised Beaches on Ports Down, Hampshire', *Proc. Hants. Field Club Archaeol. Soc.*, *33*, 17-32

Arambourg, C. (1954) 'L'Hominien Fossile de Ternifine (Algérie)', *C. R. Acad. Sci. Paris*, *239*, 893-5

Arambourou, R. (1976) 'Les Civilisations du Paléolithique Supérieur dans le Sud-Ouest (Landes)' in H. de Lumley (ed.), *La Préhistoire Française*, *2*, CNRS, Paris, pp. 1243-51

Ardrey, R. (1961) *African Genesis*, Collins, London

Arkell, A.J. (1949) 'The Old Stone Age in the Anglo-Egyptian Sudan', *Occ. Paper Sudan Antiquities Service*, *1*, Khartoum

Avnimelech, M.A. (1967) 'A Preliminary Account of the Geological Situation of the Prehistoric Site near Hazorea', *Man*, *2* (3), 457-61

Barbetti, N. and Allen, H. (1972) 'Prehistoric Man at Lake Mungo, Australia, by 32,000 years BP', *Nature*, *240*, 46-8

Bartstra, G.-J. (1978) 'The Age of the Djetis Beds in East and Central Java', Note in *Antiquity*, *52* (204), 56-8

Bar-Yosef, O. (1975) 'Archaeological Occurrences in the Middle Pleistocene of Israel' in K.W. Butzer and G.Ll. Isaac (eds), *After the Australopithecines*, Mouton, The Hague, pp. 571-604

— and Tchernov, E. (1972) *On the Palaeoecological History of the Site of Ubeidiya*, Israel Academy of Sciences and Humanities

Baudet, J.L. (1959) 'Dunes Acheuléennes dans le Nord de la France', *Quärtar*, *10-11*, 277-81

— and Jepsen, E. (1968) 'Industries Lithiques de la Baie de Jammerland, Sjaelland', *Rev. Anthropol., Paris* (1968), 26-34

Beaumont, P.B. (1973) 'Border Cave – a Progress Report', *S. Afr. J. Science*, *69* (2), 41-6

— and Boshier, A.K. (1972) 'Some Comments on Recent Findings at Border Cave, Northern Natal', *S. Afr. J. Science*, *68* (1), 22-4

— and Vogel, J.C. (1972) 'On a New Radiocarbon Chronology for Africa South of the Equator', *African Studies*, *31*, 65-89, 155-82

Becker, C.J. (1971), 'Late Palaeolithic Finds from Denmark', *Proc. Prehist. Soc. 37* (2), 131-9

Behm-Blancke, G. (1960) *Altsteinzeitliche Rastplätze im Travertingebiet von Taubach, Weimar, Ehringsdorf*, Weimar, pp. 153-78

Behrensmeyer, A.K. (1970) 'Preliminary Geological Interpretation of a New Hominid Site in the Lake Rudolf Basin', *Nature*, *226*, 225-6

Bergounioux, F.M. (1958) ' "Spiritualité" de L'Homme de Néandertal' in G.H.R. von Koenigswald (ed.), *Neanderthal Centenary*, Wenner-Gren Foundation, New York, pp. 151-66

Bhattacharya, D.K. (1977) *Palaeolithic Europe. A Summary of Some Important Finds with Special Reference to Central Europe*, Anthropological Publications, Oosterhout, Humanities Press, Atlantic Highlands, New Jersey

Bianchini, G. (1969) 'Manufatti della "Pebble Culture" in Sicilia', *Rivista di Scienze Preistoriche*, *24* (1), 171-80

Biberson, P.J. (1961) *Le Paléolithique Inférieur du Maroc Atlantique*, Pub. Serv. des Antiquités du Maroc, *17*, Rabat

— (1968) 'Les Gisements Acheuléens de Torralba et Ambrona (Espagne). Nouvelles Précisions', *L'Anthropologie*, *72*, 241-78

Bishop, M.J. (1975) 'Earliest Record of Man's Presence in Britain', *Nature*, *253*, 95-7

Bishop, W.W. (ed.) (1978) *Geological Background to Fossil Man: Recent Research in the Gregory Rift Valley, East Africa*, Geol. Soc. London, Scottish Academic Press and University of Toronto Press

— and Chapman, G.R. (1970) 'Early Pliocene Sediments and Fossils from the Northern Kenya Rift Valley', *Nature*, *226*, 914-18

— and Clark, J.D. (eds) (1967) *The Background to Evolution in Africa; Papers Presented at a Symposium at Burg Wartenstein, Austria in 1965*, University of Chicago Press

—, Hill, A. and Pickford, M. (1978) 'Chesowanja: a Revised Geological Interpretation' in W.W. Bishop (ed.), *Geological Background to Fossil Man*, Geol. Soc. London, pp. 309-27

— and Miller, J.A. (eds) (1972) *Calibration of Hominoid Evolution. Proc. of*

Symposium held at Burg Wartenstein, Wenner-Gren Foundation, Scottish Academic Press

— and Pickford, M. (1975) 'Geology, Fauna and Palaeoenvironments of the Ngorora Formation, Kenya Rift', *Nature*, *254*, 185-92

—, Pickford, M. and Hill, A. (1975) 'New Evidence Regarding the Quaternary Geology, Archaeology and Hominids of Chesowanja, Kenya', *Nature*, *258*, 204-8

Black, D., Chardin, Teilhard de, Young, P. and Pei, W.C. (1933) 'The Choukoutien Cave Deposits with a Synopsis of our Present Knowledge of the Late Cenozoic of China', *Mem. Geol. Surv. China, Ser. A.11*, 1-166

Blanc, A.C. (1936) 'Scheggia di Tecnica Clactoniana Rinvenuta in Situ nel Quaternario della Valchetta Cartoni (Roma)', *Riv. Antropol. Roma, 31*

— (1958) 'Torre in Pietra, Saccopastore, Monte Circeo. On the Position of the Mousterian in the Pleistocene Sequence of the Rome Area' in G.H.R. von Koenigswald (ed.), *Neanderthal Centenary*, Wenner-Gren Foundation, New York, pp. 167-74

Bohmers, A. (1951) 'Die Hohlen von Mauern', *Palaeohistoria, 1*, 1

Bonsall, C.J. (1977) 'Gazetteer of Upper Palaeolithic Sites in England and Wales', *Res. Report of Council for British Archaeology, 20*, 423-511

Bordes, F. (1950) 'Principes d'une Methode d'Etude des Techniques de Débitage et de la Typologie du Paleolithique Ancien et Moyen', *L'Anthropologie, 54*, 19-34

— (1954) 'Les Gisements du Pech-de-l'Azé (Dordogne) 1. Le Mousterien de Tradition Acheuléenne', *L'Anthropologie, 58* (5-6), 401-32

— (1955) 'Les Gisements du Pech-de-l'Azé (Dordogne)', *L'Anthropologie, 59* (1-2), 1-38

— (1961) *Typologie du Paléolithique Ancien et Moyen*, Institut de Préhistoire de l'Université de Bordeaux, *1-2*

— (1968) *The Old Stone Age*, Weidenfeld and Nicolson

— (ed.) (1972) *The Origin of Homo Sapiens*, Proceedings of the Paris Symposium 2-5 September 1969 organised by Unesco in co-operation with the International Union for Quaternary Research (INQUA), Unesco, Paris

— (1973) 'On the Chronology and Contemporaneity of Different Palaeolithic Cultures in France' in C. Renfrew (ed.), *The Explanation of Cultural Change*, London, pp. 217-26

— and Fitte, P. (1953) 'L'Atelier Commont', *L'Anthropologie, 57*, 1-45

— and de Sonneville-Bordes, D. (1970) 'The Significance of Variability in Palaeolithic Assemblages', *World Archaeol, 2*, 61-73

Boriskovsky, P.I. (1958) 'Le Paléolithique de l'Ukraine', *Annales du Service d'Information Géologique 27*, Paris

Bosinski, G., Brunnacker, K. *et al.* (1966) 'Der Paläolithische Fundplatz Rheindahlen, Ziegelei, Dreesen-Westwand', *Bonner Jahrbuch, 166*, 318-60

Bourdier, F. (1967) *Préhistoire de France*, Flammarion, Paris

— (1969) 'Etude Comparée des Dépôts Quaternaires des Bassins de la Seine et de la Somme', *Bull. d'Informations des Géologues du Bassin de Paris, 21*, 169-220

Bouyssonie, A. and J., and Bardon, L. (1909) 'Découverte d'un Squelette Humain Moustérien à la Bouffia de la Chapelle-aux-Saints (Corrèze)', *L'Anthropologie, 19*, 513-18

Bowen, B.E. and Vondra, C.F. (1973) 'Stratigraphical Relationships of the Plio-Pleistocene Deposits, East Rudolf, Kenya', *Nature, 242,* 391-3

Bowen, D.Q. (1978) *Quaternary Geology: a Stratigraphic Framework for Multidisciplinary Work*, Pergamon Press

Brain, C.K. (1958) 'The Transvaal Ape-Man-Bearing Cave Deposits', *Mem. Transvaal Museum, 11,* 1-131

—— (1970) 'New Finds at the Swartkrans Australopithecine Site', *Nature, 225,* 1112-19

Breuil, H. (1939) 'Le Vrai Niveau de l'Industrie Abbevillienne', *L'Anthropologie, 49,* 13-34

—— (1952) *Four Hundred Centuries of Cave Art*, Montignac (English edn)

—— and Koslowski, L. (1932) 'Etudes de Stratigraphie Paléolithique dans le Nord de la France, la Belgique et l'Angleterre', *L'Anthropologie, 42,* 27-47

Brock, A. (1978) 'Magneto-stratigraphy East of Lake Turkana and at Olduvai Gorge: a Brief Summary' in W.W. Bishop (ed.), *Geological Background to Fossil Man*, Geol. Soc. London, p. 480

—— and Isaac, G. Ll. (1976) 'Reversal Stratigraphy and its Application at East Rudolf' in Coppens *et al.* (eds), *Earliest Man and Environments in the Lake Rudolf Basin: Stratigraphy, Palaeoecology and Evolution*, University of Chicago, Chicago and London, pp. 148-62

Broom, R. (1936) 'A New Fossil Anthropoid Skull from South Africa', *Nature, 138,* 486-8

—— (1937) 'The Sterkfontein Ape', *Nature, 139,* 326

—— (1938) 'The Pleistocene Anthropoid Apes of South Africa', *Nature, 142,* 377-9

—— (1949) 'Another New Type of Fossil Ape-man', *Nature, 163,* 57

—— and Robinson, J.T. (1949) 'A New Type of Fossil Man', *Nature, 164,* 322-3

Brothwell, D. and Higgs, E. (1969) *Science in Archaeology: a Survey of Progress and Research*, Thames and Hudson, 2nd edn

Bryan, A.L. (1969) 'Early Man in America and the Late Pleistocene Chronology of Western Canada and Alaska', *Current Anthropology, 10* (4), 339-65

Butzer, K.W. (1965) 'Acheulian Occupation Sites at Torralba and Ambrona: Their Geology', *Science, 150,* 1718-22

—— (1968) *Environment and Archaeology*, London, 2nd edn

—— (1969) 'Geological Interpretation of Two Pleistocene Hominid Sites in the Lower Omo Basin', *Nature, 222,* 1133-5

—— (1970) 'Contemporary Depositional Environments of the Omo Delta', *Nature, 226,* 425-30

—— (1971) 'The Lower Omo Basin: Geology, Fauna and Hominids of Plio-Pleistocene Formations', *Naturwissenschaften, 58,* 7-16

—— (1973) 'Re-evaluation of the Geology of the Elandsfontein (Hopefield) Site, South-western Cape, South Africa', *S. Afr. J. Sci., 69,* 234-8

—— (1974) 'Geo-Archaeological Interpretation of Acheulian Calc-Pan Sites at Doornlaagte and Rooidam (Kimberley, South Africa)', *J. Archaeol. Science, 1,* 1-25

—— and Isaac, G. Ll. (eds) (1975) *After the Australopithechines. Stratigraphy, Ecology and Culture Change in the Middle Pleistocene*, Mouton, The Hague, Paris, pp. 1-911

Calkin, J.B. (1934) 'Implements from the Higher Raised Beaches of Sussex',

Proc. Prehist. Soc. East Anglia, 7, 333-47, Figs 1-26

Campbell, B.G. (1964) 'Quantitative Taxonomy and Human Evolution' in S.L. Washburn (ed.), *Classification and Human Evolution*, Methuen, London, pp. 50-74

— (1965) 'The Nomenclature of the Hominidae, Including a Definitive List of Hominid Taxa', *Occ. Paper Roy. Anthropol. Inst.*, 22, 1-34

— (1974) *Human Evolution*, Aldine, 2nd edn

Campbell, J.B. (1977) *The Upper Palaeolithic of Britain: a Study of Man and Nature in the Late Ice Age*, 2 vols, Clarendon Press, Oxford

— and Sampson, C.G. (1971) 'A New Analysis of Kent's Cavern, Devonshire, England', *Univ. Oregon Anthropol. Papers*, 3, 1-40

Capitan, L. and Peyrony, D. (1928) *La Madeleine – son Gisement, son Industrie, ses Oeuvres d'Art*, Paris

Cardini, L. (1930) 'Il Paleolitico Superiore della Barma Grande ai Balzi Rossi', *Archivio per l'Antropologia e l'Etnologia*, 60-61, 1-461

Carney, J., Hill, A., Miller, J.A. and Walker, A. (1971) 'Late Australopithecine from Baringo District, Kenya', *Nature*, 230, 509-14

Casteret, N. (1952) *Ten Years Under the Earth*, Penguin Books

Chang, Kwang-Chih (1977) *The Archaeology of Ancient China*, Yale University Press, New Haven, London, 3rd edition, pp. 1-535

Chavaillon, J. (1970) 'Découverte d'un Niveau Oldowayen dans la Basse Valle de l'Omo (Ethiopia)', *C.R. Séances Mensuelles, Bull. Soc. Préhist. France*, 67, 7-11

Chavaillon, N. (1971) 'Les Habitats Oldowayens de Melka-Kontouré', *Actes du VIIe Congr. Panafr. Préhist. et. Quat.*, Addis Ababa

Chernysh, A.P. (1961) *Palaeolitigina Stoanka Molodova V*

Childe, V.G. (1942) *What Happened in History*, Penguin Books

— (1944) *Progress and Archaeology*, Watts, London

— (1950) 'Cave Men's Buildings', *Antiquity*, 24, 4-11

Chmielewski, W. (1961) *Civilisation de Jerzmanowice*, Instytut Historii Kultury Materialne Polskiej Akademii, Nauk, Warsaw (in French), 1-92, Plates I-XXIV

Clark, J.D. (1954) *The Prehistoric Cultures of the Horn of Africa*, Cambridge University Press

— (1958) 'The Natural Fracture of Pebbles from the Bakota Gorge, Northern Rhodesia, and its Bearing on the Kafuan Industries of Africa', *Proc. Prehist. Soc.*, 24, 64-77

— (1959) *The Prehistory of Southern Africa*, Penguin Books

— (1962) 'The Kalambo Falls Prehistoric Site: an Interim Report', *Actes du IVe Congres Panafrican de Préhistoire et de l'Etude du Quaternaire*

— (1963) 'Prehistoric Cultures of Northeast Angola and Their Significance in Tropical Africa', *Diamang. Publicaçoes Culturais*, 62, Lisbon

— (1966a) *The Distribution of Prehistoric Culture in Angola*, Companhia de Diamantes de Angola, Lisbon

— (1966b) 'Acheulian Occupation Sites in the Middle East and Africa: a Study in Cultural Variability', *American Anthropologist*, 68 (2), 202-29

— (ed.) (1967a) *Atlas of African Prehistory*, University of Chicago Press

— (1967b) 'The Middle Acheulian Occupation Site at Latamne, Northern Syria (first paper)', *Quaternaria*, 9, Rome, 1-68

— (1969a) 'The Middle Acheulian Occupation Site at Latamne, Northern Syria (second paper). Further Excavations (1965): General Results, Definitions and Interpretation', *Quaternaria, 10*, Rome, 1-71

— (ed.) (1969b) *Kalambo Falls Prehistoric Site. 1 The Geology, Palaeoecology and Detailed Stratigraphy of the Excavations*, Cambridge University Press

— (1975) 'A Comparison of the Late Acheulian Industries of Africa and the Middle East' in K.W. Butzer and G. Ll. Isaac (eds), *After the Australopithecines*, Mouton, The Hague, pp. 605-59

— and Kurashina, H. (1979a) 'Hominid Occupation of the East-Central Highland of Ethiopia in the Plio-Pleistocene', *Nature, 282*, 33-9

— and Kurashina, H. (1979b) 'An Analysis of Earlier Stone Age Bifaces from Gadeb (Locality 8E), Northern Bale Highlands, Ethiopia', *S. Afr. Archaeol. Bull., 34*, 93-109

Clark, J.G.D. (1975) *The Earlier Stone Age Settlement of Scandinavia*, Cambridge University Press

Clark, W.E. le Gros (1949 and many later editions) *History of the Primates*, British Museum (Natural History)

— (1959) *The Antecedents of Man*, Edinburgh University Press

— (1964) *The Fossil Evidence for Human Evolution*, University of Chicago Press, 2nd edn

Clarke, R.J. (1976) 'New Cranium of *Homo erectus* from Lake Ndutu, Tanzania', *Nature, 262*, 485-7

—, Howell, F.C. and Brain, C.K. (1970) 'More Evidence of an Advanced Hominid at Swartkrans', *Nature, 225*, 1219-22

Clottes, J. (1976) 'Les Civilisations du Paléolithique Supérieur dans les Pyrénées' in H. de Lumley (ed.), *La Préhistoire Française, 2*, CNRS, Paris, pp. 1214-31

Cole, G.H. (1967) 'The Later Acheulian and Sangoan of Southern Uganda' in W.W. Bishop and J.D. Clark (eds), *The Background to Evolution in Africa*, University of Chicago Press, pp. 481-528

Cole, S. (1954) *The Prehistory of East Africa*, Penguin Books

Coles, J.M. and Higgs, E.S. (1969) *The Archaeology of Early Man*, Faber and Faber, London

Collins, D. (1969) 'Culture Traditions and Environment of Early Man', *Current Anthropol, 10* (4), 267-316

Combier, J. (1967) *Le Paléolithique de l'Ardèche dans son Cadre Paléoclimatique*, Delmas, Bordeaux

Cooke, C.K. (1966) 'Re-appraisal of the Industry Hitherto Named the Proto-Stillbay', *Arnoldia (Rhodesia), 2* (22), 1-13

Coon, C.S. (1951) 'Cave Explorations in Iran, 1949', Philadelphia University Museum Monograph

Coope, G.R. (1975) 'Climatic Fluctuations in Northwest Europe since the Last Interglacial, Indicated by Fossil Assemblages of Coleoptera' in A.E. Wright and F. Moseley (eds), *Ice Ages: Ancient and Modern, Geol. Journal Special Issue*, no. 6, Liverpool, Seel House Press, pp. 153-68

Coppens, Y., Howell, F.C., Isaac, G. Ll. and Leakey, R.E.F. (eds) (1976) *Earliest Man and Environments in the Lake Rudolf Basin: Stratigraphy, Palaeoecology and Evolution*, University of Chicago Press

Corvinus, G.K. (1970) 'A Report on the 1968-69 Excavations at Chirki-on-Pravara, India', *Quaternaria, 13*, 169-76

— (1975) 'Palaeolithic Remains at the Hadar in the Afar Region', *Nature, 256,* 468-71

— (1976) 'Prehistoric Exploration at Hadar, Ethiopia', *Nature, 261,* 571-2

Cubuk, G.A. (1976) 'Erste Altapalaolithische Funde in Griechenland bei nea Skala, Kephallinia (Ionische Inseln)' in *Colloque 8, IX° Congres, Union Internationale des Sciences Préhist. et Protohist.,* Nice, pp. 152-77

Curtis, G.H., Drake, R.E., Cerling, T.E. and Hampel, J.H. (1978) 'Age of KBS Tuff in Koobi Fora Formation, East Lake, Turkana, Kenya' in W.W. Bishop (ed.), *Geological Background to Fossil Man,* Geol. Soc. London, pp. 463-9

Dart, R.A. (1925) '*Australopithecus africanus:* the Man-ape of South Africa', *Nature, 115,* 195-9

— (1948) 'The Makapansgat Proto-human *Australopithecus prometheus'*, *American J. Phys. Anthropol.,* 6, 259-84

— (1959) *Adventures with the Missing Link,* Hamilton, London

— and Beaumont, P. (1969) 'Evidence of Iron Ore Mining in Southern Africa in the Middle Stone Age', *Current Anthropol.,* 10 (1), 127-8

Day, M.H. (1969) 'Omo Human Skeletal Remains', *Nature, 222,* 1135-8

— (1977) *Guide to Fossil Man,* Cassell, London, 3rd revised edn

—, Leakey, M.D. and Magori, C. (1980) 'A New Hominid Fossil Skull (L.H.18) from the Ngaloba Beds, Laetoli, Northern Tanzania', *Nature, 284,* 55-6

—, Leakey, R.E.F., Walker, A.C. and Wood, B.A. (1975) 'New Hominids from East Rudolf, Kenya', *American J. Phys. Anthropol.,* 42 (3), 461-76

Delporte, H. (1976) 'Les Civilisations du Paléolithique Supérieur en Auvergne' in H. de Lumley (ed.), *La Préhistoire Française,* 2, CNRS, Paris, pp. 1297-304

Desbrosse, R. (1976) 'Les Civilisations du Paléolithique Supérieur dans le Jura et en Franche-Comté' in H. de Lumley (ed.), *La Préhistoire Française,* 2, CNRS, Paris, pp. 1348-57

Devore, I. and Washburn, S.L. (1963) 'Baboon Ecology and Human Evolution' in F.C. Howell and F. Bourlière (eds), *African Ecology and Human Evolution,* Wenner-Gren Foundation, Aldine, Chicago, pp. 335-67

Drake, R.E., Curtis, G.H., Cerling, T.E., Cerling, B.W. and Hampel, J. (1980) 'KBS Tuff Dating and Geochronology of Tufaceous Sediments in the Koobi Fora and Shungura Formations, East Africa', *Nature, 283,* 368-72

Drummond, H.J.H. and Paterson, T.T. (1962) 'Soan, the Palaeolithic of Pakistan', *Memoir, Dept. of Archaeology in Pakistan, 2*

Dupont, E. (1866) 'Etudes sur les Fouilles Scientifiques Exécutees pendant l'Hiver de 1865-1866 dans les Cavernes des Bords de la Lesse', *Bull. Acad. R. de Belgique, ser. 2, 22,* 31-54

Efimenko, P.P. (1958) *Kostienki I,* AN SSSR, Moscow, Leningrad (in Russian)

Emiliani, C. (1967) 'The Generalized Temperature Curve for the Past 425,000 years', *J. Geol.,* 75, 504-10

— (1968) 'The Pleistocene Epoch and the Evolution of Man', *Current Anthropol.,* 9 (1), 27-30

Evans, J. (1897) *The Ancient Stone Implements of Great Britain,* London, 2nd edn

Evans, J.G. (1975) *The Environment of Early Man in the British Isles,* Paul Elek, London

Evans, P. (1971) 'Towards a Pleistocene Time-scale', Part 2 of *The Phanerozoic Time-scale – a Supplement,* special publication of the Geological Society,

5, London, pp. 123-356

Evernden, J.F. and Curtis, G.H. (1965) 'The Potassium-Argon Dating of Late Cenozoic Rocks in East Africa and Italy', *Current Anthropol.*, *6* (4), 343-85

Fejfar, O. (1969) 'Human Remains from the Early Pleistocene in Czechoslovakia', *Current Anthropol.*, *10* (2-3), 170-3

Felgenhauer, F. (1959) 'Willendorf in der Wachau (1956-1959)', *Osterreichische Akademie der Wissenschaften zu Wien, Prëhistorische Kommission, Mitteilungen, 8-9*

Fitch, F.J., Hooker, P.J. and Miller, J.A. (1976) ^{40}Ar/^{39}Ar Dating of the KBS Tuff in Koobi Fora Formation, East Rudolf, Kenya', *Nature*, 263, 740-4

— and Miller, J.A. (1970) 'Radioisotopic Age Determination of Lake Rudolf Artefact Site', *Nature*, *226*, 226-8

— and Miller, J.A. (1976) 'Conventional Potassium-Argon and Argon ^{40}/ Argon ^{39} Dating of Volcanic Rocks from East Rudolf' in Y. Coppens *et al.* (eds), *Earliest Man and Environments in the Lake Rudolf Basin*, University of Chicago Press, pp. 123-47

Fleming, S. (1976) *Dating in Archaeology: a Guide to Scientific Techniques*, Dent, London, pp. 1-272

Fox, R. and Peralta, J.T. (1972) *Preliminary Report on the Palaeolithic Archaeology òf the Cagayan Valley, Philippines, and the Cabalwanian Industry. Seminar on the Southeast Asian Prehistory and Archaeology*, Manila, pp. 1-39

Freeman, L.G. (1975) 'Acheulian Sites and Stratigraphy in Iberia and the Maghreb' in K.W. Butzer and G. Ll. Isaac (eds), *After the Australopithecines*, Mouton, The Hague, pp. 661-743

— and Butzer, K.W. (1966) 'The Acheulian Station of Torralba (Spain): A Progress Report', *Quaternaria*, *8*, 9-22

— and Echegaray, J.G. (1970) 'Aurignacian Structural Features and Burials at Cuerva Morin (Santander, Spain)', *Nature*, 226, 722-6

Freund, F. (1952) 'Die Blattspitzen des Paläeolithikums in Europa', *Quartar Bibliothek*, Bonn, pp. 1-330

Fridrich, J. (1976) 'The First Industries from Eastern and South-eastern Central Europe' in *Colloque 8, IX° Congres Union Internationale des Sciences Préhist. et Protohist.*, p. 8-23

Garcia, L. Pericot (1942) *La Cueva del Parpallo* (Gandia), Cons. Sup. Invest ci Inst. Diego Velasques, Madrid, pp. 1-351

Garrod, D.A.E. (1955a) 'The Mugharet el-Emireh in Lower Galilee: Type Station of the Emiran Industry', *J. Roy. Anthropol. Inst.*, *85*, 141-62

— (1955b) 'Palaeolithic Spear-Throwers', *Proc. Prehist. Soc.*, *21*, 21-35

— and Bate, D.M.A. (1937) *The Stone Age of Mount Carmel: Excavations at Wady el Mughara*, *1*, Oxford University Press

— and Kirkbride, D. (1961) 'Excavation of the Abri Zumoffen, a Palaeolithic Rock Shelter near Adlun, South Lebanon, 1958', *Bull. Musée de Beyrouth*, pp. 7-45

Ghosh, A.K. (1969) 'Development Pattern of Palaeolithic Culture in India' in M. Ters (ed.), *Etudes sur le Quaternaire dans le Monde*, VIII Congress INQUA, Paris, pp. 1033-8

Gill, E.D. (1966) 'Provenance and Age of the Keilor Cranium: Oldest Known Human Skeletal Remains in Australia', *Current Anthropol.*, *7* (5), 581-4,

6 plates

Girard, C. (1976) 'Les Civilisations du Paléolithique Moyen en Basse-Bourgogne (Yonne)' in H. de Lumley (ed.), *La Préhistoire Française*, 2, CNRS, Paris, pp. 1115-9

— (1978) 'Les Industries Mousteriennes de la Grotte de l'Hyène à Arcy-sur-Cure (Yonne)', *Supplement Gallia Préhistoire*, 11, CNRS, Paris

Goodall, J.V. Lawick (1971) *In the Shadow of Man*, Fontana, Collins

Goodwin, A.J.H. (1928) 'The Archaeology of the Vaal River Gravels', *Trans. Roy. Soc. S. Afr.*, 16, 77-102

Goury, G. (1948) *Origine et Évolution de l'Homme*, Picard, Paris

Grahmann, R. (1955) 'The Lower Palaeolithic Sites of Markkleeberg and Other Comparable Localities near Leipzig', *Trans. Amer. Phil. Soc.*, 45, 511-687

Graziozi, P. (1960) *Palaeolithic Art*, London (English edn)

Grigor'ev, G.P. (1967) 'A New Reconstruction of the Above-Ground Dwelling of Kostienki', *Current Anthropol.*, 8 (4), 344-9, Figs 1-3

Gruet, M. (1976) 'Les Civilisations du Paléolithique Moyen dans les Pays de la Loire' in H. de Lumley (ed.), *La Préhistoire Française*, 2, CNRS, Paris, pp. 1089-93

Guichard, J. (1976) 'Les Civilisations du Paléolithique Moyen en Périgord' in H. de Lumley (ed.), *La Préhistoire Française*, 2, CNRS, Paris, pp. 1053-69

Hammen, T. van der, Maarleveld, C.C., Vogel, J.C. and Zagwijn, W.H. (1967) 'Stratigraphy, Climatic Succession and Radiocarbon Dating of the Last Glacial in the Netherlands', *Geol. Mijnb. (Amsterdam)*, 46, 79-95

Harris, J.W.K. and Bishop, W.W. (1976) 'Sites and Assemblages from the Early Pleistocene Beds of Karari and Chesowanja', *Proc. Colloque V, IX Congress de UISPP*, Nice, pp. 70-117

— and Herbich, I. (1978) 'Aspects of Early Pleistocene Hominid Behaviour East of Lake Turkana, Kenya' in W.W. Bishop (ed.), *Geological Background to Fossil Man*, Geol. Soc. London, pp. 529-47

— and Isaac, G. Ll. (1976) 'The Karari Industry: Early Pleistocene Archaeological Evidence from the Terrain East of Lake Turkana, Kenya', *Nature*, 262, 102-7

Hauser, O. (1909) 'Découverte d'un Squelette du Type Néanderthal sous l'Abri Inférieur du Moustier', *L'Homme Préhistorique*, 1, 1-9

Hay, R.L. (1976) *Geology of the Olduvai Gorge: a Study of Sedimentation in a Semiarid Basin*, University of California, Berkeley, Los Angeles and London

Heim, J.-L. (1976) 'Les Néandertaliens en Périgord' in H. de Lumley (ed.), *La Préhistoire Française*, 1, CNRS, Paris, pp. 578-83

Heinzelin de Braucourt, J. de (1962) *Manuel de Typologie des Industries Lithiques*, Institut Royal des Sciences Naturelles de Belgique, Brussels

Hole, F. and Flannery, K.V. (1967) 'The Prehistory of Southwestern Iran: a Preliminary Report', *Proc. Prehist. Soc.*, 33, 147-206

Hollin, J.T. (1969) 'Ice-sheet Surges and the Geological Record', *Canadian Journal of Earth Sciences*, 6 (4), 903-10

Horowitz, A., Siedner, G. and Bar-Yosef, O. (1973) 'Radiometric Dating of the Ubeidiya Formation, Jordan Valley, Israel', *Nature*, 242, 186-7

Howell, F.C. (1959) 'Upper Pleistocene Stratigraphy and Early Man in the Levant', *Proc. American Phil. Soc.*, 103, 1-65

— (1966) 'Observations on the Earlier Phases of the European Lower

Palaeolithic', *American Anthropologist, 68*, 88-201
— (1969) 'Remains of Hominidae from Pliocene/Pleistocene Formations in the Lower Omo Basin, Ethiopia', *Nature, 223*, 1234-9
— and Bourlière, F. (eds) (1963) *African Ecology and Human Evolution, Viking Fund Publications in Anthropology, 36*, Wenner-Gren Foundation, Aldine, Chicago
— and Clark, J.D. (1963) 'Acheulian Hunter-gatherers of Sub-Saharan Africa' in F.C. Howell and F. Bourlière (eds), *African Ecology and Human Evolution*, Aldine, Chicago, pp. 458-533
—, Cole, G.H. and Kleindienst, M.R. (1962) 'Isimilia: an Acheulian Occupation Site in the Iringa Highlands, Southern Highlands Province, Tanganyika', *Proc. 4th Pan African Congress, 1960*, pp. 43-80
— and Coppens, Y. (1976) 'An Overview of Hominidae from the Omo Succession, Ethiopia' in Y. Coppens *et al.* (eds), *Earliest Man and Environments in the Lake Rudolf Basin*, University of Chicago Press, pp. 522-32, Plates 1-23
— and Wood, B.A. (1974) 'Early Hominid Ulna from the Omo Basin, Ethiopia', *Nature, 249*, 174-6
Howells, W. (1964) *Mankind in the Making*, Mercury Books, London
Hughes, A.R. and Tobias, P.V. (1977) 'A Fossil Skull Probably of the Genus *Homo* from Sterkfontein, Transvaal', *Nature, 265*, 310-12
Hume, G.W. (1967) 'Comments on the Geology and Archaeology of the Bard Sir Valley' in J.R. Caldwell (ed.), *Investigations at Tal-i-Iblia NSF Project GS-1324, Illinois State Museum Preliminary Report, 9*, 108-10
— (1976) *The Ladizian. An Industry of the Asian Chopper-Chopping Tool Complex in Iranian Baluchistan*, Durrance, Philadelphia
Ikawa-Smith, F. (1978) *Early Palaeolithic in South and East Asia*, Mouton, The Hague
Inskeep, R.R. (1976) 'A Note on the Melkbos and Hout Bay Raised Beaches and the Middle Stone Age', *S. Afr. Archaeol. Bull., 31*, 26-8
Isaac, G. Ll. (1976) 'Plio-Pleistocene Artifact Assemblages from East Rudolf, Kenya' in Y. Coppens *et al.* (eds), *Earliest Man and Environments in the Lake Rudolf Basin*, University of Chicago Press, pp. 552-64
— (1977) *Olorgesailie. Archaeological Studies of a Middle Pleistocene Lake Basin in Kenya*, Prehistoric Archaeology and Ecology Series, University of Chicago Press
— (1978) 'The First Geologists – the Archaeology of the Original Rock Breakers' in W.W. Bishop (ed.), *Geological Background to Fossil Man*, Geol. Soc. London, pp. 139-47
— and Brock, A. (1974) 'Palaeomagnetic Stratigraphy and Chronology of Hominid-bearing Sediments East of Lake Rudolf, Kenya', *Nature, 247*, 344-8
—. Harris, J.W.K. and Crader, D. (1976) 'Archaeological Evidence from the Koobi Fora Formation' in Y. Coppens *et al.* (eds), *Earliest Man and Environments in the Lake Rudolf Basin*, University of Chicago Press, pp. 533-51
—, Leakey, R.E.F. and Behrensmeyer, A.K. (1971) 'Archaeological Traces of Early Hominid Activities, East of Lake Rudolf, Kenya', *Science, 173*, 1129-34
Jacob, T. (1967) 'Recent Pithecanthropus Finds in Indonesia', *Current*

Anthropol., *8* (5), 501-4

— (1972) 'The Absolute Date of the Djetis Beds at Modjokerto', *Antiquity*, *46* (182), 148

Johanson, D.C. and Taieb, M. (1976) 'Plio-Pleistocene Hominid Discoveries in Hadar, Ethiopia', *Nature*, *260*, 293-7

Jolly, C. (ed.) (1978) *Early Hominids of Africa*, Duckworth, London

Keeley, L.H. (1977) 'The Functions of Palaeolithic Flint Tools', *Sci. Amer.*, *237* (5), 108-26

— and Newcomer, M.H.J. (1977) 'Microwear Analysis of Experimental Flint Tools: a Test Case', *Archaeol. Sci.*, *4*, 29-62

Keller, C.M. (1973) 'Montagu Cave in Prehistory: a Descriptive Analysis', *Anthropol. Records*, *28*, 1-98, Figs 1-53, Plates I-LIII

Kernd'l, A. (1961 and 1963) 'Übersicht über ein Forschungsstand der Ur- und Frühgeschichte in der Sowjetunion 1', *Berliner Jarbruch für Vor- und Frühgeschichte*, *1*, 172-90, *3*, 112-79

Klein, R.G. (1966) 'Chellean and Acheulian on the Territory of the Soviet Union: a Critical Review of the Evidence as Presented in the Literature', *Amer. Anthropol.*, *Special publication*, *Recent Studies in Palaeoanthropology*, *68* (2), 1-45

— (1969a) 'The Mousterian of European Russia', *Proc. Prehist. Soc.*, *35*, 77-111

— (1969b) *Man and Culture in the Late Pleistocene: a Case Study*, Chandler, San Francisco

— (1974) 'Environment and Subsistence of Prehistoric Man in the Southern Cape Province, South Africa', *World Archaeology*, *5* (3), 249-84

— (1975) 'Middle Stone Age Man-Animal Relationships in Southern Africa: Evidence from Die Kelders and Klasies River Mouth', *Science*, *190*, 265-7

— (1976a) 'A Preliminary Report on the "Middle Stone Age" Open-air Site of Duinefontein 2 (Melkbosstrand), South-western Cape Province, South Africa', *S. Afr. Archaeol. Bull.*, *31*, 12-20

— (1976b) 'The Mammalian Fauna of the Klasies River Mouth Sites, Southern Cape Province, South Africa', *S. Afr. Archaeol. Bull.*, *31*, 75-98

Klima, B. (1954) 'Palaeolithic Huts at Dolni Vestonice, Czechoslovakia', *Antiquity*, *28*, 4-14

Koenigswald, G.H.R. von (ed.) (1958) *Neanderthal Centenary 1856-1956*, Wenner-Gren Foundation, New York

— and Ghosh, A.K. (1973) 'Stone Implements from the Trinil Beds of Sangiran, Central Java, 1 and 11', *Verhandelinoen Konikl. Ned. Akademie van Wetenschappen, series B*, *76* (1), 1-34

Koslowski, J.K. (1972) 'Archaeological Materials. In Studies on Raj Cave near Kielce (Poland) and its Deposits', *Folia Quaternaria*, *41*, 61-149

— and Kubiak, H. (1972) 'Late Palaeolithic Dwellings made of Mammoth Bones in South Poland', *Nature*, *237*, 463-4

— *et al*. (1974) 'Upper Palaeolithic Site with Dwellings of Mammoth Bones – Cracow, Spadzista Street B', *Folia Quaternaria*, *44*, 1-110, Plates I-L (in English)

Kretzoi, M. and Vértes, L. (1965) 'Upper Biharian (Intermindel) Pebble-industry Occupation Site in Western Hungary', *Current Anthropol.*, *6* (1), 74-87

Kroeber, A.L. (ed.) (1953 and later edns) *Anthropology Today*, University of

Chicago Press

Kuhn, H. (1958) *On the Track of Prehistoric Man*, Arrow Books, London

—— (1966) *The Rock Pictures of Europe*, Sidgwick and Jackson, London 3rd edn

Kukla, G.J. (1977) 'Pleistocene Land-Sea Correlations 1. Europe', *Earth Sci. Rev.*, *13*, 307-74

Lacaille, A.D. (1947) 'Châtelperron: a New Survey of its Palaeolithic Industry', *Archaeologia*, *92*, 95-119

Lacorre, F. (1960) *La Gravette. Le Gravétien et le Bayacien*, CNRS, Laval

Laming, A. (1959) *Lascaux*, Penguin Books

Leakey, L.S.B. (1952) 'The Olorgesailie Prehistoric Site', *Proc. 1st Pan-African Congress on Prehistory 1947*, Oxford, p. 209

—— (1953) *Adam's Ancestors*, Methuen, London, 4th edn

—— (1959) 'A New Fossil Skull from Olduvai', *Nature*, *201*, 967-70

—— (1965) *Olduvai Gorge, 1951-1961*, Cambridge University Press

—— (1968) 'Bone Smashing by Late Miocene Hominidae', *Nature*, *218*, 528-30

—— (1969) 'Fort Ternan Hominid', *Nature*, *222*, 1202

——, Tobias, P.V. and Napier, J.R. (1964) 'A New Species of the Genus *Homo* from Olduvai Gorge', *Nature*, *202*, 7-9

Leakey, M.D. (1970a) 'Stone Artefacts from Swartkrans', *Nature*, *225*, 1222-5

—— (1970b) 'Early Artefacts from the Koobi Fora Area', *Nature*, *226*, 228-230

—— (1971) 'Discovery of Postcranial Remains of *Homo erectus* and Associated Artefacts in Bed IV at Olduvai Gorge, Tanzania', *Nature*, *232*, 380-3

—— (1972) *Excavations in Beds I and II, Olduvai Gorge*, *3*, Cambridge University Press

—— (1975) 'Cultural Patterns in the Olduvai Sequence' in K.W. Butzer and G. Ll. Isaac (eds), *After the Australopithecines*, Mouton, The Hague, pp. 477-93

——, Clarke, R.J. and Leakey, L.S.B. (1971) 'New Hominid Skull from Bed I, Olduvai Gorge, Tanzania', *Nature*, *232*, 308-12

—— and Hay, R.L. (1979) 'Pliocene Footprints in the Laetolil Beds at Laetolil, Northern Tanzania', *Nature*, *278*, 317-23

——, Hay, R.L., Curtis, G.H., Drake, R.E., Jackes, M.K. and White, T.D. (1976) 'Fossil Hominids from the Laetolil Beds', *Nature*, *262*, 460-6

——, Hay, R.L., Thurber, D.L., Protsch, R. and Berger, R. (1972) 'Stratigraphy, Archaeology, and Age of the Ndutu and Naisiusiu Beds, Olduvai Gorge, Tanzania', *World Archaeol.*, *3* (3), 328-41

Leakey, M.G. and Leakey, R.E.F. (eds) (1978) *The Fossil Hominids and an Introduction to Their Context, 1968-1974, Koobi Fora Research Project*, *1*, Clarendon Press, Oxford, pp. 1-191

——, Tobias, P.V., Martyn, J.E. and Leakey, R.E.F. (1969) 'An Acheulian Industry and Hominid Mandible, Lake Baringo, Kenya', *Proc. Prehist. Soc.*, *35*, 48-76

Leakey, R.E.F. (1970) 'Fauna and Artefacts from a New Plio-Pleistocene Locality near Lake Rudolf in Kenya', *Nature*, *226*, 223-4

—— (1971) 'Further Evidence of Lower Pleistocene Hominids from East Rudolf, North Kenya', *Nature*, *231*, 241-5

—— (1972) 'Further Evidence of Lower Pleistocene Hominids from East Rudolf, North Kenya, 1971', *Nature*, *237*, 264-9

—— (1973a) 'Evidence for an Advanced Plio-Pleistocene Hominid from East Rudolf, Kenya', *Nature*, *242*, 447-50

—— (1973b) 'Further Evidence of Lower Pleistocene Hominids from East Rudolf

North Kenya, 1972', *Nature, 242,* 170-3
— (1974) 'Further Evidence of Lower Pleistocene Hominids from East Rudolf, North Kenya, 1973', *Nature, 248,* 653-6
— (1976a) 'An Overview of the Hominidae from East Rudolf, Kenya' in Y. Coppens *et al.* (eds), *Earliest Man and Environments in the Lake Rudolf Basin,* University of Chicago Press, pp. 476-83
— (1976b) 'New Hominid Fossils from the Koobi Fora Formation in Northern Kenya', *Nature, 261,* 574-6
—, Butzer, K.W. and Day, M.H. (1969) 'Early *Homo sapiens* Remains from the Omo River Region of South-west Ethiopia', *Nature, 222,* 1132-8
— and Walker, A.C. (1976) 'Australopithecus, *Homo erectus* and the Single Species Hypothesis', *Nature, 261,* 572-4
Lenoir, M. (1976) 'Les Civilisations du Paléolithique Supérieur dans le Sud-Ouest (Gironde)' in H. de Lumley (ed.), *La Préhistoire Française, 2,* CNRS, Paris, pp. 1252-6
Leroi-Gourhan, A. (1967) *The Art of Prehistoric Man in Western Europe,* London (English edn)
— (1976) 'Les Structures d'Habitat au Paléolithique Supérieur', in H. de Lumley (ed.), *La Préhistoire Française, 1,* CNRS, Paris, pp. 656-63
— and Brézillon, M. (1972) 'Fouilles de Pincevent. Essai d'Analyse Ethnographique d'un Habitat Magdalénien (la Section 36)', *VIIe Supplement a Gallia Préhistoire,* 2 vols, CNRS, Paris
—, Brézillon, M. and Schmider, B. (1976) 'Les Civilisations du Paléolithique Supérieur dans la Centre et le Sud-est du Bassin Parisien' in H. de Lumley (ed.), *La Préhistoire Française, 2,* CNRS, Paris, pp. 1321-38
Lorenzo, J. (1958) 'Préhistoire et Quaternaire Récent au Mexique. Etat Actuel des Connaissances', *L'Anthropologie, 62,* 62-83
Lowe, C. van Riet (1952) 'The Vaal River Chronology: an up-to-date Summary', *S. Afr. Archaeol. Bull., 7,* 135-49
—, Söhnge, P.G. and Visser, J.L. (1937) 'Geology and Archaeology of the Vaal River Basin', *Memoir Union of South Africa Geological Survey, 35*
Lumley, H. de (ed.) (1972) 'La Grotte de L'Hortus', *Mem. Etudes Quaternaires, 1,* 1-668
— (ed.) (1976a) *La Préhistoire Française, Tome 1, 2,* CNRS, Paris
— (1976b) 'Les Premières Industries Humaines en Provence' in H. de Lumley (ed.), *La Préhistoire Française, 1,* CNRS, Paris, pp. 765-96
— (1976c) 'Les Civilisations du Paléolithique Inférieur en Lanquedoc Mediterranéan et en Roussillon' in H. de Lumley (ed.), *La Préhistoire Française, 2,* CNRS, Paris, pp. 852-74
— (1976d) 'Les Structures d'Habitat au Paléolithique Moyen' in H. de Lumley (ed.), *La Préhistoire Française, 1,* CNRS, Paris, pp. 644-55
— and Boone, Y. (1976) 'Les Structures d'Habitat au Paléolithique Inférieur' in H. de Lumley (ed.), *La Préhistoire Française, 1,* CNRS, Paris, pp. 625-76
Lynch, T.F. (1966) 'The Lower Perigordian in French Archaeology', *Proc. Prehist. Soc., 32,* 156-98
McBurney, C.B.M. (1960) *The Stone Age of Northern Africa,* Penguin Books
— (1967) *The Haua Fteah (Cyrenaica) and the Stone Age of the South-east Mediterranean,* Cambridge University Press
Mackereth, F.J.H. (1971) 'On the Variation in Direction of the Horizontal

Components of Remanent Magnetization in Lake Sediments', *Earth Planet Sci. Letters*, *12*, 332

Madsen, E. (1963) 'Primitiv Flintkultur ved Isefjord', *Aarboger for Nordisk Oldkyndighed og Historic* (1962)

—— (1968) 'Un Site Danois à Silex Préhistorique Primitifs', *Rev. Anthropol. Paris* (1968), 14-22

Maglio, V.J. (1972) 'Vertebrate Faunas and Chronology of Hominid-bearing Sediments East of Lake Rudolf, Kenya', *Nature*, *239*, 379-85

Malez, M. (1974) 'Ober die Bedeutung der Entdeckung von Geröllgeräten in den Villafranchiumschichten der Sandalja 1 in Istrien (Kroatien, Jugoslawien)', *Bull. Scientifique*, *A 19* (3-4), 79-80

Mania, D. (1974) 'Bilsingsleben Kr. Artern-eine Altpalëolithische Travertinfundstelle im Nördlichen Mitteleuropa (Vorbericht)', Zeitscrift für Archäeologie, *8*, 157-73

Marett, R.R. (1916) 'La Cotte de St Brelade', *Archaeologia*, *67*, 75-118

Marshack, A. (1971) 'Notation dans les Gravures du Paléolithique Supérieur: Nouvelles Methodes d'Analyse', *Mem. Bordeaux Uni. Inst. Préhist.*, *8*, 1-123

—— (1972) 'Cognitive Aspects of Upper Palaeolithic Engraving', *Current Anthropol.*, *13* (3-4), 445-78

—— (1979) 'Upper Palaeolithic Symbol Systems of the Russian Plain: Cognitive and Comparative Analysis', *Current Anthropol.*, *20* (2), 271-311

Martyn, J. and Tobias, P. (1967) 'Pleistocene Deposits and New Fossil Localities in Kenya', *Nature*, *215*, 476-80

Mason, R.J. (1962) *The Prehistory of the Transvaal*, WUP, Johannesburg

—— (1965) 'Makapansgat Limeworks fractured Stone Objects and Natural Fracture in Africa', *S. Afr. Archaeol. Bull.*, *20* (77), 3-16

—— (1967) 'The Archaeology of the Earliest Superficial Deposits in the Lower Vaal Basin near Holpan, Windsorton District', *S. Afr. Geog. J.*, *49*, 39-56

Mathiassen, T. (1948) *Danske Oldsaker. 1. Aeldre Stenalder*, Copenhagen

Mellars, P.A. (1969) 'The Chronology of Mousterian Industries in the Périgord Region of South-West France', *Proc. Prehist. Soc.*, *35*, 134-71

—— (1973) 'The Character of the Middle to Upper Palaeolithic Transition in South-west France' in C. Renfrew (ed.), *The Explanation of Culture Change*, Duckworth, London, pp. 255-76

—— (1974) 'The Palaeolithic and Mesolithic' in C. Renfrew (ed.), *British Prehistory, a New Outline*, Duckworth, London, pp. 41-99, 268-79

Merk, C. (1876) *Excavations at the Kesslerloch near Thayngen, Switzerland: a Cave of the Reindeer Period*, Longmans Green, London, pp. 1-65, Plates I-XV

Merrick, H.V., Heinzelin, J. de Braucourt, Haesaerts, P. and Howell, F.C. (1973) 'Archaeological Occurrences of Early Pleistocene Age from Shungura Formation, Lower Omo Valley, Ethiopia', *Nature*, *242*, 572-5

—— and Merrick, J.P.S. (1976) 'Archaeological Occurrences of Earlier Pleistocene Age from the Shungura Formation', in Y. Coppens *et al.* (eds), *Earliest Man and Environments in Lake Rudolf Basin*, University of Chicago Press, pp. 574-84

Meszáros, Gy. and Vértes, L. (1955) 'A Paint Mine from the Early Upper Palaeolithic Age near Lovas (Hungary)', *Acta Archaeologica Academiae Scientiarum Hungaricae*, *5*, 1-34

Miller, J.A. (1972) 'Dating Pliocene and Pleistocene Strata Using the Potassium-

Argon and Argon ⁽ᵃ⁾/Argon ³⁹ Methods' in W.W. Bishop and J.A. Miller (eds), *Calibration of Hominoid Evolution*, Scottish Academic Press

Mitchell, G.F., Penny, L.F., Shotton, F.W. and West, R.G. (1973) 'A Correlation of Quaternary Deposits in the British Isles', *Special Report No. 4*, Geol. Soc. Lond., pp. 1-99

Mohapatra, G.C. (1966) 'Preliminary Report of the Exploration and Excavation of Stone Age Sites in Eastern Punjab', *Bull. Deccan Coll. Research Inst.*, 25, 221-37

Molleson, T. (1976) 'Remains of Pleistocene Man in Paviland and Pontnewydd Caves, Wales', *Trans. Brit. Cave Res. Ass.*, 3, 112-16

Mongait, A.L. (1961) *Archaeology in the U.S.S.R.*, Penguin Books

Moure-Romanillo, J.A. and Cano-Herrera, M. (1979) 'Tito Bustillo Cave (Asturias, Spain) and the Magdalenian of Cantabria', *World Archaeology*, 10 (3), 280-9

Movius, H.L. (1949) 'The Lower Palaeolithic Cultures of Southern and Eastern Asia', *Trans. Amer. Phil. Soc. (N.S.)*, 38 (4-1948), 329-420

— (1950) 'A Wooden Spear of Third Interglacial Age from Lower Saxony', *South Western Journal of Anthropology*, 6 (2), 139-42

— (1956) 'New Palaeolithic Sites near Ting-Ts'un in the Fen River, Shansi Province, North China', *Quaternaria*, 3, 13-26

— (1966) 'The Hearths of the Upper Perigordian and Aurignacian Horizons at the Abri Pataud, Les Eyzies (Dordogne) and Their Possible Significance', *American Anthropologist*, 68 (2), 296-325

— (1975) 'Excavation of the Abri Pataud, Les Eyzies (Dordogne)', *Bull. Peabody Museum*, 30, 1-305

— (1977) 'Excavation of the Abri Pataud, Les Eyzies (Dordogne)', *Bull. Peabody Museum*, 31, 1-167

—, David, N.C., Bricker, H.M. and Clay, R.B. (1968) 'The Analysis of Certain Major Classes of Upper Palaeolithic Tools', *Bull. American School of Prehistoric Research*, 26, 1-58

Mturi, A.A. (1976) 'New Hominid from Lake Ndutu, Tanzania', *Nature*, 262, 484-5

Müller-Karpe, H. (1966) *Handbuch der Vorgeschichte. 1. Altsteinzeit*

Mulvaney, D.J. (1975), *The Prehistory of Australia*, Penguin Books

— and Golson, J. (eds) (1971) *The Racial Affinities and Origins of the Australian Aborigines*

Murty, M.L.K. (1969) 'Blade and Burin Industries near Renigunta on the South-East Coast of India', *Proc. Prehist. Soc.*, 34, 83-101

Musil, R. and Valoch, K. (1968) 'Stranská Skála: its Meanings for Pleistocene Studies', *Current Anthropol.*, 9 (5), 534-41

Newcomer, M.H. (1971) 'Some Quantitative Experiments in Hand-axe Manufacture', *World Archaeology*, 3 (1), 85-93

Oakley, K.P. (1949 and many later edns) *Man the Tool-maker*, British Museum (Natural History)

— (1956) 'Fire as Palaeolithic Tool and Weapon', *Proc. Prehist. Soc.*, 21, 36-48

— (1957) 'Tools Makyth Man', *Antiquity*, 31, 199-209

— (1962) 'Dating the Emergence of Man', *Adv. of Science* (Jan. 1962), pp. 415-26

— (1964) *Frameworks for Dating Fossil Man*, Weidenfeld and Nicolson, London, pp. 1-355

288   *Bibliography*

—, Andrews, P., Keeley, L.H. and Clark, J.D. (1977) 'A Reappraisal of the Clacton Spearpoint', *Proc. Prehist. Soc.*, *43*, 13-30
— and Campbell, B.G. (1967) *Catalogue of Fossil Hominids. Part I: Africa*, British Museum (Natural History)
—, Campbell, B.G. and Molleson, T. (eds) (1971) *Catalogue of Fossil Hominids. Part II: Europe*, British Museum (Natural History)
—, Campbell, B.G. and Molleson, T. (eds) (1975) *Catalogue of Fossil Hominids. Part III: Americas, Asia, Australasia*, British Museum (Natural History)
Obermeier, H. (1924) *Fossil Man in Spain*, New Haven
Okladnikov, M.A.P. (1953) in H.L. Movius, *The Mousterian Cave of Teshik-Tash*, Cambridge University Press
Osborn, H.F. (1924) *Men of the Old Stone Age*, London
Otte, M. (1977) 'Données Générales sur le Paléolithique Supérieur Ancien de Belgique', *L'Anthropologie*, *81* (2), 235-72
Ovey, C.D. (ed.) (1964) 'The Swanscombe Skull. A Survey of Research on a Pleistocene Site', *R. Anthropol. Inst. Occ. Paper*, *21*, 1-215, Figs 1-65, Plates I-XXV
Paddayya, K. (1977) 'An Acheulian Occupation Site at Hungsi, Peninsular India: A Summary of the Results of Two Seasons of Excavation (1975-6)', *World Archaeology*, *8* (3), 344-55
Partridge, T.C. (1978) 'Re-appraisal of the Lithostratigraphy of Sterkfontein Hominid Site', *Nature*, *275*, 282-7
— and Brink, A.B.A. (1967) 'Gravels and Terraces of the Lower Vaal River Basin', *S. Afr. Geographical J.*, *49*, 39-56
Patterson, B., Behrensmeyer, A.K. and Sill, W.D. (1970) 'Geology and Fauna of a New Pliocene Locality in North Western Kenya', *Nature*, *226*, 918-21
Pei, W.C. (1934) 'A Preliminary Report on the Late-Palaeolithic Cave of Choukoutien', *Bull. Geol. Soc. China*, *13*, 327-58
Peyrony, D. (1934) 'La Ferrassie', *Préhistoire*, *3*
Pfeiffer, J. (1970) *The Emergence of Man*, Nelson and Sons
Piggott, S. (1950) *Prehistoric India*, Penguin Books
Pilbeam, D.R. (1975) 'Middle Pleistocene Hominids' in K.W. Butzer and G. Ll. Isaac (eds), *After the Australopithecines*, Mouton, The Hague, pp. 809-56
Powell, T.G.E. (1966) *Prehistoric Art*, Thames and Hudson
Pyddoke, E. (ed.) (1963) *The Scientist and Archaeology*, Phoenix House, London
Ranov, V.A. (1974) 'Palaeolithic from Soviet Central Asia' in K.L. Mukhopadhyau (ed.), *Perspectives in Palaeoanthropology*, Calcutta
Renfrew, C. (ed.) (1973) *The Explanation of Cultural Change, Models in Prehistory*, Duckworth, London
Rigaud, J.P. (1976) 'Les Civilisations du Paléolithique Supérieur en Périgord' in H. de Lumley (ed.), *La Préhistoire Française*, *2*, CNRS, Paris, pp. 1257-70
Robins, G.V., Seeley, N.J., McNeil, D.A.C. and Symons, M.R.C. (1978) 'Identification of Ancient Heat Treatment in Flint Artefacts by ESR Spectroscopy', *Nature*, *276*, 703-4
Robinson, J.T. (1954) 'The Genera and Species of the Australopithecinae', *Am. J. Phys. Anthropol.*, *12*, 181-200
— (1960) 'The Affinities of the New Olduvai Australopithecine', *Nature*, *186*, 456-8

— (1961) 'The Australopithecines and Their Bearing on the Origin of Man and of Stone Tool-Making', *S. Afr. J. Science*, *57*, 3-13

— (1972) *Early Hominid Posture and Locomotion*, University of Chicago Press

— and Mason, R.J. (1962) 'Australopithecines and Artefacts at Sterkfontein', *S. Afr. Archaeol. Bull.*, *17*, 87-125

Roe, D.A. (1968a) 'A Gazetteer of British Lower and Middle Palaeolithic Sites', *Res. Report Council British Archaeol.*, *8*, 1-355

— (1968b) 'British Lower and Middle Palaeolithic Hand-axe Groups', *Proc. Prehist. Soc.*, *34*, 1-82

— (1975) 'Some Hampshire and Dorset Hand-axes and the Question of Early Acheulian in Britain', *Proc. Prehist. Soc.*, *41*, 1-9

— (in press) *The Lower and Middle Palaeolithic Periods in Britain*, Routledge and Kegan Paul, London

Rust, A. (1937) *Das Alsteinzeitliche Rentierjägerlager Meiendorf*, Neumünster

— (1943) *Die Alt- und Mittelsteinzeitlichen Funde son Stellmoor*, Neumünster

— (1950) 'Die Höhlenfunde von Jabrud (Syrien)', *Offa-Bücher*, *8*, 1-154, Figs 1-110, Plates 1-9

— (1958) *Die Jungpaläolithischen Zeltanlagen von Ahrensburg*, Neumünster

— (1962) *Die Artefakte der Altonaer Stufe von Wittenbergen*, Neumünster

Sacchi, D. (1976) 'Les Civilisations du Paléolithique Supérieur en Languedoc Occidental (Bassin de l'Aude) et en Roussillon' in H. de Lumley (ed.), *La Préhistoire Française*, *2*, CNRS, Paris, pp. 1174-88

Sackett, J. and Gaussen, J. (1976) 'Upper Palaeolithic Habitation Structures in the Sud-Ouest of France', *Colloque XIII, IX° Congres U.I.S.P.P.*, pp. 55-83

Sampson, C.G. (1962) 'The Cape Hangklip Main Site', *J. Sci. Soc. Univ. Cape Town*, *5*, 24-31

— (1968) 'The Middle Stone Age Industries of the Orange River Scheme Area', *Memoir National Mus., Bloemfontein*, *4*, 1-111

— (1974) *The Stone Age Archaeology of Southern Africa*, Academic Press, New York and London

Sandford, K.S. and Arkell, W.J. (1929-1939) *Prehistoric Survey of Egypt and Western Asia*, 4 vols, Univ. Chicago Orient Inst. Pub.

Sankalia, H.D. (1969) 'Problems in Indian Archaeology, and Methods and Techniques Adopted to Tackle Them', *World Archaeology*, *1*, 29-40

— (1971) 'New Evidence for Early Man in Kashmir', *Current Anthropol.*, *12* (4-5), 558-62

Schaller, G.B. and Emlen, J.T. (1963) 'Observations on the Ecology and Social Behaviour of the Mountain Gorilla' in F.C. Howell and F. Bourlière (eds), *African Ecology and Human Evolution*, Aldine, Chicago, pp. 368-84

Schmid, E. (1969) 'A Mousterian Silex Mine and Dwelling Place in the Swiss Jura' in F. Bordes (ed.), *The Origin of Homo sapiens*, Unesco, Paris, pp. 129-32

Schmider, B. (1971) 'Les Industries Lithiques du Paléolithique Supérieur en Ile-de-France', *Supplement 6 to Gallia Préhistoire*, Paris

— (1975) 'Bibliographie Analytique de Préhistoire pour le Paléolithique Supérieur Europ*é*an', Tome *1*, *Index*, Tome 2, *Catalogue des Publications Analysées*, CNRS, Paris

Schwabedissen, H. (1954) *Die Federmessergruppen des Nordwesteuropäischen Flachlandes*, Neumünster

— (1973) 'Archaeological Research; 1: Palaeolithic and Mesolithic Periods', *Eiszeitalter u. Gegenwart*, *23-24*, 340-59

Seddon, J.D. (1966) 'The Early Stone Age at Bosman's Crossing, Stellenbosch', *S. Afr. Archaeol. Bull.*, *21*

— (1967) 'Some Early Stone Age Surface Sites around Stellenbosch, S.W. Cape', *S. Afr. Archaeol. Bull.*, *22* (2), 57-9

Semenov, S.A. (1964) *Prehistoric Technology*, Cory, Adams and Mackay, London

Serizawa, C. and Ikawa, F. (1960) 'The Oldest Archaeological Materials from Japan', *Asian Perspec.*, *2* (2), 1-39

Shackleton, N.J. and Opdyke, N.D. (1976) 'Oxygen Isotope and Palaeomagnetic Stratigraphy of Pacific Core V28-239 Late Pliocene to Latest Pleistocene', *Memoir Geol. Soc. America.*, *145*, 449-64

Shackley, M.L. (1980) *Neanderthal Man*, Duckworth, London

Shapiro, H.L. (1976) *Peking Man*, Book Club Associates, London

Sieveking, A. (1971) 'Palaeolithic Decorated Bone Discs' in G. de G. Sieveking (ed.), *Prehistoric and Roman Studies*, British Museum, pp. 206-29

— (1979) *The Cave Artists*, Thames and Hudson, London

— and Sieveking, G. (1962) *The Caves of France and Northern Spain: a Guide*, Vista Books, London

Simonnet, R. (1976) 'Les Civilisations de l'Epipaléolithique et du Mésolithique dans les Confins Pyrénées de la Gascogne et du Languedoc' in H. de Lumley (ed.), *La Préhistoire Française*, *2*, CNRS, Paris, pp. 1412-19

Singer, R. (1958) 'The Rhodesian, Florisbad and Saldanha Skulls' in G.H.R. von Koenigswald (ed.), *Neanderthal Centenary*, Wenner-Gren Foundation, New York, pp. 52-62, Plates XX-XXIII

— and Wymer, J.J. (1968) 'Archaeological Investigations at the Saldanha Skull Site in South Africa', *S. Afr. Archaeol. Bull.*, *23*, 63-74

—, Wymer, J.J., Gladfelter, B.G. and Wolff, R. (1973) 'Excavation of the Clactonian Industry at the Golf Course, Clacton-on-Sea, Essex', *Proc. Prehist. Soc.*, *39*, 6-74

Smith, P.E.L. (1966) *Le Solutréen en France*, Bordeaux

— (1971) 'Mélanges de Préhistoire, d'Archéocivilisation et d'Ethnologie Offerts à André Varagnac', *Ecole Pratique des Hautes Etudes – VIe Section Centre de Recherches Historiques*, Paris

Smith, R.A. (1911) 'A Palaeolithic Industry at Northfleet, Kent', *Archaeologia*, *62*, 515-32

— (1926) *A Guide to Antiquities of the Stone Age*, British Museum

Soergel, W. (1926) 'Das Alter der Paläeolithischen Fundstätten von Taubach-Ehringsdorf-Weimar', *Mannus, Leipzig*, *18*, 1-13

Solecki, R.S. (1953) 'A Palaeolithic Site in the Zagros Mountains of Northern Iraq. Report on a Sounding at Shanidar Cave. Part II', *Sumer*, *9* ,0-93

— (1963) 'Prehistory in Shanidar Valley, Northern Iraq', *Science*, *139*, 179-93

— (1972) *Shanidar. The Humanity of Neanderthal Man*, Allen Lane, Penguin Press

Sonneville-Bordes, D. de (1960) *Le Paléolithique Supérieur en Périgord*, vols I-II, Bordeaux

Sorensen, P. (1962) *The Thai-Danish Expedition*, Copenhagen

—, Shouls, M.M. and Laming, D.J.C. (in press) 'The Archaeology, Geology and

Significance of Pebble Tool Finds in Lampang and Phrae Provinces, Northern Thailand', *Preliminary Publication Series*, Scandinavian Institute of Asia Studies, Copenhagen

Sparks, B.W. and West, R.G. (1972) *The Ice Age in Britain*, Methuen, London

Stekelis, M. (1960) 'The Palaeolithic Deposits of Jisr Banat Yaqub', *Bull. Research Council Israel*, Section G (Geo-Survey), *9G* (2-3), 61-87

—— (1966) *Archaeological Excavations at Ubeidiya, 1960-1963*, Israel Academy of Sciences and Humanities

——, Bar-Yosef, O. and Schick, T. (1969) *Archaeological Excavations at Ubeidiya, 1964-1966*, Israel Academy of Sciences and Humanities

Sulimirski, T. (1970) *Prehistoric Russia: an Outline*, John Baker, London

Swanscombe Committee (1938) 'Report on the Swanscombe Skull: Prepared by the Swanscombe Committee of the Royal Anthropological Institute', *J. Roy. Anthropol. Inst. Lond.*, *68*, 17-98

Swanson, E. (ed.) (1975) *Lithic Technology: Making and Using Stone Tools*, Mouton, The Hague

Terra, H. de and Movius, H.L. (1943) 'Research on Early Man in Burma', *Trans. American Phil. Soc.*, *32* (3), 265-464

—— and Paterson, T.T. (1939) 'Studies on the Ice Age in India and Associated Human Cultures', *Pub. Carnegie Inst., Washington*, *493*, 1-354

Thévenin, A. (1976) 'Les Premières Industries Humaines en Alsace' in H. de Lumley (ed.), *La Préhistoire Française*, *2*, CNRS, Paris, pp. 810-16

Thibault, C. (1976) 'Les Civilisations du Paléolithique Moyen du Sud-Ouest (Pays Basques et Béarn, Landes, Gironde)' in H. de Lumley (ed.), *La Préhistoire Française*, *2*, CNRS, Paris, pp. 1048-52

Thompson, G.C. (1946) 'The Aterian Industry: its Place and Significance in the Palaeolithic World', *J. Roy. Anthropol. Inst.*, *76*, 87-130

Thorne, A.G. (1971) 'Mungo and Kow Swamp: Morphological Variation in Pleistocene Australians', *Mankind*, *8*, 85-9

—— and Macumber, P.G. (1972) 'Discoveries of Late Pleistocene Man at Kow Swamp, Australia', *Nature*, *238*, 316-19

Timms, P. (1974) *Flint Implements*, Shire Publications, Aylesbury

Tixier, J. (1961) 'Les Pièces Pedonculées de l'Aterien', *Libyca*, pp. 6-7

Tobias, P.V. (1967) 'The Cranium and Maxillary Dentition of *Australopithecus (Zinjanthropus) boisei*', *Olduvai Gorge*, *2*, Cambridge University Press

Tuffreau, A. (1971) 'Quelques Aspects du Paléolithique Ancien et Moyen dans le Nord de la France', *Numero Spécial du Bull. de la Soc. de Préhistoire du Nord*, *8*, 1-99

—— (1978) 'Les Industries Acheuléennes de Cagny-la-Garenne (Somme)', *L'Anthropologie*, *82* (1), 37-60

Turner, C. (1970) 'The Middle Pleistocene Deposits at Marks Tey, Essex', *Phil. Trans. Roy. Soc.*, *B*, *257*, pp. 373-440

Twiesselman, F. (1958) 'Les Néanderthaliens Découverts en Belgique' in G.H.R. von Koenigswald (ed.), *Neanderthal Centenary*, Wenner-Gren Foundation, New York, pp. 63-71

Ucko, P.J. and Rosenfeld, A. (1967) *Palaeolithic Cave Art*, Weidenfeld and Nicolson, London

Valoch, K. (1968) 'Evolution of the Palaeolithic in Central and Eastern Europe', *Current Anthropol.*, *9* (5), 351-90

Vandermeersch, B. (1976a) 'Les Sépultures Néandertaliennes' in H. de Lumley (ed.), *La Préhistoire Française, 1*, CNRS, Paris, pp. 725-7
— (1976b) 'Les Néandertaliens en Charente' in H. de Lumley (ed.), *La Préhistoire Française, 1*, CNRS, Paris, pp. 584-7
Vértes, L. (1955) 'Neue Ausgrabungen und Paläolithische Funds in der Höhle von Istalloskö', *Acta Archaeologica Academiae Scientarium Hungaricae, 5,* 111-31
— (ed.) (1964) 'Tata, eine Mittelpälaolithische Travertin-Siedlung in Ungarn', *Archaeologica Hungarica, S.N., 43*
— (1965a) 'Typology of the Buda Industry – a Pebble Tool Industry from the Hungarian Lower Palaeolithic', *Quaternaria, 7,* 185-95
— (1965b) 'Discovery of *Homo erectus* in Hungary', *Antiquity, 39* (156), 303
— (1975) 'The Lower Palaeolithic Site of Vértesszöllös, Hungary' in R. Bruce Mitford (ed.), *Recent Archaeological Excavations in Europe*, Routledge and Kegan Paul, London and Boston, pp. 287-301
Waechter, J. d'A. (1952) 'The Excavation of Jabrud and its Relation to the Prehistory of Palestine and Syria', *Ann. Rep. Lond. Univ. Inst. Archaeol., 8,* 10-28
— and Conway, B.W. (1969) 'Swanscombe 1968 Interim Report on New Excavations in the Barnfield Pit', *Proc. Roy. Anthropol. Inst. Gr. Brit. and Ireland for 1968*, pp. 53-61
—, Newcomer, M.H. and Conway, B.W. (1970) 'Swanscombe 1969, Barnfield Pit, Kent', *Proc. Roy. Anthropol. Inst. Gr. Brit. and Ireland for 1969*, pp. 83-93
—, Newcomer, M.H. and Conway, B.W. (1971) 'Swanscombe 1970', *Proc. Roy. Anthropol. Inst. Gr. Brit. and Ireland for 1970*, pp. 43-64
Wainwright, G.J. (1964) *The Pleistocene Deposits of the Lower Narmada River and an Early Stone Age Industry from the River Chambal*, Dept. of Archaeology and Ancient History, Baroda
— and Malik, S.C. (1967) 'Recent Field Research on Problems of Archaeology and Pleistocene Chronology in Peninsular India', *Proc. Prehist. Soc., 33,* 132-46
Walker, A. (1976) 'Remains Attributable to Australopithecus in the East Rudolf Succession' in Y. Coppens *et al.* (eds), *Earliest Man and Environments in the Lake Rudolf Basin*, University of Chicago Press, pp. 484-9
Walker, D. and Sieveking, A. (1962) 'The Palaeolithic Industry of Kota Tampan, Perak, Malaya', *Proc. Prehist. Soc., 28,* 103-39, Plates IX-XX
Warren, S.H. (1951) 'The Clactonian Flint Industry: a New Interpretation', *Proc. Geol. Ass., 62,* 107-35
Washburn, S.L. (ed.) (1962) *Social Life of Early Man*, Methuen, London
Waterbolk, H.T. (1972) 'Radiocarbon Dates from Palaeolithic Sites in Western Europe, Compared with the Climatic Curve of the Netherlands' in F. Bordes (ed.), *The Origin of Homo sapiens*, Unesco, Paris, pp. 245-52
Watson, W. (1950 and many later edns) *Flint Implements*, British Museum
Wendt, W.E. (1976) ' "Art Mobilier" from the Apollo II Cave, South West Africa: Africa's Oldest Dated Works of Art', *S. Afr. Archaeol. Bull., 31,* 5-11
West, R.G. (1956) 'The Quaternary Deposits at Hoxne, Suffolk', *Phil. Trans. Roy. Soc., series B, 239,* 265-356
— (1968) *Pleistocene Geology and Biology, with Special Reference to the*

British Isles, Longmans, London

Willey, G.R. (1966) *An Introduction to American Archaeology*, Prentice-Hall, New Jersey

Wolberg, D.L. (1970) 'The Hypothesized Osteodontokeratic Culture of the Australopithecinae; a Look at the Evidence and the Opinions', *Current Anthropol.*, *11* (1), 23-37

Wolpoff, M.H. and Lovejoy, C.O. (1975) 'A Rediagnosis of the Genus Australopithecus', *J. Hum. Evol.*, *4*, 275-6

Woo, J. (1966) 'The Skull of Lantian Man', *Current Anthropol.*, *7* (1), 83-6

Wood, B.A. (1976) 'Remains Attributable to *Homo* in the East Rudolf Succession' in Y. Coppens *et al.* (eds), *Earliest Man and Environments in the Lake Rudolf Basin*, University of Chicago Press, pp. 490-506

Wright, H.E., Jr and Howe, B. (1951) 'Preliminary Report on Soundings at Barda Balka', *Sumer*, *7*, 107-18

Wymer, J.J. (1968) *Lower Palaeolithic Archaeology in Britain, as Represented by the Thames Valley*, pp. 1-429, Figs 1-110, Plates I-XXXVI, John Baker, London

—— (1974) 'Clactonian and Acheulian Industries in Britain – Their Chronology and Significance', *Proc. Geol. Ass.*, *85* (3), 391-421

—— and Singer, R. (eds) (in press) *Excavations at Klasies River Mouth, South Africa, 1966-1968*, University of Chicago Press

Zeuner, F.E. (1958) *Dating the Past*, Methuen, London, 4th edn

—— (1959) *The Pleistocene Period*, Hutchinson, London

Index of Sites

A page number such as 56. .59 means that the text is interrupted by other matter.

General Index

A page number such as 22. .25 means that the text is interrupted by other matter.

Indices compiled by Freda Wilkinson.